PRINCE

THE DAY I WAS THERE

Alison Howells DiMascio & Sue Houghton

Published in Great Britain 2024 by Spenwood Books Ltd
2 College Street, Higham Ferrers, NN10 8DZ

Copyright © Alison Howells DiMascio & Sue Houghton 2020, 2024

All rights reserved. No part of this publication may be reproduced, stored in a retrieval system, or transmitted in any form or by any means, electronic, electrostatic, recording, magnetic tape, mechanical, photocopying or otherwise, without prior permission in writing from the publisher.

The publisher makes no representation, express or implied, with regard to the accuracy of the information contained in this publication and cannot accept any responsibility in law for any errors or omissions.

The right of Alison Howells DiMascio & Sue Houghton to be identified as authors of this work has been asserted by him in accordance with sections 77 and 78 of the Copyright, Designs and Patents Act 1988.

No part of this book may be reproduced in any form without permission from the publisher except for the quotation of brief passages in reviews.

A catalogue record for this book is available from the British Library

This edition © Spenwood Books Limited 2024

ISBN: 978-1-915858-30-6

' When you don't talk down to your audience, then they can grow with you. I give them a lot of credit to be able to hang with me this long, because I've gone through a lot of changes, but they've allowed me to grow, and thus we can tackle some serious subjects and try to just be better human beings, all of us '

Prince Rogers Nelson

Contents

Introduction	6
Early days	8
UK debut	15
1999	21
Purple Rain	22
Hit n Run USA	33
Parade	38
Sign o' the Times	47
Lovesexy	50
Nude	64
Diamonds & Pearls	74
Act I & II	83
Interactive	95
Ultimate Live Experience	100
Jam of the Year	111
Newpower Soul	115
Celebration/Xenophobia	124
One Nite Alone	129
Musicology	137
Perf4rming Live 3121	152
Superbowl XLI	156
Earth/21 Nights	158
Montreux 2009	178
20Ten	179
Welcome 2...	183
Live Out Loud	194
Hit and Run	196
Piano & A Microphone	244
I Heard The News	248
Acknowledgements	259

INTRODUCTION

From the first time I heard '1999' I was hooked, intrigued by an artist who looked unlike any other person in the charts and whose sound was so unique to me. No one else understood it and I was ribbed at school for my love of Prince, and for having his pictures covering all of my schoolbooks. The only one who didn't was my friend Sue Houghton, and that's where our journey together began. We experienced our first concert together in 1986; the *Parade* tour, where all the chairs had black and white balloons on them. After that, I could never get enough of seeing him live. It was addictive.

In 1987, the *Sign o' the Times* tour was cancelled in the UK and I was devastated, not only because I missed it but also because I had persuaded my mum to take me to London to camp out to get tickets against my dad's wishes who, as an old fashioned Italian, wouldn't have approved of his daughter camping in London overnight.

The last time we saw him was in 2015 at Autism Rocks, at Koko's in London. So Sue and I saw our first and last Prince gigs together, although of course we didn't know that at the time.

INTRODUCTION

Whether it was the stripped down tours of *Parade*, *Nude* and *One Night Alone* to the extravagant tours of *Sign o' the Times* and *Lovesexy* and, more recently, the *Hit and Run* shows where there could be only a few hours notice, each tour was unique. Not just in the layout on stage or the personnel of the band, but even in the songs he chose to perform that night. He always changed the set on the spur of the moment, and sometimes missing a gig may have meant you missed that one song that he wouldn't perform again for years, perhaps never. Regularly catching as many gigs as I could meant catching many rarely performed songs too. During his 21 night stint at the O2, I saw 16 of the main shows and went to eight after shows; after a few nights the security guards were greeting me by name. Probably the most amazing part of the shows at the O2 was that after most people had left he would sometimes decide to come back on and play to the few who had remained.

Over the past 37 years I have met hundreds, maybe thousands, of Prince fans and one of the most enjoyable aspects of all of this is swapping stories and experiences with them. Each person has a story to tell. Some saw him hundreds of times; some only had the chance to catch him once. Either way, their stories are what make this such an interesting community. Some live their lives consumed by the love of Prince. Others just enjoy his music. What we all have in common is the unforgettable privilege of seeing the genius of our time.

Prince was part of a select few who were a master of several instruments, a writer and performer who influenced a huge range of musical genres, and a man who always stayed true to what he believed in and always spread the gospel of love, positivity and music. This book is a reflection of those stories, collected together to show the real fan experience.

Alison Howells DiMascio
Portsmouth, UK
November 2019

UNKNOWN VENUE

C1977, ATLANTA, GEORGIA

I WAS THERE: LESLIE LADD

It was about 1977. I had attended one of the many Parliament-Funkadelic shows I enjoyed during that era. I was and still am friends with George Clinton, MudBone, Bootsy and gang and they had tour passes waiting for us. My roommate and I drove to Atlanta from Chattanooga, where we lived, to enjoy the show. We hung out at our usual place, the side of the back stage area, and enjoyed the funk.

On the other side of the stage there was an unusual looking small young guy who really caught my eye. After the show, my roommate and I hung out with the gang as they cleared up the equipment

Leslie Ladd saw Prince at a Parliament-Funkadelic show before he was famous

and at one point we were standing in a semi-circle chatting and a record producer friend of my roommate introduced us to the interesting guy and told us that he was going to be a big star. George Clinton had taken him on several stops of the tour to help promote him.

The first thing I noticed was how shy he was, never looking you in the eye. The second thing was how little he was. I was only 5' 5" and I was a tad taller than he was - he was not wearing tall heels. He did speak to say hello but he spoke softly and hard to hear with all the backstage hoopla going on. I didn't see him perform but it was not long after this that we started hearing his music on the radio. If I had only known, I would have initiated a conversation with him and more closely followed his progress.

His music and dancing were great sources of fun. I was very sad when he passed. I was happy he was able to induct George and PFunk into the Hall of Fame.

George Clinton: He came to a show we did, that would've been '77, and he was looking like Bootsy, all Funkadelic, and Warners was telling him he was *the* new artist. The same [management] people who had Earth, Wind & Fire brought him to the show for us to check him out, and I just met him for a minute… When he first started out, he was wearing what looked like waiter costumes. I told him, 'Your whole thing is cool, except for the waiter suits. Looks like you work in a nightclub or restaurant.'

WARNER BROTHERS RECORDS

1977, BURBANK, CALIFORNIA

I WAS THERE: NIGEL MOLDEN

I never saw Prince perform live but met him in the very early days when he was about 18. In 1977 I was the General Manager of Warner Brothers Records in the UK. In that role I visited the headquarters of the company in Burbank, California about twice a year. I would be there for a few days and would meet not only with the executive responsible for international coordination but also with the other senior managers and vice presidents. On one occasion I received a message to drop by the A&R office on the lower ground floor to meet a new artist that had been signed by the company. The approach was always very positive within the company and, on this occasion, it was only different in that the new artist was very quiet and undemonstrative. The A&R person introduced me to him and explained that 'he just calls himself Prince'. To be accurate it was not at all unusual for the company to sign an unknown artist but I do remember that this young man had a very striking appearance very similar to the image which we all came to recognise. In less than a year, of course, he was on his way to becoming a major artist.

MACY'S

1977, SAN FRANCISCO, CALIFORNIA

I WAS THERE: DONNA NASH

I met him at Macy's in San Francisco. He was doing a photo shoot for his first album cover way before he was 'Prince'. He was sitting on a bed, in the mattress. He was very nice. He played me a sample of 'Soft and Wet' on cassette tape and promised to send a copy of album when it was pressed. He did. I love that album. It was always special to me. I played it to all my friends, telling them, 'This is a new guy just coming out.'

Signed to Warner Bros. on the strength of his one-man band demos, Prince didn't take the traditional route to stardom by building a local word-of-mouth following in clubs. After playing in the cover band Grand Central while in school, he had not booked a single gig under his own name by the time he released his 1978 debut, *For You*. Released on 7 April 1978, it reached 138 on the *Billboard* chart.

CAPRI THEATER

5 – 7 JANUARY 1979, MINNEAPOLIS, MINNESOTA

Prince made his live debut at the Capri Theatre, Minneapolis. Warner Bros executives attended the show but decided Prince and the band needed

A ticket for Prince's first ever show

more time to develop his music. Warners wanted to see him onstage to determine if the instrumental skills that dazzled them on tape could translate to a live setting. Prince booked the Capri Theater in North Minneapolis for three nights. The opening night was a warm-up gig and the executives would come to the second night. Tickets were $4 and only around 300 of the 507 seats were occupied, the vast majority by former school friends, musicians and cousins. Prince performed a 60 minute set and exhibited his extraordinary abilities from the start, playing every instrument on stage.

The *Prince* tour ran from 26 November 1979 to 3 May 1980 in the USA, the second leg as the opening act for Rick James' *Fire It Up* tour.

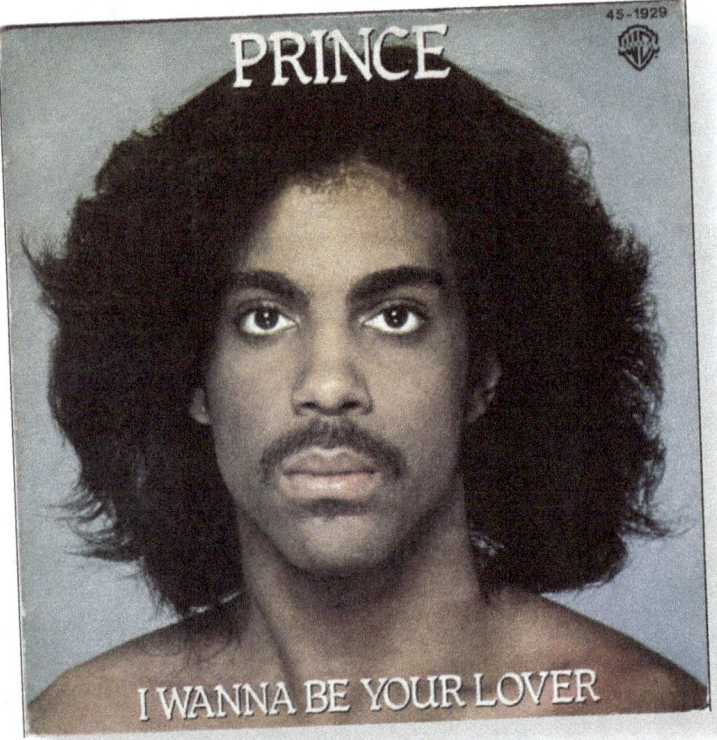

AMERICAN BANDSTAND

26 JANUARY 1980, LOS ANGELES, CALIFORNIA

Prince made his TV debut on the US show *American Bandstand*. When interviewed after his performance the singer froze and struggled to reply to the questions he was being asked.

ORPHEUM THEATRE

9 FEBRUARY 1980, MINNEAPOLIS, MINNESOTA

I WAS THERE: LIZ DODSON

Being from Minneapolis and a year younger than Prince, I was there from the beginning! My first concert was 1980 at the Orpheum Theatre maximum capacity 2600. He wore the zebra outfit. The next time I saw him was at Uncle Sam's, which is now called First Avenue, and which has a maximum capacity of 1,600, in March 1981. He wore his purple trench coat. *Purple Rain* wasn't released until 1984 so I feel like I lived that movie! That was a brief but so cherished moment in my life. When he passed away I felt like I had lost family. You have to remember Prince was ours and belonged to Minneapolis before he belonged to the world. I really didn't realise just how big he was until I went to a record store in Memphis called Peaches. They had huge album covers along the top of the building and one was Prince. I sat there with my mouth open and at that moment I knew just how much he was loved by the world!

My favourite non-concert moment was when I was out at a club called Oz in St Paul. Jimmy Jam Harris was deejaying there - he was the best at the time. Prince showed up! He came in and we left him be, no talking to him or asking for autographs. He was home and we respected that except for one woman who followed Prince, a step behind him everywhere he went. He had her going too. He abruptly stopped and she ran right into him. My side of the club fell about. He turned his head with that sly grin and left. She was too buzzed or embarrassed to follow.

I feel blessed growing up in Minneapolis and being in Prince's world!

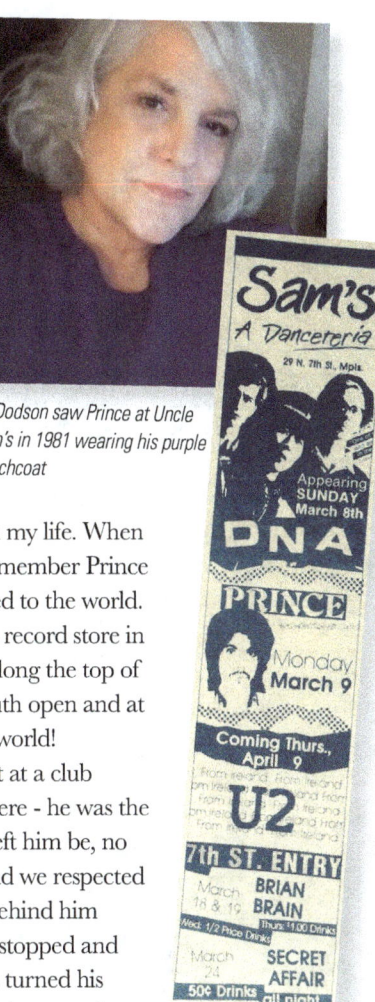

Liz Dodson saw Prince at Uncle Sam's in 1981 wearing his purple trenchcoat

Liz Dodson saw Prince twice in the early days

THE BOTTOM LINE

15 FEBRUARY 1980, NEW YORK, NEW YORK

I WAS THERE: IAN INNOCENT

I was born in London. I grew up in London and New York and I've ended up in LA. Prince is a couple of months older than I am. I was working at college radio in New York. I listened to R&B but I also listened to rock and roll. Hendrix and Funkadelic were my sweet spot. I remember hearing 'I Wanna Be Your Lover' in '77 or '78 and then we got the album *Prince* and when I listened to the album it was like, 'This is the next step for me.' I was into black rockers and he seemed like the next progression of that.

'Bambi' was the track off that album I really got into. I ended up seeing him for the first time at The Bottom Line. That's when he was the really raunchy dude with the G-string, leg warmers, the high heels and the make up, which I would say for a black artist then was kinda out there. He was awesome. That first show that I saw was like, 'Yeah, this is the future right here.' Over the years I saw him at least 30 times.

SAGINAW CIVIC CENTER

4 APRIL 1980, SAGINAW, MICHIGAN

I WAS THERE: LEMAEUL GOLDEN, AGE 10

He was opening for Rick James. I just remember being in awe of this guy. He was young and hungry and I just knew he was something special. I remember him wrecking the stage and at the end everyone chanting, 'We want Prince, we want Prince!' As he and the band were going backstage, I leaned over to my cousin Earl and said, 'Let's see if we could get back there.'

Rick James pass

Dirty Mind Oct 8

In true Rick James form he was pissed. Prince had stolen the show. That's the first time I heard 'I'm Rick James' bitch... lmao.' Anyway, I made it backstage and lo and behold there he was, this li'l guy who seemed 10 feet tall to me. I remember saying, 'Hey, you are very good' and he said 'thanks'. I then said, 'I loved your set.' I was kinda dumbfounded by his height. You have to remember I was 10 years old and we were about the same size! I remember him saying 'you're a cool li'l brother' and giving me a pick to his guitar with his name engraved on it Over my years of travel I lost the pick. But I will always have my memories of meeting the greatest to ever do it. The goat4evernourhearts.

LAKE CALHOUN

1980, MINNEAPOLIS, MINNESOTA

I WAS THERE: DEREK SMITH

I've been a fan since the beginning. There wasn't much to do here in Minneapolis summers. On Sunday we'd go to Lake Calhoun and he'd be there along with members of The Time, just hanging out. He had just finished his second album so he was kinda a big deal when you seen him out and about.

SHEA'S BUFFALO

4 DECEMBER 1980,
BUFFALO, NEW YORK

Prince played the first night of his 31 date *Dirty Mind* North American tour at Shea's Buffalo. After being told by his managers he couldn't wear spandex pants without any underwear, Prince began performing in a long trench coat, black high-heeled boots with leggings and bikini brief trunks.

The *Dirty Mind* tour began on 4 December 1980 and ran through to 11 October 1981, taking in the USA and Europe.

A newspaper review in the *Michigan Daily*, writing up Prince's 1981 Royal Oak Music Theatre show, advised readers not to miss the upcoming show at Eastern Michigan University: 'Prince is the Sex Machine of the 1980s and if you don't go, you're gonna hate yourself – maybe not now – but some time, in the middle of the night, when no one will be around to let you forget.'

BOWEN FIELD HOUSE, EASTERN MICHIGAN UNIVERSITY

20 MARCH 1981, YPSILANTI, MICHIGAN

I WAS THERE: RICHARD JACKSON

The first time I saw him was at Eastern Michigan University around the time of *Dirty Mind*. My friend begged me to go. I didn't want to. I said, 'He's not going to sound like the album anyway.' Was I wrong! He blew me away and I've been a huge fan ever since.

THE RITZ

22 MARCH 1981, NEW YORK, NEW YORK

I WAS THERE: IAN INNOCENT

The next show that I saw was at the Ritz, which was right after *Dirty Mind* came out. The Ritz is like an old music hall and I read years later that not only was Mick Jagger there but a lot of people who had heard the buzz about him. I believe that that's the show that decided the Stones to put him on that tour where he got booed off stage. That was an awesome show too. That was that young band with André Cymone and Dez Dickerson. They were just so full of energy, really raw and loud, and Prince's and Dez's intermingling with the guitars was just so awesome.

The next show after that was probably Radio City in 1989 and then I remember going down to DC to see the *Purple Rain* tour. It was the third or fourth show of the tour. That was a great show too. No matter what, he always put on a great show.

There was a period of time in the Nineties where I wasn't really feeling his music as much. He was doing the whole experimentation thing with rap which I never was really into but no matter what I knew that if I saw him he would rock my ass. He always did. I was never disappointed seeing a Prince show. I'm obsessive that way. My other favourite band is Funkadelic and I've seen them probably 40 to 50 times. So when I'm into a band I'm into a band!

What it was with Prince is that he was so diverse. When they played that video of 'While My Guitar Gently Weeps' from the 2004 Rock and Rock Hall of Fame induction for George Harrison, and he plays the guitar, people were saying, 'Wow, I had no idea he could rip it like that.' I've known for 40 years that he was a killer guitar player. Even if he didn't do anything else apart from play guitar he'd still be a bad man. So it was very cool to finally see other people catching up. Players knew, but I think there was a sense that he was more showman than musician.

The last time I saw him was at the Palladium in LA around 2012, 2013. There were a couple of shows that I want to kick myself in the ass that I didn't see. One of them was at Coachella and then there was one at a little club in West Hollywood that just happened over a couple of days where he was just doing Hendrix-like vibes all night. He was just jamming all night. I missed 3RDEYEGIRL. I would have liked to have seen them.

I never met him but I shared the same space as him a couple of times. There was a show at The Ritz where it was Vanity 6 opening for The Time and we had access to the soundboard in front of the stage. So we were hanging out there watching the show and he was there with a couple of other people. He had that purple raincoat from the *Purple Rain* period. And in the Nineties I worked at a hotel in Miami - the Marlin - which was owned by Chris Blackwell, and it had a recording studio in the hotel. Prince did some overdubbing there for *Emancipation*. He walked in a couple of times but he always had bodyguards with him. There was no way to get to him.

Musicology was the last time I saw him. It was the opening night in LA and I got really good seats for that. Eddie Murphy and his entourage were there.

When Prince died, I couldn't believe it. They didn't know at first that it was him. 15 to 20 minutes later my phone starts to blow up, because everyone who knows me knows I'm a Prince freak. People start calling me, texting me, saying, 'Did you hear?' I was completely devastated. The fact that we're the same age, that really hit home, because I'd grown up with his music. Of any other artist that I've been into, that hurt a lot. It really did.

LYCEUM BALLROOM

2 JUNE 1981, LONDON, UK

Prince made his live British debut at the Lyceum Ballroom. He would not play the UK again for five years.

During a North American tour The Rolling Stones played the first of two nights at the Los Angeles Memorial Coliseum in Los Angeles, California. Support act was Prince, who dressed in his controversial bikini briefs and trench coat ran off stage after 15 minutes due to the crowd booing and throwing beer cans at him.

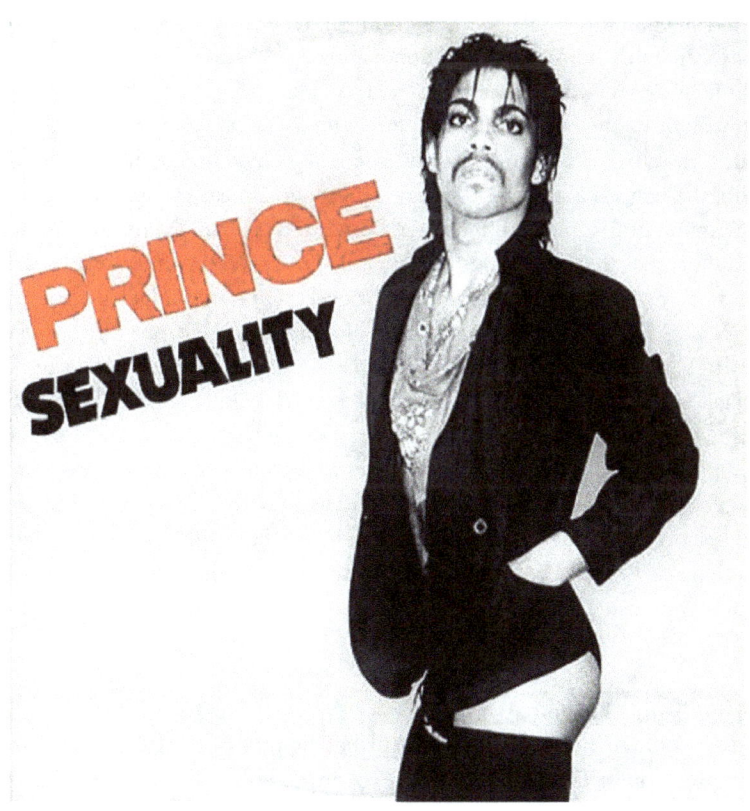

LOS ANGELES COLISEUM

9 & 11 OCTOBER 1981, LOS ANGELES, CALIFORNIA

I WAS THERE: MICHAEL POPOV, AGE 30

It was a Rolling Stones concert with The J Geils Band, George Thorogood and Prince, who opened the show. I was 30 and went with some friends, Ron and Theresa. We drove up from Huntington Beach without tickets and bought them from a scalper as we pulled off the freeway! I think we paid face value. I had never heard of Prince before and it sounded like I wasn't alone. Prince came on stage in his flashy garb and his band and played for probably 30 minutes. I just don't think we were ready for him. I say that because if it was two years later he would have left to a standing ovation. However because most people had never heard him and his style we booed him off the stage. That Prince style that became his trademark and loved by millions around the world was not initially accepted as good music and I'm sad to say that I am as guilty as anybody else who was there that day and treated this new artist with the utmost disrespect and I'm very sorry about it.

I WAS THERE: TERRY FLETCHER

The Rolling Stones have long been known to promote lesser known acts by having them perform as warm up acts. Their 1981 tour was no exception, with George Thorogood and J Geils (though hardly unknowns) and someone named Prince. I had been looking forward to seeing the Stones for the first time and arrived early to the LA Coliseum to get in a little pre-game warm up of my own. It was the quintessential October day in Southern California, hot and sunny and perfect for an all day concert. With festival seating, the crowd inside was on the rowdy side and seemed intent on sitting in the stands until the main acts came out, so it was pretty open near the stage and I wandered up to the front to grab a spot. After a while Prince and his band came out and started playing. I remember thinking to myself, 'Okay, he dresses a little differently but man can this guy play!' However I was in the minority on that front and it soon got ugly, with people throwing stuff at him and booing him pretty hard. If only they would close their eyes and just listen they would have heard an amazing talent. When Prince started singing 'Jack U Off' things got out of hand and he was literally booed off the stage. This crowd just weren't ready for Prince and I felt bad that it had come to this. I did go again on the second day and things were mildly better as word got out in the press and radio about the poor treatment he got. Although there was still a lot of booing, Prince actually finished his short set. While I am glad that I got to see this historic event I am slightly ashamed to be part of the crowd, although I wasn't part of the problem and really enjoyed and appreciated what he was doing up there. Sadly, I never saw Prince perform live again.

I WAS THERE: RICCI TERRANOVA

I was there in 1981 at that infamous concert when he played at the Coliseum, when he opened for the Stones. The J Geils Band also opened. They started hitting him with items. There were things flying up on the stage. From where I was I couldn't exactly see what they were hitting him with.

I was with my friend Richard who graduated with me from high school and we'd gone to this show and it just got really ugly. There was a darkness about this atmosphere such that I actually turned to my friend and said, 'I'm wondering if this is going to turn into a full scale riot' because it was really one of the most ugliest scenes I'd ever seen, being at a concert and having people pelt the performer with items. Later I found out they were bottles and I think on the second show when he came back on Sunday they were hitting him with chicken parts.

Ricci Terranova saw the infamous LA Coliseum show

I wasn't there for that day - I was there for the first show – because he played on Friday and was supposed to play on Sunday and then he came back for the Sunday show which I'm told was much worse than the treatment he received on the first show.

Tina Turner was backstage when this was happening. I really think that the Rolling Stones crowd was not ready for Prince. He came out very scantily clad. I don't even know if it was necessarily that he was black. I think it was very homophobic. It just seemed like they saw him as a gay man flaunting his sexuality. I think that the males that were in the front of the Rolling Stones crowd had an issuer with him. Although the n-word did come out and they were chanting 'faggot' and things like that, I really think it was not so much that he was a black artist. I think they were threatened by his overt sexuality and they perceived him to be gay. The macho Rolling Stones crowd in the front had an issue with it.

It was very disturbing to be part of that and to watch this unfolding. I never forgot it and my friend and I have talked about it. we went to so many shows. We were constantly going to concerts. We saw The Clash and The Who and Springsteen and Tom Petty. We would go to so many shows and to see this happen really stuck with me through the show. It took away from the enjoyment of being at a Rolling Stones concert. I ended up getting tickets to see the Rolling Stones again and I flew to Dallas to see them at the Cotton Bowl because I felt that I had been robbed of enjoying the Rolling Stones.

A good friend of mine named Mike Barrett who was an English teacher at a college turned me on to the album *Dirty Mind* and when I listened to that I was hooked. Both of my brothers and my family were very much into music so I grew up with an older brother who was into the Rolling Stones and the Cream and Jimi Hendrix and Janis Joplin and Buffalo Springfield – all these bands – so I really got the rock side of it. My other brother was really into R&B, funk and soul so I was being exposed to Parliament and to Earth, Wind & Fire, The Ohio Players and James Brown and I remember listening to Stevie Wonder. But I had never seen anything like Prince and I had never heard anything like Prince. I remember putting the *Dirty Mind* album on my turntable and listening to it over and over and over and when I heard the song 'Uptown', I was just captivated. Not only by the music but by him as well.

I WAS THERE: MARLA BARBIE BLAZER

I had some cool 'fashion friends' from college drama class play some EPs for me in the makeup room after class one day. I was hooked from the first song I heard! The beat was very catchy – and the lyrics! I was working part time as a dancer so I brought his stuff to the club and everybody there loved it as well.

The first time I saw him was opening up for the Rolling Stones in 1981. The last time was in '96 at the Blaisdell Center in Honolulu for his Ultimate Live Experience tour. I was with my husband and it rocked! When the Stones came in '81, the crowd was heavily classic rock and he'd not quite caught on yet. But even then, although some folk were meandering around the venue and saying he sucked, they were still moving to his music. I recall that very well to this very day. But Prince got heckled and people threw stuff at him. Bill Graham, who was the promoter, got on stage after his set and berated and lectured the audience. And security brought one of the main perps on stage and Bill Graham had him booted.

Mick Jagger: I talked to Prince once after he got two cans thrown at him in LA. He said he didn't want to do any more shows. God, I got thousands of bottles and cans thrown at me!

The *Controversy* tour ran for four months from 20 November 1981 to 14 March 1982 in the USA.

CAROLINA COLISEUM

12 DECEMBER 1981,
COLUMBIA, SOUTH CAROLINA

I WAS THERE: JOHN ADDISON

I was working a bs job loading boxes in the basement of Lord and Taylor the first time I really heard Prince. I had heard 'Soft and Wet' before, but I didn't think it was great. Then 'I Wanna Be Your Lover' exploded onto the radio playlist in the fall of '79. We played the radio loud and non-stop at work. The music truly got us through the day. That fucking intro hit your ears from everywhere. The musicians at work spent hours deciphering how Prince recorded it, how he obtained that sound. The rest of us just knew it sounded dope. 'I Wanna Be Your Lover' could have easily been a hit instrumental. Until that voice joined in. 'I ain't got no money.' Yea, Prince. We definitely know what you mean. That opening line was an impassioned plea that we all have kicked to a potential lover that was out of our league. I listened to the rest of the album, but nothing else grabbed me

Spring break '81. I was visiting my family in Charleston, South Carolina and I saw the *Controversy* album in the store. I picked it up out of curiosity. My family freaked out. 'It's blasphemy. He's reciting the Lord's Prayer.' Well, I guess I better listen.

Controversy was good. It had this bounce that you can really dance to. But then Prince put out an album by another band. The Time was the black music Prince was afraid would pigeonhole him if he recorded it. And we loved it.

I got the chance to catch the tour in Columbia, South Carolina. I wasn't ready. The crowd was my age, but from a totally different world. I was a New Yorker and Columbia was the South. And the South looooved funk music. The Time hit the stage and pandemonium broke out. They were so frigging cool. Well dressed. Good musicians. Great choreography.

Prince followed, and for me it was a let down. I didn't know his songs that well, and he was onstage, naked and hairy. When he played 'Do Me Baby', the females lost their mind and I got all jealous. How was I gonna compete with this dude? I left to have a smoke, and came back after all the screaming was over.

I took mental notes, though. From then on, my college parties always ended with 'Do Me Baby'. When we played that song, you could look and see who didn't want to be alone that night. By the time Prince started screaming at the end of the song, all we had to do was put our arm around the girl and we were in. Prince did all the talking.

COLISEUM

28 JANUARY 1982, RICHMOND, VIRGINIA

I WAS THERE: KATHY ROBINSON

I must have seen *Purple Rain* at least a hundred times. My first look at Prince on the cover of a teen magazine was love at first sight. I fell in love with 'I Wanna Be Your Lover' and loved that album and played it to death. I eventually got put out of the apartment I was living in for playing that album repeatedly. 'And too loud,' as they put it. I guess those jerks weren't Prince lovers. Oh well.

My first Prince concert was the best. It was the early Eighties. I went with my friend from work. We were at the front where you stand waiting for him to come on. The police in Richmond, Virginia were there if Prince got too exposed. We didn't care! We got to see him up close, but just not close enough. I would have loved to touch him. I wish those had been the days of cell phones. It was a great show. I got to see him about four more times. Each time was wonderful. He was the best performer. I just knew I would see him one more time as we are about the same age. I was devastated when I heard he was murdered. Yes - murdered. I have had many great dreams of Prince since his passing. The first one was shortly after that awful day. He had on a beautiful fuchsia colour and he said to me, 'I know what you want - come here', and gave me a wonderful hug. I said, 'I love you.' He said, 'I know.' He was the sweetest. I call it a crossover dream. Every dream since has been beautiful and colourful. I play his music often. He's always in my heart. Justice for Prince. It's coming, folks.

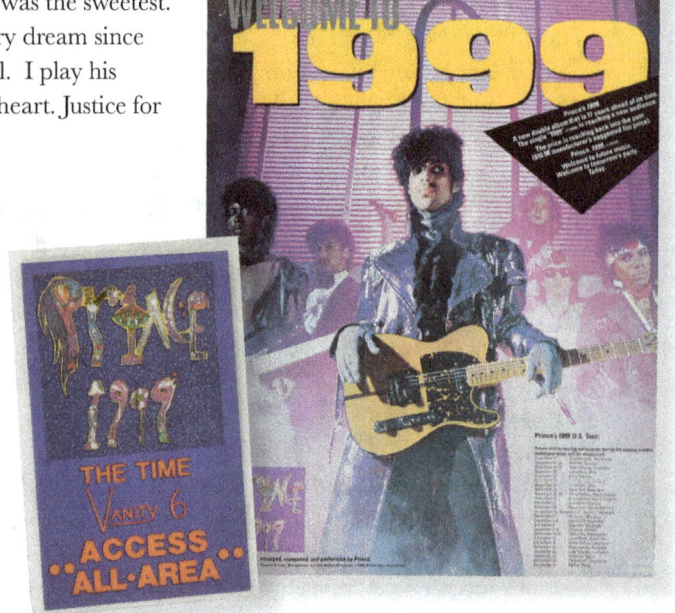

Officially named the *1999 Triple Threat* tour, the 93 show two-legged North American tour was promoting the *1999* album. It ran from 11 November 1982 to 10 April 1983. Prince was supported by The Time, who received enthusiastic receptions from the audiences, leading to Prince feeling he might be upstaged.

MASONIC TEMPLE

30 NOVEMBER 1982, DETROIT, MICHIGAN

I WAS THERE: TINA SLAUGHTER

How did I discover Prince? Well I remember hearing his song 'I Wanna Be Your Lover'. This song was constantly played on the radio. I liked the song instantly. When I first saw him on TV I was like 12 years old. He was on a dance show called *American Bandstand*. Prince was so mysterious and eccentric. I first saw him in concert in 1982. I went with my mother, my brother, a friend and her son. I was 15 years old and blown away by Prince's performance. The concert was at the Masonic Temple here in Detroit. What I remember about the show that it was attended by many people of different ethnicities. The crowd was energetic. This was the early Eighties. So punk and new wave was popular and I remember that a lot of the concert-goers had purple or rainbow hair. Some were dressed provocative. But I loved seeing Prince sing. I was in love with him and his music. Whenever I would go to his concerts, he never disappointed me.

I WAS THERE: DENNIS ROSZKOWSKI

Well, it's 8pm, and 37 years ago, I stepped into the world which has enchanted me ever since. I was at the 8pm (early) show for the *1999* tour stop at Masonic Temple in Detroit. This A U T O matically changed my concert going experience forever. What a memory!

SAGINAW CIVIC CENTER

8 DECEMBER 1982, SAGINAW, MICHIGAN

I WAS THERE: LONNIE SHARKEY, AGE 14

I had started loving him and his music after seeing him perform on *Soul Train* and *American Bandstand*. I was able to get two tickets to see the *1999* show. It was general admission. My dad drove my friend and

Dennis Roszkowski saw Prince at the Masonic Temple

me from dance classes and high school to and from the show. Vanity 6 and The Time opened for him. It was the best concert. I plastered my walls with pictures of Prince and continued to love him from there on out. I would save all my pennies to buy any Prince record I could. I also was so blessed to see the *Purple Rain* concert twice in Detroit. I was so trying to see him again when he passed.

DC ARMORY

14 FEBRUARY 1983, WASHINGTON DC

I WAS THERE: EDDIE L JONES

I was fortunate to see Prince twice - in 1983 in Washington DC and again in 2004 in Atlanta, Georgia. It was an unbelievable stage act. 1983 was raw and untamed while in 2004 he was polished. Back in 1983 I was in the Army stationed in Washington. Prince was on his 1999 tour and stopped in at the Armory. I remember him opening the show with '1999', purple coat and all. The band was on point. In 2004 my wife and I attended his Musicology tour concert in Atlanta's Phillips Arena (now the Allstate Arena). The opening act was The Time. After their 45 minutes set, it took about 30 minutes to set up Prince's stage. The intro was the preach line to 'Let's Go Crazy' and then all hell broke loose for two hours. The show was magnificent because he played his old hits and performed an acoustic set. I noticed he didn't wear his famous heels until he closed the show with 'Purple Rain'.

Up to that point, the *1999* tour was Prince's longest.

JOE LOUIS ARENA

8 APRIL 1983, DETROIT, MICHIGAN

I WAS THERE: JP MORGAN, AGE 10/11

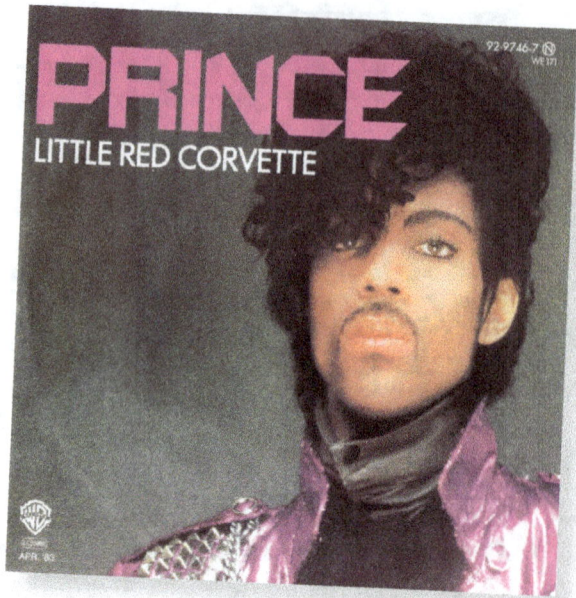

The first and only time I saw Prince was in Detroit on the *1999* tour. I went with my sisters who thought they were a bootleg Vanity 6. We had nosebleed seats. I don't so much remember the concert but what I do remember is the traffic going into Joe Louis Arena being backed up for miles! My cousin Jeff and I attended the same middle school. He was a deejay and a huuuuge Prince fan. We used to argue about who was better, Prince or RUN DMC. Mind you Jeff was a big dude, linebacker size. We convinced the principal to let us throw a concert at Roosevelt Middle School in Oak Park, Michigan. This dude came out on the stage to sing 'Sign o' the Times' with some basketball warm up pants with the buttons up the side. I almost died laughing but the kids loved it!

25 JUNE 1984

Prince released his sixth studio album *Purple Rain*, the first to feature his band The Revolution, and the soundtrack to the 1984 film of the same name. The first two singles from the album, 'When Doves Cry' and 'Let's Go Crazy', topped the US singles charts, and were hits around the world, while the title track went to number 2 on the *Billboard* Hot 100.

7 JULY 1984

Prince started a five week run at number 1 on the US singles chart with 'When Doves Cry', his first US number 1, which went on to sell over two million copies. It made number 4 in the UK.

When Doves Cry

4 AUGUST 1984

Prince started a 24-week run at the top of the US album charts with *Purple Rain*. It would go on to sell over 20 million copies worldwide, becoming the seventh best-selling soundtrack album of all time.

31 AUGUST 1984

Purple Rain opened at cinemas across the UK with special late night previews. The film grossed more than $80 million at the box office.

CHANHASSEN, MINNESOTA

LABOUR DAY, SEPTEMBER 1984

I WAS THERE: LAURA GUITAR

My cousin Sheila and I won a contest through MuchMusic. At the time it was Canada's only television music video channel. The contest was called 'Around the World in a Day'. The grand prize was airfare around the world for two people. My cousin Sheila (who was maybe 18 years old at the time) had little or no knowledge of Prince. I was 24 and owned a small restaurant. I knew I'd be entering the contest and it was at this time Sheila was diagnosed with cancer. My thought at the time was to give her 'hope' and I told her we'd enter the contest together. Hope meant she'd be around for a bit and she'd get to do those things her friends were doing and even dream about her future. We agreed that if either of our names were drawn we'd

Laura Guitar dropped in to see Prince at home

split the prize 50/50. For the contest, participants had to identify five Prince videos from one or two second sections spliced together in a montage, easy peasy for a Prince fan like myself. Plus there weren't as many videos available in those pre-Internet days. Regular post carried the 40 postcards with our entries and my answers to MuchMusic's headquarters in Toronto. The channel's rotation was eight hours, meaning whatever programming they'd done just repeated itself three times every 24 hours. I had to work the day and evening of the draw, so I stayed awake till the 2am-ish third run which included the draw to see who had won. I'm pretty sure Sheila had forgotten about it. Well of course Sheila's name was drawn! I thought I had dreamt hearing her name! We took the cash pay out instead of the airfare prize. The money enabled Sheila to realise a few little dreams and sent me to Minneapolis twice.

By 1984 I was already listening to Prince for a few years. I bought a return ticket to Minneapolis, booked a swanky downtown hotel for one night, car rental, etc. Night One I went to the First Avenue Bar (like anyone here would) for who-knows-what? A chance sighting of him? What the hell did I care? Nothing much was happening so I went to another club he reportedly often went to. You see I was attending a college programme that fall with the dream of ultimately working for *Rolling Stone* as a journalist or photographer.

Day Two I jump into the rental and navigate myself towards Chanhassen, frikken burning a tank of gas for sure by the end of the day. On a dirt road I see a kid on a 10 speed on a country road and ask him, 'Hey buddy, any chance you know if Prince lives around here?' Guy says, 'Ya, my house is on the same lake as his backs onto. Follow me' and I follow this kid to his family home. We get out of the car and he says, 'We've got a small boat at the back of our place. I can at least show you the back of Prince's property.' Uhhh yaaaa, you don't have to ask me twice, little dude. So down we go to their little dock and even littler motorboat and sure enough through the trees I see this purple ranch at the top of a little hill. It's enclosed in black security fencing. I'm like, 'Yep, that's gotta be it' and then we go back. I thank him and of course ask for the directions (what I'd seen already was not enough for moi).

I get to the front of the house and there it is in its all its purpleness, exactly what I thought it would look like. Keep in mind this is now just after *Purple Rain* hit the screen, Labour Day weekend 1984. There's a security guard outside the gate and I pulled up and ask, 'Is Prince around this weekend?' The guard says he really can't say either way but that traffic passing by this weekend is pretty quiet so... basically saying 'you never know'. I tell the guard why I'm there and ask him would it be okay for me to park away from the property 'just in case'. He says it's not a problem so long as I am discreet and if it does get busy for me to move on and return later.

So of course a few looky-loos form up, my cue to get to the hotel about two miles away and regroup. I go back around 7pm that night but stop in for gas somewhere, telling the clerk what I'm doing. The clerk tells me Prince was just there a few days before to fill up the purple bike and that Prince almost put the bike down trying to get off it. Now I'm feeling optimistic!

Back at the house I ask the guard which other clubs, etc. I might find Prince at. He tells me and I go check those out. They're nice clubs but unfortunately not for seeing our man.

Now it's Day Four, our Labour Day, and I have to return to reality - Ontario, Canada - that afternoon. The times in between were a repeat, pretty much. I drive up again, my guard buddy still at his post. I say, 'What do you think?' and he knows what I mean. By now, we're on a first name basis. He tells me, 'Today is a good day, Laura.'

Of course it's Prince and he goes into the garage side door. A few minutes pass and one of the garage doors goes up and up comes our man on his purple bike. He nods to the guard and then me and continues out of the property and down the road towards a stop sign where his road meets up with the main road. In my mind I'm saying 'WTF' and 'Nooo...!' I yell, 'Hey you! I came all the way from Canada to see you!'

And Prince turned the bike around and came back! OMG. Imagine it. I'm 24 years old and alone except for the guard. I swear to God if I had a camera or looked like something other than some nutty chick talking to his guard he would not have done so.

'Hi', he says. He was a tiny man, and so beautiful in person. I tell him my story and I ask him if he will be going into the city later that day. He says he's got a dinner to attend that evening and isn't sure. I manage 'I really love your music' and to tell him that I'd seen the movie like eight times already. He chuckled at that and said, 'Gotta go!'

I have been flying my purple flag ever since!

29 SEPTEMBER 1984

Prince and the Revolution started a two week run at number 1 on the US singles chart with 'Let's Go Crazy', his second US number 1 and a number 7 UK hit. It was the opening track on both the album and in the film *Purple Rain*.

4 November 1984 saw Prince play the first of seven nights at the Joe Louis Arena in Detroit, Michigan at the start of his 87 date North American *Purple Rain* tour. The outing marked the live debut of his new band The Revolution. The tour would go on to sell over 1.7 million tickets. The crowd hysteria and occasional cameos from the likes of

Bruce Springsteen and Madonna confirmed Prince's place as pop's star of the moment.

JOE LOUIS ARENA

4 NOVEMBER 1984, DETROIT, MICHIGAN

I WAS THERE: DESTINY ENTRESSE

I was lucky enough to see Prince many times. My first concert was on November 4, 1984 at the Joe Louis Arena in Detroit, Michigan and the last was April 9, 2015 at the Fox Theatre in Detroit, Michigan. I also saw him perform at Paisley Park in 1996 and at Northrop Auditorium, Minneapolis, Minnesota on June 13, 2000. They were all phenomenal. One does not describe a Prince concert, one must experience a Prince concert.

I WAS THERE: MANUELA RUETER

The first Prince song I heard was 'Bambi' in about 1980. I was in Ann Arbor, crashing frat parties with my best mate. We were 15. I fell in love with his sound. The music and lyrics were so different. The first popular radio play song in the US was 'Controversy'. I, along with so many others, misheard the lyrics as 'count your pussy'. It wasn't until five or six years later that I was able to see him in concert on the *Purple Rain* tour. He did several shows in Detroit at the Joe Louis Arena. I was lucky enough to see him twice that tour. The last time I saw him was in the early 2000s. It was a concert in the round, and it was supposed to be his farewell tour. He'd matured as an entertainer so much. It was, to date, the best concert of my life.

ROSEMONT HORIZON

9 – 14 DECEMBER 1984, CHICAGO, ILLINOIS

I WAS THERE: TAMARA BROWN

I remember the very first time hearing Prince and his music. It was 1979 so I had to be 8 years old. My babysitter was a big fan and she would always listen to his music. I remember the album cover was light blue and he was naked on this white horse and she would just sing and sing and sing. When I was 13, my father used to own a record shop and he had gotten a bunch of tickets for us to see Prince's *Purple Rain* tour in 1984 at the Rosemont Theatre. The record had been playing and I was familiar with it.

But to go to the concert? I was opened up wide! I was in love. I went home with laryngitis and without a voice. I screamed from the beginning to the end of that concert and that sparked my love for him.

I remember going to see *Purple Rain* the movie at 12 or 13. That was our first time being allowed to go downtown Chicago. I remember crying. I remember being amazed, just loving the music and being embarrassed. Because I was introduced to my sexuality, or to what sexuality or sexiness was through seeing Apollonia in that movie and seeing what attracted him to her. I wasn't a bad girl. I just realised that boys looked at girls in a certain way, how they carried themselves, how they moved. That's what I was introduced to.

THE SUMMIT

11 – 14 & 16 – 17 JANUARY 1985, HOUSTON, TEXAS

I WAS THERE: ROSIE BRAR JOHNSON

I saw him live numerous times and I even saw him at an after party in Austin at a country bar! I saw him in Houston. Austin. Dallas. San Antonio. I never regret seeing him everywhere in Texas every time. I mourn him daily!

I was in high school during his *Purple Rain* tour. My (young) auntie was going to see him in concert and asked if I wanted to go. My parents said yes but they were at a dinner party and explained why I wasn't there. The hosts were kind enough to inform my parents what a scandalous show I was at and I got grounded for the summer. I was forever hooked. Every time he came to Texas I went to every show he played.

When I saw him in Austin he was close enough for me to touch. He looked shy and quiet but I can only imagine how he was processing all the people around him. No one touched him or acted like fans but his presence in the room was electric indeed.

The last time I saw him was in Houston in 2004. I was pregnant with my first child. She got to hear his voice in concert too! I regret not traveling to other places to see him. I regret that with all my soul.

I probably saw him 15 times. The last time I saw him was in Houston at the NRG Stadium. It's ironic that the first and last times were both in Houston, where I'm from.

10 November 1984 saw former Rufus singer Chaka Khan at number 1 on the UK singles chart with 'I Feel For You'. Written by Prince, the song featured Stevie Wonder on harmonica and a rap by Grandmaster Melle Mel. The repetition of Khan's name by rapper Melle Mel at the beginning of the song was originally a mistake made by producer Arif Mardin, who then decided to keep it.

RIVERFRONT COLISEUM

21 – 23 JANUARY 1985, CINCINATTI, OHIO

I WAS THERE: STEPHEN JARED, AGE 17

I grew up in the upper middle west of America in the suburbs so, probably like quite a lot of white kids, I was first exposed to him through MTV. It would have been the latter half of 1983. I will never forget seeing the 'Little Red Corvette' video play. The very next day I was at school and was trying to draw from memory a picture of Prince in that video because I just couldn't get it out of my head. It was unlike anything I'd ever seen before visually and the song struck me as something very original and appealing. Then I saw the '1999' video and 'Automatic' was playing a lot and a lot of the tracks from the *1999* album and then the 'When Doves Cry' video hit MTV and *Purple Rain* came out and then I started buying everything Prince had out at that time.

There was a lot of anticipation for the *Purple Rain* record and movie and the movie just absolutely blew me away. I went to see it seven times in the theatre. When I would go to the movies it was always set in New York, LA or maybe Europe. So you would see a film where the characters are in a setting that is nothing like the suburbs of Middle America. *Purple Rain* was. When you saw Minneapolis in the movie *Purple Rain* it looked very much like Cincinnati, where I'm from. The surrounding suburbs looked like the world that I grew up in, and here was this guy who transformed himself into something unlike anybody had ever seen before, and so immensely talented.

I remember getting a book that had a lot of pictures of Prince in it. Some of these were ripped from his yearbook, from school class book photos, and he looked like a normal kid in these pictures. So how did he go from this normal-looking kid who could be sitting next to me in class to the guy who was in *1999* and *Purple Rain* within just a few years? He transformed himself into something unlike anybody had ever seen before. It was just absolutely enthralling. He just outdid himself every year. Every year was a whole new look, a whole new sound, a whole new live show, and it was just absolutely dazzling throughout the entire 1980s.

The first show I saw was the *Purple Rain* tour in Cincinnati in January 1985. I was 17. It was probably a different experience if you were growing up as a Prince fan in San Francisco or LA or maybe Chicago or New York but in upper Midwest Ohio a lot of friends who were guys looked at Prince very sceptically. He had this very androgynous look and he sang a lot with a very high voice. So there was the unforgivable risk of possibly being perceived as gay if you liked Prince or Michael Jackson even at that time. There were a lot of people who did like him but far more guys were still listening to the classic rock of Led Zeppelin and that kind of world where the question of your sexuality would never be raised.

So I didn't have a lot of friends who were really into Prince. When he died I had friends from high school on Facebook who reached out and who said, 'I'm so sorry because I know that you were a huge fan' and it made me think back as to just how unusual I was at that time, to be so hooked on him.

What I remember about that show is just being dazzled by the idea that 'there he is in the flesh right there in front of me' and watching him live, this great hero of mine. That was the overwhelming feeling.

Purple Rain, the movie, came out shortly before Christmas on video cassette and I probably watched the movie five or six times before I saw the live show. I remember leaving the show and feeling slightly and surprisingly a little let down by it. Because at that point I was such a fan and I had become so familiar with so many of his songs from earlier records that the Purple Rain show, and I think Prince admitted as much in later years long after the tour, was a case of taking the songs, which had all become huge, huge hits, and drawing them out for 10 or 15 minutes. I think the song *Purple Rain* alone went on for 20 minutes. I just felt it wasn't quite as magical as the movie was. I loved seeing him but I wasn't overwhelmed to the degree that I thought I would be by seeing him.

I WAS THERE: CATE GIACINTO-RENNER

I've loved Prince since I first heard him, so long ago. I saw him with a friend in Cincinnati in January 1985. It was freezing. It took us about an hour to get there. We had floor seats about row 15 or so. Sheila E opened for him and she was great. She took a guy from the audience up on stage with her. She had a chair for him to seat on and she sang, bumped and grinded him! The crowd went nuts. Then Prince performed the whole *Purple Rain* album. Jumping, grinding, doing splits from one level cube to another. At one point he had water streaming out of his guitar. He was fantastic! It sounded just like the album. Unbelievable. I'm pretty sure he and Sheila did a few songs together. We had a husband and wife with two young children sitting in front of us. These parents were freaking out because the whole show was so sexual. Now you would think you wouldn't bring two children under 10 to see Prince. What were they thinking? They left early!

BRIT AWARDS

11 FEBRUARY 1985, LONDON, UK

At the fourth annual Brit Awards held in London, Prince collected the awards for Best International Act and Best Soundtrack, for *Purple Rain*.

FORUM

24 FEBRUARY 1985, LOS ANGELES, CALIFORNIA

I WAS THERE: RICCI TERRANOVA

After what happened with the Rolling Stones, he chose not to support another artist and he was going to stand on his own. The second time I saw him would've been February 24, 1985 and the *Purple Rain* tour. I had already been exposed to him on MTV. They were playing 'Little Red Corvette' and '1999' and they were also showing videos of him doing 'Why Do You Want To Treat Me So Bad' and songs. I saw him at the Forum for the *Purple Rain* tour.

I was 21 years old. It was like being part of an experience. It was absolutely incredible. The ticket itself said 'wear something purple' and I remember going to the show wearing purple and going into this sea of people dressed in purple. I remember getting out of the car, going up to the Forum to get in line to get into the venue and you saw all these people dressed up like Prince, or all these beautiful women and girls all dressed in purples and lace and it was an incredible experience. The only other time I can remember such a unified fan base when somebody was so into an artist was when I saw Kiss where some people dressed up in Kiss make up and Kiss costumes.

I had great seats for that show. I paid $17.50 and I was on the floor on the first set of risers. It totally met my expectations and really transformed my whole being. It was absolutely amazing to see the show. The way he looked was incredible. I've never seen anybody dressed like that. He just looked like the epitome of a rock star to me. And the music! I don't believe there is a single Prince song that I don't like. I love his music and I've loved his music since the first time I heard it.

He tied it all together. He brought in the rock, the funk, the soul - all this music that I'd been listening to as a young man and been exposed to – he wrapped it all up and created his own style and still you could hear the influences of James Brown, Sly and the Family Stone and all these different bands that I'd been listening to.

So I absolutely had to see him again because he changed. Every time he made a new album his style would change, so you wanted to see what he was going to do, how he was going to perform with these songs.

If I had to go back and pick one show that I could go back and experience again it would be the *Purple Rain* show just because I would want to have that experience again of watching him turn into a mega superstar. That's an experience out of all the shows that I went to that I would love to get that feeling again.

But seeing him do a sound check when I was a member of the NPG Club was also amazing but the *Lovesexy* tour was unforgettable as well. And I also got to see him at a small venue called the Wiltern Theatre and that was very intimate, to see him playing in a small venue with his band.

2011 was the last time I saw him. I saw him perform the 21 night stand at The Forum. I took my wife to that show because she had never seen him before. That was the *Welcome 2 America* tour. I was there for four of the nights. I used to buy several tickets to each tour so on the *Musicology* tour I think I saw him six times. So the last time I saw him was April 2011.

CARRIER DOME

30 MARCH 1985, SYRACUSE, NEW YORK

I WAS THERE: JOEY TUCHRELLO

I saw him on the *Purple Rain* tour in Syracuse, New York when it was beamed via satellite around the world. It left me speechless!

ORANGE BOWL STADIUM

7 APRIL 1985, MIAMI, FLORIDA

I WAS THERE: PAMELA WEISS, AGE 12

The *Purple Rain* concert was my first Prince concert of a total of four in my lifetime - not enough! It was the very last leg of the tour. The Orange Bowl Stadium was listed as 'Purple Bowl' on the ticket. I was 12 years old, it was on Easter and apparently Prince was pressured to change the date because of that, but he didn't. Such 'Controversy'!

Pamela Weiss's ticket for the 'Purple Bowl'

I WAS THERE: CATHERINE MENZIES

My sister and I saw Prince perform at the Orange Bowl in 1985. My sister's boyfriend who drove a cab part time took us there. The traffic was horrible and as he was driving up on curbs and around fire hydrants to avoid the congestion, I was wondering if we would get there alive. I hadn't been in a stadium that size since my Green Bay Packer days. The energy was overwhelming. People were clapping, dancing and stomping their feet so that the aluminium bleachers were literally shaking. I was 5 months pregnant with my son and I thought the whole place might collapse. My sister bought me a purple rose that lit up in the middle and, as night fell, the stadium was awash in them. I held on to that thing for years. My sister and I still recall that night. It was a memorable adventure.

1 JUNE 1985

Prince and The Revolution started a three-week run at number 1 on the US album chart with *Around The World In A Day*.

WESTBURY MUSIC FAIR

(UNVERIFIED) 1985, WESTBURY, NEW YORK

I WAS THERE: ALISA JOSEPH

I have been blessed to see Prince in concert several times but that first time - during the *Purple Rain* tour - blew my mind! I had all his music before that so this was the cherry on top. I saw him twice at Westbury Music Fair that weekend and he has never been far from my mind or playlist since then. I took his picture into the labour room when I had my first child; he has been with me at many important events in my life. I still listen to him everyday since he left. I know he's in a better place and I hope I'm blessed to see him again.

The *Hit and Run USA* tour ran from 3 March 1986 to 3 August 1986 in the United States. It was not a full scale tour and many of the 11 shows were only announced days or even hours before they took place.

WARFIELD THEATRE

8 MARCH 1986, SAN FRANCISCO, CALIFORNIA

I WAS THERE: RED LEE

I've seen Prince 17 times. One of the first times was in the Eighties at the Warfield Theatre in San Francisco. I won a ticket on the radio. He was announcing a concert in the evening the day that I won. The radio station was having a contest and we had to call in and, if we got through, we were able to get a free ticket about 20 rows from the stage. I was at work and I called for hours and hours until I got through and I won a ticket. I was so excited I was literally beside myself. The concert was sexy, exhilarating and funky - everything you would imagine a Prince concert would be. I remember him coming out in some yellow chaps with his butt hanging out. It was so outrageous and so exciting at the same time. I don't remember too much about it except that there was loud, ridiculous screaming and that I was so happy and beside myself to see him perform.

I also saw him in the Nineties at Ruby Skye nightclub in San Francisco. It was a very small venue so it was very intimate and it was awesome to see the show in such a small space. That venue was about a block from my job at the time and I remember going into the café across the street to get lunch and the cafe staff told me that Prince and his entourage came in to eat a meal after 3am because they were open 24 hours. I literally cried about that!

15 MARCH 1986

The Bangles were at number 2 on the UK singles
chart with 'Manic Monday', a song written by Prince under the pseudonym Christopher.

19 APRIL 1986

Prince started a two week run at number 1 on the US singles chart with 'Kiss.' He also had the number 2 song, with 'Manic Monday' by The Bangles.

COBO ARENA

7 JUNE 1986, DETROIT, MICHIGAN

I WAS THERE: MICHELLE PRIETO

I saw Prince in Detroit in 1986. I was young girl about 11 years old when I first became a Prince fan. I was at my friend's house and she asked me to listen to a record she bought and it was the *For You* album. I have followed Prince ever since. I listened to the album and then I went into the *Dirty Mind* era. I followed him from that point onwards and everywhere I went I took his music with me because he was speaking the language of my life. His music had a lot to do with the way I grew up.

I went to that show with my oldest daughter's father. He and his friend queued overnight for tickets and ended up on the front page of the Detroit newspaper because the line was so backed up they were fighting to get in. When they got home with those tickets I was jumping for joy.

I couldn't wait for the concert to come. Prince wanted everyone to wear black and white to the concert. We were just a few rows from the front on the main floor. We weren't supposed to bring cameras in but I snuck a camera in and I was taking really good pictures but I got caught! I went to use the bathroom and I got caught and the police took my camera away from me. I was so mad! I said, 'I want to talk to Prince.' They said, 'Yeah, you can go and talk to him after the concert or you can go back in and watch the concert.' So I told them I would rather go back in and watch the concert and I got to sing 'Happy Birthday' to him. I'll never forget that concert. We talked about it for the longest time.

When I got news that he had passed, I was at my sister's house. She was looking after me because I was in and out of hospital and I saw something on Facebook on my phone. My aunt confirmed it, she said it was true. It was like a bad punch to the stomach. You know, I thought they were gonna kill him. I got that feeling when Prince put 'slave' on his face. I had a gut feeling then. I no longer had my best therapist in the world. You know, I lost my husband, I lost

Prince's Under the Cherry Moon movie

my best friend. I've been through a lot of bad things in my life and I have nobody to turn to apart from Prince. His music helped me get through so many things and now he's gone and I don't know how to deal with it. He was my prophet, my therapist, my doctor, my wannabe lover. He was like a husband. He was everything to me.

The premiere for Prince's *Under the Cherry Moon* movie was held in Wyoming, of all places. The band were flown in from Denver.

Lisa Coleman: The plane was a VW van with wings.

MTV aired the *Holiday Inn* after-party as a 50 minute show.

SHERIDAN COUNTY AIRPORT

1 JULY 1986, SHERIDAN, WYOMING

I WAS THERE: KERRY DOWNEY

I sang 'When Doves Cry' on the radio in Casper, Wyoming and I was voted in to win a trip to this premiere of *Under the Cherry Moon*. I sat in the theatre right across from Prince, partied with his band afterwards and then had a private moment with Prince at 2am in the morning at the airport. It's like a movie that I replay in my mind all the time. Nobody will ever be able to take that memory away from me.

MCNICHOLS SPORTS ARENA

3 JULY 1986, DENVER, COLORADO

I WAS THERE: DARLENE ARMENTA, AGE 17

The first time I went to a Prince concert was also the opening day for his movie *Under The Cherry Moon*. I dyed my hair purple. We drove from my small hometown in the mountains to Denver, Colorado to see both the movie and the concert. The concert was amazing. I screamed so much I lost my voice for two days. I also heard ringing in my ears for two days from the loud music and others screaming. It was totally worth it!

I WAS THERE: RON FEINGOLD

I'm a musician and I consider myself an educated Prince fan (friend). Prince came into my consciousness with 'Soft and Wet' and never left - to this day. Prince announced a contest on MTV in the summer of 1986 and the winner was in Cheyenne, Wyoming of all places. So Prince met the winner there, did an impromptu show and announced an arena show in Denver, Colorado (where I lived) since he was going to be close. After a night in line for a $17.50 ticket, we finally heard the sounds of 'Around the World in a Day'

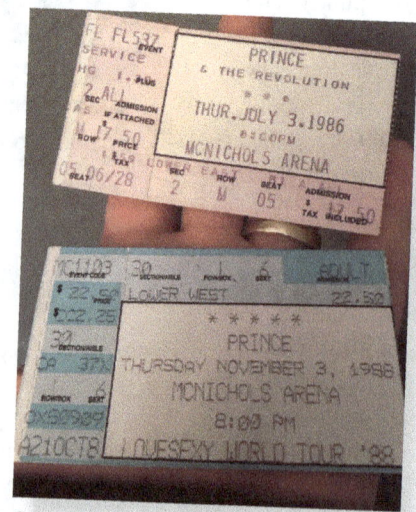

Ron Feingold saw Prince in Denver, Colorado

as he sang the first verse behind the curtain during the *Parade* tour. Never before had I heard a crowd scream like that with such a surge of energy. It was exciting and it was Love. It only got louder, much to my surprise, when he sang, 'say Papa, I think I want to Dance!' and the curtain fell and there he was - on a black and white checkered stage floor, arms outstretched soaking in our energy. I'll never forget that show and I never came down!

He came back two years later during the *Lovesexy* tour to a disappointing turnout of only 5,000 people in the arena. I eventually sat in the Ford Thunderbird that circled the stage for Prince's entrance to the stage in the round. He put that car in the lobby of the NPG store in uptown Minneapolis and I recognized it right away! I would often find myself in the listening room that was full of pillows, with Prince's drawings on the wall, and I heard the song 'Dolphin' in there for the first time as he released that song to visitors in the store.

After moving to Minneapolis in 1996 (I met my wife on a cruise ship and she just happened to be a Minnesota Viking Cheerleader at the time), we got on a secret email invitation list that announced Symbol's late night concerts at Paisley Park and we attended as many as possible. We would arrive at 1am, stand in sub zero temperatures for an hour and finally be let in by security to a sound that was already him on the stage jamming! We would watch him play and create for hours, try not to stare at him and Mayte hanging out by the stairs, and come home at 6am exhausted from a full night of the planet's finest funk!

My wife snuck a box of Captain Crunch into one show, at the Target Center in downtown Minneapolis across the street from 1st Avenue, in an attempt to either get him to take it or make him smile. He says in a song - in 'Emancipation', I think - that his favourite cereal is Cap'n Crunch. After sneaking the huge family size box into the arena (who brings cereal to a Prince show? We did!) he saw the cereal box in the hands of my beautiful wife and sang his way over as she started waving the Cap'n Crunch box faster. He then pointed at it, smiled at her and danced away. We took it home and ate it. Mission accomplished!

The shows were experiences beyond what words can help me describe. It was like a family of strangers brought together so close by the sound. I love him for that among many other reasons. May U Live 2 C The Dawn....

MADISON SQUARE GARDEN

2 & 3 AUGUST 1986, NEW YORK, NEW YORK

I WAS THERE: JENNIFER UPTON

The first time I saw him was in the summer of 1986. I was 14 years old and absolutely obsessed with Prince and The Revolution. I took piano and voice and, later, guitar lessons because of them. My uncle lived five hours north of New York City and I missed them when they played Syracuse on the *Purple Rain* tour. My Uncle who lived close to the city got me 2 nosebleed seats for the *Parade* tour at Madison

Square Garden. We were seated almost behind the stage but it didn't matter. I knew every word to every song and every dance step. A couple of months later I found out in *Rolling Stone* magazine that The Revolution had disbanded. I was gutted, but even at my young age I knew how lucky I was to have seen them live.

The *Parade* tour began with three nights at London's Wembley Arena and ran from 12 August to 9 September 1986. Taking in seven European nations and four Japanese shows, it was Prince's first foray into Europe.

Jennifer Upton and friends show of hands at Shepherds Bush

I WAS THERE: CHRIS CARRY

I wasn't a casual Prince fan. I was a hard core nut. I was (literally) in the fan club. I'd seen him play live over half a dozen times even specially travelling to the UK to see him play. The holy trinity for me is Bowie, Bruce and Prince in that order. I had spent seven hours in A&E and as a result my back was ridiculously sore. I was stressed and then I tuned onto the 7pm news. I had to stop the car. Prince. Dead? I was only listening to the new album that morning. What? Whaaat? *No. No. No.*

On Monday of that week I had acquired an eight CD bootleg set of unreleased Prince music and had been working through that. On Wednesday I was searching online to add a couple of vinyl versions of albums of his that I didn't have (*Batman* and *Lovesexy*). They were in my 'cart' but I didn't buy then because I was going to look at anything else I may have overlooked 'when I get a few minutes tomorrow'. Tomorrow never comes. Monday started with a reinvigoration and new investigation of his music and by Thursday evening it was calamity.

'All good things they say, never last.' Good god, I hated the sight of him. I read the music press from an early age (I was an *NME* subscriber!) so I probably knew a bit about him a couple of years before he hit public consciousness with the *1999* and *Purple Rain* albums. I saw the *Dirty Mind* cover, read a bit about him and instantly disliked what I saw. Now disgraced DJ Jonathan King had a music show on TV around the time that '1999' was released. He'd just concluded an interview with Lou Reed and, having been given short thrift by Lou in his general 'I hate journalists' adversarial mode, King - miffed at being found out by the razor sharp Reed - concluded the interview by saying something along the lines of, 'And now to someone infinitely more talented than Lou Reed, this is Prince...' and played the video for 'Little Red Corvette'. I was genuinely incensed about the comment that i felt badly disparaged one of my heroes. I took to an even deeper dislike of Prince after that.

Purple Rain came and went. I wasn't impressed. Prince even had the temerity to keep Bruce and 'Dancing In The Dark' off the top of the singles charts. Damn that guy! He won an award (a Brit, or a forerunner of those awards) and when he flounced up to the stage with his huge bodyguard in tow, high heels and blouse, took the award, said nothing and flounced back to his seat, I thought, 'Dick!'

Sitting with a friend of mine, Robbie Byrne, in his room listening to music one evening he took *Around The World In A Day* off the shelf. 'You *have* to listen to this, the guy is a genius' was Roberto's assessment of the situation. I duly protested, relating the J King/L Reed/Prince anecdote. Begrudgingly I took a loan of the record. I've never looked back and I can honestly say I have every album the guy ever released. The hard to get ones, the Internet only releases, 12 inch singles, CD singles, extended remixes, etc. etc. I have live album bootlegs and after show club gigs plus a plethora of songs, outtakes, demos, videos, etc. that were leaked on bootleg over the years.

I moved from Kells in Ireland to New York in late March of 1986. While I was there, Prince released *Parade*. Two shows were announced for Madison Square Gardens and I was lucky to get a ticket for the second night. I was up in the nosebleeds at the back, but I was in the room. Now, seeing Prince play a concert in NYC is a wee bit different from seeing him play somewhere like Cork. For a start, I was the only white guy in the section where I was sitting. I had relatively long fair hair then and wore a fedora hat. Yeah, this from the man who called Prince a dick. I kinda stuck out.

My experience was that NYC was not at that time a racially harmonised city. It probably still isn't. However, as with a lot of Irish people going to the US in the 80s, racism wasn't a particular issue for us. We simply didn't have much of a multi racial/cultural society in Ireland back then, so it was very rare that anything related to a racially driven incident appeared in the media nationally, let alone in the boondocks where I lived. In my own case, and in my consciousness, I was just a guy in the crowd same as anyone else.

At one stage in the show he led the crowd in a rap that seemed to turn a few heads towards me, the solitary honky. It was from 'The Roof Is On Fire' by Rock Master Scott and the Dynamic Three and seemed to be a black anthem of sorts. It goes like this: '…the roof is on fire… we don't need no water… let the muthafucker burn…burn muthafucker burn!'. O-kayyyyy.

Anyways. He played keyboards for the majority of the show, I don't remember him even playing guitar until the encore. An hour into the show, during 'Love Bizarre', Prince hollered, 'New York!' The crowd roared. 'New York!' The crowd roared louder. 'We're gonna rock all night!!' The crowd went apeshit bat crazy. The song ended. Prince stepped up to the mic and said, 'Goodnight New York, I love you.' The crowd, in unison, looked at their watches. What the fuck? An hour? He played 'Sometimes It Snows In April' at the piano and left the stage.

He walked back on stage on his own, with a guitar, for the first time that night. The lights changed colour and he delivered a 'Purple Rain' that to this day I still can't accurately describe in a way that would do it justice. Transcendent maybe?

So he played for less than an hour and 20 or so minutes. I'd have sat there all night. 'Kiss' wasn't played, which was a huge hit at the time, and I wished it had been included. At the previous night's show he did four more songs in the encore, which included 'Kiss' and 'Whole Lotta Shaking Going On'!

12 AUGUST 1986

Prince started a run of five nights at Wembley Arena, London, his first UK shows for five years.

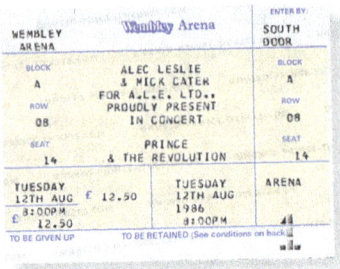

WEMBLEY ARENA

12 AUGUST 1986, LONDON, UK

I WAS THERE: NIGEL GOWINGS

I have been a Prince fan for 34 years now and saw him well over 30 times live in concert. I first got into his music at the age of 17 when a friend lent me the *1999* album to listen to. Shortly after that I went to my first Prince concert and was blown away and hooked forever. The first of those concerts was the *Parade* tour in 1986. I remember how excited I was to see this concert as I had only recently got into his music at 17. He had not played the UK since the early Eighties when he was relatively unknown in the UK and played at the Lyceum Theatre. So this would be his first gigs since the explosion of *Purple Rain* in the UK.

That night was the first of the three gigs he would play. I remember how excited my friend and I were on the tube ride from Brixton to Wembley. The show was sold out and we arrived early. We had good seats about ten rows from the front. The excitement in the arena was electric and full of anticipation. I remember that what stood out for me was how many celebrities were there to see him perform this gig from the likes of Duran Duran, George Michael, Sting, Ronnie Wood and Sam Fox, who at the time was a big model in the UK.

The show opened with the sound of Prince's voice behind the stage curtain to 'Around the World in a Day'. The moment that will always stay with me is when the he shouted out, 'London, I think I wanna dance' and the curtains opened to screams from the crowd and there was a topless Prince with a tambourine. That moment took my breath away and I was hooked forever.

He played over 26 songs that night. Although the crowd were not quite yet familiar with some of the early songs from his career, nevertheless the excitement was at full level the whole show, the climax being the two encores that he did, which included 'Kiss' and of course 'Purple Rain', which I would see him perform many times over the next 30 years.

I will always remember that night at Wembley Arena and the first time I heard the song. That was the night my bromance with Prince began, and which will stay with me forever. The critics would go on to rave about Prince and that show and his triumphant return to the UK.

I WAS THERE: ROBERT HUGGINS, AGE 16

I was lucky enough to see him three times, at Wembley Arena, Wembley Stadium and Earls Court on the *Parade*, *Symbol* and *Diamonds & Pearls* tours.

My first experience of him was at the Brit Awards in 1985 when he won for *Purple Rain* (Prince won Best Soundtrack/Cast Recording for *Purple Rain* but also Best International Solo Artist). It was so weird it was great. So I watched the film and got hooked. The next album I bought really after *Purple Rain* was *Parade*. And still to this day it has some of my favourite tracks on it. The concert at Wembley Arena for the *Parade* tour is a bit of a blur. We didn't have great seats but I remember the first track was 'Around the World in a Day'. It was my first concert. Earls Court for the *Diamonds & Pearls* tour was amazing. It was a much more intimate concert even though there were so many there. We went to the last date there and 15 minutes after the lights went off they came back on and performed a kind of jamming set, mostly covers, and you could see they just had fun. The *Symbol* tour started with 'My Name is Prince' with a dancer in a cage. Then he came on – it was so good! I live in New Zealand now and stupidly missed the *Piano & A Microphone* dates he did here just before he passed. His death happened during our night time. So I'd have woken up to the news. It was unbelievable really and so sad, as he was a genius.

I WAS THERE: NIGEL HART

There are many great performers but far fewer legends. Prince Rogers Nelson was a legend! Of the 84 shows that I was lucky enough to witness between 1986 and 2015, his were the only ones that gave you goose bumps as the lights went down on every occasion. I recall a famous quote that if Prince had just been a guitarist, he would have been one of the best and if he had been simply a singer, likewise. But the same applies to his bass playing, piano playing or any other instrument he cared

to turn his hand to. And that's before you even consider his traits as the consummate showman and entertainer, which to me were beyond comparison.

My first shows were on the *Parade* tour in August 1986, where I witnessed three sublime shows at Wembley Arena. This would be the last time he played with The Revolution, the end of an era in fact. Part soul review, part funk fest, these shows were stripped back in their simplicity, during which Prince rarely played guitar, which was unusual. I remember Sting and Ronnie Wood getting up on what I believe was the last night as they jammed out a version of the Stones' 'Miss You'.

The *Lovesexy* tour that followed in 1988 was probably my favourite tour if I had to pick one. Playing in the round on a stage that had elevated platforms, a basketball court, a bed and even a Thunderbird car that circled the stage, this was perhaps his most elaborate stage production ever! I also thought that the set lists, his look (polka dots were in!), the theming and his playing were almost other-worldly on this tour, as he switched from guitar to piano and even to drums on occasions. This was definitely one that the fans hold close to their hearts in so many ways!

I WAS THERE: MANDI INGRAM, AGE 14

I saw him over 100 times. I have a brother who is 11 years older than me and another who is nearly nine years older. One was a Motown fan and the other was listening to Prince. My family has always been very music orientated but my mum realised I was picking up on Prince when she would walk me to school and hear me singing the words to 'Soft and Wet'. I now understand her shock as I was only eight at the time! It was 1979 and she asked my brother to play something else but you know what kind of songs he was bringing out then, so I had to promise not to sing them in school anymore!

My first Prince concert was the *Parade* tour in 1986. I was 14. We went by coach and that had broken down. I thought we were going to miss the show but we made it just in time. My brother had to move me to our seats as I was stuck to the floor, and that's when my real love affair started!

On the *Lovesexy* tour I had Lenny Henry and Dawn French sitting behind me and they tried to talk to me, to ask if I was excited, and I turned round and loudly shushed them!

On one of the nights after seeing Prince at the *21 Nights* at the O2 (we did 15 of them), we were at an after gig at the Indigo 2 and I turned around to go to the toilet and nearly got knocked off my feet by Morris Hayes. I couldn't talk and my husband and brother were laughing their heads off at me.

I have made lots of friends from all around this wonderful globe because of this talented and wonderful man. I have been lucky to have a brother that I am still very close to and we travel all over the world so we have had the chance to see him loads of times. We hit one of our bucket list dreams when we went to Minneapolis and did the ultimate tour at Paisley Park. We also saw NPG and The Revolution. Our next bucket list dream is to see Sheila and Morris Day and The Time.

I WAS THERE: SHANE WETTON, AGE 15

I was 15 years old, living in North Wales. I'd first discovered Prince a few years beforehand, hearing 'Little Red Corvette' but not knowing who sang it. Slowly through 1984, as each single was released from *Purple Rain*, I liked each one a bit more until I realised that these songs I'd been singing along to were all by the same artist. My love for Prince and the Revolution was born!

In 1985 he announced he was giving up touring to 'look for the ladder' and having seen the *Purple Rain* show from Syracuse, I was disappointed. But having never seen a live concert before it would be extreme to say I was gutted. Anyway, I was sat at home one day when an announcement came on the radio to say Prince would play three nights at Wembley Arena in August 1986. It was only a few weeks away. Oh, and a mere 200 plus miles. That's a lot to a 15 year old, which is bad enough if you're in Manchester or Birmingham but from a small town in North Wales it seemed so far!

My dad tried to get tickets for me. He tried everywhere, eventually securing them from a place in Sevenoaks in Kent. I'd never heard of it but I didn't care, the tickets arrived and I was going. We had four tickets, for me and two mates plus the older brother of one – he could drive! The small matter of his leg being in plaster following an accident was a bit of an issue but he was due to have the cast removed the day before – result! Tickets cost £10 plus a small booking fee.

The day arrived, Phil had had his cast removed and we left at 9am and headed for Wembley down the M6. Or was it the M1? I can't remember! One of my mates didn't show – a mistake or what? But he had paid and made it clear he didn't expect the money back. Arriving at the Arena sometime between 1pm and 2pm, we went for a stroll around, full of excitement. Every few seconds there were touts asking, 'Need tickets? I'll buy any spares' so I asked him how much he was willing to pay. He offered me £20. Wow. I could double my money and it might get me a t-shirt! My mate said, 'Make it £25 and you have a deal' so he proceeded to give me £25 and I thought I'd pulled off the sale of the century. Little did I know people were paying well over £100 for the tickets, if not £200.

Prince arrived in a black limo with gold windows. He got out of the car, smiled, collected some gifts from a few fans and proceeded inside the arena and we sat, waited and listened to the sound check. This guy was just on the other side of a wall from me!

We were at the back of the arena but discovered the more expensive seats only started a few rows in front so we weren't that bothered. We were facing the stage head on and Wembley Arena wasn't that massive so we were happy. Prince was due on stage at 8pm but as was the norm in those days he was late. I think it was only about 20 minutes but those 20 minutes seemed like an age. The harp music died down, as did the lights, and a booming voice announced 'Ladies and Gentlemen, please welcome Prince and the Revolution' and the sound of 'Around the World in a Day' came though the speakers. Me and my mate had tried to pre-empt what he would open with. Tim thought it would be 'Let's Go Crazy' as it had been his go to opener on the *Purple Rain* tour and he hadn't toured since. I thought it might be 'Mountains', more out of hope than anything. This was obviously pre Internet or social media so there were no reviews of the previous two nights in terms of set lists apart from a couple of short news items that preferred to mention other celebrities in attendance and how Prince was controversial. The proper 'music' reviews - *Melody Maker*, *Sounds*, *NME* and the more pop-based magazines like *Smash Hits* wouldn't be out for another week so we had no idea what to expect!

The set list was perfect. The two albums since the previous tour, *Parade* and *Around the World in a Day*, covered a good amount of the set list, *Parade* especially. Then there was the 'old stuff', songs from *Prince*, *Dirty Mind*, *Controversy* and, of course, *1999* and *Purple Rain*. Hearing the band move effortlessly from one track to the next in the opening 20 minutes or so was incredible. Prince looked like he was really enjoying being in the UK but also had that glint in his eye that said 'you lot ain't gonna know what's hit you' and he was right.

Hearing songs like 'Automatic', '17 Days', 'Head'… the crowd interaction, Prince commanding the band and the crowd simultaneously. As a 15 year old being asked to chant 'the roof, the roof, the roof is on fire, we don't need no rain, let the motherfucker burn' was so bad but so good!

Of course I was just beginning my 'Prince live' journey and at the time I didn't know I wouldn't hear Prince sing '17 Days' again until the last time I saw him some 28 years later. I also really wanted to hear him sing 'Paisley Park'. I would have to wait 28 years for that one, but that was the joy of Prince, you just never knew. We got 'Little Red Corvette', the only night of the three UK dates he played it.

Then there was my first experience of a Prince encore, those unpredictable and unforgettable moments that I came to realise would always hold a special place in my memories (pretty much every encore I've witnesses has been memorable). It started with 'Miss You', with Prince joined on stage by Ron Wood and Sting, a very funky version and, as he promised at the time, he owned the song that night. This was followed by 'Mountains', which at the time was never off my turntable. I still use it as a 'go to' good mood track. And then 'Kiss', complete with the shades and the black leather jacket. Then he was gone.

Now if that had been anyone else that would have been enough, but not Prince - another encore! Yes, we expected 'Purple Rain' but he started off with the first verse and a chorus of 'Sometimes It Snows in April'. Again, this was the only night he played it. It was beautiful and led perfectly into 'Purple Rain'. I was hooked, not just at the time, but for evermore. My love of music and more importantly, live music, was formed on that one night and it would stay with me forever.

I WAS THERE: MICHELLE LANAWAY

I went up to Wembley Arena for the *Parade* tour. We were on the same side of the stage as Wendy and Lisa. We were second row. We queued overnight for tickets months before, and we took sleeping bags. We decided to queue up for tickets because going to see Prince play was the thing to do – after Madonna! People in the queue were dressed up a bit like Prince. And when you're queuing overnight there's always a bit of camaraderie and people having a laugh and if you want to go off to the chippy you go off to the chippy and someone saves your space for you. But in the morning, people tried to push in to the queue and everybody just shamed them into not pushing in.

I probably wore a lot of purple to the gig. I was into wearing a shiny gold jacket and pearls at the time. We were so excited that we were in the second row. I can still see it in my head. I can't remember what he played, but he must have played 'Sometimes It Snows in April'. Whenever I hear that song it makes me want to cry. I remember a vibe rather than exactly what he played.

After Wembley, I saw Prince at Maine Road as well. I was living in Liverpool and saw him with my friend Andrew. I thought it was really weird that you walked through all this housing estate and there was Prince playing. I remember the gig at Wembley was amazing and colourful and spectacular but the one at Maine Road being a bit dour and more about the music.

I remember really loving the film *Purple Rain* but now – that scene where the woman gets thrown in the dumpster? I think that's really appalling. I saw him on the *21 Nights* tour. It was just him and a piano in the middle of the room. It was really stripped back. We were really, really high up. It was so sad when he died. It was a real shock. He was such an inspiration for people. And of course it was performing that killed him in the end because he was in so much pain, jumping on and off speakers. So to die from a painkiller was so sad. With someone like Michael Jackson you think, 'That's going to happen,' but you thought Prince was more together. Even when he wasn't writing his own music he was inspiring so many different people.

I WAS THERE: ADELE SIMMONS, AGE 19

'I Wanna Be Your Lover' was the first song I heard from Prince and I loved it. I was 12 at the time. I saw him four times. What can I say except what a showman and a fantastic musician. His stage presence was just magical and what a dancer! These were the best live performances I have ever seen. There definitely isn't anything to compare to Prince. The first time I saw him was August 1986 at Wembley Arena for his *Parade* tour. I went with two friends from school. I remember the concert being just awesome. I bought lots of merchandise and still have the programme from the concert. All the shows I saw were fantastic. The *21 Nights* he did at the O2 was awesome.

AHOY SPORTSPALEIS

17 – 19 AUGUST 1986, ROTTERDAM, NETHERLANDS

I WAS THERE: MIEKE LAHAYE-SOMERS

My boyfriend and I were students. We discovered Prince with the worldwide broadcast live from Syracuse. Prince came to Europe for the *Parade* tour in 1986 and we went crazy. We followed him everywhere through Europe. We adored *Under the Cherry Moon*. It was a masterpiece and we decided to finish our studies at university as soon as possible and move to Nice, where the film was set, with just one suitcase between us. My boyfriend did not even speak French. We lived on the *Under the Cherry Moon* film set for seven years, married there and had a baby boy there. When Prince came to Europe, our Dutch family knew we would visit Holland too. If our French bosses said 'no' to days off we said 'yes we will go anyway' and we left for Prince concerts in Paris, Holland, Germany, etc. and we would find another job once we were back home in Nice. Prince was more important than anything else.

Even our wedding announcement cards carried the golden LOVE symbol when we married in November 1993. We made the cards with golden ink which stank. The whole room had a crazy smell that night which we thought was the ink but when we woke up in the morning we saw our apartment had been badly damaged - somebody had thrown a Molotov cocktail through the window of the vet shop underneath and the firemen hadn't warned us because we slept at the back. The funny smell was the smoke from the fire and not the golden ink for our wedding cards!

We married and had a baby boy. His first Prince concert was in my belly and we had a daughter and her first Prince concert was in my belly too. Now we are saving our dollars to honour Prince in 2021, finally visiting Paisley Park. We couldn't when he had his pyjama parties but he has been in our lives since we have been together in 1984. That is a long time and he helped us with the ups and downs... thank you Prince!

I WAS THERE: RAMON MUNTJEWERFF

I became a fan after borrowing *Purple Rain* on vinyl from the library. It absolutely blew me away so I bought it, plus some older albums. Then in 1986 Prince released *Parade* and the big news came that he was actually going to do three concerts at the Sportpaleis Ahoy in Rotterdam in Holland. I was able to get two tickets for the Monday show on 18th August 1986. I had no driving license because I had just reached 18 in June but luckily my brother who wasn't (and still isn't) a Prince fan told me he would take me.

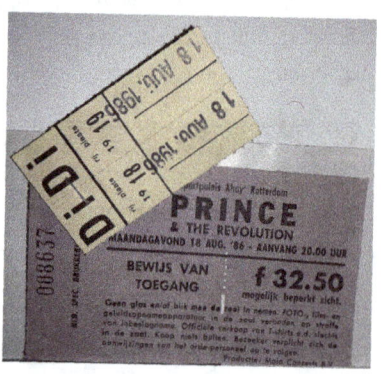

Ramon's ticket for the Sportspaleis Ahoy show

Those first minutes when 'Around the World' started playing behind the curtains and then the curtains opened and Prince jumped off the back speakers onto the stage and this was the start of one of his most funkiest concert ever, it was non-stop hits, funk, etc. Even when Prince went for a clothes change The Revolution played 'Manic Monday', which was never played before and rarely since.

At one stage two fans started fighting so Prince actually stopped playing and told them to stop or he would finish the concert. All unforgettable moments. I saw him 12 more times over the years but for some reason this is the one I fully remember and cherish so much.

My life changed after this and I got involved in the fanzine "controversy "as a area organiser and started writing stories about all things happening in Holland and because it was before Internet it was the only way to get information about Prince and be able to meet other fans. I started doing interviews with Dutch artists (like Candy Dulfer) who worked with Prince and met Wendy and Lisa from The Revolution and got my photo taken with them and it all became even more interesting when the magazine was officially recognised by Prince from number 12. 43 Controversy's were released till 1993. This was a very important era for me

ALSTERDORFER SPORTHALLE

31 AUGUST 1986, HAMBURG, WEST GERMANY

I WAS THERE: LARS RUNKEN

It was my very first Prince concert. I remember this pantomimic performance where he brushed his teeth. He fumbled something out of the front of his trousers, which was some little silver chains that he immediately threw into the audience. I wasn't one of the lucky ones who caught one but I was so damn lucky that my godfather bought me a ticket while I was on holiday in Denmark after I read that Prince was coming to Hamburg.

31 MARCH 1987

Prince released his ninth studio album *Sign o' the Times* which produced three top 10 hit singles, 'If I Was Your Girlfriend', 'U Got the Look' (with Sheena Easton) and the title track, 'Sign o' the Times'. In 1989, *Time*

Out magazine ranked it as the greatest album of all time.

The *Sign o' the Times* tour took in 34 shows. Marking the debut of what fans dubbed the Lovesexy Band, the tour ran from 8 May 1987 to 29 June 1987 and included visits to eight Continental European states.

JOHANNESHOV ISSTADION

8 – 10 MAY 1987, STOCKHOLM, SWEDEN

I WAS THERE: NIKO ECKHOFF, AGE 12

I was 12 years old, going on 13, and a pretty advanced child both music-wise and in my literary pursuits. I first heard Prince's 'When Doves Cry' on the US Armed Forces radio station in July 1984. This was considered pirate radio in Oslo, Norway where I grew up and where I lived for the first half of my life. The connection to this minimalistic piece of beauty was immediate. I felt different too. I was considered strange among my family and friends since I only listened to music and read books and papers. This was slightly before the Internet so I was lost for a few weeks until the local newspaper did a major write-up on Prince. He was in black leather boots, white flannel and full make-up in the picture. 'Music's Newest Sensation' was the headline. No kidding!

I had *Purple Rain* on cassette tape soon and that was really what kicked off my life. I was never the same after hearing Prince. I knew better now. It was okay. Everything was okay. So when 1987 rolled around, I had obsessively listened to Prince's now classic albums for a while. The show in the neighbouring country of Sweden was announced in March. To get tickets we would have to sleep on the street in front of the ticket place. The tickets included a bus ride and were about $70 at the time, which was expensive. My mom took me downtown at 3.30am and the street was alive with the then new *Sign O' The Times* album and with people in sleeping bags and hanging out, smoking cigarettes and talking. The night went by fast and in the morning I had my ticket.

When I woke up on 9 May in the early morning and got ready for the bus I was filled with a brand new feeling. I was over hyped. Having seen the VHS of the 1985 Syracuse show I knew his shows were amazing - and I was going to one! This was the third show of the *Sign o' the Times* tour. On the seven-hour bus ride from Oslo to Sweden I talked to artists and women (they were really girls probably - I wasn't even officially a teen), while some people brought beer and Prince albums played loudly on the stereo.

Madhouse, Prince's jazz project, opened the show while the venue filled up. Finally the lights went out at 8pm and Prince was playing a guitar solo in the dark while flashing lights went across the stage. I was in a trance. Two of the 'grown ups' from the bus were making out next to me. The intro - the 'Oh yeah, THAT song' - I remember clearly more than 30 years later. Then I got sucked into the energy and the songs I knew by heart and I had the best time of my life for two hours. I sometimes wonder if this is my best life experience all together outside of childhood.

I wore the t-shirt to school next day and my friends were jealous and I finally was cool. I couldn't believe it.

WEMBLEY STADIUM

25 & 26 MAY 1987, LONDON, UK

Prince cancelled his only two planned – and highly anticipated - UK shows for the *Sign o' the Times* tour because of bad weather.

WESTFALENHALLEN

1 & 2 JUNE 1987, DORTMUND, WEST GERMANY

I WAS THERE: MARK BRUTON

With the *Act 2* tour we did I think Monday, Tuesday in Birmingham, and I said, 'Right, are you ready for Saturday at Wembley? I've got you a ticket' and he goes, 'Do I have to pay for it?' and I went 'yeah', and we never made it back so had to sleep on New Street Euston station.

The *Parade* tour was first, then I went to the *Sign o' the Times* in Dortmund. I had second and third row in Birmingham, queued up all night for those, and eight times on the *Lovesexy* tour. The first London one, the last three nights in London and then the Birmingham gigs and a couple in the middle. There was a moment when he came out in a t-shirt and sat at a table eating some peanuts. Going to *Sign o' the Times* was good fun. About 30 of us went from London to Dortmund and some on to Paris. They'd do two nights and get a coach. It stopped in Cologne and then on to Dortmund.

By the time I was getting close to getting married it was tailing off, so I'd go to the Birmingham or London shows. But 31 times isn't bad!

For *Hit and Run* I went to Birmingham, KOKO and Manchester. We always said it's my wife and daughter's birthday the 9th and 10th February and I said, 'Sorry they'll be a Prince gig' thinking I would get tickets for Shepherd's Bush but I failed so had to go out for their birthday meal instead.

I WAS THERE: MIEKE LAHAYE-SOMERS

It was the *Sign o' the Times* concert in Germany with tickets as in a theatre. I had row 1, exactly in the middle, so exactly in front of his mic! I was dressed like him, a total copy, with long black leather coat, peach suit, etc., and just before the concert started my boyfriend (now my husband) bought me an ice cream which I was licking when Prince came on in front of me. He started 'Sign o' the Times' with his guitar and the look he gave me while I was licking my ice cream made me feel so ashamed I instantly dropped it on the floor!

Mieke was on the front row at Dortmund and licking an ice cream when Prince came on stage

PALAIS OMNISPORTS DE PARIS-BERCY

13 – 15 & 17 JUNE 1987, PARIS, FRANCE

I WAS THERE: VIRGINIE KRIEF

The first time I heard his songs I was very young, four years old. My parents lived in America. The first song I remember hearing is 'Soft and Wet'. Then my brother came home from the record store with a Prince disc and said, 'It's better than Michael Jackson.' I said, 'That's not possible.' He played *Purple Rain* for me and I didn't like it much. I said, 'I'll stay with Michael Jackson.' In France, there was then a new channel on TV called M6 which was playing 'When Doves Cry'. And I saw Prince and I said, 'Wow. He's better than Michael Jackson.' My brother bought all the albums from *For You* through to *Purple Rain*. My parents listened to music. My father was a big fan of Marvin Gaye. My mother listened to more French music. I was 13 when *Lovesexy* came out so I loved that album. But my favourite album now is *For You*. I saw him 13 times. The first time I saw him live was in Paris for the *Sign o' the Times* tour. He threw a rose to me and all the fans jumped on me wanting the rose! I went with my brother, who is seven years older than me. I was with him and all his friends. We were standing in the third row and we were all dancing together, doing the same moves.

NEW MORNING

17 JUNE 1987, PARIS, FRANCE

I WAS THERE: PHIL SIMMS

I've been a fan since '83 when I was 12. A friend of mine got me into him, first *Prince* and then *Dirty Mind*. In 1986 I was 14 and went to the *Parade* tour and I was interviewed for MTV because I had a long jacket on. I was a bit more of a geeky Prince fan back in the day. One thing that resonates with me going to his early tours was that it was 70 per cent women, and I was aware of that. There weren't many men there. I was reading *Sounds*, I was reading *NME*, I got into buying records (which I still do 30 years down the line), and I paid £20 back in the day for tickets to the live concert and vinyl. I then went to Paris and saw *Sign o' the Times*, and I was lucky. I was with a friend of mine and we went to a jazz club and got the wrong jazz club and they said, 'Are you looking for the Prince gig later?' and we ended up in New Morning which was high on my list of clubs because there weren't many people there so at a fairly young age we got to see a gig. I was 17.

I was lucky I was helping a plumber out and got paid quite a lot of money, with Chris Dawson from the Revolutions, he used to take a bus load of people across. I did *Lovesexy* and I think I did six gigs in total. I was always waiting for a gig to fall on my birthday. The nearest one was Maine Road in 1992 on 26th June. The highlight was the second gig at Manchester Academy where he did the *One Nite Alone* tour. A lot of people went off Prince in that era but I loved the *Rainbow* tour, my favourite album, and hearing 'Dorothy Parker' live. My last Prince gig was the 2016 Paisley Park Gala on 21 January 2016, I cried at 'Condition of the Heart', my favourite track. I was one of the lucky people. I was doing a rundown of all of the Europeans coming across and was doing the visuals and Prince was tweeting them back to me. And there was this mural and he tweeted that back to me too.

21 MAY 1988

Prince scored his first UK number 1 album with *Lovesexy*. The cover, based on a photo by Jean Baptiste Mondino, caused some controversy upon release as it depicts Prince in the nude. Some record stores refused to stock it or wrapped the album in black.

The *Lovesexy* tour ran from 8 July 1988 to 13 February 1989 taking in Europe, North America and Japan.

PALAIS OMNISPORTS DE PARIS-BERCY

8 – 10 & 12 JULY 1988, PARIS, FRANCE

I WAS THERE: SHAUN MARSH

I saw the great man on numerous occasions. I saw him in Paris a couple of times, plus Sheffield, Manchester, Birmingham and London. The 1988 *Lovesexy* tour in Bercy, Paris was the ultimate concert.

My uncle really got me into Prince. He wanted me to go to Wembley to watch the *Purple Rain* tour but I didn't know anything about Prince then. Straight after I heard the 'Girls and Boys' single I loved it and bought the 12 inch version. After that, and hearing 'Erotic City' on the B-side, I bought absolutely everything he released that I could get my hands on. I bought UK and US vinyl's, CDs, videos, DVDs, etc., some of which are quite rare. I bought anything to do with the great man. I went to his shop in Camden when it opened and bought lots of stuff from there too.

I had all the t-shirts and clothes around and even made my own for concerts after I saw someone doing the same for one of the Paris concerts. I joined a UK fan club called *Crystal Ball* which sent out awesome magazines and even got us front row priority tickets for concerts, which my friends loved me for.

Every concert I saw was unique. The guy was the ultimate professional and his bands were so tight and, boy, he put on the best shows I have ever seen to this date. The *Lovesexy* tour was my favourite, the one they showed live from Germany on UK TV. It wasn't just music, it was a complete show that got you involved and kept you thoroughly entertained. As soon as those headlights came on that Thunderbird car the show was non-stop. I regretted missing Prince's breakthrough *Purple Rain* concert so I went to every UK one I could when he came over to the UK. I'd have loved to have got into an after party show but never got the chance.

Prince was the best. An unbelievable musician who played everything, a great singer and showman and someone who always lived, ate and slept music. His output is unheard of and I hope there are many unreleased projects still to come out because I miss the guy so much... He was so cool.

The last time I saw him was in Birmingham in 2014. As always he didn't disappoint, putting on a show. Little did I know that that would be the last time I saw him live. I wish he would have brought the *Piano* tour to our shores. I would have loved the raw music with just his voice and a piano. Alas, it was not to be. I still can't believe he has gone but his great music will live on.

WEMBLEY ARENA

25 & 26, 28 & 29 JULY & 1 – 3 AUGUST 1988,
LONDON, UK

I WAS THERE: PERRY GORTON

My first encounter with Prince was watching his show from Syracuse, New York. I thought, 'Wow, I love this guy. What a performance over two hours, this guy is different!' I first got to see Prince at Wembley Arena in 1988, the *Lovesexy* tour, and it was another 'wow' moment. What a show – it was electrifying. After seeing this performance I became hooked and started to build a collection of Prince's records, memorabilia, etc. In 1990, the *Nude* tour, Prince completed 17 shows at Wembley Arena. I was lucky enough to go every night. I was definitely addicted to Prince, for want of a better word. I saw Prince on 47 occasions, built up of concerts and after show parties. Since losing Prince, my life just isn't the same although from setting up a Prince group on Facebook in 2008, Prince....The Living Legend, I get to share memories and keep his legacy alive with over 50,000 like-minded fans from around the world.

I WAS THERE: MARK HUTCHISON

1998 saw my first venture out of Scotland for a Prince gig. Me and another friend went down by train. We got to the Tube station and, it being our first time in London, we hadn't a clue which train to get. Turns out it was the purple line! Walking up to the gig, we saw Rhonda Smith behind a fence, shouted, 'hey Rhonda!' and she walked over to the fence to chat. She asked where I'd travelled from and said Prince and the band appreciated fans travelling from afar to see them play. She said, 'Enjoy the gig, and thanks for chatting.'

We were up on the second tier which turned out to be the perfect spot. Chaka Khan was on stage and we could see Prince in the sound booth playing his guitar, jamming along. You couldn't see that from down on the floor. During 'I Feel for You', Prince walked on stage still in his purple coat, saying, 'I wrote this, right? I feel for you too, baby.' The gig itself was amazing, a whole host of hits, including Prince pointing to a woman in front of us saying, 'I need a girlfriend.' The woman nearly wet herself. Then Prince said, 'No, not you.' Her disappointment was very obvious. During 'Little Red Corvette', which he played on piano, the crowd sang along. Prince stopped and asked, 'Who told you to sing?' It was Prince on awesome form.

I WAS THERE: SEAN COCKWELL

I had missed the Purple One on his 1986 *Parade* tour and I was gutted. I had only just started working full-time, after finishing college, and had yet to feel comfortable parting with cash to see an artist perform live. It wasn't just the cost of the ticket, which is comparatively meagre compared to the horrendous ticket prices of today (and that's before the additional of ridiculous fees that the awful ticket agencies fraudulently add to the cost). It was the associated costs involved of travelling to London's Wembley Arena as well as buying up a concert programme and other merchandise once there.

However after a couple of years of earning reasonably good money I felt more solvent and therefore more comfortable about using cash to see the artists I cherished perform live. By now I had seen Madonna on her *Who's That Girl?* tour and, a week before my first experience of Prince on stage, Michael Jackson, again at Wembley Stadium, in July 1988. During Jackson's *BAD* live show, his band played Prince's 'It's Gonna Be A Beautiful Night' whilst the King of Pop took a breather. This fired up passionate whisperings amongst us in the audience that perhaps both Prince and Michael Jackson would appear onstage together given that both were in residency at Wembley - Jackson at the Stadium, Prince in the Arena - but alas it was not to be.

A week later my friend Paula and I ventured up to Wembley Arena for our first live Prince experience. The *Lovesexy* tour was named after his album of the same name, released that very same year, and it was an album that saw the Purple One in a more positive frame of mind following the shelved (at the time) negativity that was his *Black Album*. The staging was central to the arena rather that at the farthest end as was normally the case, and it looked like we were going to be in for a decent view, albeit from many rows back. However my heart missed a beat when an attendant approached us and told us that we were in the wrong seats. I had visions of being further back from the centred stage. However we actually ended up being taken further forward. We were in the second row. How exciting was that!

There was no support act and we are advised to be seated promptly as the show was set to kick off at a scheduled time. As the lights dimmed and the crowd went wild, there was the sound of a car engine kicking into life and - yes - there was a car. The headlights flicked on and the car did a quick tour of the circular stage before its eagerly anticipated passengers stepped out from the vehicle onto the stage. I am not one prone to exhibiting excitement, I tend to keep it all bottled up, but upon seeing the guy that electrified me with his live performances in the film *Purple Rain* and amazed me with the diversity of his classic *Sign o' the Times* album, I was euphoric.

The next two-and-a-half hours completely dumbfounded me. After all, the week before I had seen Michael Jackson who at the time was the hottest ticket in town with his BAD tour, but Prince would have run circles around him. Whereas Jackson's show was meticulously planned to the smallest detail (not that this is a complaint) it did lack the apparent spontaneity of Prince's *Lovesexy* concert. And what's more, Prince could visibly be seen to be enjoying himself as much as his audience, whereas Jackson would probably kick himself for not pulling off a choreographed dance move.

Jackson had an annoying habit of stopping mid-song to milk the adulation to the max, on a far too regular basis. Prince was more fluid and proved to be an energetic, flawless and effortless performer. At one point it looked like his lead female dancer Cat was beckoning to Paula and myself to join them all on stage. We didn't, but my mind still reels at the possibility of what might of been if we had. Seeing Prince up close and personal is an experience that I will never forget and the subsequent tours that I had the pleasure of attending never did quite match the magnificence of that first time. That's not a fault of the performer but more the distance we were from the main stage.

I WAS THERE: DEBORAH LOUISE SAMUEL

I was lucky enough to see him several times over the years. I actually got into his music by accident. A friend was a big fan and wanted to see him live. No one would go with her so she asked me. I was returning the favour as she had attended a Human League concert with me a few years before. I saw the *Lovesexy* tour and was completely blown away by this absolutely amazing artist and performer. From that day I was hooked. The last show I saw was at the O2 Arena in London for my 40th birthday in 2007. And my favourite? His 1993 Wembley Stadium show.

I WAS THERE: RON LITTLE

In 1979 I bought the album *For You*. This album said 'all songs written, produced and performed by Prince'. How can that not impress anyone? Little did I know the effect it would have on me and my family. We even named our son Jamie Christopher, two Prince aliases - Jamie Starr and Christopher Tracy.

I got married in August 1979 and my wife Linda had never heard of Prince. I brought home a video of Prince playing live, put it on and from that moment on she was hooked. We just had to see Prince live. In 1988 that wish came true when he came over for the *Lovesexy tour* and we met him in Tower Records and he signed the album, as did the rest of the band. My wife still has that album to this day.

Believe me - Wembley Arena rocked. I have seen a lot of live bands but Prince is the best ever. But just when you thought it could not get any better - the *Nude* tour. No one is better than Prince live and Wembley Arena rocks again. I am living the dream.

Then there was *Diamonds & Pearls* at Earls Court - the same result. Fantastic! Then back to Wembley Arena which was out of this world. We have all lived a dream Prince and his music is my dream there will never be another Prince. I do remember the day he died. I shed a tear there is no shame in that after all the purple family is that close.

I do not remember the date. Prince may have passed on but his music will never die. It will outlive us all. Long live Prince and his music.

I WAS THERE: CHRIS CARRY

I was working in GE in Wembley, London and Prince announced a string of shows at the local arena, which is about a 12,000 capacity. Myself and three lads from work - Jeff, Keith and Chris (Goodwin) - headed off to the show. We took our excellent seats, row 20 from the stage, which was set up 'in the round' i.e. in the middle of the arena. As the arena filled up the row of seats in front of us remained empty. During the first song ('Erotic City'), in the darkness, a bunch of people occupied their seats and not quietly or without fuss. One of the party was a complete vision from the back. Black satin bomber jacket, the tightest black leggings imaginable (unheard of in the Eighties, not like today) and the longest black hair which was swept back from the face every few minutes.

The lads all looked down the line at me and there were a few nudge, nudge, wink, wink faces made. I didn't really pass that much remark as I was focused purely on the stage and anyone interrupting my connection to the action is generally ignored or given a withering glance. However it was hard not to physically register what looked like a vision of loveliness directly in front of me.

After a few songs more, one of the lads tugged at my elbow and nodded to my right as in, 'Bloody hell mate, look who it is?' It was Frankie Goes To Hollywood, or at least Holly Johnson, Paul Rutherford and their friends. Now I could understand the getting-to seats-when-the-lights-go-down situation, but they were also very irritating in that they still exhibited a contradictory 'look at me, look at me, I love how much I can talk and how loud I can be' behaviour.

At the first intermission, the lights went up. As the group in front began to sit down 'The Vision' turned around to us and smiled at me in a nice way, like you do when you're out at a show to the people around you. It was Pete Burns, he of the group Dead or Alive and sadly very much dead now. Yup, collective intake of breath from the four of us and a quick conversation started about the football or some other such macho-esque topic.

Prince did a blues jam, 'Blues In C' (aka 'If I Had a Harem') where he sat at the edge of the stage and played an unbelievable guitar solo, and revealed a side of Prince we'd never really ever seen before. Prince as a Delta bluesman? Wow. He also did a cover version of 'Just My Imagination' that night. Again, totally class. He finished the show with 'Alphabet Street'. This was the song where he and Kat would jump aboard a Thunderbird car that was attached to the periphery of the stage by a mechanical arm and they would then 'drive' around the stage as they waved their goodbyes. On this night they jumped aboard the 'white rad rod' (maybe a '56 or '57, it was, however, seemingly, absurd) and disappeared from view. Possibly to Tennessee.

I WAS THERE: DANIEL PAYNE

I was 11 years old in 1984. I had been brought up on good quality music. My dad was a big ELO fan and both my parents loved The Crusaders. I loved my music even at that young age and I had bought the odd single here and there and had the odd compilation album. But as yet there were no artists I was really into. I would always listen to Radio 1 and religiously watched *Top of the Pops* and loved most music. Then one day in 1984

I had the radio on and that is when it happened. Coming out of the radio was the most amazing guitar intro sound I had ever heard. It made me walk straight over to my hi fi and turn it up. Then these weird distorted vocals started and this drum beat/loop played out like I had never heard before. And then came these vocals that had this amazing layered texture to them. I remember thinking it must be two blokes duetting, as one vocal was really low and the other really high. I was totally transfixed! I rushed around to find a piece of paper so I could write down who and what it was: 'And that was the new single from Prince and The Revolution – 'When Doves Cry'.' I then remember waiting by the radio all day to hear it again so I record it on my cassette player.

In a pre-Internet time there were no resources I could go to and look this group up after hearing it on the radio. I just had to buy it because I was immediately hooked. I don't think the record had been released yet as I remember playing the tape till I nearly wore it out. But I clearly remember the excitement of traveling into town to the local Andy's record store, looking through the P section and seeing it there in all its glory - the first time I ever saw him, looking like Jimi Hendrix in round rimmed silver reflective glasses.

'When Doves Cry' was the first 12 inch I ever purchased and still to this day, 35 years later, I don't think any such record has impacted me and made me feel that way. This 12 inch also had one of his best ever B-sides, '17 days'. Again, the sound and feel to this song was just phenomenal. Then his next single was a re-release, '1999', and again I got that same feeling and again I was hooked! I purchased all of the singles he released that year and then that Christmas my auntie brought me the *Purple Rain* album on cassette, the first ever full artist album I owned.

At that point I never knew that this one man would become such an integral part of my life. From that point I brought every 12-inch released and slowly purchased and worked my way through all of his previous albums, including his side projects like The Time, Sheila E and Vanity 6.

When Doves Cry

With every album he released, Prince always managed to push my musical taste boundaries even to the point that, when some singles from a new album were released, I didn't like them - at first. I had become so addicted to his previous sound/era, eg. *Sign o' the Times*. What an album - every single song was just mind blowing. Then the *Lovesexy* album was released and when I first heard 'Alphabet Street' I remember thinking, 'Is that it? It's so sparse and so different.' But after two plays it was imprinted on my brain. It was like a drug. I just had to get home from school so I could play it over and over again.

And it was not just the man himself that enamoured me – all of his band members just had this aura about them. I was totally in awe of Sheila E, and Wendy and Lisa, especially - but that's another story.

In 1988, a BBC2 documentary on Prince and his Paisley Park studios showed the reception and the receptionist answering the phone. I somehow managed to find the number of Paisley Park studios and I would ring them every day over a period of three months and ask to speak to Prince only to be told every time that he was out touring Europe. Our phone bill was normally only about £40 to £50 and when the latest bill came through and was about £400 my mum, not knowing I had been calling America every day and thinking there must have been a billing error, went and complained to BT. They reduced it to £100. I only told her the real reason it was so large many years later!

With the news that Prince was finally coming to the UK with his *Parade* tour I just had to go but it was not to be. My mum could not get tickets. The following year he was returning with the *Sign o' the Times* tour and I managed to get tickets for the gigs, which were being held at Wembley Stadium. The request was to wear something 'peach and black'. Unfortunately this was not meant to be as the shows got cancelled due to the weather and I remember crying for weeks!

I was 15 when I finally got to see Prince in concert in 1988 when he returned to the UK with his *Lovesexy* tour. Prince was 30 years old. I cannot put into words how excited I was. I attended the concert with my sister Nadine, who also liked him. This was going to be our first concert ever. We got a coach package and so were able to meet 30 other Prince fans. This in itself was overwhelming for me as I did not know any other fans at that point.

The concert was in the round and we had pretty good seats. I remember just staring at the stage set. I could not believe that I was finally going to see him, let alone be as close to the stage as I was. Then at 7.30 the lights went out and the house erupted with screams and cheers – the atmosphere was just electric! We were lucky enough to see Prince and the band walk through a small door towards the stage and I remember my sister seeing him and saying, 'OMG there he is!' He was wearing his black and white polka dot suit. Then after a couple of minutes we could hear a car engine start up and the white Thunderbird started to circle the stage. If it was possible the crowd went even wilder and then, amidst a glaring spotlight, there he was in all of his glory – Prince Rogers Nelson! What followed was a two and a half hour show that covered a set list of his entire career. As if seeing Prince was not enough, Sheila E was also part of his new band as was the amazing Cat Glover. Mavis Staples came on and guested on 'I'll Take You There', sung during the 'I Wish U Heaven' medley. After the show I was literally speechless. I could not get over what I had just seen. We tried to get tickets for more shows but they were all sold out.

NATIONAL EXHIBITION CENTRE

5 & 6 AUGUST 1988, BIRMINGHAM, UK

I WAS THERE: HAY COOPER

The first gig I went to was '88, the *Lovesexy* Tour at Birmingham NEC. I was two rows from the front and it was spectacular. I was on holiday and my mate used to work in the city centre, in the days when you had to go and buy a ticket. He worked in a clothes shop so I said, 'You've gotta get me these tickets'. He had a young lad who worked in the shop and he sent him out straight away to go and get in the queue. And he was at the front of the queue and so we were two rows from the front. I went to work the following day and someone else from work had gone and I went, 'How amazing was that?' and he went 'shit'. He was the other side of the stage and all he saw was the back of Prince because it was all in the middle. So I loved it and he hated it.

I WAS THERE: KAREN MEE

I saw him a couple of times, at the NEC in Birmingham in the late Eighties and at the National Indoor Arena in the Nineties. He was awesome. It was the best concert I have ever attended. I remember him coming on stage, with the hat with the chains, singing 'My Name is Prince'. It gave me goosebumps knowing that I was actually there. The atmosphere was electric. I made a pilgrimage to the Hard Rock café in Barcelona to see his polka dot waistcoat. I felt sad knowing he was no longer here as it was the year he passed.

There will never be anyone else who can come close to his style and the way he performed. I was so excited when I was travelling on the bus to Birmingham to see him. I used to talk to a guy from Holland years ago and he was in a club in the Haag when suddenly Prince arrived to do a set. That must have been a surreal event. Paisley Park is on my bucket list.

I WAS THERE: SUSAN QUINN

My first ever Prince gig was the *Lovesexy* tour at Birmingham NEC. My last ever Prince gig was *Hit and Run* at Birmingham's LG Arena in 2014 and before that one I actually said to my husband, because I'd seen him in Manchester in February, 'You've got to let me go to this because I might never get this chance again'.

I saw *Lovesexy* at NEC in Birmingham on 5th August 1988 and on the 5th August 1997 I had my first child, at 11 minutes past 8 at night. Nine years earlier I was watching Prince get out of a laundry basket on stage! I remember him stepping out of that and like, 'Wow', and then nine years later I had my daughter. She went to see *21 Nights*, and no one's ever topped that. I took her to see him at Hop Farm which was a kids festival, and I took her to Birmingham and we got to the front so it were like first time she'd ever got to the front and queued for that length of time.

Birmingham wasn't as good as Manchester. It was the first time I'd ever got to the front in Birmingham. We were treated like royalty. We all had little numbers on our hands and it was like from this point you all get to come in early and buy merchandise. And then we all had to line up like cattle in numerical order to be let in. It was the first

200 who they let in early so we could get food.

I wanted to be bang in the centre, but my daughter was only small, so I said, 'We can either stand to the side or we can stand directly behind these because there's a really small boy and a small woman, so you can look over his head and I'll look over hers.' They threw a drumstick and we all went to grab it, and someone else got it and they were like 'It's her birthday!' so I passed it to her. The security man went up to him and said, 'Excuse me, it's that little boy's birthday, he'd really like that drum stick'. But it was a lie, we all said it was Louis' birthday so we could have a drumstick!

I decided when we got in early not to buy food, but while the support act were on I was like 'I feel really, really ill'. I'd been queuing for eight hours and I was like 'I've got to get outside'. I left and when I came back in after I'd had a bit of fresh air and something to eat, the security woman went 'you have to start up' and she made me go round right to the back and I just walked up to everyone and went 'Number 31!'. And I pushed past everyone to get to the front, and we had a fantastic night.

VALLE HOVIN

14 AUGUST 1988, OSLO, NORWAY

I WAS THERE: NIKO ECKHOFF

Having seen him in Stockholm in 1987, the following spring I had a girlfriend. I was 13 and *Lovesexy* was released. It was great. It was more than that. It was a journey through Prince's soul during his period of absolute peak creativity. Prince played his first Norwegian show in August 1988. It was a stadium show with 40, 000 people in a city of 350,000. I slept outside the unseated venue the night before the show, ran towards the stage when the gates opened and got something like third row. Like when I saw him in Stockholm I had this unreal feeling. This was too good to be true. 'Erotic City' kicked off the show. Even thought full songs were turned into snippets on this tour it didn't take any power out of it. Rather, it added innovation and flair. And he played 'A Love Bizarre' and even 'Sister'. These two concerts, Stockholm in 1987 and Oslo in 1988, were transformative experiences. I have been a Prince fan for 32 years. I haven't ever held onto anything like I have held on to Prince. I consider myself blessed to have experienced his golden period in bloom. I will never forget.

RIVERFRONT COLISEUM

22 SEPTEMBER 1988, CINCINATTI, OHIO

I WAS THERE: STEPHEN JARED

I saw him again four years later on the *Lovesexy* tour. That was the best show I ever saw in my life. I was third row. Prince in the Eighties just got better and better every year and dazzled you more and more with whatever new it was that he came up with. My favourite radio station would start saying 'we've got the first single off the new Prince record and we're going to premiere it right here Thursday night at 8 o'clock' and it would be on a Monday and they'd tease it all week long. And you would be waiting, 'Oh my God, it's going to be on the radio!' and you knew it was going to be something completely different from what Prince had ever done before. And sure enough it always was and it was always just jaw dropping how much he had advanced from the previous year. And after *Purple Rain* he did what he called the *Hit and Run* tour, promoting the album *Parade* and *Under the Cherry Moon* and it was one of these deals where there was no planned schedule for the tour. He'd all of a sudden announce 'tonight - or tomorrow night - I'm going to be in Lexington, Kentucky. Tickets go on sale at noon.' It would be like 11 am so it was really hard to get to that show. And for me I was still in high school and I do remember he did a show in Lexington and it was four hours away and this was on a Wednesday night and I just couldn't get there. It was announced the day before.

Stephen Jared saw Prince at Cincinatti's Riverfront Coliseum

Then the *Sign o' the Times* tour, the next tour he did, only went to Europe so there was no way for me to see that and then he released the concert film for that and of course I saw that in a theatre. For anybody unfamiliar with Prince's genius, there's where you go to to recognise just how great he was. If that doesn't do it for you absolutely nothing will.

Then he came out with the *Lovesexy* record just a few months after that concert film was released and then announced a big tour, including America, with the same band as the *Sign o' the Times* tour and so I went. It was Prince doing what he does, which is just upping his game further every tour, every record, and it was just unbelievable. What was so different about that time compared today is obviously there was no Internet so there was no way to know what the show was going to look like or what the set list was going to be. Nobody had any idea. You show up and you have no idea what you in for. He came out and did a kind of a medley of a lot of his songs and you look at the set list from many of the shows during that tour and you're talking 30 something songs. That's because he would do a couple of verses, a chorus, and then he'd jump into something else.

For a fan sitting there having no idea what to expect or to know what was coming next you just couldn't believe it. 'Oh my God, I can't believe he just did that off of *Dirty Mind* and now he's seqwayed into this and that.' There were no breaks between the songs. It wasn't like a song came to an end and then he would say 'thank you' and then a couple of seconds later begin the next song or introduce the next song. It wasn't like that. It was a continuous piece of music for about two and a half hours. There was an intermission but you just couldn't keep up with it. It was exhilarating.

The show was in downtown Cincinnati. I had a girlfriend at that time by the name of Julie Montgomery who I was at the show with, and somehow we were told what hotel Prince was probably staying at. After the show, we raced to the hotel and went to the concierge and said, 'Is Prince staying here? We were hoping to catch just a glimpse of him on his way back from the show.' And the concierge said, 'Well, I can't tell you where he staying but I can tell you that there is a club some blocks from here and we understand that he's gone there.'

So we raced to the club. It had a ground floor with a big dance floor in the middle and then it had an upstairs which was almost a complete 100 per cent wraparound balcony where you could have drinks, play games and, if you wanted to, you could look down on the dance floor on the first level. The stairs were roped off with one of those velvet ropes and you couldn't just go upstairs. We knew that's where Prince and his band were, although Prince hadn't arrived yet.

Prince had a long time keyboardist, somebody who wore a doctor's outfit with a surgical mask called Dr Fink, and my girlfriend and I recognised him. He was downstairs and we went up to him and said, 'Hey, we were at the show. You guys are so great.'

And my then girlfriend said, 'Yeah, we just really love you guys but we would love you even more if you could get us upstairs' and he said, 'Follow me.'

So he took us to the stairs and he pulled off the velvet rope and escorted us upstairs and there was all of Prince's band.

There were a handful of other people but for the most part Prince and his band had the whole of the upstairs area.

It was the *Sign o' the Times* band members and I think it was the best band in the world at that time, '87, '88. The only one that was not there was Sheila E who was the drummer for him at that time. Everybody else was there and we got to meet some of these people. He had a dancer named Cat and we went up and talked to her for a little bit. He had a sax player named Eric Leeds and trumpet player named Atlanta Bliss and they were playing pool. All of these people were right there with us.

Prince was not there yet but at some point he came in and it was one of these moments, as you've heard other people talk about. Certain stars or celebrities have this ability to just walk into the room and all heads turn. The news catches like wildfire that 'he has just entered'.

Prince came in downstairs and he had a whole group of burly guys surrounding him. He moved through the crowd a little bit, came up the stairs and my then girlfriend and I were standing there and he walked right past us. It was 1988, decades ago, and to this day I can still remember that moment and my jaw was just on the floor. 'Oh my god. There's Prince.'

I could literally just have reached out and touched him. And he moved past us to another cordoned off area with velvet ropes and a small square space on that upstairs balcony. There was a chair there and it was obviously set up for Prince. He went over and he sat down and he watched the people, the crowd down below on the dance floor, for quite a while. Every once in a while a band member or somebody else would go over and whisper something in Prince's ear and he would give a short reply and then they would walk away. For the most part it was just Prince watching these people dance down below him for maybe 20 or 30 minutes and then he got up to go.

You knew he was leaving because all these burly guys got up and started surrounding him again. And as he was now passing my girlfriend and I, my girlfriend just reached out and grabbed his hand and said, 'We think you're great, man!'

I was just on automatic at that moment not knowing what to do and what to say and I grabbed his hand and I couldn't even speak. My jaw was just hanging open.

Prince had this look that he gave people sometimes, this sly kind of smirk, that was a little condescending but also very endearing, and he just gave me that look. Because he could see that I was speechless and that I didn't know what to say to him. I don't know what you say to somebody that you just idolise so much.

JOE LOUIS ARENA

30 & 31 OCTOBER 1988, DETROIT, MICHIGAN

I WAS THERE: THERESA SPATZ, AGE 23

I saw him in Detroit. *Sign o' the Times*! I had been a fan since I was 16 so by then I was 23 and very excited to see him! I dressed in a black cami with a black lace skirt and purple leggings and I wore black leather boots.

My girlfriend was supposed to go along but she cancelled at the last minute. I was so determined to see my teenage crush I went alone and I danced all night and had a blast! I tried to go see him at the after party that night but I got lost and ended up downtown

Theresa Spatz saw Prince in Detroit

asking crackheads for directions! I always thought when I was young he would meet me and we would ride off into the sunset. He was so talented. Who could not love Prince?

I WAS THERE: JOHN CARLTON YOUNG

He's in my top three of all time. I was going to college at Central Michigan University. I had *Purple Rain* on cassette tape. It was magic, man. I saw the *LoveSexy* tour. That was a theatrical show with a lot of lights. It was like a Broadway show. The Prince magic showed through. He was dynamite. A few years later - I don't think it was an announced tour – I found out he was going to play this place in Michigan called Pine Knob and me and my wife got tickets ten rows back. It was a small venue for him. I think it only held 15,000 people. He was just awesome that night. He blew me away with his workmanship, his craft and his charisma.

John Carlton Young saw Prince at the Joe Louis Arena in Detroit

PACIFIC COLISEUM

17 NOVEMBER 1988, VANCOUVER, CANADA

I WAS THERE: MICHELLE WEBB

Prince symbolized a tremendous menagerie of music and life experiences for me. The 1980s for a teenager in Canada had its share of British punk music, metal bands and in my case American R&B and Funk. My first experience at a Prince concert was the *Lovesexy* tour in Vancouver, British Columbia. This $30 concert ticket may have been the best money spent in my entire life. Sheila E was playing percussion and Cat, the enigmatic dancer, performed alongside Prince. On the floor I stood, in awe, of the performer that to date has never disappointed. Incredibly, I could not find anyone to go with me to this concert. In my world, most young 20somethings were listening to metal bands, ska, punk or oldies. I actually hid my Prince fandom from most of my peers. I convinced a friend that was a boy (I shudder to say 'boyfriend') to come along. He was not impressed and even acted 'jealous' and left before me! I was glad he left. I ran as close to the stage as I could. It was magical.

My next Prince concert was many years later during the *Welcome 2 Canada* tour. Living in the US, I made a pilgrimage (in my mind) to Vancouver with my husband and young adult kids. The show was at Rogers Arena on December 16, 2011. I was nervous to see my beloved Prince with my husband as he disliked Prince. Walking from our hotel to the arena, the streets were filled with Prince fans and I felt I was among my people. Finding our way to our seats, the energy in this arena was different than any other concert I had been to. This was truly a once in a lifetime moment. Prince, incredibly, connected with the huge arena full of people like he was each person's longtime friend. He performed 'Purple Rain', the obvious anthemic song of the night, amidst falling purple, gold and silver confetti, soaring guitar riffs and flags waving from the stage. Prince in 1988 was famous like all popular artists during that time. Prince in 2011 was iconic and enthralling, yet notably humble. And to think we were even treated to Maceo Parker's funk and soul on the saxophone. I was not even born when he was playing with James Brown in the 1960s or Parliament-Funkadelic in the 1970s.

THE SUMMIT

27 NOVEMBER 1988, HOUSTON, TEXAS

I WAS THERE: GREG SCHRODER

I'd been married to my wife for only a year and she was a little hesitant that her 29-year-old husband was still geeking over a pop star like Prince. Her first concert was the *Lovesexy* tour in Houston. I'll never forget looking at her when Prince played 'Purple Rain' and seeing her waving her hands in the air with a smile on her face as big as Texas. I knew she got it then! And thank God she did, because she's been stuck with me (and Prince) for 31 years now!

3 FEBRUARY 1990

For the first time ever, the UK top three singles featured acts neither British nor American, with Ireland's Sinead O'Connor, Australia's Kylie Minogue and Belgium's Technotronic occupying those slots. Sinead O'Connor was at number 1 with 'Nothing Compares 2 U', written by Prince.

21 APRIL 1990

Sinead O'Connor started a four week run at number 1 on the US singles chart with her version of 'Nothing Compares 2 U'. The track was also number 1 in 18 other countries.

RUPERT'S NIGHT CLUB

30 APRIL 1990, MINNEAPOLIS, MINNESOTA

Prince played a concert at Rupert's in Minneapolis. The $100 a head ticket proceeds all went to the family of his former bodyguard Charles 'Big Chick' Huntsberry, who had died from a heart attack.

2 June 1990 saw the start of the *Nude* tour, comprising 51 shows in Europe and another five in Asia. It was a greatest hits tour and a stripped back production. Starting in Rotterdam in The Netherlands and concluding on 10 September 1990 in Yokohama,

Japan, and promoting *Batman* and *Graffiti Bridge*, Prince once again chose not to tour North America. The London shows comprised a total of 12 sold out nights at Wembley Arena.

WEMBLEY ARENA

19 JUNE 1990, LONDON, UK

I WAS THERE: DANIEL PAYNE

A new band and my second Prince show. It was completely different to the *Lovesexy* show and had a more stripped down set. I had waited two years to see him again and boy was it worth it. Rosie Gaines, Michael Bland! What more could you ask for? I saw him twice in June, and Mavis Staples was support both times.

Daniel Payne

I WAS THERE: SAM BLEAZARD

My earliest memories of Prince are from the early Eighties, when I was a kid at high school. People were into break dancing, and putting a big piece of cardboard down in the street and listening to Grandmaster Flash and Melle Mel's White Lines - even in Scotland! I liked Michael Jackson when *Thriller* was at its peak. And I remember watching a BBC2 show – it might have been the *Old Grey Whistle Test* – when they played a clip of *Prince and the Revolution: Live* and I can remember being interested in that, and then there being a family debate about whether it was appropriate for me to watch it. I was 10, going on 11 at the time.

Then I was aware of other things, like seeing Prince's 'Little Red Corvette' video on TV and people comparing him to Michael Jackson, and I remember saying to my mum at the time, 'Oh god, this guy's awful. He's never going to be as good as Michael Jackson. I really don't like him at all.' But then I saw bits of the *Live in '85* show and the first songs I heard were things like '1999', which was reissued on the back of his 'Purple Rain' success, and then 'Let's Go Crazy', which I thought was unbelievable. I was still at primary school and I can remember just being so excited at those songs. I also remember being in HMV in Edinburgh and asking to buy either the *1999 or the Purple Rain* LPs and my parents saying they were probably too rude.

In the mid to late Eighties all of Prince's live shows were at their peak in terms of creativity and critical reviews. I became interested in all of his single releases too, and I remember my uncle coming to my house one day and bringing back the 'Girls and Boys' seven inch, and I also remember watching his TV special for *Parade* on Channel 4. Although I was still too young to go and see the concerts, I went to see the *Sign o' the Times* concert movie, and I can remember that having a massive effect. I went to see it at the Cameo Cinema in Edinburgh and it blew my mind. I used to 'borrow' the Parade LP from my sister, and my best friend used to bring his sister's copy of *Sign o' the Times* round to our house.

Prince was brilliant in terms of experimentation so when he released 12 inch singles he often created mini-albums out of them. He would extend songs and explore different aspects of them through remixing, and of course he was so prolific, so most of the B-sides were rare tracks from his vault. Some of those B-sides also became great songs in his live set – 'She's Always in my Hair' is just one example.

He spanned the mainstream and the underground because, and I don't know if he did this deliberately, a lot of bootlegs surfaced through Prince because he was so prolific. *The Black Album* became this whole thing. A lot of my friends in high school had copies of *The Black Album*, and I actually had a copy of it at the wrong speed! In the process of endless bootlegging and second or third generation copies, Prince's voice was speeded up every so lightly and he sounded Mickey Mouse-like, so I listened to *The Black Album* for years at the wrong speed. When it eventually came out officially it sounded like the wrong speed to me, as if it was too slow.

That all led up to me being allowed to go down to London in 1990 to see him with my best friend, Gavin. The first time I saw him live was at Wembley Arena. He had a record-breaking run of nights there. I saw him twice on that tour, at Wembley and then at the Birmingham NEC.

My parents separated when I was between primary and high school, and the whole *Purple Rain* narrative was all part of a very angsty period in the mid 1980s. Teenagers were looking for something. All my friends were listening to REM and U2 and stuff like that and I thought that was pretty boring. Prince had a whole kaleidoscopic universe of things going on - leaked material from his underground vault, great live shows, interesting albums, every single different to the last. There was a lot to get into and as a teenager there was a lot of depth to it. He was never just the pop guy. There were all sorts of things going on with it. It was like being part of something mysterious and secret.

Those first shows that I saw were around the post-*Batman* period, so Prince was still a massive commercial artist when I first saw him. It's quite well documented now that the Nineties weren't a great time for Prince. He negotiated bigger and bigger record deals but his commercial power was on the wane by the end of the decade.

I WAS THERE: DEBBIE COPPINGER, AGE 16

My first gig was the *Nude* Tour at Wembley. My mum and dad took me because I was 16, and obviously *Lovesexy* happened before and I begged to go but they said I was too young. I've been obsessed since '87 when I was 14. I remember my dad took me mainly to ogle at all the half-naked women that he used to have on stage and then NPG turns up and there were three men dancing! So he was very disappointed. Him and my mum sat down all the way through whilst I jumped about like a loony.

Then it was *Diamonds & Pearls* which would be '92.

My last gig was 2014 and *Autism Rocks*. The Manchester Academy Saturday show on 22nd February was my favourite ever because, other than the after show at the Indigo, it was the closest I'd got to him. I was surrounded by people who felt the same as I did. I wasn't next to 20,000 people who only know 'Purple Rain'. Everybody was in the same boat and he was on fire that night. He was phenomenal – three hours and 15 minutes of pure heaven. It was my eldest son's first gig as well. Three of my four kids who are Prince fans now.

I had a bit of a stalker when I was younger. We were work mates and we house shared, but I'd moved back with my mum and dad and there was a knock on the door and he was standing there and said, 'Debbie, get your coat on, I'm taking you somewhere. Trust me, you're gonna love this.' Then we got the train to Wembley. That was a lovely surprise.

I WAS THERE: GUÐBJÖRG ÖGMUNDSDÓTTIR

It was the first week of July 1990 at Wembley Arena, London and the *Nude* tour. I had seats way in the back but the sound was awesome there! Prince did a great set, but what I can never forget is his whole performance of 'Purple Rain' and the unbelievable guitar solo during that song. It just blew me away completely and I had goosebumps all over! Prince was one of the best performers in history. His dancing while performing, singing and playing was par to none and it was such a waste to lose him so early. Some people in the very last row behind us that were trying to steal from the people in front of them! I have never had that happen at a concert before or since. Fortunately me and my friend got wise to them but I am afraid some other people had worse luck.

I WAS THERE: VON SALTER

I had the pleasure of going to see him twice. The first time was in 1990 at Wembley Arena. It was the first time in many years I had been to a pop concert and I was a little nervous. The last time I had been to something so big was a David Cassidy concert at White City Stadium in 1974 where a young girl in crowd unfortunately got crushed and died. So I was very apprehensive about going. Prince was as popular as David, probably more so. But things had changed and I was no longer a teenager. Security was tight and we were not even allowed to take water bottles in. We were searched and bottles were taken off of us.

We travelled on a coach from Devon with *Graffiti Bridge* playing all the way. I couldn't believe how tiny he was and how graphically sexual he was. It was an amazing night which I will never forget. The atmosphere was amazing, with so many people dressed like him with satin trousers with the buttons. And people with the same hairstyle.

I then saw him again in 2007 at the 02 Arena. I took my younger daughter. He was a little bit more laid back by then and didn't flaunt sex so much. He was still brilliant.

I WAS THERE: GINA JOYCE

My obsession with Prince first started after watching the *Purple Rain* movie. I was 29 years old and married with two young children. I already loved his music, *1999* being the first album I'd bought. I played it to death - they were called LPs back then, not vinyl.

It's ironic that on those rare early Prince TV appearances at award ceremonies, my first impression of him had been that he was a bit of an arrogant, jumped-up idiot! That huge mop of curly hair, over-the-top sparkly outfits, never smiling, but instead wearing that sulky expression on his face, like he obviously didn't want to be there. I'm sure there are many non-Prince fans that still conjure up those images and so who will probably always still see him in that light. People either loved him or loathed him – there was never anything in between - and I think that still stands to this day.

Of course us true fans know that off stage he wasn't arrogant at all - far from it. He was extremely shy, softly spoken, very polite, kind and generous, and had an amazing sense of humour, quite the joker, often setting people up and playing pranks. Once on stage though he became this different person, confident, sometimes with an aggressive streak, his passion for the music clearly visible in his facial expressions and amazing performances.

I then watched *Purple Rain* for the first time. I was mesmerised by every performance in that movie, watched it over and over, and was hooked. I wanted to hear and see more. At this point I'd no idea just how much more of his stuff was out there, including pre-*1999* albums, until I later started searching and - dare I confess? - started buying bootlegs.

The award winning *Sign o' the Times* movie was also a game changer for me. Every performance was totally amazing. I could watch 'Forever in my Life' from that movie repeatedly and not tire of it - his emotional screaming into the mic, then wiping a tear away, and nobody could wear a hat like Prince did! Yet I hated that song when I first heard it, and thought it monotonous and tuneless, which actually it is. But you have to really listen to the lyrics and, like most of Prince's songs, they are so much better live when you are actually watching him, rather just listening to the official track on a CD. I love 'Controversy' live at any of his shows, but again was never keen on the official single. I rarely listen to his official stuff on discs, although I have to buy them for my collection. I really only listen to live recordings from his shows.

Exact dates, etc. are all a bit of a blur and a bit sketchy now the years have passed, but a couple of years later they broadcast the *Lovesexy* concert on TV. I recorded it on our VHS recorder (I still have it) and was amazed at the huge scale of the concert, his incredible performances and the choreography, which included of course the legendary Cat and Sheila E. They had broadcast it on TV on a Sunday, a holy day, so many complaints were made afterwards due to the suggestive content. I watched that concert back-to-back too. His 'Purple Rain' and 'The Cross' performances were very powerful and emotional, but all of it was amazing.

In 1990 my eldest sister and I went to Wembley for the *Nude* concert. I hadn't bothered checking the stadium seating plans and we had seats right up in the lap of the gods and right over to one side on the left. Prince looked like a dot. We watched the large screens throughout the show, but I was still on a high afterwards. They had shown a video of his extended 'Thieves in the Temple' new single, again with amazing dance moves, and I bought it as soon as it was released.

I WAS THERE: JAMES MERRITT

I was 10 years old back in 1990 when Prince was on the *Nude* tour. I attended one of the Wembley Arena dates in London with my parents who were massive Prince fans and had been to many concerts before and after this one.

Before the set started, one of Miko's groupies came to my parents at our seats that were dead centre of the front row and said that Miko (Prince's guitarist) would like to talk to me. They were very quick to usher me over to him and he proceeded to say hello and shake my hand and then give me a signed red plectrum. This for me as a 10 year old boy didn't mean a great deal but for my parents was huge.

The concert then started and I danced away to the songs that I was used to hearing blare from the speakers in my parents' dining room. Prince then started to play the tambourine with two of his backing dancers. Once finished he threw one my way which my dad just missed with the tips of his fingers and it fell to the people behind us. Then the first of the backing dancers threw his to the right of the crowd. Needless to say we were a little gutted by this. Prince then looked at me on my dad's shoulders and pointed. He threw the final tambourine my way. It hit me in the mouth and fell into my dad's hands. This was the icing on the cake for me and my parents. We still have the tambourine in our possession and will treasure it forever.

NATIONAL EXHIBITION CENTRE

30 JUNE 1990, BIRMINGHAM, UK

I WAS THERE: CRAIG LEVERINGTON

At the NEC in Birmingham, Prince stood on his piano and ran his fingers from his chin to his chest, asking seductively, 'Do you wanna bite of my apple?' In my excitement, and during an oddly quiet moment, I leapt from my seat and shouted at the top of my voice, 'No, but I'll suck your plums!'

I WAS THERE: NATHAN STANMORE

I first heard Prince when a friend played *Purple Rain* to me. I went to over 20 concerts plus after shows. I went to at least one concert but mostly two or three every time he was in the country from 1990 to 2014. My first concert was the *Nude* tour. I got stuck in Birmingham as the train stopped and I couldn't get home. Dad had to get out of bed to get us. I missed *Lovesexy* and *Sign o' the Times* never happened here. I saw the *Ultimate Live Experience* or *Gold* tour where he didn't play crowd favourites like 'Purple Rain' and he was doing everything on that tour. I still have some of the gold glitter from being front row or second row at most of those concerts.

I got given a piece of paper for an after show and we rushed out of the concert to Birmingham and dumped the car. But we got to the venue to find it was cancelled and then we spent two hours trying to find the car as we forgot where we dumped it!

The Emporium after show was my favourite. He came out and we sang all night and he played for us for over two and a half hours. That meant no sleep for 30 hours for me to see him!

I was there at the last concert he did in the UK. I missed a drumstick from Hanna by a whisker. It's not seeing him in concert that hurts more than the lack of albums being released for me. Seeing him in concert was the best time. Plus I found I understood a new song or album when he played it in concert.

I was also at the opening of the shop in Camden and met the band. Then me and a friend went into the shop at another time and got talking to the shop manager. She said, 'Are you real fans?' We said yes and she said, 'If you are around tonight, I have some tickets to the premiere of a film that has Prince music in it.' She gave us the tickets and me and my friend went to Leicester Square to watch the film. We didn't know until it started but it was the premiere of *Girl 6*.

PÁIRC UI CHAOIMH

7 JULY 1990, CORK, IRELAND

I WAS THERE: LOUISE STAFFORD, AGE 14

I've been a fan of Prince for 30 years. I first saw him live in 1990 when he came to my home town of Cork city in Ireland on 7 July - a month after his birthday. It was my first proper gig. My aunt had bought me the ticket for Christmas for the princely sum of £19. I was beside myself with excitement! The *Batman* album had been played on repeat at my friend's house all year so there was a lot of hype about this gig and especially a superstar such as himself coming to Cork, where we hardly got any big names playing.

So I went to the concert at the Páirc Uí Chaoimh stadium which was just down the road from where I lived. I could walk down. I was with three other girlfriends of mine. It wasn't a particularly hot summer's day but it was dry and slightly overcast. Prince made his entrance onto the stage with his opening song 'The Future' and the whole stadium went nuts! I couldn't believe my eyes and that he was really here in front of me. I was mesmerised. He moved around the stage like he owned it, which of course he would do as you could clearly tell this was where he was meant to be, dancing and doing his funky moves getting the crowd into it.

As he played through all his hits, intertwined with his more recent releases at that time, he would do various things to entertain us like he would make us imagine his microphone and stand was a lady that he would pleasure in a sexual way. To my young eyes that was shocking but I knew this was Prince and he was all about being the rude boy. There was another moment in the concert where he stopped to mime having a cigarette break. It was very clever and enjoyable to watch him play around like that.

Another moment that stuck out for me was when he played 'Nothing Compares 2 U', which only a few months earlier our own Sinead O'Connor had made world famous. But of course when he went in for the chorus in his own style - probably the way he wrote it and that way it was meant to be sung - the crowd started to sing over him in Sinead's style which he didn't like at all! He actually stopped playing and spoke into the mic to say, 'Whose song is this anyway?' so I kind of cringed at that point in the show because I felt my people were disrespecting him. But maybe most of the audience didn't know he wrote the song. My last memory of this amazing concert was at the end when he played 'Purple Rain' and it actually started to rain! I thought, 'Oh here we go, typical Irish weather ruining the day.' But when he played the same song during the Super Bowl half time set he did in 2007 the same thing happened, so it brought me back to my experience which I thought was pretty cool.

I WAS THERE: LINDA WILLIAMS, AGE 16

I went to my first Prince concert at 16 in Cork. I had just split up with my boyfriend but we still went together, with friends. It turns out he went and caught Prince's tambourine, but he would not give it to me even though he knew I was Prince's biggest fan. He said he'd keep it until we got back together. Well, after 28 years and both with kids and exes, we reunited and are very happy together. And guess what? He kept it for me and framed it with the tickets and set list.

WEMBLEY ARENA

24 AUGUST 1990, LONDON, UK

I WAS THERE: DANIEL PAYNE

I saw him again on the *Nude* tour on the 20 and 24 of August, when Lois Lane was support. The 24th was the last night of the *Nude* tour in the UK and he started with 'Partyman', which was normally done near the end of the show. Again, the crowd were ecstatic.

MAINE ROAD FOOTBALL GROUND

21 AUGUST 1990, MANCHESTER, UK

I WAS THERE: KATE SULLIVAN

I must have seen Prince about five times and I couldn't give you a proper memory. The first time I saw him was on the *Parade* tour with my friend Jane at Wembley Arena. I was a massive fan. The black and white film for *Parade* was really pretentious and terrible but *Parade* was such a fantastic album. I remember him wearing peach and black. That might have been the *LoveSexy* tour.

I don't remember whom I went to Maine Road with. I got absolutely leathered at that gig because it was the day I passed my driving test. I had the driving test first thing in the morning, passed it and then went to the gig and went on the piss. I don't remember there being a brilliant atmosphere. I was pissed though, so I don't remember very much at all! I also had tickets to see the *Sign o' the Times* tour and it was cancelled. I remember the outcry when we didn't get our booking fee back.

I saw him at the O2 on the *21 Nights* tour and got pissed at that one as well! This woman in front of us was dancing really badly. We were very high up and I was leathered and I turned around and looked at the bloke next to me and said, 'I wish she'd sit down!' And he said, 'I know, and she's a shit dancer!' I had the worst hangover in the world the following day. Despite that, my boyfriend made me get up for breakfast because he said I'd feel better for it. I didn't!

I don't think Prince did anything off *Sign o' the Times* on that whole tour. We got 'Kiss' and 'Raspberry Beret' and a lot of noodling.

I missed the chance to see him in Manchester in 2014. My friend Mark Doyle, my Twinnie, texted me and said, 'Do you want to come and see Prince at the Academy? I've got two tickets.' But we were away. He was lost before his time. He might have written another really brilliant album. He was a real talent.

WEMBLEY ARENA

24 AUGUST 1990, LONDON, UK

I WAS THERE: MARK WARE

As a teenager I narrowly missed seeing the *Lovesexy* tour. My first experience of Prince live was the *Nude* tour at Wembley Arena on 24th August 1990. The passion of his live performance from someone at the top of his game was absolutely awesome. Of course I had to stay beyond the house lights coming on just to be sure Prince wouldn't return for a further encore. This resulted in me and my date for the night missing the last train back to Cobham and having to walk from Esher station!

I WAS THERE: LEE BETTLES

I first heard him in 1998. The VHS of the *Sign o' the Times* concert tour had come out and it was playing on a TV screen in HMV. I looked up and saw it and I thought, 'That's really good.' By pure fluke I happened to be going by a market stall and I heard somebody playing what I now know to be a live version of 'Housequake', a bootleg recording recorded at the Small Club. It was an after show with about 300 people that was recorded about 3am in the morning in Holland. I went straight back to HMV and bought the VHS. I was hooked.

I hadn't bought the latest Prince album because I was behind. *Lovesexy* had just come out so then I bought *Lovesexy* and I had this wonderful journey of going backwards from *Parade* to *Purple Rain*, *Around the World in a Day* and all those, right back to the first album. And I loved every minute of it. Then I just devoured everything.

I'm a disabled person. I've got cerebral palsy and I remember asking my mother if I could go and she said no. I was 17. I was walking on crutches and she wouldn't let me go on my own. It was one of those 'wrap me up in cotton wool' kind of things. I was buying bootlegs. I was buying everything I could possibly get my hands on and what really irritated me was that my brother was going to Donnington on his own. In the end she said, 'You can go if you can find somebody to go with you.'

One of my teachers at school found out that I wanted to go and I went with one of her daughters. We had an amazing night. She was a night nurse so she slept all the way there.

1990 was the *Nude* tour and it was a back to basics, stripped back tour of greatest hits because he'd just done *Lovesexy* and was drained by all the message and everything out of that.

It was just phenomenal. I could not believe that I was in this mythical presence. Every time you felt that you were in the presence of something not of this planet. He did two hours. He did a massive run at Wembley. And every night he was extending the show by five minutes. So by the time I got to see him, which was towards the end of the run, it was two hours. When it was finished I remember turning to the lady that I was with and saying, 'So when's the next one?'

PAISLEY PARK

SOMETIME AROUND 1990, CHANHASSEN, MINNESOTA

I WAS THERE: ANDREA FOY

Back in the early Nineties, the Atrium in Paisley Park was where Prince had his first private parties. You had to have a gold pass to get in! There were directions on back of the pass for people to find Paisley. It was not commonly open like it was in recent years. I received my pass at Glam Slam, his club in Minneapolis. The bodyguards would walk around and hand out the passes, mostly to women. We had to drive about 30 minutes to get to Chanhassen where Paisley was. He had food and drink at the first few parties. He also performed a couple of times on a tiny stage. The first parties were about 10 to 30 people and they were the best parties. There Prince could be relaxed and have fun. They felt like an old high school gym party. Security was all around but they did not bother anybody, unless they really tried to bother Prince.

Most of the time he already had a companion with him. On nights when he was alone, some women would try and talk to him. Some would succeed and get to talk to him or stand with him for a little while others would get turned away by the bodyguards. One night I walked up to him while he was standing next to the DJ table. I expected the bodyguard to stop me, but to my surprise and horror, he just stood there. I looked at Prince. Those eyes were looking back at me. He had an amused look on his face. 'Would you like to dance?' I asked, sure he'd say no. 'Maybe later,' was his deep whispered response. I went back to the floor and joined my friends, just pleased I talked to him, and he talked back. I was happy he didn't say no but was sure it was a no.

I almost fainted about 20 minutes later when he walked over and told me to 'come over here.' He wanted to dance on the edge of the dance floor, maybe so he could escape if needed. It was like having an out of body experience. I didn't think he would dance with me and I was terrified. After the one song, he smiled and said, 'Thank you.' I said it back and he left so quickly. I didn't know if Prince was just being polite. All my friends gave me hugs, and I did see him walk past on the second level of Paisley, looking down at us.

This was our second dance, there was that night in Paris... read more in my book!

PRINCE: THE DAY I WAS THERE

Ticket for Prince's Blenheim Palace show. Photo thanks to Anita and Shane Wetton

BLENHEIM PALACE

31 AUGUST 1991,
WOODSTOCK, UK

HE WASN'T THERE: LEE BETTLES

Because I came back in one piece, from then on my parents couldn't really stop me. I bought tickets for Blenheim Palace. That didn't happen. It was supposed to take place on 31 August 1991, headed by a group called Diamond Promotions. It was a one off gig. He was only doing that one show in the whole of Europe that year, and the show was pulled a week before the gig. Basically, the promoter had run off with all the money. Prince refunded fans out of his own pocket. Those that had bought tickets would be able to see him on the *Diamonds & Pearls* tour which followed the next year.

Fans who missed out on seeing Prince at Blenheim Palace could claim a complimentary ticket for the following year's Diamonds & Pearls tour

On 9 November 1991, Prince and the New Power Generation started a two week run at number 1 on the US singles chart with 'Cream', a number 15 hit in the UK.

The *Diamonds & Pearls* tour started on 3 April 1992 and ended three months and 50 shows later on 12 July 1992. It took in 18 Asian and Australian shows - his first there - and another 32 in Europe. It included 10 UK shows, playing to a combined audience of more than 200,000 British fans.

The Diamonds & Pearls tour

WALDBÜHNE

31 MAY 1992, BERLIN, GERMANY

I WAS THERE: MIKE MURTAGH

I was serving at RAF Gatow in Berlin when Prince came to town. Berlin was a terrific place to be at that time, when Germany was still going through its post-Cold War transition, as well as hosting gigs by practically all major bands of the time, Prince being one of them. It was great to be able just to get a bus to a big gig, instead of mounting an expedition, to which I was more accustomed, never having lived previously in a major capital city!

The venue is an open-air amphitheatre and, luckily, it was a beautiful evening. Still air and perfect conditions for outdoor concert. The support band was Was (Not Was), an in-vogue, dance pop, post-disco band whom, to my surprise, I enjoyed far more than I was anticipating. But, of course, Prince was the legendary main attraction - and with justification, being a strong song writing talent and, we were told, an excellent stage presence. I don't pretend that I was a massive follower but it was Prince, after all, and I was intrigued by word that he had been collaborating with my musical hero, Miles Davis, who had died the preceding September.

It turned out to be a bit of a strange performance - for me, anyway. On the one hand, you had a terrific stage performer and musician at the top of his game - fantastically entertaining - and yet, on the other, you had irritating breaks in the gig, where Prince would disappear from the stage for a series of costume changes. This served to disrupt the flow of the performance and prevented it from reaching its natural (and potential) heights. Just as the musical tension was building and the audience were really getting into it, off he would go for yet another distracting costume change, leaving us frustrated and dissatisfied, with the band noodling around until his return.

There were probably not as many such interludes as I think I remember - it was a while ago - but there were still sufficient for them to have had a major effect on my enjoyment of what was otherwise an enjoyable gig. I have a real grouse about this sort of thing! It's a major reason why I veered away from what became known as prog rock. The music should be able to stand on its own, which Prince's could, but it became a bit of a triumph of style over substance and, in my opinion, that's not right. The costume changes and the spectacle appeared to be more important than the music and, for a musician of Prince's musical stature, that's almost criminal! Good gig but it could have been great.

EARLS COURT EXHIBITION CENTRE

15 - 24 JUNE 1992 , LONDON, UK

I WAS THERE: DANIEL PAYNE

The 15th was the opening night of the UK *Diamonds & Pearls* tour and, after the incredible success of his *Diamonds & Pearls* album, this show was back to his expected theatrical expertise. Carmen Electra was due to be the support act but this was cancelled. He previewed his new track, 'Sexy MF'. On the 24th, 'Chain of Fools' was performed as part of the encores.

I WAS THERE: MICHELLE JUSTICE

I saw him many times, from my first concert in 1990 to my last (sadly) in 2014. There was nobody could compare as a live performer. I first heard Prince when I was 9 in the radio, hooked by 'When Doves Cry'. I begged my Mam for some money to go swimming with my friend and a bit extra and bought the 7-inch record on my way home. Ever since I was hooked, plastered my bedroom with posters and hoped one day I'd see him in concert. It wasn't until I was sixteen and the 1990 *Nude* tour at Manchester Arena. My sister and her husband took me. I couldn't believe I was actually going to see him live. It was fantastic but I enjoyed many others after more up close - as well as up close with his minder! Over the years I saw him in London, Sheffield, Edinburgh and again in Manchester for the final time in 2014.

For London's Earls Court and the *Diamonds & Pearls* tour, I won the tickets in a newspaper

Michelle Justice first saw Prince at Earls Court

competition. I did not expect to be so close to him but I could see the soles of his shoes. I was so excited I took out my smuggled in camera. Rather than being discreet, I couldn't help but snap away. What a sight - him appearing on stage with Diamond and Pearl on a descending brass bed. Next thing I knew, I nearly fell over as my camera was yanked out of my hands by a huge, burly minder! He opened my camera, pulled out the film, opened it, pulled out all the roll in front of me and then handed my camera back to me without saying a word.

I WAS THERE: SARAH LEE

Every single Prince concert I've been to has been special, but my first has always held the greatest memories for me. It was 1992 and my friend Michelle and I were kind of new to Prince. I'd discovered him with *Graffiti Bridge*, but we both fell in love with *Diamonds & Pearls*, playing it until we knew each word and every beat of every song. Sadly, as we'd just missed the *Nude* tour, we had to wait a couple of years before going to our first show. But as always - even years later when I discovered Prince could keep you standing around for hours before he hit the stage at an after show - he made it well worth the wait.

We went to one of his Earls Court shows and were so wowed by his typically impeccable performance, and that of the NPG as they would go on to be called, that when the house lights came up at the end we simply had to sit there for a moment. While the crowds drifted away, the dazzling finale of '1999'/'Baby I'm a Star' and 'Push' had us fixed in our seats, unable to move as we tried to process Prince's incredible talent, and giggle like the teenage girls we were as we recalled the way he fixed his doe-eyes on us in the crowd (okay, it wasn't on us, but we felt a connection nonetheless) and writhed his perfect body around the stage during 'Insatiable'. Stuck between our racing teen hormones and the thrill of our first show we sat basking in the afterglow of his purple kingdom, attempting to describe our highlights to each other.

But we didn't realise the highlight of the night was still to come. Minutes later some of the musicians appeared on our side of the curtain. Then Tony M came out and grabbed the mic and in a flash Michelle and I joined the few people left in the auditorium - around 100 of us - clambering over rows of seats to get to the front of the stage, as drums kicked off the music again and Tony opened his rap with the words 'Step, step to the mic'.

We were suddenly at the front with the NPG stage right. Rosie blasted out her vocals to back Tony up in the chorus to a song we'd never heard before. The room was rocking and we were jumping up and down in time to the music. We flashed excited smiles and hugged each other, for the split second we could take our eyes from the stage. But something was missing - Prince wasn't there. I consoled myself that this seemingly impromptu performance was still awesome, but deep down I was sad he wasn't part of it.

However, it turns out the song we were hearing had a thrashing guitar section, and soon Prince was there making his electric guitar talk like only he knew how. We were feet from our new idol, getting an extra concert performance, and simply couldn't believe our luck. As the song ended, the band waved to the few of us left in the arena and coolly walked off the stage. Prince had already snuck off, of course, as was his style.

Truly, as overwhelmed with excitement as we were, we needed to sit down again. The experience had us absolutely ecstatic, but by now the staff were ferrying those of us that had caught this extra performance out the doors.

The greatest mystery for us though was the name of the song. There was no Shazam in the 1990s, of course, and it was some months later before I happened on it. When I found 'Money Don't Matter 2 Night' on offer somewhere I snapped it up, only to discover 'Call The Law' - and memories of that wonderful night - on the B-side. 'Call The Law' is still one of my favourite songs, and as I prepare to go and see the Original NPG in concert tomorrow, more than 27 years after I first heard it, I'm hoping they perform it again. I know if they do, the room will be jumping!

I WAS THERE: PAUL SHELDON, AGE 26

I like Prince from when I heard 'When Doves Cry'. I saw him on the *Diamonds & Pearls* tour at Earls Court. About 10 of us went on the wrong night but they let us stay. The show was amazing. Prince was such a great guitar player. Being a rock fan, I was shocked at how good he was while dancing at the same time. He would have fitted in any rock band on the planet.

I WAS THERE: LAURA SUTCH

When people ask, 'What was your best Prince gig?', It's impossible to answer. Every single gig had a different impact at the time, but you always left with the exact same feeling - one of complete awe and speechlessness at the extraordinary talent you'd observed. I have vivid memories of leaving Earls Court in 1992 and, as I was walking down the stairs, I started to hear music again. Prince had decided it wasn't the end of the show and started playing. I don't think I'd ever run so fast back into the venue! He did it again at the opening night at the O2 in 2007, and I leapt over 20 rows of chairs to run stage side and get as close to him as I'd ever be.

There are no words that do justice to explain the Manchester Academy gig in 2014. All I can say is I feel blessed to have witnessed this amazing man doing what he was born to do, in such an unbelievable way. From start to finish the whole performance was over three hours of perfection.

'Purple Rain' was never my favourite track, but hearing it live was something to behold. When he played it at the Roundhouse gig in 2014, it was exactly how he'd described it, like some sort of religious experience only those who were there to witness it could understand.

MAINE ROAD FOOTBALL GROUND

26 JUNE 1992, MANCHESTER, UK

I WAS THERE: BABS NEW

My first time seeing Prince live was 1992 at Maine Road, Manchester City's old football ground. It was the *Diamonds & Pearls* tour. He was amazing and, as you can imagine, very energetic. He danced on his piano and also - being Prince - had a bed on stage too! It was a scorcher of a day and I can remember waiting outside to go into the ground and hearing Prince and his band the NPG rehearsing with the song 'Thunder'. This added to our excitement and eagerness to get inside as it sounded fantastic. Once inside we ran to try to get as close to the stage as possible.

I think the best thing for me was actually seeing Prince for the first time after all the years of listening and loving his music. Also I felt like he was singing just to me, like I was the only person there. The man was a genius. I saw him again at the O2 in London in 2007 when he did his 21 nights *Earth* tour. It was just as brilliant but I didn't feel the intimacy as it is such a big venue.

I WAS THERE: PAUL AIDEN, AGE 10

Maine Road is where it all started for me and was not only my first Prince gig but the first concert I had ever attended. I was only 10 years old, about to turn 11, and it was my last few weeks of junior school in the UK. My best friend at school, Jake, suddenly out of nowhere said, 'Would you like to go and see Prince in concert?' He was going with his family and, luckily for me, his sister couldn't go so there was a spare ticket. Of course I said yes immediately. I was very familiar with the *Batman* and *Diamonds & Pearls* albums. I couldn't wait and started wearing out my prized cassette of *Diamonds & Pearl*s in the days before the show. I was so excited.

To see any big show with 50,000 or so people in the crowd at such a young age would have been special with all the lights and sound but what I saw really blew my mind. He wasn't just like a super hero, he was a super hero. The way he was dressed, the style, his command of the audience, the sounds, his guitar playing, his guitar, the songs, the moves, his piano playing... I'm pretty sure he even jumped on the drums... I remember at one point being on my friend's dad's shoulders so I could see the entire stage - including a floating bed!

The band were outstanding and, apart from Rosie Gaines, I have been fortunate to have met them all touring since Prince's passing and told them what they mean to me. It's almost hard to sum up the impact that show had on my life. It was staggering, utterly inspirational. I remember knowing all the tracks from *Diamonds & Pearls* but also a 'Tom Jones cover version' song, 'Kiss', which I realised shortly after was his own song, and a brand new song entitled 'Sexy MF'. I decided at that moment, seeing Prince in 1992, that I wanted to play music for a living and I still do that today heading into my late 30s.

I flew out to Minneapolis to see the NPG and Stevie Wonder do a tribute to Prince in October 2016 and when they played 'Sexy MF' along with Mayte Garcia dancing, I got very emotional, bringing back memories of this gig where it all started! I went on to see Prince live in concert 21 times including incredible after shows and secret events and I even drove to another country to see him. My favourite tour was *One Nite Alone* but there was nothing quite like the first time. It was like being transported to another planet and luckily one I was able to travel to many times. Thank you Prince.

CELTIC PARK

28 JUNE 1992, GLASGOW, UK

I WAS THERE: JACQUELINE HARDY

I first heard of him in the mid Eighties and I was quite interested in this little man who dressed in a quirky way, but at that time everyone did. I found him to be quite unusual and different from all of the other Eighties pop stars or musicians in that he didn't seem to be tongue-in-cheek like the rest. He seemed serious and I think that was reflected in his music.

I saw him at Celtic Park in 1992, which is a lifetime ago! He was a very small man on a very large stage but managed to fill the stage and stadium with ease. I can't remember set lists, etc. but I do remember it being a brilliant show and there being a piano and if memory serves me right a huge bed! It was probably one of my first stadium gigs. Everyone charged through the security to get into the pitch. The sound was also brilliant.

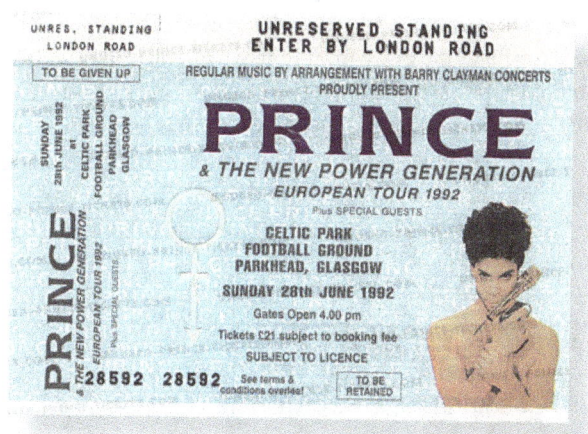

As I got older, he was still there (unlike most of the others) and still producing really original and cool sounds. Had he still been alive he would still be making really good music as he definitely had staying power and originality.

I WAS THERE: SHEENA SEVERN, AGE 20

I first got into Prince when I was around 12 or 13. My older sister had the *1999* album and I used to play it all the time when she was out! When *Purple Rain* came out, it was the first album I bought with my pocket money. Every album that came out after that was amazing. *Parade* is my favourite as it brings back great memories of listening to it every day on the school bus, and of getting the t-shirt.

I first saw him live in the summer of '92, at Celtic Park in Glasgow. I was 20 years old and travelled up to Glasgow from my hometown of Stranraer. I went with my friend Emma and my cousin Tom. We queued for hours and got near the front. I'll never forget the first moments of that gig... The song 'Thunder' kicked it off and when he came on stage I literally peed my pants - this has always been a long standing joke!

I saw him nine times in all. The best one for me was the after party in '95 at The Garage in Glasgow!

PALAIS OMNISPORTS DE PARIS-BERCY

10 JULY 1992, PARIS, FRANCE

I WAS THERE: NICOLA WAKLEY-WAKE

As with so many people, my first experience of listening to Prince was the *Purple Rain* album. My Mum bought it for me on cassette (I still have it!) and my love affair began. Ridiculed by my peers as he was different, most parents thought he was perverted (my husband still does – he's not a fan!) but none of these things deterred me from my infatuation with Prince. Once *Purple Rain* was devoured, I needed more - it wasn't enough! Considering I was only 11 years old, maybe 12, this wasn't an easy task! As I didn't really get consistent pocket money; it took time. But he was always worth the wait.

I first saw Prince live on the *Diamonds & Pearls* tour in Paris in the summer of 1992. It was my first time away from home, with my best friend at my side. I had just turned 18 and it was the best birthday present ever! He did not disappoint. He was barely a dot on the stage from where we were sitting, but it was quite a ride. At one point the stage show included a double bed that was suspended over the audience with him on it. I also don't think he was alone. My love for him was now on another level.

As my working life and career took hold I didn't manage to see him live again for quite some time. But with so many albums flowing, it didn't matter too much.

THE SUMMIT

29 DECEMBER 1992, HOUSTON, TEXAS

I WAS THERE: KATHRYN MELTON

I took a friend of mine's young teen daughter as a favour because she wanted to go and her dad did not. I had no expectations but I was blown away. OMG he played the piano like a virtuoso. It was just beautiful. A bed rose up from the stage with him on it being 'sexy'. It was a little weird being there with a young girl but I totally enjoyed the show and was a Prince fan from then on!

GLAM SLAM

31 DECEMBER 1992, MINNEAPOLIS, MINNESOTA

I WAS THERE: LYA RIVERS

It was December 31, 1992 when I met Prince. Okay, back up for full disclosure. Shannon and I drove up to Minneapolis on New Year's 1992 and stayed at a hotel

Lya Rivers met Prince at Glam Slam, Minneapolis in 1992

downtown close to Prince's new nightclub, Glam Slam. We heard he was going to be there. Dressed to the nines, we ran six blocks in high-heeled shoes to enter Glam Slam. Prince was there but only on the second floor, entry to which was prohibited. Thankfully, Shannon cajoled her way past security up the stairs as I snuck in behind her. Grabbing a drink, we walked around the exclusive second floor attempting to fit in. Finally, Shannon leaned into me and whispered, 'OMG, there he is!' I whipped left and right, screaming, 'Where? Where?' Shannon grabbed my arm assertively. 'Calm down! He's right behind you.' I turned around and there he was, sitting in a booth with those eyes looking right at me and a cheeky grin that I will never forget. I smiled back then turned around as my knees buckled under me. For the rest of the night, Shannon worked the crowd as I kept my composure and exchanged a couple of furtive glances. I couldn't take my eyes off him for a second. At one point, he casually walked up to the railing overlooking the dance floor below and I followed suit. Three bodyguards checked my movements periodically so I wouldn't get too close. Shannon popped up later and proudly stated she had secured an invite to Prince's after party at his Paisley Park Studio by cornering one of his female entourage wearing a bright red cat suit in the women's bathroom. Score!

We drove all the way to Chanhassen, only to sit in the parking lot because I didn't have the guts to go in. Watching limos pull up with lavishly dressed people striding in, I protested, 'I can't go in!' Little did I know at the time; those after-hours parties were numerous and everyone was welcome. Shannon insisted, 'Lya, if we don't go in, you will regret it for the rest of your life.' Shannon was right. We didn't go in. We drove back to our hotel that night crestfallen. I missed the opportunity of a lifetime. But, I still 'met' my Prince, which I will never forget.

BALTIMORE CIVIC CENTER

5 MARCH 1993, BALTIMORE, MARYLAND

I WAS THERE: LINDA TRIOS, AGE 17

My first time. I had very little knowledge of Prince. I knew his first hit and I knew '1999'. I was 17 years old. My boyfriend worked at WWIN AM/FM in Baltimore which was an R&B station. His cousin was a big Prince fan and invited us to a concert to see him. Our seats were way in the back, up in the nose bleed section. The Time and Vanity 6 played. Prince came on. I remember the purple bed, the neon heart and the shiny purple coat. I was not a big fan before, but he was utterly mesmerizing. I couldn't take my eyes off him, it was like he reached out and took hold of my heart and mind. When he did 'Do Me Baby', a lady in front of me waved her panties around in the air. My boyfriend and his cousin thought that was so funny, but I completely understood. I've never been the same since.

The *Act I* and *Act II* tours by Prince and The New Power Generation were undertaken between 8 March 1993 and 7 September 1993 in North America and Europe respectively to promote the *Love Symbol* album.

SUNRISE MUSICAL THEATER

9 MARCH 1993, SUNRISE, FLORIDA

I WAS THERE: BARBARA ROGERS, AGE 22

My first time seeing Prince in concert was the opening night of the *Act 1* tour in Sunrise, Florida. I was 22 and so excited. I sat about 10 rows back from the front and Mayte was sitting right in front of me, in her costume, with two bodyguards. That was awesome for a first show. I also camped out over 24 hours in front of Sears to purchase my tickets. My friends at the time thought I was nuts. This was before I found my Florida NPG family. Little did I know but a lot of my family today were at that concert. We were destined to become Purple family through our Prince.

TURTLE'S RHYTHM AND VIEWS

12 MARCH 1993, ATLANTA, GEORGIA

I WAS THERE: TROY MOTES

I attended the first four shows of Prince and the NPG's 1993 *Act I* tour. It was his first US tour since the 1988 *Lovesexy* tour, so anticipation was high! The first two shows were in Sunrise, Florida, and the next two were in Atlanta, Georgia. All four shows were a blast, but that week's highlight for me was the afternoon before the second Atlanta show.

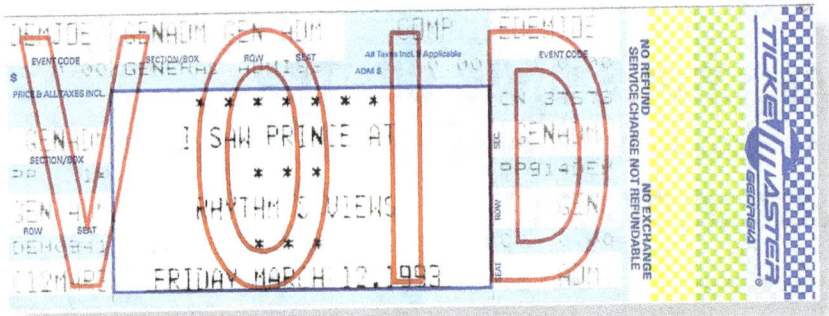

Troy Motes ticket for Turtle's Rhythm and Views

It had been reported the night before that Prince would be signing autographs the next day at a local record store, Turtle's Rhythm & Views. My friend and I showed up early, but there were already a few hundred people in line. It was a cold day, with a bit of rain. Although the weather wasn't good the crowd was great and everyone was excited. We stood in line for several hours and the line eventually wrapped around the block. There were probably at least a few thousand people there. Camera crews from MTV and *Entertainment Tonight* both showed up and interviewed fans. Eventually, the people at the front of the line slowly entered the store. Several minutes later, the first lucky fans burst out of the store and were celebrating the fact that they had met the man. As a handful of people continued to come out of the store, a few came over and talked to those of us still waiting in line. They showed us their autographs, and we all thought it was weird that Prince didn't sign his name, but instead drew the unpronounceable 'love symbol' which was the title of his latest album. Little did we know that Prince would be changing his name to that symbol less than three months later.

The line moved incredibly slowly, and we were worried that we weren't going to get inside. Eventually we made it through the doors, and we could barely see Prince and the NPG on the other side of the crowded store. The latest album was blasting over the sound system. The line snaked through the aisles of the store, through the bins of CDs and cassettes. After what seemed like forever, we eventually got close to where Prince and the band were seated. Prince was wearing a red outfit and sunglasses. He was seated at the middle of a long table with all the members of the NPG. There were instruments set up on a tiny stage right behind them, which belonged to a local band that was scheduled to play later that day. Just when it looked like we would be approaching the table, Duane Nelson, Prince's stepbrother, announced that Prince would not be signing any more autographs!

Our disappointment quickly vanished when we saw the table the band was sitting at being moved and the members of the NPG began tuning the borrowed instruments on the tiny stage. The fans that had gotten autographs were ushered out of the store. We got as close to the stage as we possibly could. I was mashed up against a bin of CDs, but I didn't care! I was about to see Prince and the NPG perform live in a record store of all places, from only a few feet away!

The music started with a loose, mostly instrumental version of 'Delirious'. Afterwards, over the opening chords of 'Sexy MF', Prince said something like, 'I don't want y'all singing the bad words, alright?' When he got to the refrain of the song, he said, 'Now don't say it... say it!' After the crowd chanted the chorus, he said, 'We got babies in the house, don't do that!'

Prince was smiling, and obviously having a great time. After 'Sexy MF', he said, 'We'd like to stay, but we got a show to do.' Many people in the crowd yelled 'One more!' A few moments later, Prince whispered in a couple of band members' ears and they played one final track, 'My Name is Prince'. It was a really unique, raw version of the song, without all the sampled backing tracks used in the regular concert version. When the song was over, Prince and Mayte were gone. The mini-concert had lasted 15 minutes.

On our way out the door, a member of the staff gave out souvenir tickets that said 'I saw Prince at Rhythm & Views'. The local newspaper estimated that about 500 fans had gotten autographs and left the store before the mini-concert, and about another 500 fans witnessed the actual performance. Although my friend and I didn't get his autograph, seeing Prince perform in such a unique environment from only a few feet away was an extraordinary experience that I will never forget.

FOX THEATER

12 MARCH 1993, ATLANTA, GEORGIA

I WAS THERE: MAISHA T G-DEJEAN

I was attending grad school in Atlanta in 1993 and one morning on the local radio station, they were giving out tickets to the brand new Prince tour (*Act I*) if you could stump the DJs with a trivia question about Prince. I wanted to clinch those tickets, so when I got through on the phone, I asked some obscure question from the liner notes of an album like *Lovesexy* or *Graffiti Bridge*, eg. who was the sound engineer on a song that wasn't released as a single. The morning show hosts were a little pissed at me, because they had to search for the answer for the rest of the show - but I still got those tix!

The show was at Atlanta's Fox Theater and we were on the orchestra floor. He was going by the love symbol name now and Mayte was in the crew. They dropped glitter and flower petals, and actual mock newspapers during the song 'Morning Papers'. When he invited women on stage to dance with him, I waved at security and one beckoned me to come, but I couldn't make it through the crowd. Being only 5'1" I think I would've been perfect to accompany him. Alas, it was not meant to be....

So at the end of the show, my friend and I left the theatre to find wet snow staring to collect on the streets. I stayed overnight since my boyfriend had the car and awoke to find about a half-foot of snow on the ground. The city was paralysed! They called it the Blizzard of '93. Local news stations had almost 24 hour coverage and warned folks to stay off the streets. But my boyfriend was fearless (plus we were from the North and thought it was silly) and came to pick me up via the deserted freeways.

I found out later that Prince's next date in South Carolina was cancelled and he spent the rest of the weekend holed up in the Hotel Nikko, where he was spotted playing the lounge piano by other stranded guests! What a weekend....

I WAS THERE: MARK HEAD

I was around 11 years old when I first heard of Prince. While listening to the Top 40 countdown there was this song that for some reason just really grabbed my attention. Then came the video. You see I was a self-admitted MTV junkie (back when the M actually stood for music). Something about seeing the artists perform the songs I had been listening to really struck me. So when I saw this guy in the purple coat just owning the performance I was struck. Then came '1999'. I needed to hear the rest of this album. I got it and the ominous voice at the beginning scared the crap out of me. But I was totally hooked. Something about the things this guy was singing about really connected with me. It wasn't just the blatant sex references either, although as boy hitting puberty there is no doubt that was also a draw. I shouldn't have been so enamoured with this guy – I was a young white boy from the Deep South and he was a black musician from the way north! Then came *Purple Rain* and the whole country had Prince mania. I desperately wanted to see this man and his extraordinary band live but the closest they came to me was a three-hour road trip and my parents were not having any of that. I was also incredibly interested in music and thought I wanted to be a musician (turns out a lack of talent is really a hindrance to that) and I had gone back and researched and digested everything I could find about this man. I discovered that his talent was just incredible.

Then he announced that he did not plan to do a big tour again. I thought I would not get the chance to ever see him live. He of course backed off of that and finally in 1993, as I was finishing college, he announced a tour and again the closest he was coming to me was a three hour drive. But this time I was 21 and could drive myself!

I got a group of friends that all wanted to go and we obtained tickets (barely – they sold out fast) for the show in Atlanta, Georgia at the Fox Theater. My seats were about as far from the stage as you could get but it didn't matter. I was there – I was watching this incredible artist live and life was good. At one point the lady next to me asked if I knew every song, I replied, 'Yes ma'am, except for that brand new one he just played.' It was the most incredible live performance I had ever seen. I was struck by the incredibly diverse audience as well. Young, old, black, white, all together singing and dancing and having a great time. The whole thing was surreal. I knew of the after shows he was notorious for having in those days and I was able to find out where he was going to be after the show but we weren't dressed appropriately for the venue's strict dress code and started the drive back. This also happened to be the date that the Deep South experienced a blizzard. Somewhere about 20 miles from home we hit a patch of ice and slid off the road into muddy icy slush and could not get out. We all spent the night in the vehicle. We were able to get to a nearby business and use a phone to call my parents and once the weather cleared up some my father and one of my accompanying friends' father finally made it to us on a tow truck to pull us out. As he got out of the truck he yelled to me, 'Was it worth it?' My reply was, 'Every minute of it.'

I was able to catch him live over the years seven more times. All of them were incredible shows.

RADIO CITY MUSIC HALL

24 MARCH 1993, NEW YORK, NEW YORK

I WAS THERE: CHRISTINA WITHERS

I went to many Prince concerts. My first concert was his *1999* tour, which I saw at both Madison Square Garden and at the Greensboro Coliseum. I had floor seats for both. His music dared you to sit still. And I lost the dare every single time.

One of my most favourite concerts was the *Symbol* concert. One of my sisters worked at Warners. She would hook me up with everything Prince related – everything! He was playing Radio City and I was with my sister and the Warner 'suits' in the Golden Circle. NPG and Prince started and I was on my feet, edging my way to the aisle so I could dance. Sometime around the third song, I turned to find my sister in the aisle getting down with the suits! My sister is 16 years older than me and she never went to a Prince concert before. That night she was baptised in the waters of Lake Minnetonka!

MAPLE LEAF GARDENS

30 MARCH 1993, TORONTO, CANADA

I WAS THERE: MARLEY RAE

I only saw him twice in concert. My first time was at Maple Leaf Gardens just eight days before my 21st birthday! I can't remember what I wore, only that I went with a boy. And I remember buying lots at the souvenir stand after the concert. Although we were in the nose bleed section, to see him live was a dream come true.

BILL GRAHAM CIVIC AUDITORIUM

11 APRIL 1993, SAN FRANCISCO, CALIFORNIA

I WAS THERE: JACE WITMAN, AGE 22

My first time seeing Prince was in 1993 during the *Act 1* tour in San Francisco. I was 22 at the time and had many failed attempts to see Prince before that. My friends and I sat in front of a local record store in a nearby strip mall all night for tickets. We weren't first in line, but we had a close enough spot that we were pretty sure we would get tickets. I can't imagine doing anything like waiting all night in a line to get concert tickets now, but it was a different time back then. This of course was before the Internet and smart phones allowed the process to be done anywhere.

Jace Witman had many failed attempts to see Prince

The wait paid off. My friends and I got eighth row centre seats, and we paid the standard ticket price, not some crazy scalper price. Standing in line for that concert now reminds me of standing in a line for a ride at Disneyland. Even waiting seemed like part of the experience, especially seeing all the women (and some men) dressed in lace bodysuits and wild clothing that was out-dated even then.

Once inside the venue, the wait seemed to be forever, but it was never boring. There was electricity in the air, and it was the first time I felt what it was like to be in a Prince audience. We were all the same, and we all knew it without having to say anything to one another.

The lights went out and the building erupted in screams, as if the entire audience was on a roller coaster. 'My Name is Prince' was the opener of that show and his band at the time, the NPG, was loud. Michael B's drum set was moving so much air that I could feel his kick drum in my chest. Prince appeared, his face covered by his gold chain mask. There he was, my hero, and I watched in disbelief that it was all happening. We were close, but I was sceptical until he finally took off the chain mask. The crowd erupted again, maybe because - like me - they were now sure it really was Prince in the flesh.

The show was broken up into two sets, including an intermission. Most of the first half was material from the *Symbol* album, which I loved. Near the end of the first set, he performed two of my favourite B-sides, 'She's Always in My Hair' and 'Irresistible Bitch'. I'm sure my mouth hung open the whole time. I couldn't believe what I was hearing and seeing. In that moment I felt something that I've only really felt at other Prince performances. I was in the right place at the right time.

My friends and I connected after the show and drove 90 minutes or so home to Sacramento. We talked about the show the entire way home and for days that followed. That was my first time seeing him, after years of trying, and I made up for lost time. I saw him over a dozen more times after that.

NATIONAL INDOOR ARENA

26 JULY 1993, BIRMINGHAM, UK

I WAS THERE: DANIEL PAYNE

The opening night for the *Act II* tour. Unfortunately he had adjusted the set list dramatically from the *Act I* tour and not as many songs from the new album were played, but the energy of the show and the new set list were amazing! He previewed several new tracks – 'Come', 'Endorphinmachine' and '2gether' including the lyrics for 'Race' and 'Johnny'.

I also saw him on 31st July at Wembley Stadium, the first and only show he ever performed at the stadium. It was great to see him in a stadium environment and with 75,000 other fans!

I then saw him at Wembley Arena on 7 September, the last gig of the *Act II* tour. This show was just electric! Prince had already performed live on Radio 1 earlier that day and was due to perform an after show gig after this last show at Wembley Arena. From the second the show started, with Mayte dressed as Prince coming through the audience in a cage whilst miming to 'My Name Is Prince', he really was on fire that night. His energy was just off the scale and the audience lapped every second of it up! This show was so much better in the arena rather than the stadium – the sound and the lighting was just so much better.

He performed 'The Sacrifice of Victor' one song before the end before being carried off by his band mates.

MEADOWBANK STADIUM

29 JULY 1993, EDINBURGH, UK

I WAS THERE: NICOLE DONKIN

I saw him twice and went to an after show party in London too. I stole my dad's *Purple Rain* vinyl when I was 11. He had a lot of vinyl and I loved *Purple Rain*. So it was my dad's fault! For my 18th birthday my parents got me and my friend tickets for his concert at Meadowbank Stadium in Scotland. It was quite an adventure going on the bus. 4 Non Blondes were the support act. I loved that concert, we were so near. I could see he wore make up. My friend, who was my next door neighbour, was only 16. We were at the front of the stage. We talked a security man into giving us a wristband that got us into the front rows. It was amazing. There were cameras recording the show. Me and Keeley were dancing and the cameraman was on us and laughing at us. I have this show on CD and love watching it.

Nicole Donkin saw Prince at Edinburgh's Meadowbank Stadium

Mayte came on the stage first dressed as Prince and everyone thought it was Prince. She was dancing around and she fell over. Two minutes later Prince appeared on stage. During 'Let's Go Crazy', lots of streamers were let's off. We had them round us. The concert was two hours and he did lots of old songs. When the concert finished we were late getting back to the bus. The driver was talking to a policeman. We got on and people cheered and looked in envy at our wristband and the streamers we still had on. We got right to the front. I remember some press photographers being behind us.

At the O2 in London, I went with my partner. The shape of the O2 made the sound amazing. We went to the after show party after this concert, in the Indigo Room. Prince came on stage at the after show, but only for one song as too many people were taking photos and he stomped off.

I love Prince and his talent as a musician, singer and performer got me hooked. I was brought up around lots of music. My dad would always say music artists should play music and write it. Not like some modern day acts now. I am so happy he liked Prince and he can never argue that Prince was rubbish. It seems he got me into Prince.

I was at home the day Prince died. My friend saw it on the news and texted me. I was devastated. I turned the news on and cried. My husband came in and hugged me. I remember seeing how he had nearly overdosed on the plane weeks before. And thought, 'My God, I will never see him in concert again.' It upset me so much that he was alone and so weird he had died in his elevator. I wish I could turn back time. Prince's music always cheers me up. I have depression and when I am down Prince always makes me happy. I am so lucky to have seen him. My friend Keeley is still a fam and my hubby is too. Hopefully my son will like him. If not I will teach him to like someone talented that writes and plays music.

I WAS THERE: SAM BLEAZARD

I saw the *Diamonds & Pearls* tour at Earls Court, and I saw him in Edinburgh in 1993, the only time he played in my 'hometown'. It was brilliant. It was at Meadowbank Athletics Stadium and it was a great show, which began with his dancer Mayte being lowered onto the stage, disguised as Prince.

I WAS THERE: MARK HUTCHISON

I grew up not in a deprived area but not in a place you'd consider privileged. Money was always tight. So starting high school I found myself in this mix of classes, personalities and opinions. One guy in my year was a Prince fan and I ribbed him for it. The usual stuff – 'he's gay', 'his songs are crap', etc. The guy hated me, but we got talking. Eventually. Sometime in late 1992 he handed me a cassette and says, 'Play that from where it is on Side A. The song is called '7'. I think you'll like it.' So I gave it a chance. Before I knew it, I was listening to the entire album over and over. It was eye opening. About a week later I decided to go and buy a Prince CD. *Parade* was in the bargain bin at my local music store so I bought it. I heard 'Mountains' and decided right there and then that I would buy every album this guy has ever released. And I did, including the ones he didn't release! Me and that guy from school are now the best of friends. We have shared so many Prince moments together, whether at home or at a Prince gig. We created and forged memories and an amazing friendship. That's how I got into Prince's music.

1993 comes along. Prince is playing Edinburgh so I want to see this. My aforementioned friend is looking pleased with himself as I pass him standing at the front of the queue. Until I say, 'Thought you were in the seats?' He replies, 'I am.' To which I say, 'Yeah, that's the standing queue.'

And so, my first concert, Edinburgh, Meadowbank Stadium 1993. My local ice cream man noticed I had a Prince t-shirt on and asked if I was going. I had no idea he was playing Scotland. After a brief conversation he said, 'Get a ticket, we'll take you.' I live in Kirkcaldy. 25 miles or so from Edinburgh. So I get the ticket and he takes me to the most amazing experience of my life. I'm 15 years old and watching Prince just blow the place away. He introduces 'Purple Rain' by saying, 'See the man with the blue guitar?' and Levi strums the 'Purple Rain' intro. From that moment, every chance I got I just had to see him live.

The last time was at the SSC Hydro in Glasgow in May 2014. Tickets sold out instantly so a £65 ticket cost me £198. But I would've sold my right arm for it and I managed to get on the front row. I took some pictures that are very special to me and which were taken very discreetly due to the usual no pictures rule at Prince concerts. It was amazing!

I WAS THERE: SHONA MCDONALD

Before Prince I was into David Bowie and The Jam and all that kind of music. I was brought up on Stevie Wonder and Ray Charles, really good music, rather than electronic or manufactured music. I was introduced to his music by a friend of mine in 1988. It was the *Sign o' the Times* album. I just fell in love with it. I thought it was the best thing ever. I drove my son to primary school and we would sing 'Starfish and Coffee' together on the way to school and he just loved it. But when I showed him the videos of 'Purple Rain' and things like that he thought, as most people did, 'Oh, he's gay' because he was so effeminate and small and freaky. I didn't think that at all. I thought he was stunning and I just continued my whole life to buy every single CD that came out and tried to go to every concert I could.

I first saw him in Glasgow on the *Lovesexy* tour. He loved the fans. I have never seen anybody try to engage with an audience like he did. Then I saw him again in Edinburgh, where I lived, at Meadowbank Stadium, which was actually a very small running stadium. When they said Prince was coming to Edinburgh I thought, 'Wow, it must be Murrayfield.' They actually closed the stadium down and re-vamped it.

I was right up close at the front. It wasn't overly packed. It's probably the best concert I've ever been to just because of the intimacy of it. You could really see him up close doing his thing. He came out and started to jump around between all the instruments and the drums, jumping around and dancing, and then he started to strip off, to take his clothes off, and - it wasn't him! It was a female! It's just what he was - he was a showman so of course you get a double cheer with the artist coming onto the stage.

When he did *21 Nights* in London I took my son for his 21st birthday. I could almost cry because I was only going to see him for one night. You could hardly see him he was so tiny. You ended up watching it on the screen and you don't want to do that because you can do that at home. He just looked like a wee dog jumping around on the stage. But when it was all over and we were leaving he came out on the stage on a big motorbike and he rode around the stage for a couple of minutes.

Then I saw him at the Hop Farm Festival with Larry Graham and 3RDEYEGIRL. That was brilliant. The last time I saw him was in Glasgow and I went with my nieces and nephews. I can't remember the venue.

When he died I was in my flat with my youngest sister. I have five sisters. Because I've passed him down to all of my family now - my son, my nieces, my nephews all love him. I got a text from my sister. We sometimes have a joke with each other and she went, 'Oh my goodness, Prince has died' and I went, 'Stop it.' Because that happened a few times. 'You don't say things that aren't true.' I was gutted when I found out it was true. It's been a while now. You just never knew anything about Prince because it wasn't in the tabloids. He wasn't in the papers so you only heard about him if you listened to his music or if he was doing a concert. I don't know anything about the drugs he was supposed to have taken but look at the way he danced and performed. His body must've been absolutely exhausted. I don't know, if he didn't want to have surgery, what the problem was. I don't know if he overdosed on painkillers. He wasn't a drug-taking rock star. He was always very clean. He even sacked people on his crew who were taking drugs. When I saw the last pictures of him I thought maybe it was just his time his time to go. He just performed his whole life. He was a workaholic. He just worked, worked, worked. He was a leader. Everybody else follows. These rappers? They're just ripping off magical artists like my Prince and Stevie Wonder.

WEMBLEY STADIUM

31 JULY 1993, LONDON, UK

I WAS THERE: PAUL HEWITSON

I was lucky enough to see him a few times over the years, beginning in July 1993 with Wembley Stadium, then G-MEX in Manchester in March 1995, Wembley Arena in August 1998, Manchester Apollo in October 2002 and finally on 23 May 1014 at the First Direct Arena in Leeds. As a 14 year old, I wasn't really into music. I used to tape the Top 40 off the radio on a Sunday night, but that was about it.

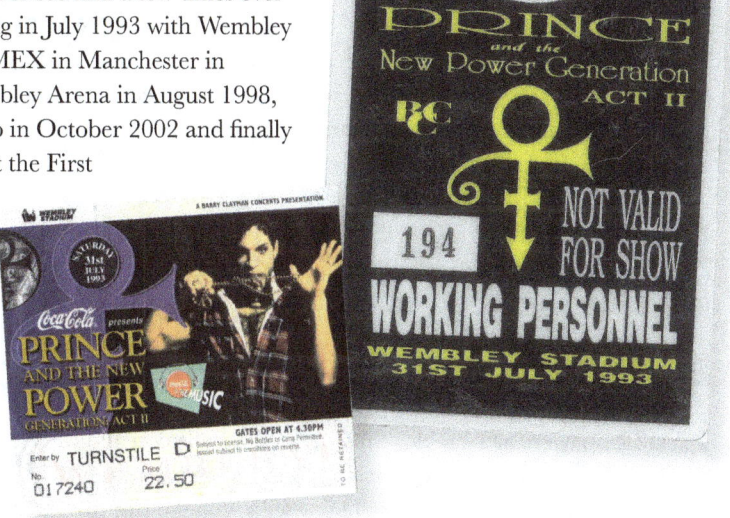

I had a friend who was into a wide variety of music - ZZ Top, Zappa, B52s, Velvet Underground - and Prince, amongst others. He used to go on at me to listen to it all and I'd listen to some just to shut him up! I didn't really listen to the Prince stuff until the day that *Batman* was released. He rushed out, bought the tape and came round that afternoon. It was playing for a while and I liked it. I played it from the beginning and I copied it. I listened to it two or three times that night. That was the moment! I went out and bought a copy the very next day from Our Price Records. I've been hooked ever since. In the following weeks, I went out and bought a tape each week, starting with *Dirty Mind*. It started with cassette albums and cassette singles then vinyl, CD singles, anything! I had to have everything I could get my hands on. Now I have a room devoted to my collection!

THE FORUM

1 AUGUST 1993, LONDON, UK

I WAS THERE: MARK WARE

On 31st July 1993 I went to *Act II* at Wembley Stadium. This was followed by my first experience of a Prince after show gig. This was in the early hours of 1st August at the Forum in Kentish Town North London. This was a 'queue- up-and-pay-£10-on-the-door' after finding out the location by word of mouth at the Wembley gig. I believe a number of 'celebrities' were in attendance. The only one I recall bumping into was Sid Owen (Ricky Butcher from *Eastenders*). Chilling on the dance floor area seeing the stage prepared for the intimate gig, I saw Prince enter the venue via a side fire door wearing a vivid pink jump suit.

Just a few weeks later I attended the final *Act II* gig at Wembley Arena (The Sacrifice of Victor) on 7th September followed by the very special after show party and gig at Bagley's Warehouse in Kings Cross. The event was known as *The Dawn*. I recall picking up the tickets for this from the Virgin Megastore. This event was infamous for ticketing issues which resulted in more people than tickets sold which made for an uncomfortable atmosphere ahead of the band taking to the stage, with overcrowding in the main room. However, the gig was well worth the wait with guest vocals including The Steeles and Mavis Staples and a show which lasted about two and a half hours and ran until about 4am.

BAGLEY'S WAREHOUSE

8 SEPTEMBER 1993, LONDON, UK

I WAS THERE: HAZEL DEWHURST

Nude was my first tour, so I was quite late to the party really.

In 1993 we were at Wembley Stadium in the afternoon and we had tickets to most of the gigs that summer and we'd heard about the legendary after shows and never thought we'd ever get a look in. We got sat in our seats with the Controversy Fan Club in the stands and were handed tickets to a private after show party at The Forum in Kentish Town. So we legged it like women possessed, not quite believing our luck. He came on about 2 o'clock in the morning. There is no recording that exists of it anywhere. He stage dived and all the crowd stepped back and parted and he fell on the floor!

I went to Bagleys, the one everybody talks about in London, where we all thought we were going to die because it was oversold. It was really, really hot. It was after another show in London so it was sold separately, and it was before health and safety. It was incredibly hot, the rumour was that he didn't want to go on but by then there would have been an absolute riot. And when he did he was in a foul mood but the performance was incredible - it's what they used for 'The Sacrifice of Victor' video.

I also went to Minneapolis in '92 but as soon as he heard we were coming he buggered off so we didn't see him. But we met the band and did all the tour round the sites and other things and we were given a private listening party for the *Symbol* album which was a little bit special. And the Glam Slam nightclub was open then so I met his mum in the toilets. Yeah - I stalked his mum in the toilets!

PRINCE'S HOUSE

6 APRIL 1994, LOS ANGELES, CALIFORNIA

I WAS THERE: LIZ WALTERS

In late 1993, my sister - who's a huge Prince fan - showed me this ad that said that Prince was 'seeking the most beautiful girl in the world'. She asked for some pictures and I thought nothing of it. At the time I was a dancer at Disneyland, so she sent in a snap of me as Princess Jasmine and a couple from my prom night, waiting for my date in the front yard of my parents' house. Weeks went by and I then got a letter from Paisley Park, saying my image had been selected and it may be used in the video or in print. I signed off on its usage, and never saw anything about it, until going into a record store the day the single 'The Most Beautiful Girl In The World' was released. That was one of the most insane feelings ever, to walk in and see your face amongst a collage of women's faces on a Prince song!

Fast forward a few weeks later. The song goes gold. My sister, who was in the fam club, found out they were having a party for the song at Glam Slam in Los Angeles. She told me to call Paisley Park and see if we could get on the guest list. 'Tell them you're one of the girls on the cover!' So I did. And we got on the list. And the search was on for the perfect tight gold dress!

We show up, the Glam is packed. She walks over by a group of men, and she knows who they are. 'That's Duane, Prince's brother, that's so and so…' and all of a sudden we see HIM. Sitting in the corner at a little table, one hand on his cane. After her talking me into it, I walk over to Prince with all the bravado the almost 20 year old me could muster. 'Hi, you don't know me, but I'm one of the girls on the cover.'

'Honey I know, I put you there.' I DIED.

So he asked me to sit down, and it's like the entire club, celebrities included, faded away. We chatted and he asked if I was still dancing at Disneyland. I told him I was. As we were finishing our chat, he said he wanted to see me again. I asked if he had a pen so I could write down my number. He replied, 'I can find you.' I DIED AGAIN. Then I replied, 'Well, I can be found.'

A few days later, I had just gotten home from my college classes when my mom told me, 'Someone named Terry from Paisley Park called for you. Here's the number.' OMG what? I ran to the garage phone for privacy and immediately called the number. After a few transfers to 'the boss', I was greeted with a very deep 'hello'.

'Hi! How are you?' I said. And there began the most insane phone conversation that old yellow wall rotary phone ever had. We talked about each other, our interests, what I wanted to do with my life, art, love, and music. I likened him to the Wizard of Oz because he's bigger than life, but today, he's just a guy I'm talking to on the phone. I asked him how do I address him, since he had recently changed his name to the love symbol. 'However you address me, I'll answer,' he said.

He asked if he could see me that night, and transferred me to his driver Oscar, so I could give him directions to my house in Orange County, about an hour from the Bel Air mansion he was living in at the time. By the time I hung up from that call, I was freaking out! 'What am I gonna wear? OMG, Prince is sending a car, he's sending a car to come get me! Mom, can I go to Prince's house?'

My sister made it over in record time, hair and makeup fully done. When Oscar shows up he makes it clear Prince only wants to see me, not my sister, and no, not even if she waits in her own car. Sorry sis, I'll tell you all about it!

Of course I called my friends to tell them what was happening! And of course they showed up to my house, but we had just left, so my parents told them to catch us on the way to the freeway. We were sitting at a stop light, and I was admiring the pillows in the limo with the symbol on them and the Tootsie pops in the arm rests. My friends pull up alongside us and roll down the window.

'Liz, is that you?' I rolled down my window and screamed! I yelled out, 'Please don't follow us!' Oscar just laughed and shook his head.

The drive up to LA was exciting and I was a nervous wreck. When we pulled into the gated driveway, I got out of the car and saw him walking towards me, smiling, wearing a red suit with the matching boots. He looked gorgeous. We shook hands. He noticed my grunge era Doc Martens and said, 'Nice boots.' I looked at his and said, 'Nice heels.' 'Touché', he said, and we went inside.

To the right of the door inside was a giant neon sign of his symbol. He had a pool table, with big windows looking out at the skyline. He asked if I was hungry, I said no. So we sat down to talk. We talked about favourite shows growing up. Mine was *What's Happening!!* He liked that show too and said the character Shirley was his favourite. He put the TV on. It was just after Kurt Cobain had shot himself and we were watching Courtney Love on MTV, speaking tearfully to fans. He asked me if I thought he was going to heaven. I said, 'I'm Catholic, and killing your self is a mortal sin, so maybe he wouldn't. We both agreed it was the most tragic thing ever.

We played pool, and he wagered I would give him my Princess Jasmine watch if I lost, which I did. 'Keep your watch,' he said. 'Can you imagine what they'd say if they see Prince wearing a Jasmine watch?' We sat and talked, side by side, alone in his house. His eyes were so terribly beautiful, coated by the longest lashes, and he smelled like lavender. I reached over and touched the symbol on his chain, and he let me. He was so funny, so charismatic, so down to earth, and yet, so Prince.

Oscar walked back in and hands him a bag from Tower Records. He pulls out a VHS copy of the movie *Aladdin*. I was stunned. 'So I can watch you', he said. We talked some more and he asked me to make a video of myself dancing and send it to him. We hugged, and I walked out to the car.

How the hell do you go back to classes the next day after that?

A little while later my sister and I were back at Glam Slam. He was supposed to be giving one of his secret shows that night. As we were approaching, I saw Oscar standing outside the car. 'Oscar!' I called out. He turned to me and remembered me! 'Liz! How are you? How's mom and dad?' 'Good!' I said. 'Is he inside?' 'Sure is, wanna go see him?' And with that, he led us past the velvet ropes into the VIP area of the back room at Glam Slam. We were right in front of Prince as he performed that night to less than 100 people. He sang 'The Most Beautiful Girl In The World' and looked right at me the whole time. One of the most memorable nights of my life. AGAIN!

Time went on and he married Mayte. I finished college and continued to dance and act. He told me once he thought I would be a great actress because I 'have no barriers. You say what you mean.' I took that advice with me on every audition.

I saw him in concert a few times after that, the very last being at the Grove in Anaheim. My friend and I were right on the floor, in front of the mic stand. I was close enough to get his sweat on me, and he performed a 17-minute 'Purple Rain' for his finale. Another unforgettable night, thanks to Prince.

I'm so grateful for those memories, those moments, that attention, and his welcoming arms into his home. There will never be another genius like him.

PAISLEY PARK

1994, CHANHASSEN, MINNESOTA

I WAS THERE: KEFLE J CALLENDER

It was the summer of 1994. I was at Prince's club, Glam Slam, in downtown Minneapolis. I was there on a Thursday night because that was the '18 and up' night. On this night Prince was in the building. Prince was in his club often when he wasn't on tour and it was always awesome to see him whenever he was in the building.

Kefle Callender saw Prince at Paisley Park

When the club night ended all the bouncers who were working for Prince were telling everybody that Prince is performing tonight out at Paisley Park. I was like, 'Really? I'm definitely going.' My Uncle Samson had let me drive his Cadillac on this night, which was so cool. I saw one of my friends named Leslie exiting out of Glam Slam and I asked her if she'd like to come and see Prince perform tonight with me and she said yes. When we got out there, there was like 100 people standing in line. So I parked the car and we got in line with the people. Back then last call was at 12.45am and the clubs let out at 1am. It took 30 minutes to drive out to Chanhassen from downtown Minneapolis and it was way worth it. When the doors opened up, the bouncers who worked at Glam Slam were the same bouncers who worked out at Paisley Park. When the doors opened up they started frisking people at the door and at that time we were being charged only $20 to get in. Cash only.

When 2am rolled around, everybody was inside and Prince approached the stage. The first song he opened up with was 'Pussy Control' and my mind was blown. Prince played nonstop until 6am in the morning and the show was unbelievable. From that night began a 19 year experience of me going out to Paisley Park for concerts and parties.

Thank you, Prince, for everything you gave us.

16 April 1994 saw Prince have his first UK number 1 with 'The Most Beautiful Girl In The World', his 37th single release. It was his first release since changing his stage name to an unpronounceable symbol.

GLAM SLAM

7 JUNE 1994, SOUTH MIAMI BEACH, FLORIDA

I WAS THERE: TROY MOTES

My friends and I attended the concert at the grand opening of Prince's Glam Slam club in South Miami Beach on June 7, 1994. The concert was billed as 'The World's First Interactive Party' and as Prince's 'first' birthday (it had been one year since he had changed his name to the unpronounceable 'Symbol'.)

We arrived at the club late in the afternoon. The doors were supposed to open at 10pm and we were told Prince wouldn't hit the stage until after midnight. We waited outside the club in the heat and humidity for what seemed like forever, catching glimpses of band members and members of the crew as they were going in and out of the front doors. We asked one guy who was coming out of the club if we could stand inside to escape the heat. He didn't really seem to care, and he let us in. We stood in the corner in the entrance of the club, trying hard not to look imposing. There were many large photos of Prince and different pieces of artwork all over the floor which hadn't been hung up yet. We heard the sound of instruments tuning in the next room and the band began jamming on 'Interactive'. About this time another guy who worked in the club asked us why we were there. We said we were told by someone else that we could stand inside. He tried to get us to leave, but we insisted we were told it was okay. He left to ask if it was all right if we could be there, and the music stopped about this time. A few minutes later, Michael B and Sonny T walked through the room and spoke to a few people. Then, without warning, Prince strolled in the room followed by his bodyguard. He was wearing a black and red outfit and seemed to be locked in thought. I don't remember him speaking to anyone, he was just casually examining the club and the artwork on the floor. My friend and I both had birthday cards we were going to give him, but we were afraid we would be kicked out if we approached him. In fact, I had gotten him a card for a one year old, since the show was being billed as his 'first birthday'. Prince walked right past us and right on out of the room. At that point, the guy who worked in the club told us we had to leave 'now'.

After many hours of waiting, and watching the line grow around the block, the doors opened a few minutes after 10pm. We were allowed into the entry area where we had spotted Prince earlier, but the doors to the actual club with the stage weren't opened until 11.15. After a performance by a weird local dance troupe, we were finally allowed to rush the stage, and we got in the very front. Since this was the 'world's first interactive party', there was a satellite link up with Prince's other Glam Slam clubs in Minneapolis and Los Angeles, and footage from each club was being broadcast on huge video screens in the other clubs. We were forced to watch the silly interplay between the hosts at each club, until Prince and the NPG finally hit the stage at 12.25am (technically missing his birthday!).

Prince was wearing a long white robe/shirt thing that had pictures of the Eiffel Tower on the legs of his pants. The word 'SAVED' was written on the right side of his face. There were many amazing moments during the show, but the definitive highlight for me came right after the performance of 'Space'. I was waving a birthday card in front of Prince that said 'Happy Birfday 2 O+>' and finally he looked at me and asked, 'And what's that say?' I yelled, 'Happy birthday' and continued to wave it in front of him, and he asked, 'Happy birthday?' I tossed it to him and it fell on the stage by his feet. I yelled, Read it!' and he bent down and picked it up. He said, 'This is my birthday, huh?' and he opened it. He looked at the card and said, 'You know how old I am? One!' He read the card to himself, turned to me and said, 'I appreciate it.' Wow! He then spoke about how he was spiritually reborn a year ago, and how it was his first birthday. People threw cards to him all through the show, but he didn't bother to look at any others. I think he liked the fact that I had gotten him a card for a one year old.

The rest of the show was phenomenal, and almost everything he played was unreleased at the time. The crowd sang 'Happy Birthday' to him a few times, and at one point Mayte brought a cake out for him and spray-painted the number '1' on his robe. The show ended at 2.55am. The entire experience and my 'close encounter' with Prince are memories I will treasure for the rest of my life.

THE PALLADIUM

14 JULY 1994, NEW YORK, NEW YORK

I WAS THERE: ANJA LÜDERS

A friend called my friend from New York. We lived in Germany. She said, 'Prince will play New York Palladium in 48 hours. Are you going to come?

Anja Lüders (left) flew to New York at short notice. Her boss thought she was crazy

I have tickets for you.' So I called my boss to say that I had to fly to New York from Berlin because Prince was playing two gigs at the Palladium. He thought I was crazy but gave me leave. From the first gig we got home at five in the morning. At 8am we got a call that Prince was playing a charity gig at 12 noon. We were dead tired and did not have a ticket but we went to check it out.

Kids arrived with their free tickets (you could not buy tickets for the show). I remembered my own school time and how sometimes we were taken to boring places we were not really interested in. That is why I chatted up three kids to sell their tickets to me. They did because they did not know Prince well. They would rather have the money.

We were stood on the first row. Prince came out and saw us, three white grown ups on the first row at a charity concert for black dancers. You could tell he was pissed. I could not bear him hating me because we loved him so much. I asked my friends if we could leave but they said, 'Not even Prince gets us away from a Prince concert.'

They were right. I stayed too.

The *Ultimate Live Experience* tour brought Prince to Europe from 3 to 30 March 1995.

WEMBLEY ARENA

3 MARCH 1995, LONDON, UK

I WAS THERE: DANIEL PAYNE

This was the first night of the *Ultimate Live Experience* tour, and I saw two more shows there and the last night too. These were amazing shows with performances of the as yet unreleased *The Gold Experience* album and with a fabulous stage set. Mayte was flying over the ground, sprinkling gold glitter during the song 'Gold'. Unreleased videos and music were played before each show on loop – 'Zannalee', '18 and Over', 'Empty Room', 'The Same December' and 'P Control'.

SCOTTISH EXHIBITION AND CONFERENCE CENTRE

13 & 14 MARCH 1995, GLASGOW, UK

I WAS THERE: MARK HUTCHISON

This was a very different gig. The whole 'slave' thing was going on. So the promo videos ran as a 'warm up' act. The great coincidence is, Prince opened that gig with the song he closed the '93 Edinburgh gig, 'Endorphinmachine'. It was a rocking start to a concert. The whole gig was amazing but there wasn't a lot of greatest hits. By this time my collection of bootlegs was pretty vast so I was able to enjoy some lesser-heard songs. The two songs that stood out were 'Pussy Control', where he announced, 'Beautiful girls, raise your hands, beautiful women, raise somethin' else. Y'all need pussy control' and 'Pink

Cashmere'. He just walked out on stage, no band, and started, 'Oooh, here I go again, falling in love all over' and then the band came in.

I WAS THERE: TRACIE NEWTON

I have been a fan of Prince since I was 12 years old, in 1985. I honestly can't remember what it was about him, but I was hooked. While all my friends were following the likes of Duran Duran, I was following Prince, Terence Trent Darby, etc. I had tickets to see him in 1993 in Edinburgh but ended up out of the country. So I jumped at the chance to see him in 1995. As expected, he was spectacular a non-stop showman. I was beyond excited at finally getting to see him live. The atmosphere was outstanding. I've been to many concerts in my 46 years, but that will always be my best.

SHEFFIELD ARENA

16 & 17 MARCH 1995,
SHEFFIELD, UK

I WAS THERE: LAURA WADE, AGE 26

I remember being in my best friend's house. We were big Duran Duran fans. We were 15 years old. Her brother came in and said, 'Just listen to this guy and see what you think.' That was it - Duran Duran was out and Prince was in! We loved him, his music was different. He always seemed to get talked about in a negative way in the media. *Purple Rain* was fab. The album was unbelievable. My

Laura Wade saw Prince at Sheffield Arena

friend was lucky. Back then her parents gave her spending money, so she imported many albums from America - Vanity 6, The Time, Apollonia and The Time. It was great because I got to tape them.

We first went to see him in Sheffield. I was 26 years old at the time and couldn't believe I was seeing him. His wife Mayte was on the stage dancing too. I cried all the way through.

The second and last time I saw him was in Leeds in 2014. When I heard he was here again I just had to go. My husband promised me he would get two tickets as soon as the ticket lines opened. 20 minutes into it he messaged me and said the computers were down and he can't get through on the phone. The ticket price was - I'm sure - £40. I panicked so much I went through a ticket agent. It took me ages but I was the happiest person in the world. I called the husband and said, 'I got the tickets!' He said, 'How much?' I said, 'Don't worry – only £200 pounds.' He put the phone down on me. I would have paid £1,000 for them.

Prince was touring with 3RDEYEGIRL. The concert was out of this world, the fans were lovely and friendly and I cried all way through (again). Sometimes as a fan you think to yourself, 'I'm sure Prince just looked and smiled at me.' I'm sure he did at that last concert but I will never know. I always thought I'd never get to see him again after that and I didn't.

NATIONAL EXHIBITION CENTRE

18 & 19 MARCH 1995, BIRMINGHAM, UK

I WAS THERE: SIMON HOULDERS

I saw him twice, in '95 at the NEC and 2003 at the Hammersmith Apollo, for the *One Nite Alone* tour. The first album I had, on cassette, was *Controversy*. I was 12 and I listened to it obsessively. I can't remember where I got it from but even though I didn't get all the references, it really spoke to me. And so for every birthday and Christmas from then on I would ask for a Prince album. *Diamonds & Pearls* always evokes feelings of Christmas, because I got it as a gift and played it to death.

The *Symbol* (Love Sign) album was the soundtrack to my teens, and the first time I saw him live, in '95, was between this and *The Gold Experience* albums. He was really late to the concert. They kept playing Ice Cube and George Clinton's 'Bop Gun' on repeat (I believe it was recorded at Paisley Park), and the crowd kept doing the Mexican wave. Because of his late appearance, my dad and I had to leave to get the train, and so missed some of the concert. At the show was the first time I heard 'Pussy Control', and I remember Mayte dancing with the sword balanced on her head, and the stage set, like in the 'Gold' video, with the conveyor belt at centre stage.

In 2002, I went with my partner for my birthday to the Hammersmith Apollo in London, for the *One Nite Alone* tour. It was a much more intimate venue than the NEC. At one point Maceo Parker came into the audience, right by me, to squeeze his horn! I don't recall the whole set, but it was really special, and I'm just grateful I got to see him in a more intimate setting.

WEMBLEY ARENA

21 & 22 MARCH 1995, LONDON, UK

I WAS THERE: MICHELLE JUSTICE

For the *Gold Experience* (*Ultimate Live Experience*) tour I saw the show in Glasgow, went straight on to Sheffield two nights in a row and then on to London. Whilst at the London show he said, 'Continue the party at…' and named a club, which I'll have to rack my brains for to remember what it was called! I remember I paid £100 on a taxi across London to get me there! He was there but didn't play. He just sat up in a balcony, had a few drinks and left. Still, it was amazing to watch him there!

THE POINT

30 MARCH 1995, DUBLIN, IRELAND

I WAS THERE: TANYA LOFTUS DURKIN

Back in March 1995, I brought my friend Victoria to see Prince live! She wasn't a fan but I had seen him play live once before and he was amazing so I wanted her to experience this. I was a huge fan of course. It was at The Point in Dublin and it was the *Ultimate Live Experience* tour. I was beside myself with excitement and wore my best purple hot pants and gold attire. The gig was phenomenal - Prince and Mayte had such chemistry and it was very funky! My friend got word that Prince was doing a secret after show at the Pod nightclub so we made our way over. We queued for what seemed like forever and couldn't get in as it was too busy.

Now my friend Victoria worked in radio and knew a couple of people she worked with would be in the club but of course without mobile phones in those days there was no way of contacting them. So we asked the bouncer to announce it in the club or let one of us in to find them but he wasn't having it and Victoria forgot her radio ID. So feeling deflated, we just hung around for a while and then my friend spotted a white limo driving down the side of the club.

We walked down and waited and waited outside the side entrance. It felt like hours but it was about an hour. There were a few bodyguards on walkie talkies conversing with people inside the club. There were only a small handful of people hanging around. Then there was a bit more activity with the bodyguards so we felt something was happening. Next moment the side door swung open and Mayte came out by herself and got into the limo and off she went!

Then limo number two pulled up and after maybe 20 minutes the door swung open again, there was a flash of a long yellow coat and it was Prince! We quickly walked up to near the limo and I wanted to say, 'Thank you for the funky music.., and I love you' but I was completely speechless. It didn't seem real - my music idol! I also didn't know how to say 'Symbol'!

Well he stopped, looked at my friend and myself and took my hand and said, 'Ladiez' in his deep voice. His eyeliner was immaculate and his face and hair full of gold sparkle - I was in awe! With that the bodyguard quickly moved us away as if we were going to jump into the awaiting car and - like that - in a flash he was gone!

On a high was an understatement of how I felt the next morning. I woke up and looked at my hand! It all seemed so surreal. What a feeling. To this day, when I think of it it brings back the feelings of excitement and the most amazing night! His music made such a huge difference in my life. I will never forget this genius of a man! Forever In My Life.

THE POD

31 MARCH 1995, DUBLIN, IRELAND

I WAS THERE: MAUREEN O'SULLIVAN, AGE 22

Prince and the NPG had just played two amazing nights at The Point and we were front and centre for both shows. Those shows embodied the sexy, funky quintessential Prince – a moving icon - with an epic NPG line up and his most beautiful girl in the world, Mayte. They weren't playing the hits. And we couldn't be happier. We rejoiced in hearing 'Endorphinmachine', 'Get Loose', 'Now' and we wanted nothing more than to 'Get Wild'. We were on a Purple High as we rushed from the venue on the promise (and hope) of access to an after show.

It was a freezing cold night on the streets of Dublin but we refused to move an inch. It was of little consequence that it was the early hours of the morning and I was wearing hot pants and high-laced boots. I would have gladly risked hyperthermia to access a Prince after show. A thing of legend that occurred in other countries to other people but my boyfriend Mark (now my husband) and I were in the queue for what was our first ever opportunity to be part of one.

The Pod was hosting a celebrity event earlier in the evening of March 30th. Unsurprisingly the celebrities present did not want to leave, but Prince was adamant about getting his fans inside. A bouncer informed us that the celebrities were being cleared out to make space for us fans. This only made us love him more. Finally, around 3am the queue started moving. That rush of pure adrenaline and fear that perhaps we wouldn't get in or that maybe it was too late for him to play now - it made the whole experience more exhilarating. We were 22 and we would have stood on that pavement all night if we had to, but not getting in would have been torture.

They were collecting the entry fee: £16 in a biscuit tin. It's funny what things stick in your memory. The opening notes of 'The Cross' started playing and the crowd protested the hold up by two girls not willing to pay. Someone in the queue was recording meaning that my protests were immortalised in a bootleg of the show.

Finally, we were in! I remember squeezing Mark's hand in disbelief, working our way through the crowd in a venue that felt like an underground cave. Stone walls curved around the band crowded onto a tiny stage. Bono was on the mike singing 'The Cross'. This didn't fit with the set lists at the time and his rendition was completely unique, including new lyrics about Easter time. But after all it was Dublin, U2's town, so having him there was a surreal touch.

'The Cross' faded out to much noise from the crowd. Prince started the show with a little teaser of 'People Get Ready' before bursting into 'The Jam'. The reality hit us that this was Prince's playground and he was showing off his band. He called out to his small crowd 'Ireland!' and we screamed back 'Yeah!' Our tiny number sounded like a thousand and in answer, he hits us with 'I believe in you, Ireland!' and again we responded 'Yeah!' ' I wanna hear your voices tonight!'

Prince erupted into 'Glam Slam Boogie' with the whole crowd singing 'Oooh ee oooh,

oooh ee oooh' until Prince joked 'What you singing for? I didn't give you the cue.' He seemed to be genuinely having fun. 'You like funky music?' he challenged us and our response came instantly, 'Yeah!' 'You're gonna have to prove it tonight.'

Starting with James Brown's 'Get Up', the set list that followed could be used as blueprint for what an after show should be. The whole show was nothing less than a funk-fuelled-trip. Highlights included the perfect after hours song with a perfect introduction, 'This song is not a song, this song, oh Lord if you don't mind, is a 'Funky Design'.' He could have played it for a week (and they almost did).

'The Most Beautiful Girl In The World' was a wonderful surprise and although it felt out of place with the evening, hearing Prince sing this song in this tiny venue was dreamlike. When Prince asked if there were any youngsters in the house, we knew that '18 and Over' was up next. The whole crowd was buzzing as upon Prince's command the guys sang '18 and over, I want to bone ya' and the ladies sang 'oh yeah, oh yeah'. Prince was playing the 'Bone-Ranger' and it was all too crazy to be real. He followed this with a mad version of 'Get Loose' fused with 'Bustin' Loose' with extra percussion from James 'McGoo' Gregor then flowing straight into an outstanding 'Santana Medley'. And when Prince said he would send us home 'with a ballad' we almost believed him.

But the only way to end the night was with 'Get Wild' and a few hundred fans waving their Wild signs high at about 4.30am. Needless to say I never wanted that show to end. As we spilled out into the Dublin streets to the cold morning air I had the call back 'Blow your mind, blow your mind, everybody tripping on a funky design' looping in my truly blown mind.'

When I listen to certain tracks from this *Gold* era I am transported back to being in that little crowd jumping up and down to 'Get Wild' and singing along to '18 and Over'.

Many years and many shows later, I have met fans who were there that same night. One person who shared the memory before we ever knew each other was a woman named Angela, someone who is now one of my closest friends. Having had the chance to chat to some of the members of the NPG over the last few years I've had to ask about their memories of that night. Morris confirmed it was one of his favourite after shows, Tommy reminisced about drinking with Bono, Michael B shared a crazy story about busting a snare drum early in the set and continuing a solo while James E McGregor had to get on his back to fix it while 'Go Michael, Go Michael, Go Michael' was being chanted by the oblivious crowd. Hilariously, this was encouraged by Prince, who knew perfectly well the instrumental issues that had just occurred. This Prince after show was worthy of its legendary status and I feel something beyond being blessed that I was there.

GLAM SLAM

8 JUNE 1995, MIAMI, FLORIDA

I WAS THERE: TROY MOTES

After seeing Prince's birthday concert at Glam Slam in South Miami Beach in 1994, my wife and I were fortunate enough to attend the two shows he performed there in 1995

Troy Motes got a couple of guitar picks from Glam Slam in Miami

also. The show scheduled for June 7, 1995 actually started at 1.30am on June 8th and ended at 3.35am. After resting most of the day, we decided to explore the neighbourhood around Glam Slam. We walked by the front of the club around 6.30pm and saw about 100 people standing around the main entrance. After chatting with a few people, we found out that they needed 150 extras for a music video they were filming, and they would even pay us! Most of the people were local models and actors who answered a casting call that had been made by a local talent agency, and weren't necessarily Prince fans. A couple of people coached us on how to fill out the necessary paperwork, and we were in! NPG Records hats were handed out for free to some people. We found out the video they were filming was for 'The Good Life', a track from the NPG's *Exodus* album which had been released in Europe a few months prior. After waiting until about 8.30pm in the entrance area, we were given some brief instructions to file into the club casually to avoid tripping over wires and camera equipment. Then the doors to the club were opened and we headed toward the stage. We ended up in the very centre of the front row, right in front of Prince's microphone!

Prince was standing directly in front of us, with his back to the crowd, strumming on his 'one-eyed' bass guitar. He turned around and jokingly acted as if he was surprised we were there. He was 'disguised' as Tora Tora, the pseudonym he had been using when he performed as a member of the New Power Generation. He was wearing a long black robe with the NPG logo on the front, as were the rest of the band. His face was covered with a sheer scarf and he was wearing a black top hat. To top it all off, he was wearing a wig of black shoulder-length hair. He went to the microphone and said, 'Thanks for helping us out.' About 10 minutes passed as he walked around onstage strumming on his bass and talking to the director and the band. Prince stood directly in front of me and my wife for several minutes, and we literally had to move our hands away from the stage a bit so he wouldn't step on them. Finally, the director announced they were ready to begin filming. They did a great lip-synced performance of 'The Good Life'. The director came back out and said everything looked good, but they wanted to film it again. He wanted the audience to show a little more energy - clapping hands, dancing, etc. About a minute into the second performance, Prince's bass was turned on, so he was playing live bass over the studio version of the song. When the song was over, Prince left the stage. They began repositioning the cameras as Morris Hayes and Tommy Barbarella started messing around on Morris's keyboards. Eventually, just the two of them started a groove of Sly and the Family Stone's 'Don't Call Me Nigger, Whitey' and they both played it on the same keyboard. The crowd applauded when they were through.

Sonny Thompson ran up to Tommy's keyboards and played a few notes of something and the crowd cheered him on. Then they filmed Sonny sitting in his chair at the back of the stage lip-syncing the song, with Mayte dancing in the foreground. Afterwards, Prince reappeared onstage (without the Tora Tora disguise) and was talking to the director. It seemed like Prince was very much in charge of the production. He walked to the edge of the stage, still talking to the director. Prince then called Sonny over and Mayte followed him. They all stood at the front of the stage talking for a few minutes. Prince then said to the crowd, 'Do you think y'all can hold him up?' while he pointed to Sonny. The crowd cheered and Sonny laughed, but he seemed apprehensive. Prince said something to him like, 'Turn around, bend your knees, and just fall back into the crowd.'

The director said they would practice one time, so Sonny fell into the crowd and we held him overhead. Sonny made a comment that we should 'watch the family jewels!' He got back onstage, laughing and hitting high-fives with the audience. Prince then grabbed Mayte and said something like, 'Would you rather hold her up?' and acted like he was going to throw her in the crowd. They then played the song back, and filmed Sonny falling into the crowd as he was passed around and back to the stage. He stood there for a few moments, clapping his hands and singing the song. Some footage of Mayte dancing on top of the speakers in front of the video screens on the right side of the stage was also filmed. After this, a majority of the crowd was taken to another part of the club to be filmed dancing to the song. At some point, my wife noticed a small box of Prince's guitar picks were right in front of us, beside his guitar rig. I won't incriminate her by saying she grabbed a few picks while no one was looking. After a while, Prince reappeared in a gold outfit and he started rehearsing a scene in the corner of the club with a tall, scantily-clad woman. He acted like he was kissing her, while she was slipping a wad of money out of his pocket. This footage was apparently for the 'Pussy Control' video (which was never released), and they filmed it a few times while the crowd was still being filmed dancing to 'The Good Life' on the main dance floor. Awhile later, the woman who was filming the scene with Prince came onstage along with some other dancers. The other women dancers were topless, except for tape over their breasts. They were filmed performing an energetic dance sequence to a portion of 'Pussy Control' three or four times. At about 11.20pm, we were told to exit through the door in the back of the club, where we turned in our vouchers to get paid. We had been inside the club for around three hours while they were filming.

After we left the club, we immediately got in line for that night's concert. That show didn't start until 2.30am the next morning, and it ended at 4.45am!

A couple of months later, my wife and I each got a $75 check in the mail from Unique Casting Company. The memo section on the check said 'Prince Music Video'. When

'The Good Life' video premiered, we were both so excited to see ourselves in several shots throughout it. It's still something we love to tell people about. We were actually in a Prince music video, we were paid for it, and we won't admit to taking home two of Prince's guitar picks as souvenirs!

PAISLEY PARK

9 SEPTEMBER 1995, CHANHASSEN, MINNESOTA

I WAS THERE: ADAM STANLEY

People who had tickets were let in first, relatively early at 9.15pm. We walked right up to the front and we directly in front of his mike. Only one person separated me from the stage. Surprisingly, the gig started at 11.45pm. He started with the 'Purple Medley' and with that there was a huge surge and all hell broke loose. My legs were sore next morning from trying to stand my ground. The kids like the 'Purple Medley'! The highlight of the night was 'Pussy Control'. As soon as it started I was shouting and one of the large (did I say large?) black ladies said, 'That's my song!' Ok, it rocked. Even funkier! We were all doing the chorus. He went from 'Pussy Control' into 'Letitgo' and did all of it.

He was in a great mood, having lots of fun. I was close enough too see that his cuticles were in much better shape than mine. I caught eye contact with him a few times. He ended with 'Get Wild' about 1.15am. There was no encore.

PAISLEY PARK

27 OCTOBER 1995, CHANHASSEN, MINNESOTA

I WAS THERE: ADAM STANLEY

This was the video shoot for the Love Symbol concert. We got there about 10.30pm and walked right in and even got a good spot about 10 to 12 feet away from the stage. It was really cool to see all the cameras and stuff. On one side of the soundstage they roped it off and had about 20 guitars hang in the air. It looked like a cool piece of art! They did crowd shots for about 20 to 30 minutes, a comedian did a routine and then Nona Gaye did a song from the Marvin Gaye tribute album. Prince came out and did 'The Return of the Bump Squad', 'The Jam', 'The Ride' and 'Bambi'. End of show. It was scary the number of people I recognised. The comedian was Dave Chappelle, I think. Who knew? Certainly not me.

The *Gold* tour took place in Japan and ran from 8 to 20 January 1996.

On 14 February 1996 The Artist Formerly Known As Prince married Mayte Garcia in a Minneapolis church. He also composed a special song for his wife, 'Friend, Lover, Sister, Mother, Wife', which she heard for the first time when they had their first wedding dance. Garcia had appeared on the US television programme *That's Incredible!!* At the age of 8 as the world's youngest professional belly dancer. She came to the attention of

Prince in 1990 when her mother submitted a video cassette of Mayte performing. The couple split in 1998.

PAISLEY PARK

26 AUGUST 1996, CHANHASSEN, MINNESOTA

I WAS THERE: ADAM STANLEY

One of the great things about living about living in Minneapolis is that everyone has a Prince story. I was lucky enough to see him six times, either in a club or at Paisley Park, which is just as magical as people think. This show was Tha Bomm! We waited outside for about two hours before we got in. We got inside, went right up to the front of the stage and waited for three hours. Basically, we were on the left side, about five to ten feet away from his mic, and I was one foot away from his monitor. The stage was about two feet high so we were in a perfect place. Mr Hayes was about three feet away from me and Michael B was about 15 feet away, towards the back. Prince came out and played guitar from behind the screen that was still showing videos. It sounded like 'Sometimes It Snows In April' but he was just noodling around for a couple of minutes and then he played it. Sadly he played '7' and 'Dolphin'. He played 'Killer Peach' for a long, long time. He played all of 'Bambi' and did this amazing version of 'Race' where he and Tommy just jumped around playing their axes. Then he started play the keyboard riff from 'Girls and Boys', like he had at the Berlin show the previous November. He went up to the mic and sung a verse and chorus. It was the shit!

Then they just kept playing around. During the keyboard intro to '7', which was the fourth song of the set, 'Around The World In A Day was played. When he did 'Girls and Boys', I was starting to think that it was going to be a *Parade* tour-like show, with not too many complete songs. For the last 40 minutes he just jammed. He started to do 'I Hate U' and went right into '319' that broke down into 'Superhero'. He did most of 'Billy Jack Bitch'. There was no 'Pussy Control', but he did a cool version of 'Dark'. He played the small eye bass for 'Days of Wild' which ended the set, but even that broke down to a song that no one knew.

The *Love 4 One Another Charities* tour was a 21 date North American tour to promote Prince's charity of the same name and his album *Emancipation*.

BOUTWELL MEMORIAL AUDITORIUM

18 JANUARY 1997, BIRMINGHAM, ALABAMA

I WAS THERE: MICAH MANN

Growing up as a young gay boy in North Alabama was scary. I felt different from as far back as I can remember. I wanted to be me. I wanted to be expressive. I wanted to be free. Then I discovered Prince around 1985 and I wanted to be Prince! I learned every lyric from every new album within two or three days of its release. I hunted down the back catalogue of works I had missed prior to *Purple Rain*. I learned those also. I mastered his falsetto (I was a pre-teen so that part was easy). I managed to 'impersonate' his bass, his runs and his screeches, 'huhs' and his 'do me babies'.

In high school, I found a 'love symbol' necklace at a record store, bought it, and wore it proudly down the hall between classes. An androgynous necklace in a rebel flag sort of town wasn't common. Neither was my admiration for Prince's music. When I left for college, I worked for a time on campus in the student centre just one floor below the Ticketmaster office. I heard Prince was coming to a nearby town. The year was 1997 and the *Love 4 One Another* tour was popping up all over. I bought seven tickets for $30 a piece. On a college student budget mind you. I drove around and gave six of those tickets to friends that I had known for almost as long as I had known Prince. They knew I knew his music. They knew my passion. They knew this was going to be a moment to remember.

Eight rows back from the stage surrounded by friends that loved me, Prince broke into 'Purple Rain' and I broke into tears. He was newly released from his slave of a record contract and he showed it. I sang my heart out. Every lyric to every song. My cheeks hurt afterward from smiling so much. Prince on stage was magnificent. He was free. He was expressive. Up on that stage... Prince was me!

The *Jam of the Year* tour began on 1 July 1997 and concluded on 22 January 1998. Focused entirely on North America, it took in 65 shows.

MARINE MIDLAND ARENA

13 SEPTEMBER 1997, BUFFALO, NEW YORK

I WAS THERE: LINDA K SCHMIDT

We were in Minneapolis. My daughter Angela worked for the airline and we would fly out every once in a while to different concerts. We'd go and see Prince and then come back the next morning. This show was in Buffalo and we went out there. We were transferring in Detroit and my daughter said to me, 'Mom, we need to run to the next desk.' I said, 'Why?' and she said, 'Just come on - let's fly.' So we ran to the next desk and she said, 'Do you have any first class seats available?' The guy on the desk rang someone up and then said to us, 'I guess Prince bought out the rest of first class.' So we got to first class and we were on the left side on row five. And before you know it here comes Prince and his bodyguard and they sat on the other side on the first row. We didn't bother them. We didn't say anything.

At one point he got up to go to the men's room and I said, 'He's going to the bathroom' and she said, 'Yes, mother, he probably has to whizz.' He sat there the whole time of the flight with a yellow legal pad and he was writing. We landed in Buffalo and he and his bodyguard got off the plane and my daughter said to me, 'Mom, look under the seat.' And I looked under his seat and under his seat was his white fedora that he had been wearing. I went up and I grabbed it and I put it under my shirt.

Linda Schmidt models the fedora she and daughter Angela rescued for Prince

We got off the plane and I said, 'We're going to go to jail. There's going to be people everywhere looking for that hat.' So we go outside and there's all kinds of guys standing there talking up their sleeves and looking in taxis and looking everywhere and I said, 'I told you, they're looking for that hat.' So we get to the hotel room and we thought, 'What are we going to do with this hat?'

So we took pictures of us wearing the hat, and pictures of the hat, and my daughter went and got some posterboard and we made signs that said 'you forgot something' and 'we came from Minneapolis' and then we thought, 'We can't do that.' We decided that we couldn't keep it because it wasn't ours. 'We've gotta give it back.'

So we took a laundry bag from the hotel, wrapped the hat up in a pillowcase so nobody could see it and put it in the laundry bag. We got into the venue and we were in the fourth row watching the concert. We were trying to get it to him.

There was venue security there but we finally found a guy from Minneapolis who was one of his guys. And my daughter went up to him and opened the bag and showed him the hat, and he said, 'Where did you get that hat?' and she said, 'He left it on the plane.' He took it from her and he took it out of the bag and he handed it up to Prince on the stage. Prince put it on his head and he finished the show.

After the show, the Prince security guy who was from Minneapolis comes up to us afterwards, taps us on the shoulder, hands us a VIP pass and says, 'There's going to be a little after party and he would like you ladies to go there.' So we took our VIP passes and we went there and there's a line of about 600 people long trying to get in. But there was only one line. We thought, 'There's got to be a VIP line.' So we walked around everybody and up to the front, showed them our passes and said, 'Is there a VIP line?' And the guy on the door said, 'Oh, you're here. Wait a minute, wait a minute.' And he got on his headset and he called somebody and this huge guy comes out and he says, 'Ladies, he's been waiting for you. Follow me.' And he parted the crowd inside like the Red Sea and we went into an area that was cordoned off and you had to go up three steps where there were purple tablecloths and purple candles and the whole works and he says, 'Here they are', and they take the rope down and they start to go up the steps and he said, 'I don't know what you two did but you must've done something.' And he looked at me and he said, 'Are you his momma?'

Then he said, 'You're supposed to sit anywhere you like.' So we pick a table and we sit down. After about three or four minutes my daughter says to me, 'Mother, do not turn around but a door is opening behind you and Prince and his bodyguard are coming out here and they're headed right towards us.' I said, 'You are kidding me. I'm about to wet my pants!'

Prince walked right up to me, took off his sunglasses and grabbed my hand and said, 'I cannot thank you enough for returning my hat. It's of great sentimental value to me.' And I said, 'You're more than welcome. I was afraid somebody was going to steal it.' He went to my daughter and he kept looking at her and looking at her and he said, 'Thank you so very much.' She said, 'It's nice to finally meet you.' She had worked at Glam Slam in Minneapolis in security, and when he had the NPG store in Mall of America, and I think he recognised her but didn't know from where.

So he ended up sitting down with his bodyguard and the bodyguard calls over the server and he says, 'He would like to buy these ladies a drink.' I ordered a bottle of water. My daughter ordered a diet Coke. The bodyguard ordered a 7 Up or a Sprite for him and Prince and we chatted a little bit for a couple of minutes and then I thought, 'What do we do now? He doesn't

Jam of the year pass

want to be sat with us. The classy thing to do would be to say, 'Well, we must get going now' and leave.'

So we said, 'We have to get going' and when we stood up he stood up, and he said, 'Thank you so much again. Thank you, thank you.' And we said, 'You're more than welcome.' They opened up the ropes and we went down through the crowd. People were saying, 'What were they doing up there?' They were playing videos at the after party and I said, 'What are we going to do? Stand here and watch videos? We're out of here.'

A couple of days after that he was on the *Today* programme and he was wearing the white fedora.

After that we got to any after parties we wanted to and we could park right next to the front door. In Las Vegas we got VIP passes and I was elbow to elbow with Jack Nicholson. We're in the video for 'Rock and Roll is Alive! (And it Lives in Minneapolis)'. Prince asked us to stay for the video. And every time we saw him after that he'd either point or smile and he'd wave.

CORONADO THEATER

18 OCTOBER 1997, ROCKFORD, ILLINOIS

I WAS THERE: BENJAMIN RIECK

I was attending the second and final date of the NPG Ballet's performance in Rockford, Illinois. The opening night was the evening prior in Detroit, Michigan, after which Prince and his entourage dined with Stevie Wonder. I believe that I was attending the last day of the tour due to poor performance of ticket sales. I still have my ticket stub and a beret as merchandise. We found our seats and, seeing as we were early to the performance, I sought out the restroom. The restroom was located pretty far back in the theatre. As I exited the restroom, there was a commotion at the front of the theatre. There was cheering and fanfare to welcome Prince into the building. He would walk through the theatre to the staircase, where he would ascend to take his place in the front row to take in the show. As the reality of the situation caught up with me, I realised that I was about to have a once-in-a-lifetime opportunity to view my musical hero, up close and personal. As he made his way up the stairs I yelled to him the only thing that crossed my mind: 'Vegetarians rule!' He turned around and smiled and continued up the stairs. It wasn't 15 minutes of fame, but it was a memory of a moment that will live forever.

THOMPSON-BOLING ARENA

6 NOVEMBER 1997, KNOXVILLE, TENNESSEE

I WAS THERE: DEBORAH SLUSS

I saw him in Knoxville, Tennessee. It was him and a piano and that was all. He performed great though. In hindsight, I believe it was around the time his baby died. I think that's why it was just him and the piano. He had a load of guitars he played too.

He sang religious types of songs along with his hits. He sang, 'What if God was one of us?' ('One of Us'). I absolutely loved him.

PAISLEY PARK

1998, CHANHASSEN, MINNESOTA

I WAS THERE: BEN UMBREIT

I was in Minneapolis for a wedding around 1998. We had an afternoon off and I convinced a friend to drive out with me to Prince's recording studio so that I could see it in person and take some pictures. I knew about Prince's tight security measures and I was all ready to just stand on the sidewalk outside of the compound's fence to take my photos. My friend, however, wasn't as scared as me about the security and said we should just walk up to the studio and see if anyone was home. I reluctantly agreed and walked nervously beside him to the front door. The front was made of glass and there was a little entryway before a second set of glass doors led into the main part of the building. Inside on the wall was a telephone.

Ben Umbreit saw Prince play at Paisley Park

My friend then had the crazy idea of entering through the first set of doors and picking up the phone and dialling the front desk. The phone ended up ringing somewhere within the studio and I just stood there frozen, wondering if Prince was simply going to materialise in front of us. Instead a woman came to the door and asked if she could help us. I suddenly remembered that they used to do tours so I asked her if that was still the case. She politely said no, but that he was probably going to be jamming that night and that we would probably be able to watch. She said to come back around 11 that night!

My friend and I were absolutely overjoyed for the remainder of the evening, knowing that we might actually be able to witness one of Prince's legendary late night jam sessions at Paisley Park. I called another good friend and had him meet us at our hotel before driving out to the studio. When we got there, there was already a small line of people waiting. I remember a security guard coming out to give some instructions and these women in front tried to hand him a big bag of candy for Prince. The man's response was, 'Prince doesn't eat candy anymore, but I'll give it to his bandmates.'

After a while we were let into the complex. The main soundstage was in use by another act so we all gathered in the small loading zone next to it. There was a small, one-foot-tall stage to the side of the room with some drums and a microphone set up. We immediately stood next to the microphone, which was literally three feet from me and at chin level (I'm 6'4"). I saw another guy stand next to me and I asked him if Prince was going to be literally right there in front of us singing. He nodded in the affirmative. The room then filled up and the wait was on. Of course several hours passed, tiredness set in and you began to wonder if this would be one of Prince's infamous 'no shows'. I remember looking around the room, observing the people, and then turning back to the stage and suddenly seeing Prince literally a few feet from my face. His eyes were closed and he gave a quick count off to the drummer (Kirk Johnson) who had taken his seat at the drums, before launching into a two-hour jam session. He hardly sang and pretty much tore into the guitar the entire show. I remember one of my friends saying, 'I had no idea he was this good.'

At one point Prince put down the guitar and stood behind some bongo drums. He told the crowd that he had heard that people were saying he was out of touch. Then, while quietly playing the bongos, he said, 'I think I AM the touch.' He then had us chant to him that he was the touch. It was a magical experience and by far the best musical moment of my life.

ARAGON BALLROOM

24 APRIL 1998, CHICAGO, ILLINOIS

I WAS THERE: TAMARA BROWN

I was introduced at 8, fell in love at 13 and I saw him too many times in concert to name. He was back in Chicago at the United Center and I did not have tickets. And that day we heard he was doing an after show at the Excalibur Theatre for $19.99. We lucked up and we got tickets. I couldn't believe it was a whole 'nother concert for $19.99. It was awesome.

Another time I saw him after he and Mayte got married. They came here to Chicago to see Lenny Kravitz at the Aragon Ballroom. Me and my girlfriend were all dressed up, all garbed up, and we were at the front. I'm five three, at the time I might have been 100 pounds, and so it's always easy to slither directly in front of the stage.

And so we got to the front of the stage for when the concert started, and we were all sexy and funky in our little outfits, and a security guard came and he said, 'get your shit and come with me'. And we looked at him and said, 'we ain't going nowhere. We are absolutely dead centre on the stage for Lenny Kravitz.' We weren't going anywhere. But he said, 'Get your shit and go upstairs right now. Prince is upstairs.'

So I don't know if Prince told him to go downstairs to get us or what, but we went upstairs. And as soon as we hit the top step, Prince was not five feet away, all giggly huggy lovey with Mayte. And I started acting like a fan, going, 'Oh my god, oh my god.' My friend was like, 'Calm down before we get kicked out of here.' And I instantly got my shit together. And as soon as I did, Prince looked over and he waved at us. That was the fucking bomb! They didn't call anybody over but us to come up there.

I have the guitar pick from when Prince called me onstage, because when we were leaving and the security guards finally told us to leave, I looked down on the floor and there were all these guitar picks. I wrote the date on the pick.

At a Prince concert, he would look down and say, 'Who wants to come up here with me?' We were not directly at the stage. We were maybe second or third row. Prince was asking, 'Who wants to come up here?' and my eyes were buggng out of my head. I was trying to wave and flail my arm as high as I could, and Prince scanned our area. The feeling of having him look in your eye and point you out? I don't remember anything! I just remember being lifted out of the crowd! As soon as they set me down I was barefoot. I don't know where my shoes were. And I just had on some jeans and this sheer see-through top. I did not wear a bra with it. It was real cute. And I got on that stage and I danced like it was my job. And as soon as I started dancing I could hear the crowd. They felt my energy. We were up there dancing and dancing. This security guard came to get us and Prince said, 'leave them alone'. It seemed like we were up there forever. When we first got there we had to edge our way to the stage and people had attitude. When Prince finally let us go, the crowd parted like the Red Sea. People thought I was part of the show. I said, 'No, I'm a fan just like you.'

He called me on stage a second time at the Rosemont. This was the year that his drummer's child died and they had had to reschedule the show. I went to that show with another girlfriend and I dressed really, really sexy. This was after Prince said he was a Jehovah's Witness and he wouldn't be performing a lot of the songs any more. Again, we were in the front row. This time we were seated. He said, 'I'm looking for people. Who wants to come up here?' and he looked at me. He walked up and down the stage and he looked me dead in my eyes three times and I think he would have chosen me. But I had on this really short dress and I figured this would have been my ass out had he pulled me up there. Had I been more demurely dressed he would definitely have chosen me.

Another time I saw him at the United Center two nights in a row, maybe four years before he died. I still haven't been to Paisley Park yet. It's still hard to read any of the literature, like the fan magazines and stuff. I've been given books and stuff as Christmas gifts. I can just now in the last couple of years really listen to the music. But he impacted my life greatly and my son, who just turned 26, is a lover of Prince's music and I'm glad that I was able to pass on the music. I am just sad that I was not able to go to a concert with my son. That would have been even more of a bonding experience.

WEMBLEY ARENA

26 AUGUST 1998, LONDON, UK

I WAS THERE: DANIEL PAYNE

This was the *Newpower Soul* tour. It was also the 35th and last time Prince played Wembley Arena and it was a 12,000 capacity sell out. Chaka Khan and Larry Graham and NPGCS were the support act. Prince ran on stage during Chaka's performance of

'I Feel For You' to sing one verse and then also joined Larry Graham on 'Free'. During Larry's show, Larry walked among the audience while he slapped the bass!

HIPPODROME CASINO

27 AUGUST 1998, LONDON, UK

I WAS THERE: SAM BLEAZARD

As the Nineties wore on Prince seemed to get more and more disaffected. He wasn't happy with the way his releases were being promoted. Maybe he felt Warner Brothers weren't pushing his material enough. He also started being a bit more self indulgent. And then the whole 'Slave' thing distracted everyone from his music. I saw a couple of really interesting after shows at that time though. One was a really late night show at the old Hippodrome in London's Leicester Square, which was – at the time - a pretty run of the mill disco. Very few people were at the show and it was very unusual for a whole number of reasons. That's one that really sticks in my mind.

I got a tip off that Prince was going to do an after show in London after his main show at Wembley Arena and during that show, or just before the end, they had the habit of announcing something over the PA, 'Prince will be playing in London later tonight', or they'd sometimes leave flyers on the first few rows to spread it by word of mouth. It wasn't a particularly warm lead or a strong rumour – we followed the instruction on a whim – but the other Prince fans I was with were convinced. They'd heard that he was going to play at the Hippodrome, which I thought was unusual anyway. At the time it was a cheesy, drinks promo kind of place, a really mainstream club right in the centre of London and about as far away from the height of cool as you could get.

Four or five of us crushed into this guy's Mini and we sped across London, thinking there'd be tons of people trying to get in to this after show. When we eventually got parked, we went up to the front door and there was nothing at all to suggest that Prince was playing. We wandered into the foyer where there was a badly photocopied A4 piece of paper with his love symbol motif on it, which said, 'Prince, Hippodrome, playing here tonight'. There was one woman sat at a desk. We said to her, 'Is Prince playing here tonight?' She said, 'Yeah, yeah, Prince is playing here tonight. Look at the sign on the wall.' To which I thought, yeah but it's just a piece of A4, really badly photocopied. It doesn't look like Prince's kind of promotional material. We said, 'How much is it?' and she said, 'it's £25 to get in', so we went inside. It was about 11.30pm at this point. The Hippodrome then was a typical central London nightclub of the time with lots of neon lights, different levels, staircases and floors. And the place was completely empty so I was immediately sceptical that Prince was actually going to turn up there. It certainly didn't look promising.

We'd been there for an hour or two and the deejay was playing lots of Prince songs - things like 'Kiss' and 'Gett Off' – and he kept saying, 'Is everybody looking forward to Prince?' It just seemed like a really bad joke. It didn't seem plausible at all. It got to about 1.30am, quarter to two, and I can remember saying to people who were there,

'I'm going to head off. This looks ridiculous. We're being had here.' There can't have been more than 100 to 150 people there and it was already seriously thinning out.

But at some point after two in the morning we were still there. We were standing in front of this little raised step – you couldn't even call it a stage. Someone then came out of a door at the back of the room with a little snare drum in hand and plonked it down on the stage. Over the next few minutes this fairly rudimentary kit started coming out of the woodwork - keyboard, keyboard stand, rest of the drum kit, one or two instruments - and we started getting excited. People started clustering near the area.

And then at about 2.45 in the morning, Prince appeared with his band and a few other musical guests. He was wearing massive mirror shades like Bono used to wear, the bug-eyed sort that made you look like an insect, and he had this really strange hair style and a fur coat on.

Larry Graham was there, along with some of the founding members of Sly and the Family Stone. There was no ceremony about it. Prince just wandered on almost as if it was a practice or a rehearsal room he used, and they started playing a jazz funk instrumental thing. They got straight into it and just started jamming. He didn't talk to the crowd too much but he was talking to the sound man. I would say he was not in the best of moods and was quite grumpy about the sound. He kept saying, 'interesting sound man we've got this evening' and this became a theme for the first 20 minutes, testing the sound just through jamming. And they did that until they were happy with it. He then went on to play an amazing show that last until almost five in the morning. Prince and his band played lots of unusual things. There's a really odd track called 'The War' which is almost like a Gil Scott Heron thing, quite heavy and full of Prince's concerns for the world – war and drugs etc. It's almost like 'Sign o' the Times' if he'd stretched that out to a 20 or 25 minute spoken word thing, quite murky. He was talking to the crowd about what they felt the UK was like, had it contributed to major wars? It was quite a strange thing to play, quite a cult thing amongst fans. So that in itself was unusual. He also played some Sly and the Family Stone stuff, such as 'Thank You For Talkin' To Me Africa'.

It was one of the first times I'd been up quite close to Prince. He had plasters on his fingers and he made a joke with the crowd at one point, saying he'd been playing his guitar so much that his fingers were cracking. It was so surreal, because it was so late at night and the venue was so odd.

At the end of the concert, there was a set of stairs up to a room in the back of the club. When the concert stopped, everybody was really tired anyway because we'd stayed up all through the night. I can remember he stood at the top of those stairs for a while as people were chatting and the lights came up. He turned around and stared at the crowd for two or three minutes in complete silence. It was the strangest thing. Eventually, he just turned and walked out the door.

We filed out into the morning – I actually got the first tube train home that day – but it was still dark when we filed out onto the cobbled street round the back of the club. There was a limousine or some sort of expensive car with tinted windows parked there. Four or five of us were wandering away and the window of the car went down and a little leather glove with a cane waved out the window. It was the final surreal moment of that night, just before the sun came up.

I WAS THERE: OWEN HOWE

I thought Mayte stage dived onto my head at the Hippodrome after show in London in August 1998. The following night, Prince did the same at the Café de Paris gig. Three times in a row. But when I checked with a friend who was also at the after show it turns out Mayte did not jump on our heads that night – it was actually Prince! It happened three minutes and 50 seconds into 'Days of Wild'. Mayte wasn't even there as far as my friend can recall. She was at the Brixton gig two days later though as my friend briefly met her after he was pulled up to dance on stage at the close of the concert.

WEMBLEY ARENA

28 AUGUST 1998, LONDON, UK

I WAS THERE: NADEEM MASOOD

On 28 August 1998 my brother and I attended Prince's *Jam of the Year* show at Wembley Arena, London. He hadn't graced our shores for well over three years - a very long absence at that time - so we were naturally excited to be seeing him again. Before the show we were chatting about what we may see that night in terms of set list. We each chose one song we would love to see him perform. My brother wanted 'I Could Never Take the Place of Your Man', which he had never before performed in the UK, and I really wanted to see 'The Ride', a song which I believe he debuted live at an after show in London in 1993.

The show began and we were having a great time. It was in full flow when he went into my brother's choice, which we of course appreciated. As he broke it down at the end we heard the opening guitar licks of 'The Ride'. Just imagine my shock at this coincidence, almost as if he had heard us talking about it. He'd been performing 'I Could Never Take the Place of Your Man' quite regularly over the previous year or so, so there was a good chance he would do so that night too, but 'The Ride' had never been a regular feature in his sets. To hear them back-to-back after we chose them both was really very special and something I will never forget.

I WAS THERE: GREGG WHITE, AGE 16

My first ever Prince gig, back in 1998, was the *Jam Of The Year* world tour at Wembley Arena. I was 16 and Prince had already become a major constant in my life. I begged my Dad to continuously try for tickets while I was busy at school and his persistence paid off! I remember the first moment Prince walked onto stage after Larry Graham's support, wearing his purple cashmere jacket with huge white fluffy sleeves as he strutted across the stage. 'That's not really him', I said loudly into my father's ear. 'That's some sort impersonator.' I think my adolescent brain had decided that Prince was not actually a real person but some sort of hyper-being from another realm that was real in image and voice but not in actual human matter. And then, 'This is the joint I've been waiting for all night…'

My mouth dropped open in conjunction with hysterical screams from the crowd. My father then asked, 'Still think it isn't him?'

CAFÉ DE PARIS

28 AUGUST 1998, LONDON, UK

I WAS THERE: MATT OSGOOD

I was there, both times the Greatest of all Time decided to grace London's Café de Paris in 1998 and in 2014.

28th August 1998 was a gloriously warm summer's night in London UK and a gig that was an invitation-only performance taped for a TV special on Channel 4. Access was through an old database from the previously officially endorsed Prince fanzine, *Controversy*. I phoned from a landline and paid via credit card for a pair of tickets. In full 'SLAVE' on the cheek mode and riling against the music industry and Warner Bros contract, this gig was from an era when his antics were seen as tiresome and the music press had long since moved on to grunge and BritPop, etc.

Their loss, as whatever people think about his records at this time, not once did he stop being an A+ live artist and playing blues tracks like 'The Ride' or angry tracks like 'Days of Wild' and 'Mad', or tracks he'd grown up loving, now alongside his heroes such as 'Sweet Thing' with Chaka Khan and 'Thank You (Falettinme Be Mice Elf Agin)' and 'Everyday People' with Larry Graham - a real treat to behold.

I attended with my sister-in-law and her ex, but not my best mate who really I should have attended with and for which I still take a lot of stick but that's another story... As ever with Prince, there was a lot of waiting around and we got a small booth and, as students just venturing out into the world of work, we found out just how expensive prices in London were for drinks, so we sipped slowly!

The show was promoting the last NPG album, *New Power Soul*, which was really more of a Prince LP than anything else, and mostly over looked at the time but it has class tracks such as 'The One', 'Come On' and hidden track 'Wasted Kisses'. Only 'Come On' was played that night. Needless to say, the pinch of the cost of drinks was soon forgotten and the place was jumping when Prince and the band finally came on stage. The special guests of note were Chaka Khan, Larry Graham and band, Doug E Fresh.

The night ended late and with us missing our last train home to St Albans and thus sleeping outside of the old front, covered area on Kings Cross, with one very happy mega Prince fan and one more casual Prince fan getting increasingly unsettled by the more transient population around Kings Cross at the time until we got a circa 5am train home!

I WAS THERE: PAUL F KENNY

I'm from Edinburgh and back in 1998 I was lucky enough to get a ticket for the secret gig (it wasn't announced until about 12 noon on the day and a radio station leaked it). We arrived at the Café de Paris at about 12 noon, were first in line and I was first in when the doors opened so I managed to run and grab my spot right at the front in the middle. It was an amazing show and during 'Mad' Prince asked, 'Are you going to catch me?' I have watch thousands of hours of Prince live and seen him live 10 times, and not once have I seen him stage dive - but he did! It was an amazing night, one that I will never forget. That week I was also at Wembley, the after show at the Hippodrome and at Brixton. It was a totally amazing week.

Newpower Soul Tour

BRIXTON ACADEMY

28 AUGUST 1998, LONDON, UK

I WAS THERE: HASSAN RAZZAQ

I went to the *Newpower Soul* tour. He did a show at Wembley Arena but I went to the Brixton gig the day after. He had his hair in that little ponytail and that was such a good gig. There were two or three thousand people in there. He was just so energetic, the amount of times he was jumping off the piano, sliding across the floor, doing splits every 10 seconds.

REGENTS PARK

29 AUGUST 1998, LONDON, UK

I WAS THERE: LOUISE KING

Prince was in London, dressed as an old man. He was in one of the London parks and I walked behind him. I didn't realise who it was. I was talking to some girls at the time, one of them being Manuela and a friend. It wasn't until later on that I found out that it was him. I was gutted!

STUDIO 54, MGM GRAND

1 & 2 JANUARY 1999, LAS VEGAS, NEVADA

I WAS THERE: BENJAMIN RIECK

One of many purple experiences over the years was a trip to Las Vegas for what Prince called *1999: The New Masters*. He would be having a party at the Club 54 at the MGM Grand in Las Vegas. I was living in my hometown of Chicago at the time. I made arrangements to travel to Las Vegas with my girlfriend at the time. The timing of the show was just after the New Year had come, and in Chicago that can mean bitter cold and/or snow. We first secured tickets to the show and then travel/lodging. Prince added a second show for a consecutive night to presumably extend the party. We wavered on whether to secure the extra expense of another set of tickets for Club 54. We decided that it would be worth it and this paid dividends, as The Time performed the first night, and Prince would end up performing for the next night, the one for which we were not sure about buying tickets. As the time to travel arrived we boarded our flight out of Chicago O'Hare. We didn't pay any attention as the travel was originally booked, but we had a layover in Minneapolis before we made our way to Las Vegas. When we touched down in Minneapolis, I chose to stretch my legs and visit some of the shops in the terminal. After walking around a bit, I made my way back to the plane. One of the people-moving carts passed by me, going in the same direction that I was going, and I did a double take as I watched it go by. Members of the New Power Generation were headed toward my gate, to get on the same plane I was on to go to Las Vegas! I found my seat where my girlfriend was waiting to find out we were sitting behind Mr Hayes! I couldn't believe our fortune as we watched him sit between strangers and offer to let them watch the movie he was viewing on his laptop, offering them headphones to plug in to his experience. My mind was on fire trying to soak up the experience of what I was being exposed to. I wanted to find the nerve to ask for an autograph, as this experience would surely never come again. As the flight continued, we learned that Prince was aboard and possibly one of the last people to get on the plane. Also, members of the New Power Generation would walk through or stop by to speak with Mr Hayes.

At some point, I got out my camcorder to record what I could of the experience. Finally finding my nerve, I asked Morris for an autograph. I handed him a Prince fanzine called *Uptown* to capture his signature. These periodicals were considered to be bootleg and not official, so we had to hide them away. Mr Hayes said that he hadn't seen this one yet, so he wanted to look through it before providing his autograph. I filmed him paging through the magazine and then he autographed the cover for me. As the flight came to an end and we were filing off the plane, I was trying to capture what I could in the form of recording the band's walk from the plane. Among the images was Rhonda Smith stopping along the way at a candy store, filling a bag with loose candy and pouring the bag's contents into her mouth. We never saw the Purple One on the flight – he was the last to enter and the first to exit.

Prior to attending either of the night's events, we found Prince merchandise in the gift shop, with the logo for the *1999 New Master* embroidered on them. As we prepared for the actual event, the attendees were packed into the venue. It was general admission and standing only and we took our position close to the stage. The temperature was so hot from the bodies packed together that people were having trouble breathing and cold bottles of water were being purchased and passed to the concertgoers. This particular line up of the band included Larry Graham on bass, who actually left the stage and performed in and amongst the crowd. As he thumbed his bass, we all gathered around to encourage his furious playing. As his guitar pick slipped from his hand, a melee ensued and I emerged from the scramble with this prized memento. Months later I took the autograph and guitar pick and fashioned them into a remembrance of the event that I gave to my girlfriend, even though we were no longer together. Our love for Prince's vision and music binds us still.

MILL CITY MUSIC FESTIVAL

6 SEPTEMBER 1999, MINNEAPOLIS, MINNESOTA

I WAS THERE: KELLIE FOURNIER

I saw Prince at the Mill City Music Festival in Minneapolis in September

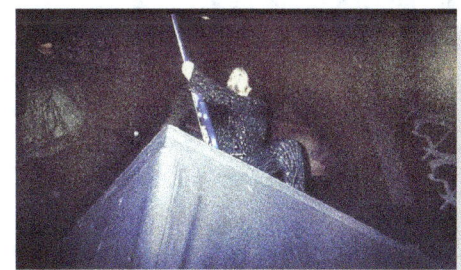

Prince at the Mill City Music Festival

1999! My date and I got to the show early and managed to get right up front next to the stage. I had snuck in a disposable camera (no photos allowed) and got one picture of Prince. It's not the best quality photo but I cherish the memory of the day and his sparkly outfit.

MERMAID THEATRE

15 NOVEMBER 1999, LONDON, UK

I WAS THERE: DIANE ELIZABETH RHULE

The Mermaid Theatre was great because it was a showcase for the *Rave Unto the Joy Fantastic* album. He was in a great mood. There were lots of celebrities in amongst a very small crowd. He called me and Beck up on stage to sing 'Kiss' with him.

PAISLEY PARK

18 DECEMBER 1999 (AIRED 31 DECEMBER 1999), CHANHASSEN, MINNESOTA

I WAS WATCHING: JANICE DORIGHT

This was a pay per view concert. It was remarkable. I totally remember going through all kinds of changes trying to find someone with cable while visiting with family in North Carolina. I managed to get the show paid for so I could see it. I was the only one there that had any love for Prince. If they only knew the phenomenal talent that would totally emerge from this guy. I'll bet they were so glad after having to watch that show. I made everybody in the house watch it!

CELEBRATION #1
PAISLEY PARK STUDIOS

7 JUNE 2000, MINNEAPOLIS, MINNESOTA

I WAS THERE: DANIEL PAYNE

I was lucky enough to get VIP tickets for the week of the first ever celebration. This included a VIP tour of Paisley Park studios, where we were shown around the complex, including the underground car park where they filmed the 'Sexy MF' video, and we had VIP early access every day to Paisley Park. We landed in Minneapolis on June 7th and we drove straight to Paisley Park. We were allowed to park in the main car park directly outside.

We went in and it is true what they say – there was just an amazing aura and atmosphere about the place. I remember standing in the lobby talking to one of my friends – and then all of a sudden the atmosphere in the room just changed. I turned around and there he was, only metres away from me and drinking a milkshake, looking 100% as Prince! We were then in the main concert room and I could see a very tall lady walking about and lots of people were going up to her. It turned out to be Macy Gray. Then after about an hour Macy performed a full show for about 40-50 of us on the sound stage.

While watching her I looked to the left of the stage and on a high riser I could see a large sofa and there he was again, watching the whole show. Half way through he jumped down and started to play the keyboards. As the week progressed more people arrived from around the world.

One night as Prince ran through the audience I managed to touch his arm and got severely told off by the security guard! But I touched him. I don't think I have washed it since! I also got to meet Dr Fink and Bobby Z who were inside the complex.

I WAS THERE: SAM BLEAZARD

I went to Paisley Park twice. The first time it took place there were six consecutive nightly parties at Paisley Park, plus a closing jam at Northrop Auditorium by Prince and special guests on June 13. By this time, Prince was starting to rebuild his image and his reputation. He was releasing albums that were better thought of. He had dusted himself down, and was talking about abandoning the whole symbol thing and calling himself Prince again. '1999' had been a big anthem for the millennium anyway, and there was an upsurge in interest.

At the height of my being a Prince fan there was a network of people who kept in contact pre-dating the explosion of the Internet. Round about 2000, this underground network of Prince fans (I heard about it through a guy I knew at the time) said Prince was thinking of letting a certain number of his fans from all over the world into Paisley Park for a week-long musical celebration. The idea of that sounded so incredible anyway that it was a bit of a Willy Wonka thing: the gates of a fabled place were going to open.

It was $250 to go, which essentially gave you access to Prince's recording complex for a week. People at the time were asking, 'Is that good value? Is it worth going?' If you average that out it was roughly £30 a night to have full access to a Prince-hosted music festival, on his sound stage. It sounds bizarre now, and it was one of those things that didn't make it to the mainstream media.

The first year we went was an amazing experience, but although Prince must have liked the idea of having his fans around, he couldn't quite figure out how to make it work. So although we got access to Paisley Park every night, and it was fascinating, Prince didn't play live. He had his motorbike from *Purple Rain* on display, his guitars laid out on stands, he had his Linn drum machine from *1999* just set up, which you could play on. He had Apple Macs set up with lots of tracks on that no one had ever heard, old tracks from his studio recordings. His staff were around and inviting us to, 'Click and vote on tracks that you want to hear and Prince will compile them into an album for you.' That became *Crystal Ball II*.

On reflection, although that was incredible in itself, it was a bit of a disappointment because every night we wanted to hear Prince play. And in his studio complex there was a massive soundstage area which was pretty blank apart from all these props, costumes and instruments from his career. But then he had a smaller performance space. It was classic rock star stuff. He had these massive doors that must have been about 20 or 30 feet high with the symbol on but when these doors opened it was like he had his own little night club with a tiny little stage, stairs up to a DJ booth and a little stepped area in the middle of the room with sofas on it - very Prince! The first year we went, we went into that room every night and it was really packed out, really crammed.

There were DJ sets and Prince would often be there playing videos of his live performances, or hanging out. He wouldn't really talk to people but he would be in and out or milling around, he seemed pretty relaxed. People like Macy Gray played, and other artists from Minneapolis, like Mint Condition. On the seventh night he played at the University of Minnesota. It was a great show. He had Q-Tip from A Tribe Called Quest, soul singer Angie Stone and various musical guests, which included two or three members of The Revolution joining the show to jam.

NORTHROP AUDITORIUM

13 JUNE 2000, MINNEAPOLIS, MINNESOTA

I WAS THERE: DANIEL PAYNE

This was an amazing one off show that started with 'Anna Stesia'. Bobby Z, Marc Brown and Dr Fink were in attendance. They all got up to perform with him on the track 'America' and while they walked towards their stage Prince looked (in a nice way) at Dr Fink as he was dressed in his Dr's gear and he commented that they all looked 'shapely' and resembled the look of the *Around The World In A Day* era. Q-Tip, Doug E Fresh, Angie Stone and Maceo Parker and Larry Graham all guested with Prince during the show.

The *Hit 'n' Run* tour ran from 7 November 2000 to 6 May 2001 and comprised 33 shows across the United States played over two legs. It was Prince's first tour after abandoning the Symbol name. This was followed by *Prince: A Celebration* which was a six-show tour that took in five cities.

One Nite Alone was released on 14 May 2002. Prince's 25th studio album. It included a cover of Joni Mitchell's 'A Case of You', retitled 'A Case of U'.

In 2002, the second *Celebration* event to be staged at Paisley Park was held.

XENOPHOBIA: 7 NIGHTS ALONE WITH PRINCE

21 – 27 JUNE 2002, MINNEAPOLIS, MINNESOTA

I WAS THERE: TRENTON LUNDY

I arrived and saw my friend Sky was DJing on the outside stage. I went up and hung out with him and some friends of mine from London saw me and took me to the front of the house. There was a news station there asking people what they expected from Prince for that seven day celebration. She asked me and I said, 'I want the funk, the whole funk, and nothing but the funk.' I was very happy because people started clapping for me! Every night he gave a concert, each night was a different style of music. As the show began, they would show clips of people answering the question about what they expected. Every night I was excited because I just knew that they would play mine since people clapped for me. By the fifth night, they hadn't shown my clip and I was a little offended. I was so mad I didn't even want to stay and see the show. As I was pouting and walking towards the door to leave, Prince comes on stage and says, 'So you want the funk, the whole funk and nothing but the funk? Well, here it is!' That whole night they played funk and I was truly amazed that he didn't play my clip but answered me directly. Then, at the last song, Prince and the band didn't exit the back of the stage like normal but walked through the crowd, singing and shaking tambourines. He walked right up to me, bumped into me and smiled. I will never forget that night!

I WAS THERE: SAM BLEAZARD

We went back to Paisley Park two years later and it was much better organised. I saw him play for seven nights straight. Prince had set up his massive soundstage in the rehearsal area, which was a big open square space and it worked a lot better. It was really superb. You had seven shows from Prince and every night there was a really great support act. Nora Jones was starting to break through and she played a really lovely piano set. That was the night Prince came out and just played acoustic guitar for an hour. I think I heard some fans squealing with delight when they saw that. The feeling was '…are we actually going to hear Prince just sitting there on his own with an acoustic guitar?' That was one of the best shows I ever saw. It was unbelievably good, and although there are one or two clips of him playing acoustic guitar online, they don't compare to what I saw that night.

He played a different style of music every night at the 2002 *Celebration*. He wasn't showing off. He was scratching an itch. He had played an hour's worth of acoustic guitar, and then he came back out for a second half to do effectively a Ray Charles thing steeped in R&B, a big band show with horns. Another night it was pure Led Zeppelin and Jimi Hendrix, really hard rock, where he turned the Marshalls up to 12! Then another night he would play hits, or build a piano show with flutes and other instruments. They were quite unique things. He was so good and he played so many styles of music that it was difficult to process at times, even if you were really into it, because it was hard to fathom that one person could do all that. He could sound like Ray Charles one minute and then he could sound like a U2 or REM and then he could sound like Hendrix and then he could sound like James Brown. He really was that good, when he was stretching out behind closed doors.

There were a lot of Americans in the crowd who had taken road trips to get there. So you got people from different states that couldn't come for the whole thing but were driving in for two days or taking long flights to get there. The audience was 250 to 300 people so it wasn't massive. It was very relaxed and you could wander around. It wasn't a big crush or anything, because he'd limited the numbers. From that point of view it was an amazing experience.

He had an American guy called Bernard Allison open for him, who played a really good set. That night was quite unusual because Prince was there with his girlfriend at the time, and sat in the back corner of the room where they'd set up a little elevated area. There was an older couple with them as well. Prince had his shades on, was holding his cane and seemed happy to be low-key at the back of the room. Bernard got a bit mischievous though, and at one point thought, 'Oh Prince is in the room. This is great' and he started wandering through the crowd with his wireless guitar. I turned around to see Prince and the people he was sitting with and I thought, 'This is going to make him feel uncomfortable!' So the guy wandered up to him – 'I'm going to play a brilliant solo right in front of one of my heroes' – and Prince picked up a bottle of water and just started squirting the guy with it. The message seemed to be, 'Don't come any closer. This is my private space. Get back on stage. I'm with my date!'

One night the band did an amazing funk set. The support that night was Victor Wooten, who has got to be one of the best bass players in the world. He was playing with his brother, but also played in a band called Bela Fleck and the Flecktones at the time. It was clear that Victor had raised the performance bar a bit and the impression I got was that Prince then felt he had to come out and up his game a little bit.

On other nights the drummer and singer Sheila E would be there, and some of his former band members. They filmed little bits of it, and I got the feeling he was using us as a test group, testing material on us for his next world tour.

If there was a negative to all of this, it was that by the end of that week it was becoming a bit like the church of Prince. On the seventh night, you could already sense the opening of his show had religious undertones to it. Prince was very keen to leave some sort of spiritual message with his biggest fans. People had come from all over the world to hear his sermon, people who had stuck with him through thick and thin, and kept listening when his popularity had dipped. I remember he played a version of 'Purple Rain' that was almost like being in church. There was quite a difference in how the Americans and the Europeans in the audience saw that. The Europeans I spoke to tended to be more cynical about such things. The Americans were a bit more evangelical. At one point, people were closing their eyes and getting into the spirit and Prince was talking about God. I stepped out at that point as I was never really into the cult of Prince. It didn't often feel very cultish, but on that one occasion – for me - it did feel like it was a bit too much. Had we heard too much in that one dose? It was an amazing experience nonetheless.

What was really interesting was that it was one of the few times you saw Prince at his most relaxed. Over the seven days you would see him bob in and out, wandering through the sound stage with guitars, in and out of the studio. And he would talk to the crowd during performances. He would talk about musicians like Miles Davis or what his relationship with his dad was like. Miles had done a special painting for him and he was telling people that they'd hung it upstairs in Paisley Park. He talked about how eccentric he was, how they'd had musical conversations and how they'd recorded stuff together.

After one of the shows, Prince asked the audience if they'd like to follow him down the road in their cars to the local cinema. This was about midnight or one in the morning –

'I've booked it out. I'm going to see *Minority Report*. Who wants to come?' Some people were asking, 'What? Is this a joke?' We didn't go, because we didn't religiously follow him everywhere, but quite a few of the fans went and sat in there with him, watching a Tom Cruise film and eating popcorn. That was part of his eccentricity.

Prince's *One Nite Alone...* tour began on 1 March 2002 and concluded on 29 November 2002. It took in 64 shows in total in North America, Europe and Asia.

HAMMERSMITH APOLLO

3 – 5 OCTOBER 2002, LONDON, UK

I WAS THERE: MICHELLE JUSTICE

I was there for the *One Nite Alone* tour at London's Hammersmith Apollo with the horn section, which was amazing. He invited people up on stage. I was at the front but was so in awe my legs went to jelly. I couldn't get up there! By the time I plucked up the courage, everyone was getting ushered back down. But the drummer gave me his drumsticks at the end of the show.

I WAS THERE: PAUL BARNES

It was the first night of the European leg of the *One Nite Alone* tour. My friend and I arrived at the venue around 1pm, highly anticipating the potential sound check we'd read about online during the US leg. When we got into the foyer of the venue and the box office, I handed over my email confirmation of the NPG Music Club purchase. The first 15 rows were reserved for the club members on a first-come-first-served basis, so lanyards were given out. In the envelope however, there was a ticket. Mine was row N seat 42. Members were asking, 'Why do we have a ticket? We can sit where we like!' The ushers opened the doors and they let 10 people in and then closed them. They repeated this once and then they refused to let anyone else in due to a 'problem in the theatre'. Turns out someone had sat in a seat on the front row, someone else had a ticket for that seat and demanded he move, knowing full well we could sit wherever we liked... In the end, the ushers let everyone in.

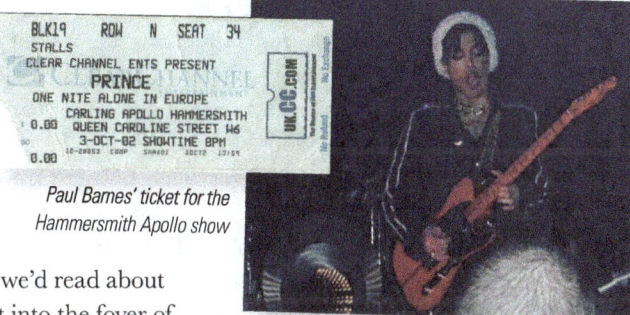

Paul Barnes' ticket for the Hammersmith Apollo show

Prince at Koko. Photo thanks to Paul Barnes

As we walked in, I and everyone else noticed Prince was sitting on the front row of the second block of seats. I took my place, fourth row centre seat. I looked over my shoulder and there sat Prince with a member of his crew, just relaxing, listening to the music, unbothered by anyone. I said to my friend, 'I have to go and talk to him, it maybe the only chance I get!!' My friend said, 'You can't!' I said, 'If he ignores me, or security moves me, so what?' So I got up and walked over! I stood over him. He looked up and said, 'Hello!' I said, 'Hi!' He said, 'I understand there was a problem with the tickets tonight?' I said, 'Yes'. 'What was the problem?' I then explained about the ticket issue.

He said, 'OK, we had a similar problem in Canada. The staff wouldn't let people in, the same. We resolved the problem by taking the trouble maker backstage! I put him in a headlock and told him you-can-sit-wherever-you-like!' I said, 'Wow, really?' He said, 'No, not really! Were you given a ticket?' I said yes, took mine out of my pocket and showed him. He took it and said 'Why did they give u this?' I said 'I don't know. I'm sat fourth row anyway'! He said, 'U seen me before?'

I listed the countless tours/shows I'd seen from *Lovesexy*, *Nude*, *Diamonds & Pearls*, *Act II*, *Gold* tour and *NewPowerSoul* to that moment. He then said, 'Well tonight, you're gonna see something you ain't never seen before!' He then stood up and said, 'OK, I'm gonna go onstage and play.' I said, 'It was great to meet you.' He smiled, and went. I sat back in my seat, shaking that I'd met my idol... I had had a chat with Prince. We had a 'normal' conversation, chatting about the issue. He was funny and charming.

When he died, I cried, as most fans did, but for me, because I met him, albeit briefly, it felt more personal somehow? A day I'll never forget for the rest of my life.

I WAS THERE: DANIEL PAYNE

We had VIP NPG Music Club tickets so got to sit in on the rehearsal. There were perhaps 20 to 30 Music Club members there in total. As we walked in, Prince and the band were rehearsing and performing 'Power Fantastic' – one of my all-time top five Prince tunes. Prince spoke to some of the Music Club members and then we also got the amazing 'Days of Wild'. I got to meet Morris Hayes and John Blackwell and got their autographs. The show was a more jazz-tinged experience and was amazing. Prince's performance of 'Gotta Broken Heart Again' was just mind blowing and he performed the best version of 'Adore' I ever heard him do, just hitting every note. He also performed (for the very first time) the unreleased 'Empty Room', probably my all-time favourite track ever, next to 'Power Fantastic'.

I WAS THERE: SAM BLEAZARD

What was interesting about the *One Nite Alone...* tour was that he went through a phase where he was trying to create a unique experience that allowed fans more access to watch the creative process close up. He created a thing called the NPG Music Club. In its simplest form, you paid an annual subscription of approximately £100 and for that, if Prince ever came to town, you got exclusive access to his shows, the best seats at his concerts, the chance to sit in on a rehearsal with his band and you would get access to rare vault tracks, with online access to stuff that he hadn't necessarily released before. It was very brief but it was brilliant while it was happening. I had a membership to the NPG Music Club.

In 2002 he played at Hammersmith Apollo for three nights. Not only did we get to sit in the first few rows but I also got to see the band rehearse each day. We went along in the late afternoon/early evening and occupied the first five or six rows of the theatre. Prince at the time was wearing almost zoot suit-type things, like pinstripe suits - very jazz era, very sharp.

There was a feeling at the time that he was becoming quite serious about his music again. During the Nineties some of the things he'd done were, on reflection, a bit throwaway. It was a really good tour, because musically it was great, really sharp, and he brought a lot of really credible players back into his group, people like Eric Leeds, who'd been the saxophone player on *Sign o' the Times* and *LoveSexy*. And Sheila E came back in to the fold once more. It was a really tight back line.

The rehearsals were amazing in their own way. You would sit there and the band would come out and play something they didn't play at the gig. One time they played an extended jam of 'D.M.S.R.' from his *1999* album. Another time at rehearsals he said, 'Does anybody want to get up and sing?' and there was a songbook at the piano and it was like, 'Okay, 'Manic Monday'. Who wants to get up and sing 'Manic Monday'?' I was too shy but a lot of people in the audience said, 'Oh – me!!' So one girl got up and sang 'Manic Monday' with him.

I WAS THERE: ALEXANDER MACINANTE

Between 1990 and 2010 I saw Prince live 25 times, including after shows. Of all the tours the one that is dearest to me is the *One Nite Alone…* tour in 2002. I flew to London to see three gigs at the Hammersmith Odeon and, as a member of the NPG Music Club, I had access to the afternoon soundchecks. The first afternoon, Prince arrived and met the fans in the concert hall before hitting the stage for the soundcheck. I shook his hand and I thought that was a dream come true, but little did I know that the following

Photos thanks to Alexander Macinante

day, 4th October, he would invite some fans on stage to sing during the soundcheck. I volunteered but he said he wanted a girl to sing 'Manic Monday'. After that, he asked again and I volunteered again but he turned me down with a smile.

After another number I lost my hopes of getting picked, but then he pointed at me and said: 'Didn't you want to sing? Get up on the stage!' In a second I was up there. He asked me what I wanted to sing. I said, 'Money Don't Matter 2nite' but he said it was not in the set. He handed me his lyrics book (!) and asked me to choose from it. I chose 'Anna Stesia' but with a smile he said, 'I'm singing it tonight...' He was very funny and down to earth and made me feel comfortable but at the same time I really didn't know what else to suggest. He said 'What about 'Shake!'?' That was a tough one for me to remember, but I was up for the challenge. He gave me the lyrics and then followed the most incredible three minutes in my life: on a London stage, with Prince playing piano and smiling at me, while at my back I had some legendary musicians like Maceo Parker, Candy Dulfer and the late great John Blackwell (who would later sign my ticket with Renato Neto). It was a dream - I can't describe it with any different word, and at the end I got a big applause from the fellow fans and Prince saying, 'Yes sir, yes sir!'

The following night, Prince spotted me and my friends in the front row and invited us to dance on stage for 'The Everlasting Now' and then again for the show finale, 'Alphabet St'. There was me again, shaking everything I got next to the Master while he was playing keys on the 'Alphabet St' jam. Incredible. And after that, the after show at the Marquee...I couldn't have dreamt anything better.

Thank you Prince for making my childhood dream true, joining you onstage, a memory that places a big smile on my face every time....

I WAS THERE: LOUISE STAFFORD, AGE 14

After seeing him play a stadium gig in Cork in 1990, the next time I saw Prince live was in London during the period I was living there, when he played at the Hammersmith Apollo. It was a much smaller, more intimate gig. He had a more jazzy feel with his band so this was a totally different experience to when I first saw him. He was more focused on playing new music so a lot of it I was hearing for the first time but it was great to see him just jamming and playing what he was into at that time. Then after a while his band left the stage and it was just Prince and his piano. He was brilliant on his own, like hearing a piano being played at some bar or hotel lobby, but then he would somehow morph whatever meandering tune he was playing into some old hit of his such as 'Do Me, Baby' and he would set the audience alight. I absolutely loved it and he just knew how to get his audience to react when he wanted us to.

Towards the end of the show he invited everyone to get up out of their seats and gather down towards the stage. My girlfriends and I made a beeline to get as close as possible. Seeing my hero up there at what felt like only two metres away from me was incredible. His stage hands were pulling fans up onto the stage to dance. My friends were trying to push me forward but I was too scared to go. The thought of being on stage next to Prince would have freaked me out. I probably would have fainted on the spot and died of embarrassment so I was safer and much happier gazing up at him within spitting distance... such a joy!

I WAS THERE: EMMA LOUISE WEBSTER, AGE 23

I was lucky enough to see Prince perform live five times in total. The first time was during the *One Nite Alone* tour at Hammersmith in 2002. I knew that he had a reputation of being a great live performer but actually seeing him live was something else! He was on stage for over two hours and it was non-stop, hit after hit. He did an acoustic version of 'Joy in Repetition' that had the whole place mesmerised!

Prince at the O2 Arena. Photo thanks to Emma Louise Webster

I also went to the opening, middle and closing nights at the O2 in 2007. I knew that he would be amazing after Hammersmith but again he just blew me away. Seeing 'Purple Rain' live brought tears to my eyes and seeing him perform it live was so emotional. I've never experienced anything like it before or since. He was constantly interacting with the crowd and had you dancing your arse off one minute to laughing the next. I honestly will never forget those nights! And every night was different so you never knew what to expect. You just knew you were going to need your dancing shoes. We went to one of the after show parties too which again was amazing. He came out to dance in the crowd and perform on stage live with the band.

I was at home with my newborn when it flashed up on my phone that emergency services were at Paisley Park so I quickly put on the news channels to see what was going on. I was gutted when they announced that he had died. You kind of put him on this pedestal and didn't think of anything happening to him. Even though you knew he was in pain, it was 'he's Prince and not like the rest of us', as crazy as that sounds.

I had lost my nan to dementia three months before he died and the song 'Free' kept my head up. That line, 'Never let the lonely monster take control of you,' was so true for me.

MARQUEE CLUB, ISLINGTON

6 OCTOBER 2002, LONDON, UK

I WAS THERE: SAM BLEAZARD

In London, Islington Council decided to create something called the New Marquee in tribute to the Marquee Club that used to be on Charing Cross Road in London. It was located in the shopping centre. This was almost twenty years ago and I don't think it's there any more, but Prince played an after show there on the *One Nite Alone* tour. It was really surreal. We were members of the NPG Music Club so we had these lanyards that Prince's fan club members wore so we got to just walk in. I remember Craig David walking in as well, and it was just in this tiny little room. Prince played a really banging version of 'Sign o' the Times'.

APOLLO THEATRE

7 OCTOBER 2002, MANCHESTER, UK

I WAS THERE: PAUL AIDEN

I've been a fan since I was about 8 or 9. I guess I went to see *Batman* and 'Partyman' and my babysitter had the album and lent me the album and I loved it. Then I missed *Graffiti Bridge* for some reason. I went into a record shop and I'd been saving money to get Michael Jackson's *Dangerous* and they were playing *Diamonds and Pearls*. *Dangerous* wasn't out and so I got into that. And then by complete and utter fluke, when I was about to turn 11, my friend in junior school said, 'do you wanna see Prince with my family?" because his older sister couldn't go. So it was *Diamonds and Pearls* in Manchester. I was on my friend's dad's shoulders and it completely and utterly blew me away. And then it was just my life ever since then.

I've been doing my Prince DJing stuff for 8 to 10 years. There was a connection with Prince when I did the Koko stuff just after he died. There was a memorial and everything. I wore a Symbol t-shirt.

I saw him in '92 when I was 10, and I ended up seeing him 21 times. I saw a few *Hit and Run* tours, I saw Electric Ballroom, Shepherd's Bush Empire, a little bit of Koko. I rushed down to Koko one night and saw the last song.

The favourite of all time though was the 7th October 2002, *One Nite Alone*, Manchester Apollo show. It was absolutely breath-taking, we got really good seats, I loved the jazz vibes. Nothing will ever beat that. There was an after show after but he didn't turn up. My second favourite was the 18th August 2007 show at the O2. Suddenly there was a keyboard set up in the middle and then he just came in wearing this huge musketeer hat and he started the after show with two Stevie Wonder covers and then 'Dorothy Parker' and it was mind blowing. And the ones at the O2 with just him and the piano, those were quite extended, there was one where he did a lot of *1999* stuff on the piano.

I went over to Paisley Park and they let me play the piano – 'The Piano' – and I got a t-shirt and a programme. I feel like I deserved that as a fan. My main memory of the Hit and Run tour was that he did 'Breakdown' with a band and just the fact that it was near the new album, *Art Official Age*, that was the last proper album for me.

I WAS THERE: KATIE TREMBATH

I was a little late getting into his music. For me it was *Diamonds & Pearls*. I thought it was just beautiful. I played it on repeat for days on end and drove my mum mad. And that was it. From that point on I went on the hunt for all things Prince. I got told a few times from my parents to turn it down. Or off in some cases, especially when playing 'Darling Nikki' on repeat so I could learn the dance he did. I was probably 11 or 12 years old and I didn't even know what half the words meant. So I was like, 'Why, what is wrong with the song?' Funnily enough, she never asked me again.

I first saw him at the Manchester Apollo. I was so excited. I bought a new outfit. The queue was so long. When he walked onto the stage I just burst into tears, I couldn't believe he was in front of me. I never sat down all night. It was the first time we heard tracks from *The Rainbow Children*. It's so good and it's still my 'go to' album. I also saw him at the O2 on 25 August 2007 in London. This was on my wedding anniversary and my husband surprised me with tickets. This was another epic show and again I never sat down. It's like his energy just passes through you.

Katie Trembath then...

...and now

POINT DEPOT

10 OCTOBER 2002, DUBLIN, IRELAND

I WAS THERE: CHRIS CARRY

Let me tell you about Pat Cusack. The most important thing to know is that Pat and I are of a distinctly similar build. We may be intellectual giants (cough!) but we're Prince-sized. Two of the whitest, and in fairness, least funky looking brothers from another other mother you'd be likely to meet. Although we've never spoken of it (the omertà of the unfunky white man) I'm sure Pat suffers the same lack of co-ordination (disco-ordination?) when it comes to physically moving ones body in time to a back beat. We'd actually been colleagues and friends for a couple of years before we realised we shared a common love for the wee Purple Genius. Like what often happens when I talk to someone and they share that they're a 'fan' of a certain artist that I like, I have to do a subtle interrogation to find out just how much they know and like that person or group. It's a thing that music fanatics who border on severe-OCD-collector-vinyl-is-god syndrome do.

I remember the great Irish musician/songwriter Peter Fitzpatrick dropping Peter Blake's name into a casual conversation when I mentioned I loved the Beatles, and I could see the inner smile of recognising one of your own in his eyes when I immediately asked him if Blake still had that striking white beard. I passed that test, the same way Pat passed my initial subtle quizzing. The dude knew his purple stuff.

Prince was great that night. It was a mixed set - *Rainbow Children* isn't one of Prince's best albums - but we were in the room and Cusack and I resisted the temptation to laugh at the other's moves. After all it would have been the equivalent of a Mexican stand off. Or Mexican dance off. But I know in my heart that Pat can dance like a mad man. Like me. In the dark. When no-one's watching. And Prince is on the stereo.

INTERNATIONAL CONGRESS CENTER
19 OCTOBER 2002, BERLIN, GERMANY

I WASN'T THERE: LARS RUNKEN
Prince played Berlin's International Congress Center in 2002 and I was in such a bad condition financially that I was not able to buy a ticket. But the *One Nite Alone* stuff moved me so much that in the late evening I took my bike and drove to where Prince and his band were performing. I just wanted to be close and to buy the tour book, but security wouldn't let me in. Eight years later, I felt kind of comforted when I was standing in the second row in the Waldbühne in Berlin in 2010 and Prince looked into my eyes from the stage in front of me. It was like he said me, 'don't be sad, don't worry, everything is very, very well.' I pass the ICC building, which looks kind of futuristic, on my bike-messenger tour every day now. Prince is always with me when I do.

The *World Tour 2003* took in Hong Kong, five Australian dates and two shows in Hawaii. It began on 17 October 2003 and wrapped on 19 December 2003.

ROD LAVER ARENA
22 & 23 OCTOBER 2003, MELBOURNE, AUSTRALIA

I WAS THERE: PAUL KOSTROMIN
I have seen Prince five times, all in Australia. I am a musician myself and have always ranked Prince as one of the all time great all round musicians/composers/entertainers. I was living in New Zealand at the time and bought tickets to the October 22nd show. The seats were pretty high up in the arena. A little while later a second show was planned as the first had sold out. I quickly purchased two more tickets, which were better and closer to the stage. I was taking my sister to the first show. She was a mild fan of Prince, but for the second show I thought I would ask my cousin - a jazz piano teacher. She was not a fan of Prince and was not keen to go, but I convinced her.

Both shows were stunning and very different. At the second show I remember Prince did an encore solo on the electric piano of a medley of his songs. The previous night was a 15 minute version of 'Purple Rain', which was huge! His band - as always - were brilliant and they were 'on' both nights. My cousin, who came to the second show, was blown away at the musicianship in the band in generally and of course how Prince would orchestrate the band. As a side note, a couple of my cousin's students got to witness Prince do an after show in a small jazz club in Melbourne in front of about 150 people. Supposedly that was unbelievable!

Prince's 28th album, *Musicology*, was sold in with tickets for the *Musicology Live 2004ever* tour, which began in Reno, Nevada on 27 March 2004 and comprised 77 shows in 52 cities, selling over 1.4 million tickets. The tour increased album sales because the CD was bundled with concert tickets, prompting *Billboard* to change its methodology for calculating album sales.

CONSECO FIELDHOUSE

12 APRIL 2004, INDIANAPOLIS, INDIANA

I WAS THERE: ANGEL GARMON

Angel Garmon saw Purple Rain over 70 times and has visited Paisley Park

I first came to know Prince during the *Purple Rain* era. I was a young teenager who was still trying to find her own identity. I fell in love with Prince immediately! I went to the movie theatre every night *Purple Rain* played. I must have seen it 70 plus times at the theatre. I wanted to be Apollonia so badly! This may sound strange but there was this club in our town that would play live bands. The outside had lights all around it similar to First Avenue does. There was a guy, much older than me, who played in a band there. He drove a motorcycle and always parked in the alley on the side of the club. I started dating him, if that's what you want to call it. I was living out a fantasy. I would pretend to myself that he was Prince and I was Apollonia. Lol! I could only have been about 13 at the time. But I was an older 13 year old - I had to grow up quick where I came from.

That's another thing I loved about this beautiful man named Prince. He made no apologies for whom he was and he wasn't afraid to wear what he wanted, to say what he wanted or to just be who he was. I loved that about him! It made me feel that it was okay for me as well. It was okay for me to just be who I was and not to worry about what others thought. His music became that background music to my life! The first and only time I got to see Prince in concert was the *Musicology* tour in Indianapolis. A guy I was dating at the time surprised me with tickets. He knew how much I loved Prince. I was in the army at this time in my life and Prince was still the background music to my life. I know Prince had a rough childhood and I related to him on that level. I was on my own at a very young age. By the time I was 19 years old I had five children, two of which were twins. No one thought I would ever do anything in my life, but I knew it was not too late and having children who I loved was not going to stop my life from progressing. I believed I could still do anything. Prince never gave up either, he knew it didn't matter where you came from or what happened to you, you still had a say in where your life went. I have always been me, regardless of what others had to say. I've always worn what I wanted to wear and did what I wanted to do. I overcame all of my obstacles in life and did better than anyone thought I would. Prince has always been an inspiration to me!

When I got to visit Paisley Park I think I was the only one there dressed like me. I know I stood out and I was okay with that because I was being myself. I know Prince would have agreed. I felt right at home. It was one of the best experiences in my life. I only wish Prince was still there with us in flesh. That would have made it perfect! I would have loved to have gotten the chance to have had a conversation with Prince. It would have been amazing!

I am now a 47 year old woman and Prince is still the background music to my life and always will be. I am still unapologetically me, just like Prince was Prince. As long as I am being who I am I know Prince would approve.

COLONIAL CENTER

21 APRIL 2004, COLUMBIA, SOUTH CAROLINA

I WAS THERE: VICTORIA ROBINSON

I was an 11 year old girl when I saw my very first general admission Prince concert in Macon, Georgia and I was completely hooked. I remember telling my best friend at the time that 'one day I am going to meet him'. She laughed. We ended up being on the front row, so we were witness to Prince stripping down to a G-string and using the bed prop during the show. The next day my mom came to me and was furious, saying, 'You didn't tell me what kind of concert you were going to!' Unbeknownst to me the city of Macon was offended by what Prince did on stage and basically said that if he didn't agree to not do that again he could not perform there. Of course, Prince chose the latter

Over the years I grew more and more in love with Prince and his music. It was pretty much all I ever listened to. After moving to South Carolina with my Dad when I was around 17, I went to my next Prince concert with friends in Charlotte, North Carolina. We were on the second row when Prince pointed me out and a guy working for him came and led me up to the stage. I was in a complete dreamlike state as I made my way to the very place that I said I would be one day. I was doing my best to keep from just freezing – and I didn't. In fact, I danced my tail off and it was amazing. I looked up at one point and here was this amazing, beautiful man standing right next to me dancing and holding the mic out for me to sing. Needless to say I was on Cloud Nine! After being on stage for a few songs I was assisted back to my seat but was given guitar picks and an after party pass. I didn't go to this because I had a couple of friends with me but I was so, so sad.

About two months later, I heard that there was a concert in my hometown of Columbia so I got online with one of the VIP seat places and purchased front row seats for myself and my sister. It was an amazing show and again I was chosen to go onstage. This time it was even more amazing and I was on stage even longer. Prince came to sing beside me and I put my arm around him when no one else ever seemed to touch him. I remember so clearly how tiny he was (and I was pretty small myself) and how beautiful his skin was up close. And I remember more than anything that no matter how sweaty he was, how long he had been performing, he always smelled like some exotic oil or flower. I can still smell it if I really think about it.

For this concert I was given a VIP pass to come backstage after the show and I was 18 and I was going! I remember feeling like a little jittery girl when being walked back but at the same time I had always known that I would be there. I remember passing many of the band and was finally introduced officially to my idol. His voice was much deeper than I expected and he told me that I was a good dancer and what he said next was just amazing! He said, 'I remember you from another show...you becoming a regular onstage. Might just want to go on tour with us!' I could barely speak as I thanked him and asked if I could hug him. He obliged, gave me a hug and a hand full of guitar picks and was then swept away by what I can only assume was media or staff. Needless to say, I was on Cloud Nine again! The man I had loved since I was 11 had actually remembered me! Not very long after this concert, I ended up getting married but I pondered often whether Prince sincerely meant that I could have gone on that concert tour. It is still just too crazy to think about!

Even though I was married, I still attended each concert that Prince did around Columbia, Charlotte and twice in Atlanta. I was picked to go onstage at most shows and I remember that Prince would say 'hi' when I would get up the stage steps and smile. I only talked to him after the concert once more, and that was after a *Musicology* show. He gave me a hug and I told him how phenomenal he was. He gave me more guitar picks and then John Blackwell gave me a drumstick. It was just unbelievable. I was approached during the concert with an after party pass but I didn't go. I was newly married and I really didn't know for sure if my Prince would actually be present or not.

The next concert in Columbia was *Welcome 2 America* and it was amazing too. This would be my last dance on the stage with my beautiful Prince and the last time he would say, 'Hi there, South Carolina girl.' I didn't even go backstage or anything after this concert because my husband at the time was with me and I knew there would be many more concerts and chances to hug Prince, except... there wasn't.

The next chance I had to see my Prince was in Atlanta for the *Piano & A Microphone* tour but at the time my mom was not feeling well so my son and I went to Macon, Georgia to visit with her instead. I remember saying to my son, 'I can't believe that my Prince is right down the road and I am not going.' I remember having this feeling that it might be my last chance. I didn't know why I felt that way. Maybe I thought that he was going to stop touring. I just don't know. I also remember feeling a strong sense of needing to spend time with my mom and wishing I could have stayed down there longer but I had to get back to work and my son had to get back to school.

Only a couple months later I received a call from an old friend who had previously worked in a very high level government job and he said that he was calling to make sure that I was okay. I asked him why and that is when he told me to sit down and to turn on the TV. I did so and within minutes my beautiful Prince's death was announced. I felt like my heart was ripped out and I cried for days. I remember getting tons of calls from friends to check on me because they knew of my lifelong love of Prince. The world lost a whole lot of magic for me that day. Almost two years to the day, I had a much greater loss and that was my greatest hero... my mom. I was completely lost and devastated. It hurts so much every day, but one of the things I often think of is how much my mom used to love to tell people about how Prince had told me that I should go on his tour. She thought that was so amazing and I smile when I think about her and Prince up in heaven talking about it.

GAYLORD ENTERTAINMENT CENTER

6 MAY 2004, NASHVILLE, TENNESSEE

I WAS THERE: MELISSA COMMON SMITH

I had wanted to see Prince in concert from the age of 16 but my mom wouldn't let me go to concerts until I was 18. By that time I was in college and couldn't afford such luxuries so I just missed it all. Fast forward to 2004. I was 34 and had an 18 month old. The *Musicology* tour was coming around near my area. My husband encouraged me to finally go but tickets in Cinci or Columbus had sold out pretty far in advance. The closest I could find was Nashville, so I recruited my 18 year old niece to go with me. On the five hour drive down there I schooled her in everything Prince, from his beginning albums up to the tour we were about to see. Needless to say it was an amazing show. After the show they announced that he would be playing at a nearby bar for an after party and encouraged the crowd to come out. I was in a city I wasn't familiar with and didn't yet have a smart phone so I wasn't sure exactly where this place was. I didn't want to take any crazy risks, walking around town with my niece if I didn't really know where to go, and I wasn't sure that aged 18 she would be able to get in if we did find it. We walked back to our hotel and turned in for the night. The next morning we were checking out and going to the parking garage when two guys rushed into the elevator at the last minute, completely full of energy and excitement. They had gone to the after show and were gushing about how amazing it was. They said Prince had come into the crowd and sat down at tables and talked to folks, and that the venue had been right around the corner from our hotel. I was so sad I missed out on that experience.

PRINCE PARTY

29 MAY 2004, LONDON, UK

WE WERE THERE: PAUL AND KAT SAVAGE

Paul: The first time we met was at a Prince party in London on 29th May 2004. I was with one of my mates, JD. We'd been out watching the football and then he decided he wanted to meet a girl called Lady Misscat. So we got to the club, Extra Time Bar, and we split up and went both ways. I went one way, he went the other, and I went to a table and I saw these girls, and I was asking, 'Are you Lady Misscat?' and she goes, 'no, but my name is Kat'. And I forgot all about finding this Lady Misscat. Five years to the day we met we got married, on 29th May, our anniversary of meeting. All our kids are Prince fans. They walk around the house singing his songs. I'm sure when they're 13 they'll probably hate us for a while, and then come back again. My first Prince gig was the 1992 *Nude* tour in Manchester.

Kat: Mine was *21 Nights* at the O2 in 2007.

Paul: I went to Wembley for the *Diamonds and Pearls* tour, the Greatest Hits tour. I got given two tickets to the after show (which was later videoed), and I said to my mate who was a bit of a Prince fan but not as big as me, 'should we go?' and he went 'but we're getting a coach back to Manchester', so we never went. I've still got the tickets. I knew nobody in London at that point - you didn't have Facebook or all the social media - but I was devastated I didn't go.

Paul: We did seven and nine after shows for the *21 Nights* tour. We were going away on holiday and we decided just to sack the holiday and we put all the money we'd saved up for the holiday towards the shows. So we planned it out most weekends, and I remember the first night we got there Kat had these shoes on that were so high.

Kat: Yeah I had these knee high boots with massive heels, because I'd never been to a Prince gig so I didn't know what to wear, and I had to keep looking down where I was going and Paul said, 'Kat, look where we are' and then I looked up and the stage and I couldn't believe it. Never in a million years did I believe we'd be that close.

Paul: She just screamed and I thought, 'yeah, she's happy now'.

Kat: Because I'd grown up with seeing Prince and thinking I'd never see him.

STAPLES CENTER

3 & 4 JUNE 2004, LOS ANGELES, CALIFORNIA

I WAS THERE: SHONDA CASEY

I have been a Prince fan since the first time I saw a picture of naked man riding on a horse while browsing through my grandfather's record collection. My grandfather was a musician and had a nice record collection that I used to entertain myself with by looking at the pictures and reading the lyrics. I asked who this beautiful man was and he let me play the record. From the first sound of the needle on the record, I was in love. When I was in high school my grandfather died. My nana would often catch me looking at that record and eventually she let me have it. Now it's my most prized possession in my music collection. My first time seeing Prince in concert was the *Musicology* tour. I paid about 100 dollars and my seats were in the nose bleed section. That's why on his *Welcome 2 America* tour I was determined to go as many times possible. Even though I made it to only three shows I got my money's worth. Each performance was amazingly mesmerizing and different and each time Prince did encores until at least midnight or 1am. It was awesome. I even dressed like Prince for Halloween last year and won first place in a costume contest.

Shonda Casey saw Prince at the Staples Center and he inspired her fancy dress costume

SBC CENTER

9 JUNE 2004, SAN ANTONIO, TEXAS

I WAS THERE: GREG SCHRODER

By 2004, our family had grown to four, with our then 11-year-old son and our just turned 8-years-old daughter. Prince's birthday was June 7 and when my wife was nine-plus months pregnant on June 7, 1996… well, I am not *too* ashamed to admit that as midnight on June 7 approached I was urging my wife to jump up and down. But our daughter Sydney did not make an appearance until the next day.

For her eighth birthday I took her to see Prince in San Antonio, Texas. As members of Prince's NPG Music Club, we had great seats on the second row, in Section F10. To those of you who haven't seen the stage, you probably have heard that it is a '+' shape. The thing is, though, that the floor area of most arenas is a rectangle. This means that there are 20 to 50 rows of seats in front of the north and south ends of the '+', but only two rows on the east and west ends. We were on the stage left side, and our second row was also the last row. Consequently, Prince (understandably) spent most of his time north and south, because there were thousands more people there. However, the horn section was right in front of us, so we got to look at Candy all night long - which was a treat! And the stairs via which the band came on and off the stage were right in front of us.

We got in our seats at 6.30pm. The pre-concert music was just awesome. All Prince and Prince protégé songs, and great songs too. A fellow with Prince's security detail walked by saw my daughter decked out in her Prince regalia, went under the stage and came back with two of Prince's guitar picks for my daughter. I thought the night couldn't get better than that. Ha! Was I wrong!

When Prince sang 'I Feel for You', he came over to our side for the second verse. When he sang, 'I wouldn't lie to you baby, I'm, spiritually attracted to YOU', he pointed right at my daughter and smiled a giant smile. We were only 10 feet away, so there was no doubt. We were higher than a kite over that!

During the acoustic part of the show, the band came down the steps right in front of us. John Blackwell hung out and talked to fans. He gave out a lot of drumsticks, and he gave my daughter two of them. Then he autographed them for her. A pick AND autographed drumsticks - things were looking up!

For the final part of the main show – before the encore – Prince would bring several ladies onstage. I had seen that at a previous show there had been a young girl about my daughter's age allowed on stage, so I told my daughter that she might get to go on stage and dance. In fact, John Blackwell invited her up, so it looked like the dream would come true. But when she was in line, one of the stage crew said she couldn't go up without her mother. Well, Mom was still in Houston, so it looked like we were out of luck. The guy was real nice, he was just concerned about my daughter's safety (in fact, before the show, he had asked me if I had earplugs for her. I did, but he had extras just in case). He said he would try to find a girl to go on stage with my daughter as a surrogate mom. However, in the rush of things, he wasn't able to get back to us.

So, I told my daughter, 'Go get in line and ask that girl up front if she will look after you.' Done and done! The gate opened and up on stage went my daughter.

My daughter danced around stage for a while. She was not shy at all; in fact, if I might say so myself she is a great dancer. She was getting down with all the girls when Candy Dulfer came over and gave her the cowbell and drumstick. My daughter played it and played it on time. Prince came over to her a couple times and said 'Play that cowbell!' and held the mic up to her.

Sydney took that as her cue to work the stage, and work it she did. During 'Life O' the Party', my daughter was at the middle of the stage and singing along when Prince noticed she knew the lyrics. Prince put the microphone up to her during the chorus. You should have seen the look on Prince's face when she belted out the chorus - all the right words, right on the beat and in the correct key! Oh man - I was screaming my head off! Prince took her by the hand and walked with her for a moment or two.

Then Maceo took the cowbell and gave her a tambourine. She played that the rest of the set, and was just having a blast! She would walk to the end of the stage and shake the tambourine to the crowd. Man oh man, I'd like to say she inherited all that funk from me, but Mom might read this!

At one point she came over to our side of the stage with Candy and they joined hands and danced together. We were all in heaven. When that segment of the show was over, Maceo took the tambourine as they herded the crowd over to the opposite side of the stage from me so that Prince could get off the stage on our side. But before they took the people off the stage, Maceo gave my daughter the tambourine back!

I was a little worried that she was on the opposite side of the arena from me now, but the same fellow who had helped us earlier took her by the hand and walked her all the way back to our seat. Like I said, he was a really nice guy. In fact, all the personnel were top-notch.

During the encore intermission, the tall people in front of us left, so I put my daughter on the front row. Standing in front of us was Inge Dulfer, Candy's mother and manager. I asked Inge if she could get Candy to autograph the tambourine. She said 'Sure!' Somebody produced a Sharpie, and after 'Purple Rain', Inge pulled Candy over and she spoke to my daughter and autographed the tambourine. They were class all the way!

As we left the arena, we (meaning my daughter) must have been stopped by, talked to and photographed by 300 people. It was insane! My daughter told everyone how she had been touched by Prince on her left hand, and by Candy on her right hand, and that she was never going to wash those hands. Needless to say, I was one proud papa! But it gets better…

AMERICAN AIRLINES CENTER

11 JUNE 2004, DALLAS, TEXAS

I WAS THERE: GREG SCHRODER

An incredible guy named John gave me tickets to the show in Dallas. My daughter and I met my wife there. Keep in mind – I called my wife after the San Antonio show, described Sydney's exploits there in great detail, and the first thing my wife asked was, 'Are you drunk?' I'm not sure she believed a word of my story, until we all walked into the American Airlines Center and my daughter was mobbed by the patrons. It seemed like hundreds and hundreds of the people in Dallas had been at the San Antonio show and they all remembered Sydney. Most of them thought she was with the band!

I had two sets of tickets for this show. My wife and daughter's seats were on the front row of the same side section we'd sat in at the San Antonio show, but nearer to John Blackwell. My seat was on the seventh row at the 'front' part of the stage. During the first part of the show, my wife came over to my seat and showed me the wrist bands that her and our daughter were wearing, and said they had been picked to go up on stage. Of course, I got excited.

During the dancing part of the show, they were not on stage. I was a little worried, thinking that something had happened, but I was also a little confused when she showed me her wristband and said it was for getting on stage. In San Antonio, everyone on the front row was given a wristband so that security would know who was supposed to be on the front row and who wasn't, and that's what I thought my wife's wristband might be for. Turns out I was right, and they didn't get to dance on stage.

So I was kind of bummed because I thought that would be a huge disappointment to my daughter, and I was preparing my 'don't worry baby, you still got to do something special in San Antonio' speech for when I met up with them after the show.

I went to our pre-arranged meeting place in the lobby and waited for them. Imagine my surprise when my daughter walks up not wearing a frown, but an ear-to-ear smile. The reason? She was carrying one of John Blackwell's cymbals! It was almost as big as she was!

During the show, John had given my daughter a couple of drumsticks. She already had two from the San Antonio show, so she gave one to a fellow who didn't have one. But not long after that, someone took her other stick off her seat and just stole it right out from under her. After the show, as John was autographing drumsticks, my daughter told him what happened. He said, 'Wait right here - I've got something better for you.' He went onto the stage, took out one of his cymbals, and autographed it for her. Incredible!

The show itself was amazing. The set list was just about the same as San Antonio, except for the acoustic part. Prince played 'Something in the Water (Does not Compute)' and 'Motherless Child'. I was freaking out, and after the show told my wife that there couldn't have been 10 people in the arena who had ever heard of 'Motherless Child'. She said the people sitting next to her had become friends with John Blackwell and had asked him to ask Prince to play that song, and he did! That was great, but it gets better....

CENTURYTEL CENTER

12 JUNE 2004, BOSSIER CITY, CALIFORNIA

I WAS THERE: ASHLEY PURDION

I started listening to Prince when I was very young, probably 5 or 6. My aunt loved him and so I wanted to love him too. My parents were younger so we always had MTV or VH1 on and every time a music video of his would come on, I made sure to watch it. When I turned 13 and got my first CD player, my aunt gave me tons of his CDs. Most I shouldn't have listened to due to content, but I did anyway!

My parents loved concerts and music so really instilled that in me at a young age too. I got the tickets one afternoon. My dad printed them off and handed them to me and I didn't realise what it was. It wasn't my birthday yet but it was a birthday present. When I realised, I started jumping up and down. It seems like it was months and months until the actual concert. We didn't have the best seating but we had a bird's eye view. The excitement everyone had when he came out was unlike any concert I have ever been to, even now. He had on high-heeled boots, a beautiful long sleeved shirt and flare pants in red. He was beautiful, such a small man but a huge presence. He had all of the audience singing along to all of his songs. And this was before his hip replacement so he was able to grind on the floor a bit like in *Purple Rain*. It was a beautiful concert, with no big sets or anything outrageous and just Prince and his backup group and a piano – and, of course, his guitar! I listened to the CD given out at the concert until I knew every word of every song! It is still one of my favourites of his. I also still have one of the CDs wrapped in cellophane as my mother gave me hers. I was a bit of a weird child. I had my senior pictures made in my Prince concert tour shirt. I still have the shirt.

COX ARENA

5 SEPTEMBER 2004, SAN DIEGO, CALIFORNIA

I WAS THERE: JENNIFER UPTON

I saw the *Musicology* tour in LA in March 2004. I dragged my (now ex) husband to the gig. He didn't want to be close to the stage so we were up a bit on the side. Great show. But when he came back around to San Diego that September, I bought myself one ticket through the fan club. I drove all the way down by myself blasting his tunes all the way. This was during the time when fans got the prime seats but you didn't know where you would be seated until you got to the show. The girl at the ticket booth gave me a big smile when she printed my ticket but I didn't know the stadium arrangement. I entered the stadium thinking I must be pretty far up. The usher looked at my ticket and pointed down towards the stage: 'You're down there.' I started walking down. I got to the floor and the next usher looked at my ticket. He said, 'You're up by the stage. Third row.' My jaw hit the floor. When I got to my row, there was another solo lady my age that had driven all the way from Canada. She asked, 'Can you believe these seats?' We danced and sang the whole night. At one point, Prince came over to our side of the symbol stage and played an extended bass solo for our side. My jaw dropped for the second time that night. After the gig, I drove home buzzing. A magical night.

MARCUS AMPHITHEATER

24 JUNE 2004, MILWAUKEE, WISCONSIN

I WAS THERE: JASON VOLKOFF

A friend and I went to see Prince in Milwaukee at Summerfest for the *Musicology* tour in 2004. I had seventh row centre seats and they really couldn't have been better! As we know, that tour was in the round. However, at Summerfest the amphitheatre stage is an end stage so the sound had to be reconfigured for the monitors, speakers, etc. Because of this, the show started late so my friend and I enjoyed a few of Milwaukee's greatest export - beer.

Well as the show went on we had a few more and by the end of the show I must have been 'weepily' emotional. Prince gets to 'Purple Rain' and, frankly, it really has never been one of my favourites. For me it's too slow, too long, too country-ish. Well, not that night! The lyrics finally hit me as a statement of unconditional love and I bend over as

I'm standing and begin to weep uncontrollably! Like, I finally got it.

Now, I'm six foot four and my friend is six foot two so we are hard to miss. As I'm bent over holding the bottom of my shorts and crying my eyes out, my friend tries to console me by patting me on my back. While this is happening, I look up and we are about 15 feet from the stage and Prince is looking down at us with a bemused and slightly confused look on his face like, 'WTF is going on with THOSE dudes?' A funny moment that I'll always remember!

CONTINENTAL AIRLINES ARENA

16 JULY 2004, EAST RUTHERFORD, NEW JERSEY

I WAS THERE: DONNA LOGGIA

I saw him in East Rutherford. The rule was strictly no cameras. I snuck one in after being totally searched. I was in the first row, I made friends with the security man, pulled out the camera, he turned his head and I got a photo! We also received chocolate chip cookies. During the show Prince totally looked at me and winked. No one else got the point and the wink. My friend said, 'I'll take your car home.' It didn't go that far….

Prince in East Rutherford, New Jersey. Photo thanks to Donna Loggia

PALACE OF AUBURN HILLS

31 JULY 2004, AUBURN HILLS, MICHIGAN

I WAS THERE: JOHN CARLTON YOUNG

Prince came to the Palace of Auburn Hills and I got pretty good seats. I was up off the floor but I could see from the side and had a perfect view. One of my coolest memories from that show was that I'm a big NBA basketball fan. The Detroit Pistons had won the world championship in 2004 and there was a player on the Detroit Pistons team at that time called Tayshaun Prince. Prince put a Tayshaun Prince jersey on and said, 'I know you boys got Tayshaun Prince but you got the real Prince now'. Everybody just went crazy. That night he did two of my favourite prince songs, 'Private Joy' and 'Rock City'. He was a legend and I feel fortunate and blessed in having seen him.

John Carlton Young saw Prince at the Palace of Auburn Hills

TOYOTA CENTER

6 AUGUST 2004, HOUSTON, TEXAS

I WAS THERE: GREG SCHRODER

Prince finally plays our hometown, at the 15,000-seat Toyota Center. Of course, we were there. My wife and daughter had the usual seats on the side; I was on the front row of the 'front' section again. And - once again - many, many people recognized Sydney from her previous exploits onstage. I recounted the San Antonio/Dallas stories to the fans around us, and we were all anxious to see if Sydney would get another chance to join Prince.

As the show progressed, Candy Dulfer spied Sydney and waved to her, smiled at her, and generally re-connected with her. When the audience members joined Prince onstage I looked real hard, but I didn't see Sydney. 'Oh well,' I told the people behind me, 'I guess she didn't make up there this time.'

'Really?' said one person. 'Then who is *that?*' I turned back to the stage and there was Sydney! Candy had noticed that Sydney wasn't onstage and actually had security personnel pick her up and place her onstage. I couldn't believe it! Once again Sydney played the cowbell with Maceo and the tambourine with Candy. Once again Prince gave her the microphone for the chorus on 'Life O' the Party'. And once again, Sydney nailed it! Prince definitely remembered her from San Antonio, and after she sang they went cavorting around the stage together.

The final song of that portion of the set was 'Take Me With U'. That's my favourite song of all time. It's the first song I learned on guitar; in fact, I learned how play guitar so I could play that song. So what happened when Prince played it this particular night? He grabbed my daughter's hand, they sat down on the edge of the stage and they sang the bridge together into Prince's microphone. There's my daughter, singing my favourite song, with my favourite artist. In front of thousands of people. And her mother.

15 years later and I still can't stop from crying tears of joy when I recount these stories. I cannot truthfully say Prince was a friend of mine, but I can surely say he was a friend to me and my family. The impact he had on my daughter's self-confidence just absolutely cannot be overstated. To this day, whenever she doubts herself, she is reminds herself that she sang with the greatest artist in history, in front of thousands of people – twice. You won't be surprised to learn there's just no stopping that young lady!

And then her father got to sing with Prince….

PEPSI CENTER

28 AUGUST 2004, DENVER, COLORADO

I WAS THERE: DARLENE ARMENTA

I saw him three more times. The second time was just okay. It was outside and we were too far away. The third time he held a party at a club downtown after the concert. We went but didn't get to see him. The last time was in 2004 at the Pepsi Center in

Denver. It was the *Musicology* tour. I went alone because I wanted to get a good seat. Unfortunately, he was a Jehovah's Witness then and stopped singing all the sexy songs that made me fall in love with him. A woman kept going past me to get beer before the concert. She came back right as the concert started and I grabbed her arm and said, 'That is the last time you are walking in front of me tonight. Enjoy the concert.' She must have told her friends, because when I looked over, they were all looking at me.

Billboard's 2004 review of the biggest grossing concerts of the year ranked Prince at 4, 5 and 7 and beaten only by Madonna (twice) and Elton John. His three shows at Madison Square Garden in July 2004 grossed almost $4 million. He topped Rolling Stone's annual list of the year's biggest money earners after his 2004 tour grossed over $90 million (£53 million). Madonna came in second place after earning $54.9 million (£34.3 million). Metallica were third with $43 million (£25.3 million).

WAREHOUSE LIVE

4 MARCH 2006, HOUSTON, TEXAS

I WAS THERE: GREG SCHRODER

Prince put together an album of original material for Tamar Davis and set up a tour of small clubs for her. He used the NPG for the backing band, with himself on guitar. When it was announced that he'd be playing the Warehouse Live here in Houston, you can bet I was there. And you can bet I was going to be the white guy picked to get onstage with Prince and Tamar and sing 'Play That Funky Music White Boy'!

Doors opened at 10pm so naturally I got in line at 7pm. The three hour wait was worth it, though. I knew the layout of the stage and the positioning of the artists and I was six feet from where Prince would be playing guitar. Two hours later – at midnight – Prince and the band took the stage and play guitar he did. Never before or since have I heard such playing. He was so good that I almost gave up the instrument myself right then and there, knowing that I'd never get within 1,000 miles of his proficiency.

But I had other things on my mind. Specifically, I was listening for Tamar to ask, 'Are there any white guys in the audience who think they can sing?' as that was the cue for an audience member to join them for 'Play That Funky Music White Boy'. Sure enough, about an hour into the show Tamar spoke.

She didn't get any further than 'Are there any white...' before I started jumping up and down like a maniac. 'Do you know this song?' asked Tamar. 'Are you sure you know it? If you're going to get on this stage, you'd better know this song!'

Who was she kidding? I grew up in the Seventies! I was 17 years old when that song came out. I've danced to it hundreds of times – maybe thousands! My nickname in 1978 was 'Disco Schro'. Do you think I know that song?

I jumped onstage and started vamping with The Twinz. I preened. I strutted. I hugged every female I could find. And all the while I was thinking, 'I can't remember the damn first line of the song.'

Prince started the opening riff and all I could think was, 'I know all the other lyrics but the first line is going to be something like 'Mmmpfahd dooo dah zzipp-oh fleenor'. I was also thinking, 'Then Prince might kill me.' But I was saved! From out of nowhere I heard someone sing, 'I was a boogie singer…' I looked over and I wasn't the only guy on stage. There was another guy. A big black man with dreadlocks. The complete opposite of what Tamar asked for, but who cares? He just saved my life! All the lyrics came back in a rush. He and I absolutely killed it, I must say. My trick was that during the chorus I got on my knees and held the microphone out to an audience member, letting them sing the chorus. Prince really dug that!

It was a life highlight, that's for sure. But even better than singing with Prince was afterwards meeting that big black man who'd saved my bacon. His name is Anthony and he's been my best friend now for going on 15 years.

THE MANSION

18 MARCH 2006, MIAMI, FLORIDA

I WAS THERE: RICHARD PADILLA

In March of 2006, I was in the hospital for pancreatitis. I had already bought a ticket to see Prince with Tamar in Miami at The Mansion. Due to my hospitalization, I was already cancelling my plan to go to the Prince Concert. I was released from the hospital on March 17, 2006. On Saturday, March 18, 2006, I was feeling weak due to my hospitalization and I spoken to my best friend Ronnie Christian, saying that I won't be able to go. He talked me out of not going and told me it would be good for me to go as it might bring my spirit up.

Richard Padilla drove to Miami despite suffering pancreatitis

So I changed my mind at the last minute and decided to go. I drove all the way from Fort Lauderdale to Miami and made it to become one of the first people waiting in line. Since this was a general admission show, people arrived early to get up front, me included. The wait was for hours it seemed and, with my still recovering, it was a major task.

Finally, the time came to go into the venue. I was able to secure a spot centre stage in the front. This was my second time up close to the stage since the ONA in Lakeland show where I was also sitting dead centre. Prince and Tamar came on stage to perform and the show was hot, mostly Tamar-driven with Prince on guitar. The crowd was into this hot show and I was having a blast, up front enjoying watching my musical hero on stage just a few feet away.

At one point he started to play a groove. At the time, I could not figure out what song it was. I assumed it was a classic Prince groove but I could not put my finger on what it was. Maybe it was the medicine that I was or because I was still recovering from my hospital stay but I could not figure it out. Prince asked someone from the audience to come up and sing if they knew the words. Tamar was looking for someone, while Prince was just jamming on the guitar. The first person Tamar picked was a young lady to come up, but she could not manage to get herself to stop laughing and Tamar sent her back to her spot.

Tamar then came over to the centre where I was and, like dumbstruck fool, I raised my hand. Tamar noticed me and pulled me up on stage. She asked me, did I know the words to the song? I lied and said yes, figuring I would find out what song he was playing and I would start singing. After all, I know all of Prince's lyrics so I just had to find out what song it was. I got on the mic and I looked over to my right to see Prince looking at me and nodding at me to go ahead.

Nervously, I looked at the crowd in front of me and all I could think of was, 'OMG, there is a lot of people in this room staring at me, Prince included.' Still not knowing what song he was playing, the first thing I said was something along the lines of, 'Miami, how are you doing?' etc. Tamar came over and said, 'Okay, go ahead and sing....'

At that moment, I knew I could not hide it as I still could not figure out what the song was. I then mumbled in a high squeaky voice some unintelligible words into the mic like a song. Prince looked over at me and gave me a 'WTF' look. The whole place started dying laughing. Tamar came over and took the mic and escorted me back to my spot with a little smile on her face. It should have been a moment where I would be embarrassed but I was not. I just got on the same stage as Prince and had him even notice me.

My friends from the Florida NPG all loved it. They knew that Wild Rich would somehow get involved.

The night did not end there. After he played the last song of the show, which I believe was 'Purple Rain', Prince handed his guitar down to us to pass along the front row. My picture was taken and posted to the NPGMC as the guitar was being passed along to me.

I was glad that I decided to leave hospital the previous day to go to the show as Prince provided me with the best possible medicine to recover with.

28 JULY 2006

Prince's second wife, Manuela Testolini Nelson, filed for divorce. His first marriage, to dancer Mayte Garcia, took place in 1996 but only lasted two years.

Per4ming Live 3121 was a residency by Prince at a nightclub he opened in Las Vegas, Nevada called *Club 3121*. It opened on 10 November 2006 and ended on 28 April 2007. He performed 38 shows in total.

JAZZ CUISINE

3 DECEMBER 2006, LAS VEGAS, NEVADA

I WAS THERE: JONATHAN CRAIG WALMSLEY

The Jazz Cuisine restaurant was physically adjacent to the club but their public entrances were in totally different places so it took a minute or two to walk from one to the other. The restaurant was composed of different rooms, the one nearest the entrance has the kitchen and a small adjunct dining room for about 10 people. The second main room connects the first at the far corner, and this is where the miniscule stage was set up — behind that was an atrium.

The second room is a restaurant with about 10 to 12 tables for maybe 40 people seated, and the stage, set up in the far corner of the room was only about six metres square - just enough space for a drum kit, keyboard and mic, with maybe two people standing on it at once.

We had dinner in the restaurant before the main show and whilst I did not see the band at that point, being near the public entrance in the first room, I could hear that Remato Neto and Maceo Parker sat in for a spell or two.

So, the way it went down was this — as noted by several folks, Prince referred to the possibility of playing 'next door' and 'till 5am' several times during the main concert. When '3121' (the song) was done with in the main concert, I decided to stake my place in the restaurant on the off-chance that he was telling the truth and scooted through the casino to tell the wait staff that we would like some food.

At this point, around 2.30am, the place was completely empty. The waiting person took us in and tried to sit us in the first room, ie. the one without the stage, but a polite but firm 'no thanks' had us placed in the room with the stage. We were over to towards the atrium side, about three metres from the stage. From the noise coming from the club, it was clear that the blighter was doing more encores, but we stuck to our guns more or less, and waited it out.

A couple more folks arrived to take up positions at their tables — Lisa and John were their names - and we chatted about the economics of running the place, how long he would be in Vegas and all that whilst the show wound up next door. We could hear the bassline of 'Purple Rain' rumbling through the walls and floors.

Once that was all wrapped up, a few more folks appeared, and were all seen to their tables. It really was a restaurant rather than a concert. No one was bum rushing the stage or standing. They were just sitting, ordering food and drink and generally taking it cool. I got up to go to the bathroom and just as I made it to the connection of the two rooms, Prince strides right towards me, coming straight into the room with a couple of bodyguards and friends.

I stood to one side (it seemed rude not to) and declared, 'After you, sir.' As will become apparent later, I can't help but call him 'sir' when speaking to him). He then strode in, sat at the nearest open booth, of which there were still several, and declared, 'Bring us food!'

After a little while chatting and such like, he then departed through the room's far exit towards the atrium. We were now really starting to believe that this was going to happen, and whilst it was horrendously late and we had an early flight and were tired after the long show, we started getting really excited.

Various bits of equipment made their way from the club — the bass amp, a keyboard (with gaffer tape on the back, apparently holding it together), and various guitars and effects, guitar amp, etc. Members of the band start to appear to check their stuff — Renato on keys, Josh on the bass, no-one for horns. Throughout the entire show, both horns and drums were unamplified. Such a small room did not need it.

At about 3.10am the tables were full apart from one right next to the atrium and the stage, where the band installed themselves.

At around 3.10am Prince came into the place to cheers and clapping. I shouted out, 'Bravo Maestro' (I am horrendously pretentious) and, as I did, he started laughing and playing it up with mock bows and generally soaking up the attention.

He installed himself at the band's table alongside DJ Rashida (who accompanied him all night), initially looking out into the room. But this gave him no view of the stage so he swapped sides so he has his back to most of the room but is right next to the stage and can call out instructions or lean in for a word with someone as the fancy takes him.

He is wearing a full length cream trench coat, similar to that he had on at the Versace show, although with more detail in the cut. He has his collar up. Underneath this, he is wearing a pale blue version of the outfit he wore to the UK Hall of Fame induction. He has some very bling kind of jewel-encrusted looking shoes with trademark heels. He looks immaculate.

There were maybe 50 people maximum in the room. It was a large living room kind of size and Prince was wandering about freely between the tables. Security was super-low key. Everyone is just playing it all too cool for school and it is completely amazing.

Mike Phillips gets up with Cora, Josh and Renato and they launch off into the first jam, a kind of jazz improvization which is very funky and I am later told is Thelonious Monk's 'Straight, No Chaser'.

Prince was up and down at this stage, sometimes there, sometimes out of the room. Josh is sitting on the edge of the stage next to his bass amp — there is not enough room for him to stand on stage. After that, Renato leads the band into a super-sweet jazz version of 'Gotta Broken Heart Again'. I am guessing that this was a favourite from the *One Nite Alone* tour and he does a really nice job on it. Solos from Mike, Renato (excellent) and Maceo.

Then Mike kicks off into a version of 'So What' — the band is unbelievably tight. Cora and Josh, who I must admit to having been sceptical about previously, are really excellent — both are super solid, not flashy, but highly skilful. Josh in particular seems musically self-effacing but is so fluid, fast and firm in laying down the track's foundation.

Greg takes a trombone solo, Mike takes a solo, Prince tweaks his amp, sits on the stage's edge and takes a guitar solo, Renato solos, Josh solos, Greg and Cora trade licks, Maceo steps up to round it out, the Mike takes them back into the lead line and all the horns wrap it up nice and super tight. Prince declares, 'I'm in heaven', Mike thanks Prince for arranging '3121' - 'real music for real musicians'. People are loving it and I am in music nirvana. Prince plays Miles. Holy crap! Has he ever been played that song in public before?

Something is not quite right with his guitar, though, and as the next track gets going, techs start fiddling about with it, and wheel in another set-up from the club. The next track is a funk jam. Prince takes his seat, looking out over the band. This track feels really familiar, but I can't place it, so I turn around behind me to ask one of his security guards (seated in a booth near the non-public exit) the name of the song. He says, 'I don't know - ask him…', gesturing to Prince.

I am shocked by this. I thought security people were supposed to stop people from interacting with the Principal? What if it disturbs his enjoyment, he gets up and leaves, and everyone then completely hates me? But as I look round quizzically to the guard, he says it again, 'Go ask him', so I cross the four feet between me and Prince, touch him on the shoulder and say, 'Hello there, sir! What's the name of this song?' to which he replies 'I dunno!'

It was superbly cool to have a chance to say hello, even if the conversation was A) short and B) not that informative.

Maceo solos, Prince goes and fiddles with his new amp set up, Greg and Mike both take solos too. The band is on fire. Prince moves Renato off the keys and takes them himself, and plays a break that I know, but cannot place - though at the time I am convinced it is from *The Munsters*. They set off on another funky jam number (maybe 'Sing a Simple Song'?), Prince leading on keys, Mike getting some serious vocoder action and then Morris Hayes coming back in on keys after being tracked down by DJ R at Prince's request. Freed up, Prince now takes on the guitar and lays it down, upping the tempo considerably.

A key change moves the song into 'More Bounce to the Ounce'. The funky side of things is really coming on now. The next number is really kind of strange - Prince was not around for the first time, so installs Renato back on keys, and they run through 'Gotta Broken Heart Again' again. Prince has not sung during the show and hearing this again, I have to supress a desperate urge to shout 'sing!' at him.

When it comes time for Renato's solo, Prince calls out to Cora and Josh to move to double-time, upping the funkiness once again, and Maceo jumps back in when Renato is done. Towards the very end of the song, Prince says 'testing, one, two' through the two mics that are set up on the stage, the only time he 'sings' the entire show. Prince then takes off his coat and takes up his guitar and, facing the band and away from the audience, runs through a couple of licks — the first a snatch of 'When You Were Mine', then some more noodling before settling on a fantastic version of 'Brick House'. Prince is really leading things now, and it is just him, Morris, Cora and Josh for the most part, although Maceo takes a solo or two.

Time is also getting on. It must be about 4.45am, so he ups the tempo to round the show out. The song then morphs into 'Skin Tight' and I am totally grooving. Prince is taking his guitar right up to people's tables as he plays. The room has also filled in a little more at the section where it joins the other main dining room. There are now maybe another 30 people standing in the connecting entrances, making a grand total of maybe 70 people.

As the song shift gear again into 'Love Rollercoaster' I can no longer confine myself to my seat and just get up and start dancing, as several other folks have and, to my eternal delight, Prince looks over at me, checks me out, and gives me a good point out for my 'groover's manoeuvres'. Sweet as you like!

Wrapping that up, he then calls out 'What is Hip' and the band launches into a truly ferocious version of the song, with Prince's guitar lead taking most of the melody, instead of a voice. As the song ended, Prince handed his guitar to one of the people at the table directly adjacent to the stage, and got someone to wave their hat over it to cool it down. The crowd went nuts. Prince wandered about a little, but then wrapped things up with a 'thanks for coming'. Cora and Josh got some serious audience appreciation and I was as happy as can be. It was just past 5am.

I have to say that I was pretty sceptical about the whole Vegas thing, and there was a lot about the whole set-up that I was not keen on. Las Vegas is not a nice place, and the Rio is not all that nice either. That said, the restaurant was good, and the club format/layout is very cool. It is a huge circle, with table seating on two raised levels, where people who get the VIP package or table service can sit. The main concert was very cool although we were right at the back and, it being a round room, the place did not have the best acoustics for us.

'3121' is absolutely killer live - he did such a good version of this. I really liked 'Black Sweat' too. Prince did some deep keyboard grooves at the opening of this song. It was kind of odd to have Renato, Greg and Maceo back in the band (creating a horn section with Mike Phillips) and Rhonda came on in '3121' for a solo. Did Prince now think that the *One Nite Alone* band was one of his best and was trying to re-form it?

Or was he just bringing players in for fun?

I did wonder, though, how long he would have to do this for. It looked like the Rio had invested quite a bit in this whole thing and I couldn't see how 1,000 people two nights a week could bring in all that much revenue to keep a band and club running for weeks on end.

The after show was my fourth after Bagley's in '93, the second night at the Emporium in '95 and the Marquee in '04. Short of Prince coming to my house and singing me 'Happy Birthday', I could not have wished for a more intimate concert. I got the impression that this format was more like the *3121* thing that he ran at his house in LA - really small, no barriers between artist and audience, playing whatever takes his fancy to appreciative and knowledgeable folks. It must be a little tough to have to be 'Prince' all the time and I get the sense that this was what it was about for him, just playing great music without format or necessity to please anyone but himself and his friends. He did not play once Prince song this whole show, although the band played 'Gotta…'

That said, it really was the most amazing Prince concert I have ever witnessed. The musicianship was superb but it was the burning passion for excellence that really made the difference. They wanted to kick musical ass really hard and they did. Whilst I am sad that it was probably not recorded for posterity, I am so glad that I could be there to be a part of it. And thanks to Prince, for just being so cool (even if he didn't know the name of the jam I asked him about).

SUPERBOWL XLI DOLPHIN STADIUM

4 FEBRUARY 2007, MIAMI FLORIDA

I WAS THERE: BARBARA ROGERS

My husband and I run The Florida NPG Prince group. We and a few of our friends had the opportunity to be apart of Prince's Superbowl halftime show on February 4, 2007.

Barbara Rogers and other Florida fam helped out on the half time Superbowl show

We had two weeks of rehearsals before the actual show to learn how to put the stage together. It was their most complex stage design to that point. We all had to sign a NDA and everything was hush hush. We worked in the evenings at the now Hard Rock Stadium in the parking lot pushing heavy equipment together to form that amazing Prince symbol. It was the first time he ever used it.

It was hard work but so worth it once we got to the in stadium rehearsal with Prince and the band. It was during the day. There were drones flying over trying to get a look at the stage. They allowed us (stage crew) to sit in the stands and watch Prince's rehearsals. It was an amazing experience. We got to hear what he would be doing that night and when he got to 'Purple Rain' a lot of us were in tears. We were watching history being made. Once the rehearsals were over we disassembled the stage and took it off the field.

The day of the show we met at Nova University and were all transported to the stadium on buses with police escorts. We arrived and the night got stormy. We had recorded a dress rehearsal the day before in case of a rain out. We stood there waiting and most of us said, 'they would be crazy to let Prince play in this weather.' But then at the very last minute we were told to remove our rain ponchos - we were going on with the show! We were thinking, 'Well, if Prince can get wet so can we!' Out we went.

The magic you could feel. The history we were making we could feel. We were so unbelievably proud to be members of this Prince family. 'We Will Rock You' came on and we ran to the stage as instructed and danced and sang in the rain with our Prince!

Once it was over, we were all taken back in buses and had our after party where we received long sleeve shirts and a certificate of appreciation. We were showed the recording of the show and I remember standing there soaking wet, thinking that was the most incredible experience ever, knowing we just made history with Prince and something Prince fam would remember forever - the Superbowl Halftime Show in South Florida!

My Florida NPG family included myself, Qaid Rashid, Sandra Gall, Darla Wolak, Janis Burgin, Patricia Rabinovich and Antoine Copeland.

I WAS THERE: MARTIN BLENCO

I watched this on television. Prince played to 75,000 football fans and an estimated TV audience of 140 million. The 12 minute set was performed during a rainstorm and consisted of 'Let's Go Crazy', 'Baby I'm a Star' and a covers medley of 'Proud Mary', 'All Along the Watchtower' and the Foo Fighters' 'Best of You' before culminating in 'Purple Rain'. Or was it 'climaxing' in 'Purple Rain'? During that last number, Prince's shadow was projected onto a huge white screen and some people thought the silhouette of his symbol-shaped guitar resembled a giant phallus. I don't know about that, but his performance has been rated the best halftime Super Bowl show ever and it was pretty remarkable given the weather conditions. I wish we had an equivalent here in the UK. At the FA Cup Final, which also has a huge global TV audience, we have to make do with the massed bands of the Coldstream Guards marching up and down. It's not quite the same.

RIO HOTEL

13 JAN - 29 APRIL 2007, LAS VEGAS, NEVADA

I WAS THERE: JENNIFER HIGHLAND KING

This was my first show. I was five months pregnant. We waited a long time (standing room only) for him to come out. We were in about the fourth row so I saw him really up close! It was surreal. The first thing I thought was, 'He is so tiny!' He lit up the house and the twins shook it like they were going to break something. It was amazing. Otis thought about leaving early to get in line for the after show next door but decide to stay to the end. We got in line but didn't get into the after show. We were so bummed about that. I got no merch that night.

FIRST AVENUE

8 JULY 2007, MINNEAPOLIS, MINNESOTA

Prince was forced off stage by police halfway through his set at the First Avenue nightclub during a late-night gig in his home town. The club was only allowed to stay open until 3am but Prince took to the stage at 2.45am. The singer had already played two concerts in Minneapolis before his late-night club appearance. His first performance was at a department store, where he promoted his new cologne with a nine-song, 45-minute set.

On 15 July 2007 the UK music industry reacted angrily at a decision to give away Planet Earth, the new album by Prince, as a 'covermount' with the *Mail on Sunday* newspaper. The 10 track CD was not due to be released in stores until 24 July. Stephen Miron, the newspaper's managing director, said: 'No one has done this before. We have always given away CDs and DVDs, but this is just setting a new level.'

1 AUGUST 2007

Prince kicked off the *Earth* tour which took place in August and September 2007 and comprised 21 nights at London's O2 Arena with assorted after show appearances at the adjoining O2 Indigo. Tickets for the events cost £31.21 - the same figure used by the singer to name his album, website and perfume. After completing the *21 Nights* the Jehovah's Witness was planning to take time out to study the Bible.

O2 ARENA

1 AUGUST 2007, LONDON, UK

I WAS THERE: SAM BLEAZARD

In the latter part of his career Prince was definitely developing this idea of a residency and not in the cheesy Vegas way that Elvis did it. In recent years it's become acceptable with Britney Spears, Celine Dion, Elton John and others doing it. Prince was definitely developing this idea that he'd done a few times in America. He had this thing called the *3121* concert series where he would book a venue out and play a long residency that, a bit like Paisley Park, would allow him over two or three weeks to play loads of times and play whatever he wanted on given nights. He might have a main show and then late at night he would indulge himself, stretching out and playing jazz, funk, rock and soul, just experimenting to get it all out of his system.

Although he'd done a couple of those residency type things, *21 Nights* in London was a big thing. There were posters everywhere and the O2 was still a relatively new venue at the time. Only Justin Timberlake and Bon Jovi had played there. The O2 wasn't the massive success that it is now, so he was taking a bit of a risk. The exciting thing – and I think a lot of people missed this at the time – was that he would play a stadium show, but most nights he also played in the sister venue off to the side called the Indigo at the O2. I saw him five or six times in there. For the fans, that was an incredible experience, being able to see him twice in one night and also to see very different material played late at night.

80 or 85 per cent of the tickets for those arena shows were £31.21 because it was based around his album, *3121*. He deserves some credit for that pricing strategy.

The first night Prince played at the O2 was an amazing show. I was at the first and the last of the 21 nights and both were significant. The first night because he opened with 'Purple Rain', which was an unusual thing to do, but maybe a smart move in some ways. It was the kind of thing people might have been hanging on, waiting for him to play, but I'll never forget the first night and the crackle of anticipation. It was one of these brilliant stage sets in the middle, in the round. He came up on this platform to the opening chord of 'Purple Rain'.

That night also became famous for something else, which was that at the end of the show the house lights went up and people started emptying out of the arena. I'd say 75 per cent of people who were at the arena had left when, with all the house lights on, Prince popped back up with a guitar and started playing things like 'Raspberry Beret' on this little plinth. It caused pandemonium because hundreds of people started streaming back in, jumping over chairs and hurdling rows of seats. I just stayed where I was because I was in a reasonably good spot anyway. Obviously he'd got them to switch the PA back on, and he did this mini-set with his electric guitar. That was great, to hear him play songs like 'Little Red Corvette', just him and the guitar. There were a few shows after that where people were wondering whether he was going to come back on, and it became this big thing. I think he did it a few more times.

The first after show I went to on the opening night the band came out quite late on. They were playing lots of things you wouldn't expect, gospel music, such as the old spiritual song, 'Down by the Riverside' and stuff like that. I loved it because it was all horn-led.

Prince appeared briefly in a long trench coat with dark shades on, only coming onstage for a little bit. It was almost like he didn't want to give too much straight away. I went to a few after shows on that tour. Sometimes he would have musical guests. Sometimes he would have a rapper – Common was one of the guests - up jamming with him. On a couple of the nights, he would play even longer sets after hours than he played at the O2.

I WAS THERE: DANIEL PAYNE

The anticipation for these shows was big. I remember thinking when the dates were released, 'is he gonna be able to sell all out all of these shows?' Oh my, how wrong I was. His *21 Nights* all sold out.

Daniel Payne saw Prince at the O2

I was there for the opening night on 1 August. He started with 'Purple Rain' and ran through hit after hit after hit. It was not a question of if you were going to see Prince, but more like how many times were you going to see him? Tickets were only £31.21 each, after the album of the same name. I was there on 7 August too. This was an acoustic start to the show. I had front row seats! And on 14 August he performed '1999', which he had said he would never perform again.

I WAS THERE: SHANE WETTON

I had seen every Prince tour from *Parade* in '86 through to *The Ultimate Live Experience (Gold)* in '95 but 12 years had passed since I last saw him. I didn't see the *New Power Soul* tour, he only played two nights in London's Brixton Academy, nor did I see the *One Night*

Alone tour. In fact, life was such that I didn't even discover Prince had played two nights in Manchester until a few years later - I was that far out of the loop!

By 2007 I was in a new relationship and having spent a few years saying how Prince was the best live performer ever now was the time to prove it. My partner was a big Michael Jackson fan and had seen him twice - she wasn't a Prince fan at all. We were invited to a family wedding on 4th August and a few weeks beforehand Prince had announced the *21 Nights*. Great - we could combine the two!

I booked the first night, taking my partner and her two girls, both Michael Jackson fans. Would my promise of them being blown away be accurate? Prince was, after all, 12 years older. We arrived at the O2 one member of the party light as our youngest was going through a teenage rebellious stage which resulted in her not coming to the show or the wedding. Two big mistakes, but the three of us were there and I was the biggest kid of the lot. We'd arrived early, eaten and bought some merchandise. I bought a t-shirt with his image on the front and *21 Nights* printed on the back. Apparently Prince removed it from sale the next day having seen someone wearing it and deciding he didn't like it.

To say I was excited would be an understatement. I was literally rocking in my seat, so much so the lady behind me asked my partner, 'Is he excited, does he like him?' like I was 12 years old and wasn't there!

The *Rock and Roll Hall of Fame* video played, the excitement building, and then out of the darkness the opening strains of 'Purple Rain'. His voice, oh my God, his voice. My partner still to this day talks about how she first heard him sing live. She's now a big fan but remembers those first few moments. The show was funky, it was slick. The second song, 'Girls and Boys', was one of our youngest daughter's favourites. We immediately thought how much she would love it, how she should have been there but also how she would regret it one day. Our eldest had been listening to *Musicology* a lot and when he played it, it raised the roof. Hearing all the hits for the first time live in years was so special and something I'd started to think I wouldn't see again. A few oldies followed and then a long instrumental, 'What a Wonderful World', at which point I imagine Prince was getting a well earned break before kicking in to the second part of the show.

Some newer tracks – 'Satisfied', 'Lolita' and 'Black Sweat' - were mixed with 'Kiss', 'Take Me With You', 'If I Was Your Girlfriend', and then came the moment for my wife, '7'. She already liked the track and I'd been asked so many times, 'Will he play '7'?' She heard the song start: 'All 7 and we watch them fall...' and she was happy. The way the song faded in to 'Come Together ' was another surprise but as the song is one of our favourite songs anyway it made it all the more special.

Soon he was done apart from the encores – 'Planet Earth' followed and then a second encore, a cover of 'Crazy', 'Nothing Compares 2 U' and finishing with 'Let's Go Crazy'. Prince was done - or was he? Half the arena emptied. We sat down and then across the arena floor he appeared. He walked on to the stage, acoustic guitar in hand, and proceeded to play the most intimate 20 minute encore to an arena that was about one third full – 'Little Red Corvette', 'Rasberry Beret' and 'Sometimes it Snows in April', another of our youngest daughter's favourites. She was really going to regret this. She subsequently saw Prince twice but never saw him sing this or 'Girls and Boys'. A funky finish of 'Get on the Boat', 'A Love Bizarre' and 'Le Freak' with the full band and he was done. This time he was really done. We'd seen enough. Enough to convince us we had to get tickets for another show….

I WAS THERE: DEBBIE COLEMAN

I saw Prince live in London the after party with just 100 people. It was sensational - words can't describe it. I went with two friends after work as I'm a chef. What a wonderful night. I had a spare ticket and they saw a young man with a rucksack on his back and asked him if he would like a ticket to come in to see Prince. He couldn't believe it and as it happens he was a young chef. That thrilled me. He had no money. I bought him a few drinks and then he sent me a great big bunch of flowers.

I WAS THERE: MICHELLE HOWE

I saw him live six times and was honoured to be invited to his after show party at the 02 in London at which he kissed my hand. This was the second time he did this, the first being 20 years before at another concert in Glasgow.

I WAS THERE: JONATHAN JAMISON

I was lucky enough to see him eight or nine times. Some were multiple on the same tour. My son who is 29 also saw him twice. I was also part of a fanzine called *Controversy* which was brilliant.

Summer '84 was first time I came across Prince. I was 15 years old and not really interested in music much. I was asked if I fancied going to see *Purple Rain* at the cinema but chose *Police Academy* instead! Later that summer I realised the error of my ways. I can remember revising for exams that summer and hearing 'Let's Go Crazy' on the radio and thinking, 'I like that….' After that I started to look around for his music and bought some vinyl - *Purple Rain*, then *1999*. I recorded them on tape and played that tape to death. I worked part time in a shoe shop while at school and spent every penny on his back catalogue. I remember the day *Around the World in a Day* came out. I bought it on vinyl and cassette. I was also lucky enough to get some picture discs too and basically bought everything I could, kept every newspaper cutting and recorded anything I could on VHS.

About 1987 I found out about a fanzine called *Controversy* which was put together by a lady from Croydon in the UK. It was fantastic and provided lots of information from within the Prince camp. Eventually, I'm sure, it was endorsed by him and they organised a few trips to Paisley Park.

I had a ticket for the *Sign o' the Times* tour date which was cancelled. I think my first concert was 1988 and the *Lovesexy* tour. I can't remember much about it other than I saw it multiple times and was very impressed. The next tour I saw was the *Nude* tour in 1990. Again, I attended multiple shows at different venues.

I don't have a *Diamonds & Pearls* tour programme. I have no idea why because I saw him at Glasgow and Manchester. After that, there was a huge gap until I saw him during

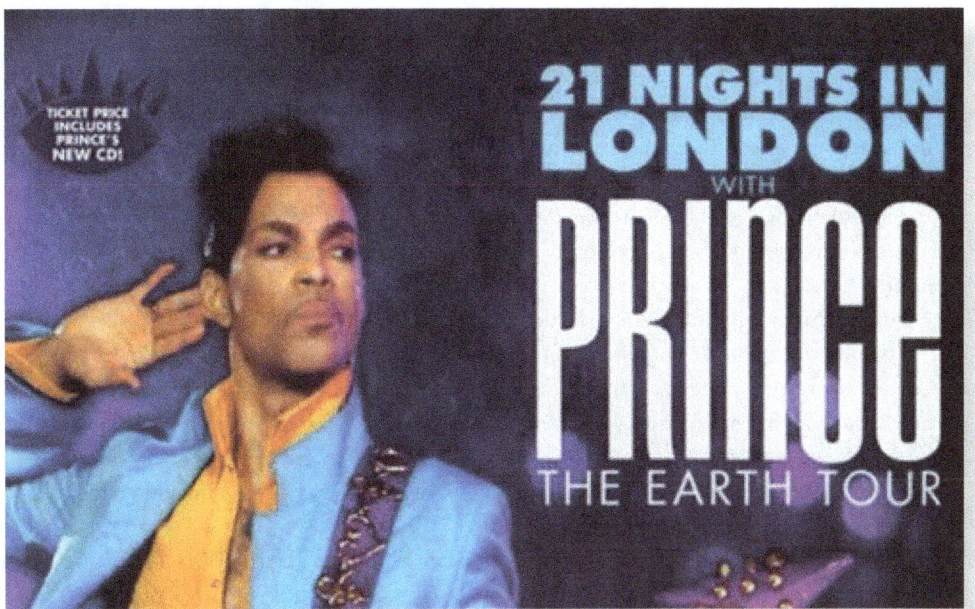

his *21 Nights* at the O2 arena 2007. This is a concert I remember very well. I took my son who was in awe at Prince live. It was an amazing night. The last time I saw him was on the *Hit and Run* tour in 2014. I can remember sitting at my computer on the day tickets went on sale and feeling so happy when I got them. This was a superb concert and he was in great form.

I prefer Prince's early music and wish I'd seen the *Dirty Mind* and *Purple Rain* concerts but feel lucky to have seen him as many times as I did.

I WAS THERE: LEEMAN JONES

Never see your heroes live as it can be disappointing. He was on a circular stage and came over to our side maybe twice. I've been a fan since 1981 and have loads of concert footage and was expecting better. Now I realise it was probably down to the pain he was suffering from. I'm glad I got to see him live and I will always be a Prince fan.

I WAS THERE: GINA JOYCE

By 2007 I had accumulated three medium-sized lidded chests full of bootleg discs, DVDs and audio. News of the *21 Nights in London* 02 *Earth* tour suddenly broke. He was coming to London again, but for 21 shows? Very exciting stuff. I was aged 52 at this point. I paid £300 for a pair of tickets off eBay for 10th August for my daughter and myself. They seemed to have better seats available than the usual ticket agents, but at a cost. I'd carefully double checked the 02 block/seating plan this time after Wembley.

Beverley Knight was the support act and sung her heart out. Prince was amazing, 'Controversy', 'Musicology' and 'Purple Rain' were my highlights. 'Play That Funky Music' whipped the fans into a frenzy and there was an encore of 'Crazy' with the brilliant Shelby J.

I ended up going another three times. Elton John made an appearance on 13th September, singing 'The Long and Winding Road'.

My husband came with me twice, my daughter once, and my youngest sister and husband were also with my husband and I for the final night on 21st September, towards the front.

The atmosphere was particularly electric on the final night, with Sky News broadcasting the opening 'I Feel for You'/'Controversy' live, the twins doing cartwheels in high heels across the stage, everyone with purple glow sticks and a mass of fans, including Prince, all jumping up and down to 'The Quake'.

I've always regretted not going to the Indigo at the O2 for at least one of his legendary after shows during the *Earth* tour, but having spent so much money already on the arena tickets we couldn't afford it. My husband has never been a Prince fan as such, although 'Purple Rain' is one of his favourite songs, but he never, ever complained about the money spent on tickets. He knew I couldn't help myself! It was a real come down for me after the *Earth* tour concerts finished.

After this I became even more obsessed, constantly on eBay (before Web Sheriff got involved via Prince), the Internet looking for bootlegs, either audio or DVD, of those O2 concerts, so I could relive them all. I was told by a Prince fan about a stall in Camden Market in London and a bloke who sold concert bootlegs. One Sunday my husband and I found him at Camden Market and I bought two O2 DVDs at £15 each – amazing! I eventually ended up with all of the O2 shows on DVD and audio.

I WAS THERE: PAULA SEWARD

Unfortunately I only saw Prince live once, when he did the long residency at the O2. I always assumed that I would be able to see him again. Obviously, it was the best concert of my life.

I WAS THERE: MARTIN BLENCO

We were up in the gods at the O2, which is never a great place to watch a show from. Prince was just a purple speck in the distance. In fact, he was so far away I don't even know if he was wearing purple. All I remember is the woman sat next to us was incredibly pissed and couldn't dance to save her life. But she didn't let that stop her!

I WAS THERE: SHELL JOHNSTON

I first got into Prince when I first heard '1999'. I loved him from the start. I was lucky enough to see him four times before he died. A memorable concert was when he announced the *21 Nights* in the O2 in London. I live in Glasgow in Scotland and had just come back from holiday so money was tight but luckily I scraped enough money to go so, waiting patiently for the tickets to go on sale, when they did I tried and tried to get through to get tickets.

Shell Johnston is Prince

When I eventually got through, I said to the guy on the phone, 'Hi, I'm looking to book six tickets for Prince at the O2,' only to be told, 'Sorry, they have sold out.' You can imagine how I felt. I was just about to say 'okay, thanks' when he announced, 'Hey, hold it - they have just added more dates.' I could have kissed him. So I got the tickets and was so excited.

To this day that gig is my all time favourite, and I've been to loads of gigs. The last time I saw Prince was when he came to Glasgow 2014. What a great gig that was. I felt as if it was only me and him there that night but when I heard he was coming to Glasgow I phoned my niece (who is also a fan), screaming down the phone that he was coming to Glasgow. She was at school collecting her child and said everyone could hear me!

When Prince announced he was bringing the *Piano & A Microphone* tour to Glasgow excited wasn't the word. On the day they were to go on sale I had two computers and three phones all set up to try for tickets, only for it to be cancelled or postponed because of touts putting them up for sale before they had even been sold. So alas that show never happened. But at least I had the pleasure of seeing him four times and they are times I cherish.

I WAS THERE: CHRISTOPHER GRIFFITHS

Being born in the late 1980s and growing up in the Nineties, I was more than aware of Prince from a young age, but not for the right reasons sadly. Michael Jackson was very much a dominant figure of music industry as far as I was concerned, from repeat plays of *Thriller* at Halloween discos, to one of my earliest memories being the ever-present *Black or White* on the TV.

As far as Prince was concerned, he was the weird guy that looked like a woman, changed his name to a symbol and 'had his lower ribs removed so he could perform sex acts on himself' according to the word on the school playground. I had very little awareness beyond that.

Late 2004 and it was at 16 years old when I heard '1999' play in a bar and in quick succession heard other key tracks like 'When Doves Cry' and 'Kiss' play on radio stations and at house parties, and I found myself quickly becoming a fan. It was a strange situation for me admitting that I liked that 'weirdo who performed sex acts on himself' but the love of this music was far greater than my worry of what people would think. Within a year I had amassed the majority of his albums and the name Prince had become synonymous with me as far as friends and family were concerned.

My journey through Prince's catalogue was incredible, discovering his musical path and how, to this day, there is a track or album than can cater for all my musical tastes; funk, rock, blues, R&B, jazz, soul and even hip hop. I underwent research reading all the books and documentaries I could find to get a better understanding of how this genius came to be. Then there was a whole other world of unreleased materials and live performances. I was in awe of the man's work ethic and craftsmanship and it was because of him I started to grow a massive appreciation of music.

Having found a few physical bootlegs and searching high and low on the likes of

Limewire and *Kazaa*, my new interest had quickly become an obsessive treasure hunt and there was so much to be discovered! Now, all that was left was to do was see the man in the flesh, although by 2005, it had been a number of years since his last UK visit and there appeared to be nothing on the horizon…

I had to wait three years before one day opening my phone at work and finding somewhere in the region of 20 text messages from friends and family informing me that he's finally coming to the UK and what's more, he's performing multiple nights at the newly opened O2 Arena! To say I was excited was an understatement. I was fortunate enough to book two nights, one with my friends who had heard enough of my preaching and one with my mother, who all endured my preaching on the word of Prince. I feel greatly fortunate that my first time would have the epic backdrop of 2006 and 2007 as a Prince fan; a number one album (*3121*), his show stopping halftime performance at the Super Bowl XLI and finally at a record breaking event of *21 Nights* in the O2 Arena.

There was coverage left, right and centre and finally on the day of August 10th, 2007 I was making my way up from Cardiff with my friends to London. I could barely keep myself together when boarding the Jubilee Line tube and heading to North Greenwich station, where the walls were plastered with Prince posters. It was all becoming real. Sat right in the gods of the 20,000 seat arena for the unbelievably insane price of £31.21, the excitement was palpable and having been a huge fan of the album, the lights went down and the heavy synthesised bass of '3121' started pounding across the arena, with the horn section of the band making their way through the stalls up to the illuminated symbol stage.

I was so excited I accidentally hit the head of the guy in front of me when shooting up out of my seat. The show itself was good and had some great unique moments including the opening track and even hearing songs like 'The Dance (instrumental)' and 'Get On The Boat' as the closing number, but whilst this was my first encounter with a Prince concert it certainly not be my last and today is not in my top three shows.

Nonetheless hearing all these songs I had played a million times in an arena environment was incredible. Then came the after show. I am more than aware how lucky I was as a 'newbie' that I got to see a main set and after show the same night in the Indigo2 Club. Not only did I get to experience the epicness of a Prince arena show, but also the intimacy and spontaneity of one of his infamous after shows, supported by Beverly Knight, her band performing extended jams of '3121' and 'Controversy' amongst other things. I had managed to prove to my friends why I was obsessed with Prince.

From this point on there would not be one tour or visit that I would miss and following a second attendance at the O2 Arena on September 1st with yet another after show, I would be dropping plans and spending money I didn't have on following him around. I would visit Copenhagen to catch his headlining slot at the 2010 Roskilde Festival, his debut and only show in Poland at the Heineken Open'er Festival the following year and a week after make a 24 hour trip to see Night Three of his shows at the North Sea Jazz Festival in Rotterdam on the promise that it would feature a unique set list, which it sure as hell did. Added to that, I would meet a lifelong friend whom is equally if not more obsessed than I.

I would not encounter a Prince show again until 2014 when I had to get out of work early on a Wednesday afternoon as the media was ablaze with sightings of 'The Purple One' across London performing a series of spontaneous mini shows in small venues like a 15 minute preview with his new band 3RDEYEGIRL at the Electric Ballroom, Camden. This would be labeled as the *Hit and Run* tour.

Like the adventure of discovering his back catalogue and unreleased materials, the hunt was back on to find where he would be performing one evening in the country's capital. Luckily I worked in Milton Keynes so only had a 40 minute train journey to get there. For the next few weeks I was keeping a close eye on social media and jumping at the last second to catch this whole new garage band style of Prince with his new group. I was fortunate enough to catch the second show at the Electric Ballroom and the second epic lengthened show at Koko the following week. It would only be a few months later that he would bring his group back to the UK to perform the *Hit and Run II* tour for the arena audiences. Two shows in Manchester and a freebie ticket to the Birmingham show led to me seeing him five times within the space of a few months.

I WAS THERE: KAYUM ABDUL

I went to a few after shows. We also went to see him at Koko for the one off gigs he did in 2014. We waited outside for six hours. I was at one of his after shows, waiting to see Prince not knowing whether he will play that evening or not. And once we saw the pedals being placed on the floor we knew he was going to show. So there I was at the front of the stage, Prince in full swing, when suddenly he stepped down and started talking to his assistant, a lady with short hair and glasses. He had his shades on and he took them off to speak to her and I was standing right next to them. I looked at Prince and thought, 'Wow, he has amazing eyes' (this coming from a heterosexual) when suddenly he looked straight at me and gave me a look like 'what the fuck are you looking at?' He was wearing a yellow jumpsuit with a hood.

I WAS THERE: SARAH HOWKINS

I saw him live twice. The first one was in the Eighties and then I saw him at the O2. For the Eighties one I wore a handmade zebra mini dress in black and white. On visiting the toilet my zipper broke. I was begging for safety pins or someone to lend me their cardigan but no one helped me. I just needed to get back to my seat and put my new

Prince t-shirt on I was clutching my dress together to stay on, feeling everyone watching me and very embarrassed. On that note, the song 'Gett Off' has the lyric 'I heard that rip when you sat down, let me work on that zipper.' It reminds me of what happened and I like to think I may have been the inspiration for his lyric - in my dreams!

For the O2 tour I made a banner which said 'Rave to the joy fantastic' amongst other things out of a lilac bedsheet. I hung it over the rails at the end, shaking the musicians' hands and telling them how talented they were. The concert was electric and I loved every minute.

Prince was so amazing - the energy of his dancing, his sexy voice, his dress sense, as a musician, composer, producer, his behind the scenes charitable deeds, his humour, his battle with Warner Bros, in his later years the spiritual messages in his songs. Nothing compares to him.

He has a song, 'Sarah'. In my dreams I like to imagine it's written about me and that he secretly found out who I was and knew about the embarrassing dress malfunction.

INDIGO AT THE O2

9 SEPTEMBER 2007, LONDON, UK

I WAS THERE: NADEEM MASOOD

This was a truly unbelievable after show that seemed to go on and on. There are a few things I remember about it, which may conjure up some memories for other people present. The show kicked off with each band member taking turns to appear on stage and getting things going. Prince came on last; he just casually walked on, wearing a pair of shades. He looked very cool and the band eased their way along with a rendition of 'Footprints'.

After Sade's 'Cherish the Day' the band performed 'The World is a Ghetto'. The horn players each got a solo, at which point Prince took a place on the left of the stage and just stood there, attentively watching (and seemingly learning), giving nods of approval and sometimes even applauding. It was great to see this incredible musician offering his band members so much respect and just enjoying what they were bringing to the stage.

A few songs later, and following the funk jam of 'All the Critics Love You in London', the opening groove of 'Chelsea Rodgers' kicked in, which was quite a moment as the crowd went crazy. I was hoping he would play it, knowing that he'd done so at previous after shows and also the last two main gigs. This was going to be a special night, evidenced only too well by the frenetic closing jam that ended 'I Wanna Take You Higher'. Already it seemed like they would be wrapping up soon, but Prince had other ideas. Before long the lights went down, Prince reappeared centre stage and demonstrated that there is indeed 'Joy in Repetition'. Just the fact that I was finally getting to hear this song made my night. The intro was slow tempo with the vocals almost spoken. One of the Twinz added backing vocals and the eventual guitar solo was fantastic, although I was a tiny bit disappointed that it didn't go on for longer, like some of his performances of this song, most notably the version he released in the *One Nite Alone* boxset.

The band then performed Tower Of Power's 'What is Hip?' during which Prince dropped his plectrum. Totally unphased, he simply continued strumming, made his way over to the mic stand, picked up another one, and seamlessly played on. Jam followed funky jam and by now people clearly didn't want this to end, and neither did Prince, explaining to the crowd that it was '...an energy exchange. You give to us, we give to you.' He wanted to hang out tonight. When 'Sweet Thing' kicked in, with Marva King on vocals, I realised that he was serious; surely he wasn't going to end the night here, so there was still more to come afterwards. I couldn't believe my luck. We were already approaching two hours.

'The Question of U' intro on guitar began. When he stopped, to go into 'The One', there were a few shouts of dismay from the crowd, who clearly wanted to hear more of 'The Question of U'. Maybe this is why he followed 'The One'/'Fallin'' with the familiar guitar solo, which he hadn't done when performing the medley at the main shows thus far. A very pleasant and welcome surprise.

After the sing-along classic 'Girls and Boys' there was another pause before the band returned for a fast tempo version of '3121', which included various intro pieces and a great guitar solo by the man himself. The near-endless show concluded in exactly the same way that the main show had done, with 'I Feel For You' and 'Controversy'. What an after show! Was it really 3am? Two and a half hours after it all began!

Prince was known for being unpredictable live, but tonight was completely unprecedented. After a blistering main show which lasted almost two hours, he came back on stage a few hours later and performed an incredibly varied set for even longer. Jamming effortlessly, he performed his own songs, covered established classics with his trademark Minneapolis sound, treated us to soulful ballads, blew the roof off with his guitar, and showcased his incredible band who supported him so capably throughout this marathon performance. I feel so privileged to have been in that room on that night, and witnessed the only man on the planet who could pull off such a feat with barely a single bead of perspiration breaking from his funk/rock/soul/jazz/blues brow. Genius.

I WAS THERE: CAMILLA NARVIK, AGE 37

I live in a small town in Sweden. 13th of September 2007 was the day I saw Prince live at the O2 Arena in London for his *21 Nights* show. I got goose bumps all over my body - what a great show! I remember the stage in the shape of the symbol and this guy singing and performing in front of us. What I remember the most is that he was playing 'A Love Bizzare' and everyone was singing and dancing. I was 37 at the time and I went alone to see the show. Prince has always been my huge inspiration since a long time. I feel lucky and blessed to have seen him live. I love Prince because he always went his own way and he made all this funky music. He had a good eye for fashion and a good ear for music. As he said, 'I am music'. 2019 was a great purple Prince year for me. I saw The Revolution in Stockholm and NPG in London. I also celebrated my 50th birthday and my birthday gift is to fly to Minneapolis and visit Paisley Park! The best birthday present ever.

Prince - thank you for all the great music you have given us.

I WAS THERE: DANIEL PAYNE

On 9 September 2007, he played the same amazing set list as he played at the Superbowl – 'We Will Rock You', 'Let's Go Crazy', 'Baby I'm A Star', 'Proud Mary' including the instrumental intro to '1999', 'All Along The Watchtower' and the Foo Fighters cover, 'Best of You'. On 13 September he did another electrifying show. Shelby J performed a fantastic mix of Cee-Lo Green's 'Crazy' which included Kylie Minogue's 'Can't Get You Out Of My Head' with special guest Elton John guesting on 'The Long and Winding Road' and a blistering encore (after the lights had gone on) of 'A Love Bizarre' and 'Chelsea Rodgers'.

That night I also went to my first ever Prince after show and there was also no promise he would perform. But after a couple of hours I could hear them testing his guitar, etc. The atmosphere was great with people still buzzing from his blistering show at the O2. Then what followed was one of my best ever Prince experiences. Being only three people away from the front of the stage I heard the ethereal sound of 'The Dance' and then 'Around the World in a Day' and in he walked. He then went on to perform an array of non-hits, with a selection of obscure tracks like 'Beautiful Strange', 'Paisley Park (instrumental)', Me'Shell Ndegeocello's 'Who Is He (And What Is He To You?)' and 'Partyup' while Shelby J did a mind blowing performance of 'Misty Blue' in which Prince walked to the side of the stage and shouted out - which you can hear on the bootleg.

The band was beyond tight and Marva King worked the crowd into a frenzy! It felt like you had been invited into his own personal living room for a private party and we were so close to the stage – it really was the most amazing experience. The sound quality was superb and the set list was just superb.

And if that was not enough, while waiting for the Thames Clipper to take us home we were waiting by the gates at the O2 and then a limousine pulled up and myself and about nine other fans just started screaming. There was a camera crew and we were being filmed – Prince then opened the window and popped his head out, sucking a lollipop and we just went crazy! Boy, would I like to see that footage!

I WAS THERE: KATRINA TAIBE

The 2007 shows are very special, but surreal to me as they happened at a really difficult time in my life. In June of that year I found out that my dad had Stage 4 lung cancer, so I had moved in with him. I tried to see Prince whenever he was in the UK since being taken to see him when I was 10 years old at Wembley Arena. My dad had taken me to my third and fourth Prince gigs during the *Diamonds & Pearls* tour, where he had remarked that Prince had great dancing girls!

I had initially bought five tickets for the *21 Nights* shows - the first night, one date in the middle and the last night, plus a couple of the after shows. I ended up going to 18 main shows and 15 after shows! It was a crazy few weeks, but I was so grateful to be able to totally escape from what was going on in my reality for a few hours, doing what I loved most. I loved coming back home to chat to my dad about the shows, usually after an after show so getting in around 4am, and he thought it was brilliant that Prince was still able to do a couple of shows a night like it was no big deal.

My dad passed away on 27th August and through my dazed grief I kept going to the shows. It was a relief to let out tears and be moved by music, not just my personal sadness. My dad's funeral was the day before my 28th birthday on September 13th. I had a ticket I wasn't going to use that evening, but my mum encouraged me to go. Elton John performed with Prince at that show, which my dad would have found 'a trip'. I met up with a friend after the show and he managed to sweet talk one of the door staff to let us in to the after show at Indigo2 later that night. We got in to the venue and took our seats upstairs when Renato Neto led the opening performance of an instrumental of 'The Dance'. I then heard a strangely familiar sitar like tune… we couldn't believe it! 'Around the World in a Day' and then 'Beautiful Strange' ran to nearly 30 minutes. It was almost a relief when things changed up a gear for 'Whole Lotta Love' and we were then teased with a snippet of 'Paisley Park'. I remember thinking how lucky I had been to get a ticket that night. Toward the end of the set Prince asked, 'Who's making pancakes this morning?' before ending the show with 'Musicology'. It was my birthday morning and I couldn't help but allow myself to think that someone had organised an extra special birthday gift for me.

I WAS THERE: BELLE DAISY

I've been a huge fan of Prince for 30 years, since I was 14. I was fortunate enough to see him in London on the *3121* tour in 2007 and also at the Hydro in Glasgow a couple of years before he died. He was absolutely amazing and a tremendous performer. The boy that was my first love at 16 was the one that introduced me to Prince when I was 14. I watched the *Live in Syracuse* VHS video and it absolutely changed my life. I was a big Michael Jackson and Motown/soul fan before that but it all went out the window from that day. I am saving my pennies to go to Paisley Park in 2021. It's top of my bucket list. It will cost me £800 to get to Minneapolis from Scotland and $40 to get in. Bargain. Sort of. I'll need $5,000 to spend in the gift shop, so I'm saving my pennies!

I WAS THERE: MARK WARE

Having attended two of the main 02 Arena gigs as part of the *21 Nights* in London summer of gigs, I attended the final after show at The Indigo (which became the *Indigo Nights* CD). When Amy Winehouse joined Prince on stage for 'Love is a Losing Game' it sent chills down my spine.

I WAS THERE: SAM BLEAZARD

I saw Prince play with Amy Winehouse. At the time it seemed quite a thing. But now it seems really loaded with significance. Nobody could have predicted that they would both be dead in such a short space of time, although it was clear that Amy Winehouse was quite a troubled person even then.

On the final night there was a great atmosphere because Prince had completed his 21 night run. There was this amazing noise in the dark and people were swinging these glow sticks around, which had been given out on arrival. It took Prince quite a while to come on. During the wait somebody threw their glow stick onto the stage and all of a sudden hundreds of people just started throwing them through the air, so they were bouncing on to his symbol-shaped stage in the dark. They were raining in. I was thinking, 'Oh dear, this is terrible, Prince is going to hate this, and he's not going to play his show!' It had a really weird effect with all these lights being thrown through the air, but the audience needn't have worried.

Eventually these were cleared away and when he came out he was in celebratory mood. He had a t-shirt on over the top of his suit and it had '21' written on it in lipstick and he tore it off at one point. Sky News was there and they broadcast six or seven minutes of the show on the night because it was such a historic thing. At the after show there was a real sense of anticipation and we were thinking, 'What's going to happen here?' I'd seen one after show when Beverley Knight was on with her band and Prince surprised her by turning up with his group.

I can remember the little velvet curtain going back and Amy Winehouse wandering out. She was already a massive star. There was a lot of screaming and people were wondering what she was going to do. I could see different members of Prince's band in the wings, and Blake Fielder-Civil, Amy's boyfriend.

You could have heard a pin drop and Prince wandered out with his blue cloud guitar, which he called the Blue Angel - it was a metallic blue version of his white 'Purple Rain' guitar. He came out with shades on and he didn't say anything, but was giving instructions to the band. They played 'Love is a Losing Game' off Amy Winehouse's *Back to Black* album and Prince accompanied her on guitar. He gave the stage over to her, and it was quite a moment. Prince then got visibly emotional and looked like he was dabbing a tear from his eye. I don't think it was a staged thing. And he made a short speech, saying, 'This girl's an incredible talent and you need to look after her.' He seemed to be saying it's your responsibility to not let this girl fade away. So it was quite a moment and I think anybody who was there will remember that so clearly. To say you saw those two performers on stage together is quite an amazing thing, especially given the fact that neither of them are still around. It was definitely one of those goosebump moments, and it is every time I think about it.

Beverley Knight was another musical guest who joined Prince onstage later in the set, performing a high octane cover of Aretha Franklin's 'Rock Steady'. Prince was in superb form, and seemed to be driving his guests to new heights as well. He was performing all kinds of stuff as the night wore on, including Janet Jackson's 'What Have You Done for Me Lately?' He was certainly in a mischievous mood and played really late – I almost got the feeling he was trying to burn the crowd out! I remember spilling out of there at about four in the morning and being so tired, because I'd been to quite a few concerts. I felt like, 'Okay, you've beaten me. I'm exhausted. I can't keep up with you any more.'

There really was some amazing stuff in that run. 2007 was such a great opportunity to see Prince, either in a stadium show or in a club environment. I just wish people who were passing fans had taken more advantage of it, as I don't think people realised how good he was. In my opinion he was the best artist of his generation.

I WAS THERE: GARETH HOWELLS

It was never the same gig twice. I was lucky enough to see him ten times, and all of those gigs couldn't have been more distinctive experiences; whether it was the festival set at Hop Farm, the funk jam in the mid-90s at Brixton Academy, or the incredible 'pop up' nights with 3RDEYEGIRL, there was always the sense that he was being immensely spontaneous and honest in his performances. He didn't always play to the audience, which could be frustrating, if you were desperate to hear a moment of 'Sometimes it Snows' or 'Dolphin' or 'I'm Yours', but that was part of the magic too. You didn't know what you were getting, but you knew he was always on top form, and always delivered an astounding performance every night he played.

My favourite shows were the 3RDEYEGIRL shows, simply because they were my favourite collaborators working behind him (and alongside him unusually) but, despite this, the one show that always makes me smile when I think of him, is the after show that followed the last night of the 21 nights at the O2.

He had already given us a powerful, emotive and extravagant set at the main O2, then rumours began to circulate that he was definitely going to be performing an after show at the Indigo venue next door. We had tickets already just in case, but clearly the news that he was definitely appearing was very exciting. What we didn't expect was a phenomenal experience watching him play some of the most unexpected, obscure songs from his catalogue that you didn't get to see in his main shows. This set displayed a man totally in the moment, very happy to be exercising the freedom he felt from playing an after show in front of the kind of fans that would recognise the most obscure songs. It was one revelation after another, with a surprise duet with Amy Winehouse in the middle of it. He freely jammed for hours, finally ending the set as the morning was fast approaching 5am. We had been in the Indigo, with our eyes glued to the stage, from 1am to 5am, after seeing him doing a full set at the O2 from 9pm earlier that night. We were exhausted, but we had experienced something truly unforgettable. I can't think of another artist that would give his audience the chance to see him from 9pm until 5am with a couple of hours gap in the middle when we queued up to settle into the Indigo next door.

Saying an artist is a one-off, or a genius is often banded about, perhaps a bit too frivolously. In the case of Prince, it is absolutely true for so many reasons. I will treasure the memories of those gigs where I saw this unique and endlessly creative man explore his musicality in front of us whenever we could get to see him. His songs and his example will stay in our present lives for a very long time.

I WAS THERE: NIGEL HART

Perhaps his most iconic London Shows were those performed 'in the round' during his *21 Night* residency at London's O2 Arena in 2007. All tickets were just £31.21 (*3121* being the title of his latest album at the time). This guaranteed a sell out crowd for every show and I managed to attend at least ten main shows along with six after shows in the smaller Indigo Club within the O2 complex that would follow his main arena shows each night.

Every single show was different, set lists being decided just half an hour before show time, as Prince kept his polished band on their toes. Seeing him hold an audience of 20,000 mesmerised in the palm of his hand each evening, sometimes for nearly three hours, and then to treat those of us lucky enough to witness one of his intimate after shows, where we could literally see the whites of his eyes as he relaxed and tore into rocked up guitar jams of 'Anotherloverholenyohead' or 'Bambi' amongst others was just a joy to behold.

I vividly remember on the last night, 21st September 2007, he played his final arena show for over three hours and then treated us to a further three hours at The Indigo, with Amy Winehouse and Beverley Knight in tow.

His energy and drive were relentless and other wordly and his performance like no other mortal or performer before him.

I WAS THERE: LISA INGHAM

I was 16 in 1982 when I first became a Prince fan, pretty much from the beginning. But I didn't go to a tour until 1990 and the *Nude* tour. At the gig I got second row. The usher walked me down and said 'that's your seat' and I was with my husband and I said, 'Are you having a laugh?' So I spent most of my time staring with my mouth open and crying. This was at Wembley. My husband used to drive me up to Birmingham from Brighton - he's not a big fan. Then for a few years I didn't see him but I saw him in '92 and '95 and then not until *21 Nights*, which I took my daughter to. We managed to stand together and sing 'Purple Rain' with him.

Lisa Ingham saw Prince at the O2

I WAS THERE: KIM WATERS

When Prince announced he was going to do *21 Nights* at the O2 in London we very excited as we had seen him many times before. My first time was *Lovesexy* when I was 16. Tony's was *Parade*. The *21 Nights* announcement meant our three children - Kerry, Lee and Cheryl - could go, although Cheryl had to miss the after shows as she wasn't 18. They had grown up with his music and knew he was something very special. Tony and I knew we would be going, but we did not know how many times. How lucky we were to be able to go to 15 main shows and 11 after shows considering that at that time we were living in Cleethorpes, a four hour drive each way.

The concerts started around 9pm and finished about 11pm. The after shows could start from 1am onwards and finish as late as 4.30am. With a four hour drive home we were ready for bed and sometimes we were going back the same day to do it all over again. The tickets were easy to get but not always the best seats. As you could print your own tickets, we kept reprinting our floor tickets and would cut the seat and level numbers off and stick them on that day's ticket. That being said it then meant you hadn't got a seat but as it was on the floor you moved about and we always found somewhere we could stand.

The staff at the 02 must have been army trained as you could hardly move from your seat. How we got away with it we will never know. But it was all worth it for we knew we were going to see something very special and have an amazing time.

One of the times, when Lee came with us we hired him a wheelchair so we could go in the disabled bay. We were the only ones in there. (He did volunteer). Then after the show Tony wheeled him back to the car while I got in the queue for the after show and waited for them. At the end of most of the main shows, if you waited around Prince would come back and do a few more songs.

By that time there was hardly anyone left and you could move down to the stage, which was in the centre. Standing there watching him perform to a small crowd you could see how much he loved it, knowing that people would wait for him to come back on.

He looked amazing every night and all through the *21 Nights* he had photos taken for a book he was doing. He hardly ever had a support act, which was good because some of them were really bad! But he had Beverley Knight as a support for two shows (Friday and Saturday) and she was very good and sang at the after shows both nights. When she was on stage with Prince at the Saturday after show she was moved to tears as she is a big Prince fan.

One of the nights we saw Elton John sitting in the audience and were surprised when he got up and sang 'The Long and Winding Road' while Prince played guitar.

We had the time of our lives. We were very sad when it all came to an end. We didn't go to the last night as were on holiday which was a shame as the after show that night was very good. But we can't complain as we did see some amazing shows. The after shows were as good and sometimes better than the main show.

I WAS THERE: SUE MITCHELL

I saw him six times, maybe more. When *Purple Rain* came out at the cinema in 1984, I went with a friend as I'd heard him on the radio. After the movie that was that, pocket money spent on the album which my dad hid away after a few weeks so I had to save and buy again! I had all his music on cassette and then vinyl and CD. I didn't really have any friends who were massive fans like myself, so I had no one to talk to about his music really. My dad did, and still does, call him 'the purple dwarf' - parents!

I went and saw him in Manchester on the *Lovesexy* tour with my then boyfriend (now husband) who also isn't a fan but enjoys some of his music and I remember being on his shoulders and Prince coming out playing that guitar and doing the splits.

I went to see him in Birmingham some years later when it was just him and a guitar and he was playing jazz and there were all cushions on stage. It was a very intimate setting due to it being a small venue. I loved it!

The next huge concert was *21 Nights* at the 02. How I would have loved to have been at a seat at the front of the stage but I think I may have cried or fainted. I went to a few gigs in between and the first and the 02 are the stand out gigs. I loved his style and the fact that he could change who or how he felt or was at the drop of a hat and not be bothered about what anyone said. And what a talent!

I remember the first interview in which I heard him speaking. I couldn't believe how deep his voice was. When I read he had launched his '3121' perfume in Macy's my hubby bought me a set (which is still in its box, unopened) and two smaller bottles so I could wear it (that's all gone now) and also the coffee table book full of amazing pictures.

I heard on the radio about his passing. I was driving. I didn't believe it. Within two minutes my dad rang me and I had a load of texts from friends who knew I was a massive fan. I still can't believe I'll never get to see him play live again.

I asked my nephew if he had anyone he ever wanted to meet that would be like a dream but which was never likely to happen and he named a footballer. Well, mine was Prince. Meeting him would have rendered me speechless and likely to faint if he spoke or even looked at me. That's my love affair with a beautiful, talented and misunderstood man who so many men assume was gay. Helloooo!?

I WAS THERE: DANIEL PAYNE

The final night of his legendary 21 night run at the O2 Arena and anticipation for this gig was off the scale. A Prince fan group was selling purple glow sticks outside of the show for all fans to light up during the gig. The opening of the show and the first two numbers were going to be broadcast live on Sky News. The atmosphere again was just electric!

Prince came on and ran effortlessly through 'I Feel for You' and 'Controversy'. The crowd just went crazy. He also performed 'Somewhere Here on Earth' and ended the gig with an encore of blistering version of 'Girls and Boys'. Three quarters of the way through the show, the dancers sprayed '21' in in red spray paint on Prince's back. Showing what a legend he was, during his mammoth run of gigs Prince also squeezed in filming a promotional video for the 'Somewhere Here On Earth' in Prague and also regularly had photo shoots with Randee St Nicholas who made the book, *21 Nights*.

I WAS THERE: NICOLA WAKLEY-WAKE

The next time I saw him was on the *Earth* tour and his *21 Nights* at the O2 Arena in London in 2007. In all honesty I was very disappointed in his performance. The stage was amazing and the setting was great but he didn't deliver like I'd hoped. He sang a few amazing songs and the atmosphere was electric but then he would leave the stage, then come back again, do a few songs and then go off again. Then, to add salt to the wound, we had tickets to the Indigo Rooms for the usual late night jamming session venue where we waited until 2.30am but he was a no show.

I WAS THERE: SHANE WETTON

We managed to get more tickets. And not just any tickets - we had tickets for the last show and the after show. The main show was good but the after show? Wow, the after show was another level.

It was late and Prince had already played over two hours in the main arena and here we were hoping and praying he would play more. The lights went down and we heard music. The curtain closed. We hoped he was there but we couldn't be sure. Then we heard 'two...one two'. That was him, he was there. The band started to play, it was a song I recognised in my head but it wasn't massively familiar, then the singer came in... It wasn't Prince but it was smooth. The curtains opened and it was Amy Winehouse singing 'Love is a Losing Game'. To say it was a moment, a moment in musical history, would be an understatement. Here we are, it's stupid o'clock in the morning, Prince has already played two hours in the arena and here he is with Amy Winehouse – and its sublime.

Prince was visibly moved at the end of the song. Sometimes you could see by his reaction that his experiences shocked even himself. This was one of these moments. We were so close to him, we could see his eyes - well, once he'd removed his shades we could.

Once Amy had left the stage Prince moved on to '7', then 'Come Together'. He was just getting going. 'Honky Tonk Women' then led in to the next guest, Beverley Knight, who knocked 'Rock Steady' out of the park. Prince obviously rated Beverley and why not? She's sensational and had supported a few of the main shows. Next up was an instrumental of 'Whole Lotta Love' and then Prince turned to the band, put his finger up to his lips and in the blink of an eye the band played 'Shhh'.

I'd seen Prince command his bands many times over the years. One finger meant one beat, two fingers two beats, a slicing motion across the neck meant stop and so on, but to witness this majesty and accuracy so close - what a man, what a leader, what a band!

The show was long. Not a lengthy set list particularly but lengthy versions of songs. 'All The Critics Love You in London' must have lasted 15 plus minutes. Pure funk one minute, pure rock the next. Pure funk followed with 'Sexy Dancer' and 'Chelsea Rodgers' and after Shelby had sung 'Misty Blue' and started to rebuild the tempo on 'Baby Love', the band started to play 'Alphabet Street'. It was funky but it was about to get funkier. After a few lines Prince stopped and asked the band to build the song bit by bit. First the bass line, then the kick drum, then the guitar... topped off with Prince's vocal. It has to be one of his funkiest recorded moments - incredible!

'Love Rollercoaster' and 'Play That Funky Music' followed and that was it. He had played for hours tonight. We weren't sure an encore would follow but we weren't moving just in case he wasn't done, and he wasn't. It was time for some rock again, a heavy version of 'Anotherlover' followed by 'Villanova Junction' which led into 'Peach', 'Rock Me Baby' and 'Stratus'. He was rocking out.

Suddenly from that rock sound he moved into a melodic mash up of 'The Question of You' and 'The One', just to tame it down a notch. A quick rendition of Janet Jackson's 'What Have You Done For Me Lately' and it was party time or time for 'Partyman' to be precise. All hail a new king, not that the old one ever went away! And he proved it by finishing off with Larry Graham's 'It's Alright'. Then he was done. It was well after 3am. We were all done! Things like this didn't happen to me, to us. They don't happen to anyone anymore!

MONTREUX JAZZ FESTIVAL AUDITORIUM STRAVINSKI

18 JULY 2009,
MONTREUX,
SWITZERLAND

I WAS THERE: GINA JOYCE

News broke of two Prince shows back to back in July. I had to go. I went with my daughter, and we stayed overnight in the Grand Hotel du Lac in Vevey, right opposite Lake Geneva, an amazing five star hotel and amazing scenery. I paid a total of nearly £1,000 for our Prince tickets for both shows (£90 per show) and one night in the hotel for us and our flights to Geneva. We arrived at the hotel looking quite dishevelled and scruffy, my daughter with a large stain on her t-shirt due to a spilt drink on the journey, and we were greeted by a posh hotel doorman in top hat and gloves! It was embarrassing, but we were giggling our heads off. Once inside, my daughter was then going around the hotel and taking photos of the amazing ballroom, the Chinese room, the antiques and the like. It really was the five star treatment with scrambled eggs on toast to die for served in our room the next morning under huge silver domes.

It was baking hot weather at the Jazz Festival. But they'd clearly also had lots of rain at some point, as the ground on entering was extremely muddy and slippery under foot. Five minutes after we'd entered I went flying, falling completely flat on the floor, and was totally covered from head to toe in brown mud. My daughter thought it was hilarious, but I was upset to say the least. I'd spent an hour getting ready and now I looked like a tramp! We found the ladies toilets, where we used stacks of wet paper towels and tried to remove some of the mud. I was then walking around the festival soaking wet during the Prince concert.

It was a complete nightmare inside, queuing for the Stravinski Auditorium nearer to the first show, with everyone pushing and shoving to get first in the queue. Some fans were getting quite rough, quite violent, we all wanted front row at the stage. We ended up a few rows from the front on the far left, which was close enough.

When Prince did 'Empty Room' he got a standing ovation with his guitar playing, a truly unforgettable moment for me, with him throwing his guitar up in the air at the end to more applause. 'Little Red Corvette' was also very dreamy and memorable, with us all singing 'slow down' with a double clap. Then it was 'Insatiable' leading into 'Scandalous': 'I'm in a palace overlooking the lake, are you with me?' (Prince was staying at the Montreux Palace Hotel) followed by 'The Beautiful Ones', which was also memorable.

We had a very long and beaty 'All The Critics' during show two, which made the crowd go totally crazy. We were all jumping up and down. Halfway through this track Prince suddenly looked extremely annoyed, looking straight ahead and putting both arms out and up in the air in an angry gesture, as if to say 'what's going on?' and then putting his finger from left to right across his throat as if to say 'I'll finish the show'. I've watched that track back on DVD many times, and I'm sure now he must have been complaining about sound issues to management or something similar. He was such a perfectionist, and if ever the sound was bad he would often refuse to play until they put it right. We'd not noticed anything wrong with the sound.

The *20Ten* tour comprised 14 European shows and one in Abu Dhabi beginning on 4 July 2010 in Denmark and concluding on 18 November 2010 in Arnhem in The Netherlands.

LA CITADELLE

9 JULY 2010, ARRAS, FRANCE

I WAS THERE: GINA JOYCE

2010 and I got news of two Prince shows – Arras in France and Rock Werchter in Belgium the day after. A friend of mine who was also a massive Prince fan invited me to go with her to France and Belgium for the shows, so we booked B&Bs and went on the Eurostar. We arrived extra early for the Arras show as we wanted to get a decent stage spot. It was a mega hot day and we were standing around with masses of fans in blazing hot sun for at least six hours, constantly applying sun block and running out of water so we were gasping!

Finally they removed the thick rope cordon and allowed us all through, a mass of fans sprinting all together through the big stone arch and into the main square to secure their spot at the stage. There were lots of drink stalls before you got to the stage area, but nobody wanted to stop and queue for water at the kiosks and risk not getting a decent stage spot. Most, including us, just stayed thirsty and dehydrated, rooted in front of the stage. People were then fainting in the extreme heat and first-aiders were carrying them out. In the end the organisers were throwing big bottles of water into the crowds and everyone was swigging from the same large bottles, then passing it to those behind them in the next row. Hygienic or what?

There was an amazing set by support act Mint Condition, followed by Larry Graham who was also excellent. He came into the crowd playing his bass and really got the crowd going. Enter Prince, who was amazing as usual. He did 'Mountains', which is one of my favourites, and he had French harmonica player Frederic Yonnet with him on this tour, who was spectacular. Stokely Williams from Mint Condition and Larry Graham joined Prince for 'I Wanna Take You Higher', with an awesome guitar duet in the middle with Prince and Larry Graham, although LG always seems to be lagging a few beats behind where he should be! Towards the end he played 'Forever In My Life', also a favourite of mine, and the crowd were flicking our lighters and mobiles on and off to the beat.

Next morning involved travel on numerous trains to Werchter in Belgium to check into our B&B for the Rock Werchter show that evening. It was very hot again. Our B&B was disgusting but they agree to cancel our booking and we found somewhere much better.

WERCHTER BOUTIQUE FESTIVALPARK

10 JULY 2010, WERCHTER, BELGIUM

I WAS THERE: ROSIE SMITH

This was the *20Ten* tour. I was at that gig with Lee Hawker and we had arrived in Werchter after an adventurous road trip from England to Belgium, via Arras in France, to see Prince twice in two days. It was a warm evening and Prince was singing 'Hot Summer'. Suddenly, it started to pour down and Prince began to play 'Purple Rain'. The rain was lit by purple lights from the stage, making the rain look purple. The purple rain poured down and Prince played his guitar and sang '…I only want to see you laughing in the purple rain….' A magical Prince moment! One of many special, happy moments seeing Prince live, for which I'll always be grateful that I was there!

I WAS THERE: GINA JOYCE

This was a similar format to the Arras show, with Mint Condition and then Larry Graham opening before Prince played a similar opening setlist as he had the day before. Halfway through the show, the heavens opened up. I've never seen torrential rain like it, with lightning. We were all totally drenched as it didn't stop for quite some time and everyone looked like they'd just got out of the shower. In the end I had to put my sunglasses on to see the stage as my eye make up had run into my eyes and was stinging

badly. A few people in the rows in front of us then put umbrellas up, blocking our view, so a few strong words were exchanged – although not by us.

Towards the end Prince did a very funky 'Partyman', leading into 'I Like Funky Music'. Prince said, 'Belgium, I'm from Minneapolis. This is how we party in Minneapolis, but we're in Belgium now and I think you can all party just a little bit harder than us –am I right?' Loud cheers from fans. 'So I wanna hear you with all your voices.' We were all then shouting 'hey, hey, hey, hey' in time to the beat. There was then an hilarious moment when Prince suddenly grabbed an air freshener spray from the side of the stage and sprayed it straight at his black guitarist at the back of the stage, saying, 'It's just too funky in here!'

We left Werchter Park totally soaked through to our underwear, but on a real high so we didn't care. As it was a huge field and we'd had so much torrential rain, the mud had now turned to muddy slush. I was wearing flip-flops and my friend sandals. We got back to our B&B soaking wet with brown muddy feet. Back in our room we took turns in showering. Then I noticed my friend was constantly looking at her mobile. She suddenly told me excitedly she'd got inside information about an after show at Viage Club in Brussels and did I want to go? Stupid question!

VIAGE AFTER SHOW

11 JULY 2010, BRUSSELS, BELGIUM

I WAS THERE: GINA JOYCE

We get dressed fast! It must have been around 1am by then and rushed outside to find a mini cab to Viage in Brussels. We arrived to find a queue of fans outside, all hoping they'll get in. We joined the long queue and finally we were admitted inside – yes!

Directly inside the main front doors were two huge staircases, one going up and one coming down, next to each other. There was a massive crystal chandelier hanging from the ceiling. The actual club was upstairs. We joined the queue with other fans on the right hand staircase and just waited and waited for hours. We were already totally exhausted. Larry Graham and band then came through the main doors and went up the left staircase to the club upstairs. He smiled, waving to us lot on the adjacent staircase, and we all cheered and waved.

Finally at 4am we were moved to the other staircase. The fans, worried they would not get into the club upstairs, all rushed together and a glass side panel got smashed, so there was some panic there for a while, us hoping it wasn't a fight. There were more queues upstairs, where they told us it was 80 euros to get in and cash only. Larry Graham and band were already playing inside, a similar set to Werchter.

The floor was all on one level, so we were all quite close to the stage and to the band. We tried to get right in front of Larry Graham and the band but it was already very packed, so we couldn't see very much. I moved to the very left side which was less packed and where I could see more. I beckoned my friend over but she was happy where she was.

Prince's band then came on. They were playing for a while, but I could not see Prince. Then I realised he was right at the back of his band, with his back to us and sitting on a stool playing guitar in a beanie hat, sunglasses and casual jacket. He looked like a little boy. Later on he came to the front. The stand out track was 'What Have You Done For Me Lately', with some great dance moves, but the whole show was amazing, although all a bit of a blur afterwards as I was so exhausted at the time. Shelby J came over to the left side where I was standing at one point and was singing literally one foot away from me, as did Prince also later on. Dare I reach out and maybe touch his arm? Definitely not!

It was an amazing night. The gig was only around 90 minutes. We came out of the venue at around 5.30am to daylight and journeyed back to our lodgings, where they were just preparing to lay the breakfast out. We stayed up, stuffed our faces until we were full and then went back to our room and slept for several hours.

Back home in London, I was relaying all this to my daughter in our garden. I took my sandals off and within 10 minutes my feet and legs swelled up like balloons. I looked like I had elephantitis. My feet and legs just kept getting fatter and fatter until I found it uncomfortable to actually walk. The following morning they were even worse so I had to go to the doctor. The constant queuing, non-stop travelling and being on my feet constantly in extremely hot weather had taken its toll. It was five days before they went back to normal.

JYSKE BANK BOXEN

22 OCTOBER 2010, HERNING, DENMARK

I WAS THERE: PABLO HERRERA MARINO

I went to four concerts – the *Parade* tour in Essen, Germany, *Lovesexy* in Copenhagen, the *Nude* tour in Kiel, Germany and finally in Herning, Denmark in 2010. I remember that the country was ecstatic when he was here in Denmark. The papers were talking about 'the real Prince' arriving. It was a long wait for that concert. He set the highest standards for how a concert should be. It was very intense. I was 14 years old when I came to

Denmark in 1983 and discovered his music a year later. It helped me to adapt to the country and to focus on something. That was good for me. It gave me an identity. I was proud, and still am, to be 'that Prince guy'.

The Welcome 2 tour began on 15 December 2010 to and ran until September 2012. Each leg of the tour was branded as 'Welcome 2' followed by the name of the continent the leg was located on.

HOP FARM FESTIVAL

3 JULY 2011, PADDOCK WOOD, UK

I WAS THERE: SAM BLEAZARD

Prince never played Glastonbury. Emily Eavis was on TV a few months back describing Prince as 'the one that got away'. The Eavis family were apparently in conversation with him or his people but at the last minute he pulled out. I think he played Hop Farm in Kent because he didn't want to be subsumed in the whole Glastonbury thing. He was saying, 'I'll do an outdoor festival but I want it to be on my terms. Hop Farm was his Glastonbury. Another amazing gig because you were standing in a field in Kent, and Prince was there. That was an especially happy memory for me because I took my four-year-old daughter along, and she sat on my shoulders with a pair of angel wings on.

Sam Bleazard saw Prince at the Hop Farm Festival

I WAS THERE: NICOLA WAKLEY-WAKE

I have to say this was the best day of my life. Well, certainly up there after marriage and babies! It was magical from start to finish and I didn't want it to ever end. He was amazing, funny - there aren't enough words to describe the experience. I could cry it was so amazing. I was with my mum and my eldest son, who was almost 12. Like I said, magical.

I WAS THERE: HASSAN RAZZAQ

It must have been around Christmas 1990 when I watched the *Graffiti Bridge* film. My auntie was a mild Prince fan and we had a VHS shop so all we used to do was watch films, and one of the films we used to watch a lot was *Graffiti Bridge*. I think I watched the film before I bought the album, so I knew the songs visually.

My first gig was the *Ultimate Live Experience* in 1996 and that was it cemented for me, it was just amazing. I was living in Preston at the time and I travelled down to London. I couldn't get anyone to come with me but my uncle – who was a mild Prince fan - finally decided he would come along with me. And it was such an amazing experience, but it was strange because at the gig I was just infatuated with Mayte. Those hot pants were just amazing! That was my first gig and I've never looked back since.

My favourite gig has to be the Hop Farm Festival in 2011 because that was the first time me and my partner went together and that was her first live gig. That was an amazing night, because he came on at about 8, 8.30pm and the sun was just setting and we watched him perform whilst the day turned into night. He was telling jokes, having the banter with the crowd, and he was taking the mick out of Sinéad O'Connor when he sang 'Nothing Compares 2 U', and he was saying, 'Yeah, with the money I made off that song I bought a house', and all that kind of stuff. He came out for like three or four hours, he did so many songs. Also, I remember that day there were a few other artists and they all said, 'I can't wait for Prince tonight'. They were more excited than the audience!

That's how I want to remember Prince. It was quite a shock because everyone was thinking Glastonbury or V-Festival but he chose Hop Farm. It was all very family-friendly, no sponsorship, and that's why he specifically found it. And they put on an extra night for him. It was such an amazing crowd, I think there were 60,000 or 70,000 people, and everyone was just fixated. I took some fantastic pictures as well. I remember Tinie Tempah, Eliza Doolittle, Imelda May, Aloe Blacc – I think he was the first one to perform that day. He looked like early Prince, '79, that sort of falsetto sound and the dance moves.

I WAS THERE: GINA JOYCE

I wet to Hop Farm with the same friend I went to Arras and Wertchter with. We arrived early afternoon, around 1pm. We didn't get to see any other bands in any of the numerous tents that day, like others did, as we just plonked ourselves down with plenty of water and food in front of the main stage, where we knew Prince would be performing that evening. We sat for around seven hours chatting in the hot sun. The first two rows nearest to the stage were already full – obviously Prince fans! - but the third row from the stage was fine. As usual we took it in turns to visit the loos so the other one could save our spot. Imelda May, Tinie Tempah and many others came on, and then later Larry Graham and band, but the sound wasn't great at all!

The nearer it got to Prince's slot the more we felt the atmosphere changing. More and more Prince fans were arriving and accumulating behind us as far as the eye could see across the fields. They were also pushing a bit until, in the end, we seemed to have hardly any arm room in our row, where some had squeezed into spaces in our row. There were people with huge purple balloons, banners, etc., most of whom were holding beers or other drinks. One bloke kept shouting, 'Where's the man?'

Prince's band finally entered the stage one by one to huge cheers from us all. Prince then came onto the stage in a pale gold top with stand up collar and matching trousers, looking very cool and gorgeous, and the crowd went crazy. 'What's happening?', he said.

They sound checked to 'We Live To Get Funky', leading into the 'Let's Go Crazy' intro – the crowd was going nuts at this point – and then 'Delirious' and many more. He gave the fans hit after hit, including a funky 'Let's Work' with some dance moves, everyone dancing and singing. Later on he played a long 'Controversy' (a favourite of mine) leading into 'Play That Funky Music'. 'Purple Rain' was amazing, with massive showers of purple confetti projected over the crowd.

I WAS THERE: KATE AMY SHINGLER

I saw the *One Nite Alone* tour at Hammersmith Apollo. I went to Hop Farm as well, that was amazing, such a hot day. I drove and it took forever to get out, but my cousin at the time lived in Kent so I drove down, saw the festival, and then on the way back I was like, 'Paul, I need some substance' so he made me a chip sarnie and a cup of tea and I went and got back on the road. I think I got back about four in the morning. Weren't people always saying 'he's gonna do Glasto' and because people were talking about it he just wouldn't do it?

I WAS THERE: CLAIRE PRIME

Although the Festival was on over a weekend, I had only booked tickets for one day as it was only one artist I really wanted to see. That one artist was Prince. The weather was ideal – warm and sunny and the fields were not muddy. On arrival we made our way to the main stage area. I declared that I was completely happy to wait here if any of the others I had come along with wanted to go and explore. Me, I would not be moving to look at other stages or tents. There was a man who brought beer around the crowds in a backpack so that was pretty ideal really!

It was the headline act that had attracted me to the Hop Farm Festival, but it was a really good line up and the music was brilliant. There was a definite buzz around. Not being a huge, well known festival, it certainly felt like a well-kept secret and it didn't have any commercial vibe, it honestly felt we had been let in on a wonderful secret.

The crowd had grown steadily throughout the day and my initial efforts of remaining as near as the front as I could get were futile, but it didn't matter. The atmosphere was electric. Everyone was there to have a good time and we were all in on this amazing music festival secret.

Completely overjoyed with excitement and anticipation, my emotions were on par with an over excited 6-year-old at Christmas. When Prince came on stage, his ethereal figure captivating the crowds, it was an exceptional feeling and the need to dance swept through my body. I can't recall if Prince said or not but even if he didn't use the words his message was clear. Now it was time for real music! Absolutely no offence to any of the previous acts as they were all marvellous and I enjoyed them all, but they were not Prince. It was, in his own words, 'You got the look'. Prince certainly did, he exuded confidence not just through his exceptional musical genius but knowing he was loved, and we were all there for him and we wanted nothing more than to dance and be witness to the phenomenal performance that he was about to provide.

Two particular moments come to mind. Firstly, when Prince invited Larry Graham on to stage with him. The crowd witnessed these two iconic musicians jamming, literally just having fun and playing like they were teenagers in their mums' garage and the crowd wasn't there. They were clearly fans of each other and respected each other enormously and the crowd were ecstatic at seeing these icons showing their slap bass skills to one another, having a funky time. It felt like such an epic yet personal moment I was witness too.

Secondly, and this moment still makes my eyes prick with tears, was when Prince announced that the crowd were there to witness 'Purple Rain'. As the words had left his mouth purple confetti fell from the sky and he began the legendary song. It was such an emotional moment. I still have a piece of 'Purple Rain' in my jewellery box.

For a couple of days after this I was an emotional wreck. Experiencing such a high that is impossible to recreate was intense but eventually I accepted that I was blessed to have been able to be there at all.

God bless you Prince. Thank you for the music and the memories.

NORTH SEA JAZZ FESTIVAL

AHOY ROTTERDAM 8 -10 JULY 2011

I WAS THERE: GINA JOYCE

This was three concerts in three days. My friend suggested we go together again so we bought our tickets and booked lodgings In Rotterdam. It was very hot weather again, with lots of train journeys again to get to our lodgings for our three night stay.

For the first show, although doors were not even opening until past midnight, we queued outside the massive venue from 6pm, sitting on the floor chatting amongst ourselves and to other fans. My friend and I were two of the first to arrive at the venue, so hopefully we'd get front row at the stage or near as. The doors finally opened past midnight. Other fans had pushed in front of us so we were not first in the queue like we should've been, but we should still have been able to get near to the front. Once our tickets were checked we ran very fast into the venue, only to find at least 12 to 15 rows of people already in front of the stage!

We suddenly realised that most of these people had been to see other artists inside the venue, so those that also had Prince tickets were let in from inside the venue before us lot outside! We were furious after six hours of queuing, but we did manage to slowly and sneakily edge forward quite a few more rows before the show started.

The lights didn't go off until around 1.15am, revealing Andy Allo on stage in black trouser suit, hair in a tight bun and dark glasses, singing the first part of Jimi Hendrix's 'Foxy Lady'. The crowd cheered. Then Prince appeared from the back of the stage playing his guitar to rapturous applause, cheers and whistles. He played some amazing guitar throughout the rest of the track. It was an amazing start to the show.

I will always remember that performance. 'Controversy', 'DMSR' and many other hits followed. The tiny and talented Janelle Monae joined Prince during 'A Love Bizarre'. She came across as a bit awestruck and nervous. Then we had 'Everyday People' with Larry Graham and another guitar duet again. It was a great first show but many people were complaining afterwards about the sound. Perhaps they were standing in a different area to where we were as it had sounded great to us.

The second show the following night was without doubt my favourite show of the three. I think this show didn't start until around 1.40am. After Prince eventually did come onto the stage he simply said, 'Good morning' and thanked us for waiting up until the early hours. He apologised for the poor sound quality the previous night.

He opened with an excellent and long 'Joy in Repetition'. Andy Allo was side of the stage doodling pictures and squiggles on a large board, which I couldn't see the point of to be honest. But we all knew she was his latest beau, so hey-ho! He was obviously loved up and wanted her on stage with him at every opportunity.

Next up was Andy Allo with her guitar singing a slow song, 'Nothing More', sung pleasantly enough (but 'just get off, we want Prince' methinks!) and Maceo Parker playing some amazing sax towards the end of it. Prince had also been playing guitar in the background.

Prince then took over the stage and the mic, playing a slow intro on his guitar leading into 'The Love We Make', my favourite Prince song of all time. I'd been really hoping he would perform this song at previous concerts, so I was in seventh heaven at that moment!

My friend and I were much closer to the stage than at the first show and slightly to the right side of Prince as we faced the stage, with an excellent view around six to eight rows back. His slow guitar intro wasn't instantly recognisable as 'The Love We Make' until he started singing. My friend and I then clapped and cheered loudly on realising what song he was singing. There were a few other cheers from fans, but not as much as I'd expected. I got the impression that a lot of the fans there were not very familiar with some of his lesser known songs, as he only seemed to get massive cheers when singing the obvious hits like 'Controversy', 'Partyman' and the like.

He sang it beautifully, with real feeling and wonderful guitar playing. The song built and built, with him saying in between 'show me your heart', then 'show your heart to me' and then the guitar playing stopped briefly with the beat still going, him singing, 'Yeah, yeah, yeah, yeah, yeah - hold it right there - don't move', then directly at us all, 'I show my heart to you - you show your heart to me' and tapping his chest/heart. We all cheered loudly in response, my friend and I both waving our arms up in the air like lunatics, swaying and singing far louder than anyone else.

Then came the amazing guitar playing again, building and building. As he was playing guitar, he was smiling as he pointed at a fan over to our far left, and then, during one of the best guitar bits, I swear to God he looked directly at my friend and I, smiling broadly and nodding his head whilst playing, as if to say, 'Yeah, alright, look at you two, you're really loving this!' Of course, it could've been the bloke behind us, but I've read many times that he got to recognise the same fans that went to his concerts, especially when they were nearly always at the front. Who really knows if he was looking at us or not, but it really felt like he was, and we were certainly showing our appreciation far more than anyone else at the time. He also threw his guitar pick towards us. My friend has it, after a mad scramble on the floor from everyone. Whenever he sang 'The Love We Make', he played the guitar sections completely differently each time. There's no two versions the same as far as I'm aware, but they are all amazing - the Monte Carlo Salle Garnier show version is one of my favourites.

He then went into 'Mountains' also one of my all time favourites. We knew that Seal was performing at North Sea Jazz on one of the other stages as it was advertised outside the venue, so I hoped he would make a guest appearance, as I knew Seal was a huge Prince fan and I'm also a huge Seal fan. And enter Seal from side of the stage! He started singing a verse of 'Mountains' but it was in completely the wrong key and didn't sound right at all. My friend and I looked at one another in shock. But his dancing and huge personality made up for it and then Prince shouted, 'Seal, thank you brother' as Seal exited the stage.

I've since read Seal mentioning that appearance and saying something like, 'I'm sure I messed it up, as I was in awe of being on the same stage'. When I read Seal's words, I knew exactly what he was referring to, as I was at that gig!

'Mountains' led into 'Come Together', where he said to a fan in the audience, 'Put your camera down, participate!' Then we had a fast 'Alphabet St', but the next track, 'Mr Man' was truly memorable, along with 'The Love We Make'.

It was quite jazzy and the band were really on form with Maceo Parker, and it was just incredible. 'Colonized Mind' was next, which my friend and I also love, and that was also amazing. Then we all thought he was doing 'Peach' due to the recognisable intro (so did Andy Allo) but he suddenly changed it to 'Johnny B Goode'! Andy Allo, at the mic with him and ready to sing, gives him this glance as if to say, 'That's not 'Peach'?' She obviously wasn't sure of the words of 'Johnny B Goode'. It was a real fun track, with him doing an Elvis leg movement and Maceo Parker playing sax. He *then* went into the 'Peach' lyrics. It was around 4am when we exited the venue.

For the third show we'd once again been queuing outside from 6pm. It started pouring with rain when we were all sat on the concrete floor queuing outside the venue. One fan had the insight to bring along with them a huge and very long plastic runner-like tarpaulin. So we were then all sitting on the floor, with both our arms above our head holding up this lengthy plastic sheet above our heads, shielding us from the heavy rain. Then someone would get up for something without thinking and someone else would end up drenched from a huge, deep puddle-like collection of water that had accumulated on the top. Fortunately not me!

We were quite near to the stage again. The show opened the Prince singing 'Laydown', which was impressive. He later did 'When Eye Lay My Hands On U', 'Empty Room' and a memorable 'She's Always In My Hair'. We then got a very funky 'Partyman' with some dance moves, then 'Controversy' and a brilliant 'Pass the Peas' with Maceo Parker.

Three amazing, memorable shows. All very different.

HARTWALL AREENA

21 JULY 2011, HELSINKI, FINLAND

I WAS THERE: HENRY KURONEN

It was a unique show for us Finns because this was his only ever show in Finland. He was supposed to come earlier but there were some difficulties with the stage because Prince wanted it to be placed exactly like he wanted. I can't remember if the stage was shaped like the famous Prince logo but I guess so. When the band started to play I knew right away that this was the real deal. He was a great showman and an amazing player who really got his audience. At the end of the show he took a few fans from the crowd to the stage to dance with him. I guess they were pretty happy with that.

MALAHIDE CASTLE

30 JULY 2011, DUBLIN, IRELAND

I WAS THERE: DANIEL GEORGE

I had been a fan of Prince from the age of 10, often singing the lyrics to 'Gett Off' without a clue about its meaning. Then when the Brit Pop era began, I began to follow the crowds for quite a few years and lost touch with Prince. I did see him at the O2 for the *21 Nights* tour, which was enjoyable but it didn't hit me as hard as I thought it would.

A few years passed and I was still in the Prince wilderness, when the *20Ten* album was released with the *Daily Mail* and I loved it! I then proceeded to fill in the gaps from *Gold* up to *20Ten* and I began to be hooked again. Prince was touring and he was playing at Malahide Castle in Ireland. I just had to go. The gig started great and I was in awe with the music and performance before me, but nothing prepared me for the slowed down version of 'Little Red Corvette'. It completely blew my mind. He toured the stage with his guitar and at one point appeared to play the keys and guitar simultaneously and my jaw was on the ground! From that day on, every time Prince was in the UK I dropped everything in my life to get to those gigs.

I've met the most amazing people through our shared love of Prince. I feel we are a very unique set of fans, with obviously the greatest taste in music! I miss those moments so much and it still hurts that we won't see him on stage again. But at least we still have the music.

In November 2011, Prince embarked upon a run of 11 shows in what was billed as the *Welcome 2 Canada* tour.

ROGERS ARENA

16 DECEMBER 2011, VANCOUVER, CANADA

I WAS THERE: MICHELLE WEBB

This concert was so impressed upon my mind that I bought tickets to see him a few nights later in Tacoma, Washington. The price was exorbitant but I felt compelled.

TACOMA DOME

19 DECEMBER 2011, TACOMA, WASHINGTON

I WAS THERE: MICHELLE WEBB

The Tacoma show on December 19, 2011, was shorter with a less enthusiastic crowd. Was this because Americans are harder to impress than Canadians? One very noticeable difference was the number of very young children that were brought with their parents. They sat on the stairs in the isles, waiving their Prince logo tambourines along to the songs they may have heard for the first time. The show ended early. Rumour has it Prince was angry at the disrespect of the crowd and the security that failed to follow his commands to have no cameras in the building. He apparently left early and went to an after party/show in the downtown area of Seattle and performed for another two hours. How fascinating to see how different the energy could be from one show to the next and is transferred from a crowd to a performer.

The *Welcome 2 Australia* leg of the tour took in eight shows.

BRISBANE ENTERTAINMENT CENTRE

18 & 26 MAY 2012, BRISBANE, AUSTRALIA

I WAS THERE: PAUL KOSTROMIN

I saw Prince again in 2012. I saw the first gig with my wife and then I took my then 15-year-old son. I said, 'You need to see Prince.' He wasn't too fussed initially. These were again two quite different gigs. The set lists were quite different and I remember Prince played his Fender Strat for most of the first gig but the Telecaster mainly in the second gig. There were

very different moods at these shows. At the first show Prince didn't seem too happy and was more going through the motions than anything. It was still brilliant, but something wasn't right. It was interesting that there were many, many people with their phones out videoing, etc. at the first gig. At the second gig there were no phones allowed, so I think Prince was maybe a little annoyed at all the people recording and videoing him?

I also remember that he did a very, very extended 'Purple Rain' encore at the first show that went on and on…. It was brilliant but as it repeated more and more that same last section of the song, I got the feeling that he was thinking, 'Fuck it, I'll just keep playing that same thing over and over' as it did go on for many minutes with the same refrain. I may be wrong, but it felt wrong.

At the second show, though, he was 'on' and there was a totally different vibe and mood in the hall. He was having a great time. Maybe all the phones had really pissed him off at the previous gig, but this time he was strutting his stuff and did some wonderful medleys of his songs. Again, as in Melbourne when I saw him before, he did an after show in town that I unfortunately didn't see, but have spoken to people that have and apparently he was having a great time!

ROD LAVER ARENA

30 MAY 2012, MELBOURNE, AUSTRALIA

I WAS THERE: STEPHEN TROISI

I got turned onto Prince via 'Controversy'. I love funk and this reeked of it. I saw him the second to last time he toured Australia at the Rod Laver Arena. It was a three hour party. After the show he was supposed to do an after-gig performance at the Hi Fi Club in the city. Fans turned up, spun Prince out and he split after 15 minutes.

I WAS THERE: HAROLD FISHER

Prince saw my daughter's tribute to him on YouTube when she was 7 or 8 years old. Jaz was only 8 when we received an email from Prince's manager asking if she could open with Prince as he was planning to visit in the future for the *Welcome 2* tour in Australia. I thought that she may be too young for all the exposure and felt it best to wait but Prince sent us tickets and still wanted to meet Jaz. Sometime after the concert the twins came up and said Prince apologised as he was attending press. I just told them to thank Prince for everything but we'd see him next time. Soon after leaving, we got a call from his manager saying he was upset as he really wanted to see her and he had security

Harold's daughter Jaz with the late John Blackwell

looking for us and asked if we could attend another concert the following weekend? I said of course!

A week later we got another bunch of VIP tickets and soon after the concert, the drummer John Blackwell, who was sitting with some NPG members, asked why Prince wanted to meet Jaz. I replied that Prince had seen her on YouTube over a year earlier. John then asked if she was the Power Fantastic girl? When I said yes, they literally rushed us. John was real excited and said Prince had been speaking about her a lot and had big plans for her. John said he would back her on drums any time she needed. When Prince saw her YouTube video, he had called all the NPG into his room and said, 'Meet my next piano player and singer.'

Then someone came into the room and said Prince wanted to meet us. I replied that it was Jaz's journey and that she could go and say hello and give him our love. After 20 minutes the person came in again to say Prince wanted to meet us too. Despite me saying it was okay, John and the band insisted so we did.

On meeting Prince, I was just amazed at how awesome he looked after such a long concert. My wife and I were lost for words. He was so funny and said I looked like I needed a jug of beer. My wife was laughing at that as I've always admired his music and I was a little shocked at actually meeting him at all. He was such a beautiful man and made us feel completely comfortable throughout our meeting.

We basically sat for almost two hours talking about life and music and planning my daughter's music career. From the outset he insisted we call him 'bro' which was really awesome and he had Jaz call him her big brother. He was so passionate about nurturing her musically and keeping her safe throughout her time with him. He even spent a long time telling us in detail how he wanted her first concert with him to be like. It was quite amazing how he made us feel it was actually happening, quite visual in every sense, and he was truly excited about it. At one point, Andy McKee came into the room and introduced himself. He said Prince had spoken about her often and it was a pleasure to finally meet the piano player Prince had often spoke about. Prince then turned and said, 'And she can sing too!'

He asked if we'd like to attend the after concert but I thanked him and said I thought she was a little too young and it was late for her, so he walked us out.

In the corridor, the band and managers were all meeting up and Prince introduced them too. He then made her promise she would visit him at Paisley Park before she turned 18. He said he would arrange a beautiful photo shoot for just him and Jaz. He then told me he would call me soon before giving us all a big farewell.

On the way home, Jaz told us after that when Prince saw her, he jumped up from his table and ran to her and gave her a big hug. They talked a bit about her music and he asked her if she could play ping pong? She replied she didn't know that song and he fell on the floor laughing! They played some ping pong and he even let her win a game!

We got an email later to say he loved meeting us and looked forward to seeing us soon. During the *Piano & A Microphone* tour we got an invite to go to the Melbourne concert but Jaz's mum was having pregnancy problems so we just said to give him our love and said we would see him next time. Sadly it was never to be as he passed away not long after.

Our baby was born 25th April by emergency and we named her Princess Saraya Paisley in his memory. Not a day goes by without thinking of our big brother, Prince. 4eva loved and missed.

The *Live Out Loud* tour took place from 15 April to 25 May 2013 in North America

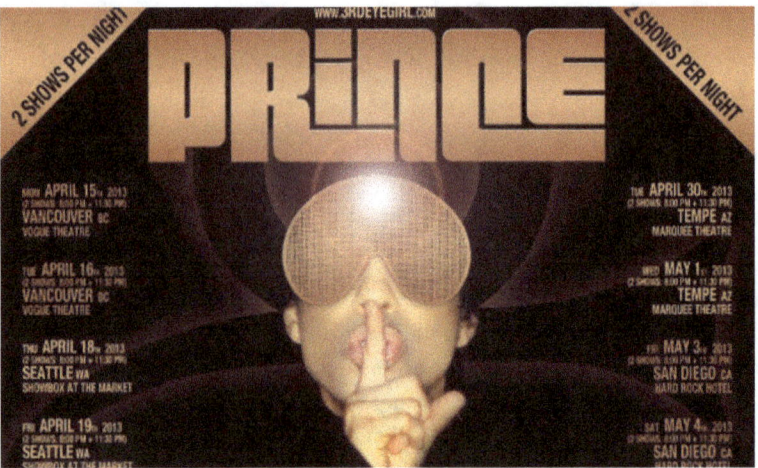

THE SHOWBOX

19 APRIL 2013, SEATTLE, WASHINGTON

I WAS THERE: MICHELLE WEBB

My last experience of seeing Prince live was at this small venue in Seattle, Washington. This famed concert venue is currently fighting for historic status, as a Canadian company wants to tear it down and put up a high rise. It felt like 1988 again as a small crowd of us gathered for drinks in the pre-show bar lounge. My husband, the former Prince hater, was now getting ready to see his third Prince concert and sat with me and watched people sip cocktails and reminisce about Prince. I felt vindicated at last. My early years of hiding my Prince obsession had come full circle. Being a Prince fan was now a symbol of the true music connoisseur.

I do admit to having too many cocktails and not enough to eat. We were crammed into the small venue and watched Prince and his girl group perform. I felt this was a different Prince, with his large Afro and preference to stay in the background for much of the performance. We even left the show before it was over. We walked through the quiet city blocks of downtown Seattle on our short journey back home across the water.

That was my last time seeing Prince. I decided not to attend his last tour - *Piano & A Microphone*. He seemed different now. I prefer to remember his two shows in my hometown of Vancouver. Nothing will compare.

STOCKHOLM MUSIC & ARTS CENTRE

4 AUGUST 2013, STOCKHOLM, SWEDEN

I WAS THERE: LEON RA LINDSTRÖM

Prince's music came into my life when I was 6 years old. It changed my life. He has been here since then and will be until the day that I die. I named my son after him - my son's name is Prince John after Prince and John Lennon. The first time I got to see Prince Live was in 1991 and it was amazing. The second time, in 1993, was at Stockholm's Globe Arena and there I was close enough to get eye contact with him while he was playing guitar. The next time was in 1998 at the Hovet in Stockholm, when he played 'Purple Rain' and sang just the first line and then played guitar solo for the rest of the song - very loud! It was epic!

The last time I saw Prince live was in 2013 with his 3RDEYEGIRL in Skeppsholmen, Stockholm. I was preparing the backstage area as I was working there, dressing the whole house in purple curtains because that was what he had asked for. It was a purple dream so to speak. Prince was a few hours late for the gig but nobody cared. Oh, and I was there for the sound check the very same morning and it was not a sound check, it was a concert for the Gods. As a sound check it is impossible to explain but the world missed out on something very rare.

I WAS THERE: FREDRIK SIXTEN

I am an acclaimed composer of sacred music. Prince is, alongside Bach, my biggest influence. Not that my music sounds like him but through his approach to music and how to compose. I say this as a scholar. I never been that amazed by other things connected to his artistry even though I can realise that he's been successful and innovative in every aspects of his creative output. He was a true genius of his time. Of course, he had to go when no-one expected it.

His journey through my life has been constant and alienable. I had the fortune of experiencing him five times live - Stockholm twice, Haag, London and Madison Square Garden, New York. Despite very different circumstances, he always surprised you. My story is that Prince always stayed present, no matter what. As a

Fredrik Sixten saw Prince in Stockholm

performer, singer, musician, artist, always present and that was 100 per cent. Never staged as many of his fellow artists, always under his conditions, never mechanical, always giving you a part of his soul, in that moment, in that hour. I remember especially Stockholm in August 2013, when he did 'Breakdown' – it was unforgettable. His cracked voice singing about a self-experienced life summarised his life and then he left us just three years later. I was so close to him, just 30 metres away. And now I can listen to that take on YouTube and retrieve it.

Prince was unique in so many ways, but perhaps the thing is that you can't bring up just one or two things. Looking back, it has to be the entirely thing about his artistry: the songs, the musician, the creator, the artist, the visionary, the God. The last one was me being pathetic, but no-one, to this day, comes near his qualifications. That's the truth.

MOHEGAN SUN ARENA

29 DECEMBER 2013, UNCASVILLE, CONNECTICUT

I WAS THERE: ANGELA BERGERON

I was at Prince's Sunday concert at Mohegan Sun (he did two nights). But my most memorable concert was when I was still in my mother's womb! She went to the Hartford Civic Center and slept on the sidewalk to get tickets, all the while not knowing about her miracle baby. Weeks later it was time for the concert. My mom's dancing having a good time while I'm inside her dancing like the Ally McBeal baby. It was during the show that I kicked her and she goes, 'I know that feeling' and realised for the first time she was pregnant with me!

After I was born and was able to speak, there was a song playing and I started humming then singing and found out it was Prince. Some lady said I was too young to know that so I pointed to my ma and said, 'Go ask her.' So I'm living proof babies learn in the womb!

The *Hit and Run* tour took place between 5 February 2014 and 14 June 2015, with UK, European and North American legs.

ELECTRIC BALLROOM

4 FEBRUARY 2014, LONDON, UK

I WAS THERE: CHOPIN GARD

For once in a Prince story, the pouring rain isn't purple. Wet February evenings in London are seldom that magical. Like many Prince stories, it starts with a rumour that 'Prince is in town' and 'he's doing a secret gig". Message boards and social media accounts were a-buzz. Even Channel 4 News was chasing him down.

It turns out the first show of this *Hit and Run* series of gigs had already happened in a small East London flat. I must confess my heart sank a little when I heard - maybe he wasn't going to be accessible to us this time. Working late my focus wasn't on the job at hand, one eye being glued to my phone the other on the door. With a tube strike and torrential rain, the last minute dash from West London was going to be painfully slow. The 'what if I miss it?' knot in my stomach was beginning to grow until – 'bing' - my phone lights up… Camden… Electric Ballroom… doors open… now!

Chopin Gard and pals went to the Electric Ballroom. Photo thanks to Prince Party UK

My hand was already grasping my coat and I was out in the parking lot before it was zipped up. Darting around puddles in a heavy downpour I arrived at the bus stop. Finally I had time to sober up enough to send an apology text to work (I wore Prince t-shirts a lot so they got it). After the longest wait for the bus came what I can only describe as the longest bus journey of my life. Every red light produced a toddler tantrum of 'I wannna go now' that I had to supress. Then somewhere half way to Camden the realisation came… I'm going to be seeing Prince tonight!

I had seen him multiple times before and it's a magical experience. My teenage years were spent playing along to bootleg live tapes from Camden, some cassettes even purchased from the weekend market in the Electric Ballroom. To be seeing him live in the same room where I got those tapes was going to be surreal.

Finally the bus arrives and I dash to the ATM to take £200 out of a hole in the wall. Nothing was said about price but I wasn't going to miss out after coming this far. I approached the venue – yes! The queue was still there – yes! There were only about 10 people in the queue – yes! I knew half the people in it. The stars had lined up perfectly.

Ultimately 50 people show up outside while the muffled sounds of 3RDEYEGIRL pounded from inside the venue. Puppy dog eyes stared at a stoic security guy that finally got the word in his ear to open the doors.

Very few things in life feel as great as the doors opening at a Prince show. It's a wave of joy that is hard to match. Worries stresses and political differences were left at that door and a group of adults old enough to know different squealed and pushed forward, each one of us about to be unencumbered by the real world. But first the question - how much is the door charge? The first couple of people ask. Now this is where the collective disbelief that we were going to see Prince after all was suddenly topped. 'It's free, no charge, enjoy.'

There is a rare moment when a Prince gig turns from a special event to a legendary night. The kind of night that becomes a 'did you go?' 'OMG, you were there when…'

This was that moment and it was set to the opening strains of 'I Could Never Take the Place of Your Man'. Spilling into the room with an interspersed group of music industry reps, we bounced our way through the polite gaps in the crowd to finally bask in the glow of a fully amped up Prince and 3RDEYEGIRL playing to a couple of hundred people like it was a stadium.

Sound after beautiful sound waved through the amps. Snap shots of that gig have flashed back in my mind many times in the years since. The moment he sang 'on your heavenly body I swear' to have the crowd shout back, 'I like it there!' This always comes to mind as I was stood next to Prince's cameraman and could hear myself on the YouTube clip he posted the next morning.

After the wailing feedback of the last song, after the last screaming applause and the house lights were lit, we regrouped. We came together, me and my friends, as we did after every gig, in part to bond and share in the thrill, in part to confirm that we really had just experienced it and that we weren't dreaming. If only to confirm it had happened we took a group photo and tweeted it out, only for it to be in the *Metro* newspaper the next day.

Walking out there was a group of young industry representatives with their eyes agape and silent. One of them quietly popped their head up and said, 'Well, that's it then, we've just seen the best gig of our lives… it's over.' I laughed to myself that this guy – no, this powerhouse - that had been doing this for nearly 40 years could still win over a new crowd.

These nights are stories now, all part of the many pieces that make up the legend of Prince and we (like the band, engineers, costume designers and international crowds) are a small part of it.

I have a family of friends formed in cold rainy queue after cold rainy queue. We laughed, sang, danced and looked after each other in those endless lines. When we get together to share our equivalent Prince gig war stories like any good veteran, you can often here us say, 'I was there when….'

I WAS THERE: SIMON MAVIN

The rumours started circulating on social media and radio early on the morning of 5 February that Prince would be playing the Electric Ballroom that night, after Prince teased it at a press event the evening before. Normally on a Wednesday I would be at work but for the for the first time in my life I was 'between jobs'. Perhaps this was a sign. Lying in bed with my morning cup of tea, my partner urged me to take a risk and go and see if I could get tickets. There started an epic adventure.

I drove down from St Albans to Camden, parked my car in a dodgy looking lock up, and sprinted to the venue, arriving at around 10am, where a queue was already starting to form. Nobody knew definitively that Prince was playing at the venue that night but as the minutes and hours passed more and more people began to arrive - the queue was now snaking around the block and the buzz was palpable. We were all increasingly convinced he would be playing that evening. My partner and I kept in contact by phone and text as she had gone to work and would eventually join me in the queue later that afternoon. After around 10 hours of standing in the queue, in the cold and in the rain, the line finally started to move. Suddenly pandemonium set in. People were pushing and queue jumpers were appearing from all angles. Before I knew what was happening we were at the venue doors, where security was trying to maintain control. In the mayhem, my partner got through and I did not. Security notified me and everyone else still in the queue that she was the last person to be admitted and the venue was now at capacity.

My partner argued that I had the money to pay for her entry and after a pause that seemed like a lifetime security waved me through. I was the last person to enter this now legendary gig. We paid as quickly as possible and as we rushed on to the venue floor, we were met with our idol already on stage, pumping out the early bars of 'She's Always in My Hair', our favourite song! This was the stuff of dreams. The gig was amazing as all the reviews testify, with too many highlights to mention.

Immediately after the show we retired to a nearby pub for a drink to reflect on what we had just experienced. The queue for the second show (yes, Prince had announced he was playing a further show that night, starting within a couple of hours of the end of the first show) was now starting to move. My partner turned to me and asked whether we should take our chances and try and get into the second gig as well. I was sceptical and said we should think about it, before heading off to the loo! While in the pub toilets my phone rang and it was my partner ringing me from the front of the queue! 'Quick, hurry,' she said. 'We can get in again if you get here this minute.' I got there with moments to spare and we did it all over again. What a night.

I WAS THERE: NIGEL HART

In an age where social media frenzy ensures that our cultural heroes are just one of us at the end of the day, Prince maintained that air of mystique, that sense of the unknown, that mystery and uniqueness that bled through into his electrifying live performances and held audiences captivated right up until his stripped down and intimate *Piano & A Microphone* dates that were to be his last.

His final shows that I witnessed were all arranged at short notice, mostly in smaller venues, and I was actually one of just 194 people who saw him at Camden's Electric Ballroom in February 2014, a free gig to tantalise an assortment of selected music journos as a sweetener for a series of *Hit and Run* dates that took in London's Koko, The Roundhouse, Shepherd's Bush Empire and further shows at the Electric Ballroom amongst others. On that run I saw him over 10 times with his superb all-female backing band, 3RDEYEGIRL.

Prince was a musical and style setting chameleon, never repeating himself, constantly changing and always evolving. Madonna and Michael Jackson were probably his closest rivals, both of whom were undoubtedly great performers, but neither were musicians. Prince also controlled everything he did, from his clothing, stage productions to musical director. His rivals relied on stylists, PR gurus and input from a plethora of others. What he leaves behind are beautiful, touching, heartfelt, mesmerising memories of a performer that really gave us his all, whether in front of a screaming stadium crowd of thousands, or an intimate gathering for the privileged few at one of his legendary late night after shows. A consummate performer, a musical maverick, who was equal parts Hendrix, Sly Stone and James Brown. A performer of such perfection and wonderment that his incomparable performances shall remain, in his own words, 'forever in my life'.

SHEPHERD'S BUSH EMPIRE

9 FEBRUARY 2014, LONDON, UK

I WAS THERE: JEFF SULLIVAN

Jeff Sullivan saw Prince at the Empire

When Prince landed on this planet, the press didn't know what to make of him. In an era of big hair, big riffs and zero subtlety, he was bafflingly labelled the 'new Hendrix' which, when declared in the same year as the *Purple Rain* soundtrack was released, seemed confusing and misleading. However, almost 30 years later Prince stands in front of an incredibly lucky Shepherd's Bush Empire audience (including me) and, with that Afro and those solos, the comparison holds a lot truer than it did when first made.

These London shows were a master class in PR from a man who still stirs rapid hype that any of his contemporaries could only dream of. The facts have been very few and far between, but after the Electric Ballroom shows, some had travelled to London from all over the country on the off chance of catching the Minneapolis Maestro in action.

It was lunchtime on February 9th 2014 that the first official show was announced via BBC 6Music that was to take place at Shepherd's Bush Empire that very same evening. I left work immediately.

The Internet resembled a voluptuous violet vulva as fans rushed to queue for the show up to six hours in advance of doors opening. As the day progressed, the news spread and with it rumours emerged including one of a £70 price tag per ticket posted by the venue itself which contradicted Prince's philanthropic pricing as declared in his press conference. As this hypocritical news outraged I of course stayed calm but others decided the opportunity was too much for too little. It wasn't until the doors opened that it was revealed that the previous price tag of £10 per ticket remained true for the night. Likely a cunning ruse to draw out only the most devoted fans to this intimate performance and to avoid dangerous crowd levels.

I didn't join the queue until 6.40pm yet still managed to get a front row view right below Prince's symbol microphone stand and pedal board, with my attendee number, 1215, scrawled across my hand in black ink. Incredibly the show didn't even sell out.

Prince kicked off proceedings blazing his way through a revamped version of 'Let's Go Crazy'. Prince's guitar and vocals sat loud and proud in a mix that made clear to the three members of 3RDEYEGIRL who the star was here. His voice sounded as clear and powerful as it did on the *Lovesexy* shows in '88. The realisation that this was really happening right in front of me finally kicked in. The set was an awe-inspiring journey through tracks old and new, reminding you just how many incredible songs Prince had released throughout his career.

Prince stomped his flashing high-heeled boot on the distortion pedal and sent my body into euphoria. No amount of dry ice, lasers or strobe lights could distract this incredibly tight outfit from the task at hand. Prince has never been one to follow trends, always striving to set his own, a leader not a follower. It was easy to forget what decade we were in as you watched the guitar acrobatics on stage and revelled in his total genius. In the two and a half hour set, Prince managed to fit in 39 songs.

Along with the *Lovesexy* and *One Nite Alone* shows, this ranked very high and totally rocked my mind. Forever changed, and I thank you for that, Prince Rogers Nelson.

I WAS THERE: CAMILLE PRINCE

My mum's a fan so I got into it through her. I've been a proper fan since I was about 14, and I had a friend in school that was also a fan. I've only seen him once. I saw him on the *Hit and Run* tour. I would have loved to have seen him in his younger days but I've never been big on media or news so I never knew when he was performing. I opened up my first Twitter account and was going to King's Cross and Camden every day to find out where he was performing. It was the Shepherd's Bush gig, February the 9th. I went on my own. I asked my cousin but when she heard it was £70 she said no, but if I'd have waited for someone I would have missed him.

I WAS THERE: MICHAEL BARNETT

I've been a Prince fan since I was 13. My first gig was '88 and *Lovesexy* in Birmingham. I was just in shock because it was my first ever gig and he was fantastic. Being a fan from that age, I was blown away. My last gig was Shepherd's Bush and that was the closest I ever got to him. Everyone was ushered in onto the floor but these guys skirted round security and I was on my own so followed, and I was 1,381 in the queue so thought there was no way I was going to be on the floor so went upstairs with them. I was on the balcony but then one of these guys shot off into a box which was empty and I followed and we were directly above George Clinton. He was on the first tier and we were on the second. We were literally overlooking Prince for two and a half hours for 10 quid. It was very expensive everywhere else, but only a tenner that night.

I did *Autism Rocks* but I still feel like Shepherd's Bush was my last gig. I didn't really enjoy that gig. When you got in there you were segregated, we were right at the top and right and the back. The best thing about that was when he started playing 'Darling Nikki'. The best tour I've ever seen but didn't go to was Hop Farm, the best one that I saw was Shepherd's Bush. *One Night Alone* at Hammersmith was great because of the jazz thing, just to see him completely different. I paid lots for the 02 three times, it was worth it, every single one was different. The first one I was up in the gods, the second one I did VIP on the tenth row and the third one I was on the third row. But after that I could never get close until I joined the Prince Army. Hop Farm was a slight regret. I wish I'd gone to it. For me, it's beaten *Parade* and *Lovesexy*, it had all the hits, his look, the band were so tight. I would have gone to *Parade* but my brother went with his girlfriend. I was a fan three years before that. My brothers were fans before me but I was under 16 and wasn't allowed to go.

I WAS THERE: SAM BLEAZARD

The Shepherd's Bush show was quite interesting because I was trying to persuade a mate of mine to go. I'd heard that there was going to be an announcement on BBC 6Music. Cerys Matthews was doing her radio show and, Prince being Prince, he was trying to create some mystery and excitement around the gig, so his three female band members went onto the radio to talk to Cerys. It was Sunday lunchtime and they were like, 'Hey guys, if you're up for it this is the *Hit and Run* philosophy. We're going to play Shepherd's Bush later this evening. The first however many people that get there will get in – first come, first served – and you're in. It won't be sold on line.'

I was in southeast London at the time and I remember saying to my wife, 'I've got to go.' It was doable in a cab. There's a speed of decision-making with these kinds of things and word of mouth meant that loads of people would go, even people who only had a passing interest. 'Wow, Prince in a small venue at Shepherd's Bush. How amazing is that going to be?' There was a lot of deliberating, but eventually I bit the bullet and jumped in a cab, not knowing if I would get in.

When I got there, there was already a massive queue around the block with hundreds of people and I was thinking, 'Well, I'm not going to get in.' But what they did was send somebody round the queue, which seemed to go for miles, and they wrote a number on the back of your hand in permanent marker. A lot of Prince fans took pictures of this and someone made a photo collage of all their hands with the numbers on. You knew if somebody wrote on the back of your hand with a marker that you were going to get in. I was one thousand and something. I think two thousand people got in in the end.

It was unbelievably exciting, the 'hit 'n' run' aspect of it. And a rumour went down the line and spread like wildfire that it was £10 to get in. I think I said something like, 'don't be ridiculous. It can't be £10 to get in. There's no gig that costs £10 to get in. That would be a loss leader for Prince.' And then I thought to myself, 'But this is the kind of thing that Prince would do to try and get headlines and to show that concert tickets are overpriced.' He was really annoyed at the time that the Internet was ripping people off through resale sites like Ticketmaster's Get Me In, Viagogo and Seatwave. He hated the fact that big organised groups were buying tickets and selling them on for huge amounts of money. He was really trying to make a statement with all the *Hit and Run* shows, just playing places and saying to people, 'If you really want to come and see me, you're just going to have to rock up before anybody else. But we will just charge you on the door.'

I remember getting to the booth and going, 'Oh, somebody down the line told me it's ten pounds to get in' and they were like, 'Yeah, that's right ten pounds.' I remember handing that ten pounds over with some incredulity. Even if you saw him play for an hour that would have been incredible. And of course, Prince being Prince, he played around 40 songs for about two and a half hours. It was unbelievable, and definitely one of the best gigs I ever saw him play.

By the time I got in, the concert was just starting. The bottom of the Shepherd's Bush Empire had already been packed out so you couldn't get in to the floor level. I preferred the balcony as an option and I remember going up the stairs to and as I walked out onto the balcony I could hear the opening refrain of 'Let's Go Crazy'. He had changed it up with his 3RDEYEGIRL group. It became more of a grungy shuffle, and not as tense as it was in his Eighties heyday. It was really good. It had a different kind of quality to it, quite heavy. There was this amazing wall of sound, like a 'whoosh' as you walked into the room.

I walked to the right hand side of the first tier balcony and had a great view of the stage. It was a brilliant spot, and I could see various celebrities packed out around the balconies.

He just played an unbelievable set full of loud rock stuff, with occasional breaks for some solo piano, and then he'd pick up a bass guitar and jam a little bit with the band. Sometimes he was jamming along with himself, playing samples and grooving along to that, but the core of it was the punk rock vibe that he was into at the time.

Prince was greatly amused and loving the fact that P-Funk legend George Clinton was there. That seemed to give him an extra 15 or 20 per cent inspiration, and he was in a really good mood. He was laughing and joking and saying, 'Do you guys really want another encore for your ten dollars?' He was making jokes about it all night.

I'd only paid ten pounds to get in and it got to the hour mark and I'm thinking, 'okay' and then it was an hour and a half, and then it got to two hours plus. He played three or four encores. I think he was trying to make a point, saying, 'I know you've all paid 10 quid to get in here but I'm going to completely blow your socks off, and it's going to make you think that other concerts are bad value.' There was definitely some kind of mischievous aim to the whole thing.

And he kept referring to George Clinton, saying, 'Do you know who that guy is?' And he'd say, 'George, this is for you.' Because George's band Funkadelic were a heavy black rock group from the late Sixties and early Seventies so Prince obviously loved all that music. George Clinton was delighted as well. He was wearing a wide-rimmed hat and a cream suit. He didn't have the coloured dreadlocks at the time. He was loving all that attention and waving down to Prince. There were lots of other celebrities there too, models like Cara Delevingne. And it was a great set list.

I WAS THERE: ROBERT GOUGH

I fell into being a fan in 1992 at the age of 14. I saw him many times in various UK venues and he was always amazing. For the Shepherd's Bush Empire gig in 2014, it was announced on Twitter that someone was playing that night but there was no actual confirmation. It just said that the first people queuing outside the venue would get in. I raced across London to join a queue that was 300 long when I arrived and ended up being 4,000 long. We didn't know whether he was actually there or whether he was going to perform. I queued for nine hours and Prince released a video of the queue on YouTube. In the end we got in and paid £10 a ticket. A maximum of 1,000 people were there. The concert also had George Clinton watching from above - Prince called him out. Ironically, I then queued next to George and his wife (or whoever the woman who was with him was) in the KFC across the square after the gig because he was so hungry!

I WAS THERE: JENNIFER UPTON

I was #696 in the queue to see Prince at Shepherd's Bush Empire. It was so cold he sent hot chocolate out for all of us. It was the fifth and last time I would see him play live. George Clinton was about 15 seats away and I saw him order a kebab nearby after the gig. 'Do you want vegetables on this?' 'Naw, man… just meat.'

Jennifer Upton was 696 in the queue

Prince's appearance at the 420 capacity Kings Place in King's Cross, London saw him perform two shows, opening both sets with a handful of acoustic numbers including 'Raspberry Beret' and a cover of The Clash's 'Train in Vain'.

KINGS PLACE

14 FEBRUARY 2014, LONDON, UK

I WAS THERE: HASSAN RAZZAQ

I went to the *Hit and Run* tour. I went to see him at Kingsway, in Kings Cross, and the capacity was 500. When I got into the venue the stage was really small, but he managed to get all three of the girls on and himself and he played I think for 50 minutes non-stop rock, and he played 'Endorphin Machine' and - oh my god. There were just 500 people in there and he did two shows that night. And it was Valentine's Day and the queue was massive. We didn't get into the first show and people were starting to walk away and we were like, 'No, no, stick around he might do a second show', so we just hung around hoping. That was a really good show but just a bit too short - it was 70 quid! Shepherd's Bush was £10 and he bought hot chocolate for everyone waiting in the cold, all the fans got one. That time in London everywhere you went it was just, 'Where's Prince playing tonight?' and he played Shepherd's Bush which was a few thousand and then Kingsway which was 500. It was just what he was feeling. He played two or three nights at Electric Ballroom. If you were a Prince fan and you were in London it was just amazing. He was releasing singles every single week on iTunes. He was all over the music press. He didn't do any TV appearances but he was all over the print media. I remember lots of stories in the *Metro* about where he was next performing.

I remember the Brit Awards, because we didn't know he was going to come on the show, and he was the first presenter with 3RDEYEGIRL and that's when he announced the Manchester gigs and as soon as he said 'Manchester', the tickets went live. I think a lot of artists have followed announcing their gigs at short notice, and I think he wanted to announce gigs the night before or the morning of.

Hit and Run was the last time I saw him, but as European fans – especially UK fans – we've been spoiled with shows. I think he really loved his UK fans, there was something special there. I personally think the European fans respected him more and the US fans took him for granted more, and he liked the vibe more here.

21 Nights was quite special. I think the first couple of days he didn't do the after shows and fans were quite upset, but I think he spoilt us in that way because he didn't have to perform. A lot of the after shows they just played CDs of his new stuff. I think one of the unique things about his European tours was that he'd play the new stuff and fans would love it. On the *21 Nights* tour he played stuff from his *Planet Earth* album. You think of another artist who treats his fans like that with £31 tickets or a £10 ticket. I mean, you can't see Ed Sheeran for less than £100. And giving away free copies of the album was just genius. I think he knew he was gonna sell out all the shows. I think Billboard got pissed off because he was in the top 10 album charts for weeks because you got a free CD with the ticket; he was always ahead of the music business.

KOKO

16 FEBRUARY 2014, LONDON, UK

I WAS THERE: DANIEL PAYNE

This show was only announced on 14th November and tickets could not be purchased online to avoid ticket scalpers. So fans had to turn up on the day – some people had started queuing up at 10.30pm the previous night! We got there about 10am. After queuing all day and not knowing if we were even going to get in or even how much it was going to cost, the admission price of £70 was announced to us queuing and then we slowly started to go in in at around 6pm.

There was another new band - 3RDEYEGIRL – and they were amazing. Prince performed what was going to be show one of three shows that day. Lianne La Havas was a guest and performed the amazing 'Lost and Found'. Marcus Anderson also guested on 'Something in the Water (Does Not Compute)'. As we left, the next queue of people were lining up for the following show.

RONNIE SCOTT'S JAZZ CLUB

18 FEBRUARY 2014, LONDON, UK

I WAS THERE: KAREN HODGSON

I queued up for 13 hours in Ronnie Scott's to see him, and when I got in I got right up by him and he was on the keyboard right by me, and I looked at him and I said, 'Prince, you're a handsome dude'. And he looked at me and smiled. This was in 2014, the *Hit and Run* tour. That was the best, because I had eye contact with him. I just melted on the spot because he heard what I said. I couldn't believe it. For days after, I was just saying to everyone, 'Guess what?' That was my favourite gig of all time, but I've seen him countless times. The *Nude* tour, the first time I was there, we had eye contact again. I remember I was in the crowd and everything went black and you had to sit down and he just looked at me and I just went 'woah' and sat down. That's never happened to me ever. The *Nude* tour was Birmingham NIA. My favourite look of Prince was the *Nude* tour with the long hair.

I WAS THERE: LEE HAWKER

It was 8.45am and my mobile rang. It was my friend Daniel George telling me excitedly that the rumours were true and that Prince was to perform at Ronnie Scott's Jazz Club in London Soho that evening. We had discussed this the previous night at the gig in Koko. I ruled out even bothering to try and go due to the fact that they were a members priority club and the small space would easily be filled. Dan was staying nearby and woke early to investigate. The rumours were confirmed by a roadie and also that Prince had hired the club privately to allow fans in and to keep members out.

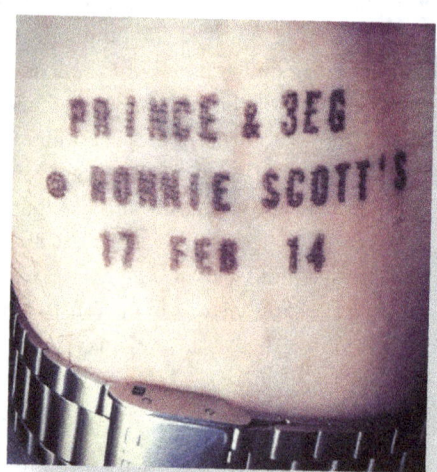

Lee Hawker's stamp that was used on the inside of the Plectrum Electrum album cover

Despite being absolutely shattered from the two Koko shows the previous day, where I travelled throughout the night and started queuing at 6am, I flew out of bed and headed for the tube, praying I would make it in time before word spread.

I arrived at Ronnie's at 9.30am. There was already a queue of about 50 people, all with the obligatory numbers written on their hands for queue position. I became number 57. This 'fan controlled' system had worked well up until now. However, when I saw a group of guys write their own numbers on and push in, I knew that this wouldn't work for such a prestigious event. I was determined not to miss out on the arguably the hottest event in London that summer. At 10.30am, with the queue getting longer, I started to worry, especially after spotting three people with number 36 on their hand. After securing our places in the queue with other trusted fans, I dragged Dan around

Chinatown to find a cool purple dragon stamp or something similar. Having no luck whatsoever, we found a Rymans and bought a text/number rubber stamp. Whilst having a sneaky pint we decided to write 'Prince & 3EG @Ronnie Scotts 17.02.14'. It looked official and everyone agreed. I then set about the queue administering the stamp to as many people who had patiently stood in line. Because of my large build and black jacket, many fans thought I was a Prince crew member and this gave us a well needed laugh. The legitimate fans now had a stamp they could show off and tell the push ins and chancers that it was required.

This stamp was featured on the *PlectrumElectrum* album cover art which reminds me of the night and also makes me proud in a way that I contributed something that Prince signed off.

As the crowds grew I found my place in the queue and waited. The hours slowly rolled by and there were crowd surges, arguments, scuffling, angry shop owners and Ronnie's staff trying to keep control and stop the widening queue from blocking the road. Mounted police and TV crews also joined the melee. The paparazzi were also out in force with their long lenses which added to the excitement brewing. I tried to avoid all media as I had phoned in sick for work that day - like you do!

By late afternoon the queue was hundreds long and stretched way around the block and out of sight. Everyone was tense, as it was obvious most fans would not even have a chance of getting in. By 7pm many people had lost their place in the ever tightening queue. Families and couples had become split and it wasn't fun. The niceties of saving a place for your queue neighbour for a toilet or food break had gone. When the rain fell many people had had enough and quit. Like Duracell bunnies Dan, Unique and myself held firm. Our plan was that when the crowd surged left to view a celebrity arriving, which they had started to do, we would move right towards the wall and the door. This worked well for us. I didn't see one famous person arrive nor did I care, as I was moving closer to the door. The hours dragged and the showers continued. I was shattered, hungry, cold and wet and I questioned my sanity. Prince was the only person that I would do this for!

At 15 minutes past midnight, the doorman finally opened the doors and people trickled in. Dan, Unique and myself all made it through with the first 15. The exhilaration once in as I rushed to the stage was indescribable. We positioned ourselves next to the keyboards...

Suddenly he appeared and was bouncing around like a teenager. In a second all of my tiredness and wet clothing were all forgotten about. My 15 hour wait was worth it before he had even sung a note. He looked sensational. The 90 minute set flew by. When he was at the keys he was an arm's length from me. It was mesmerizing being that close to him and witnessing his genius. He transformed the mundane and effortlessly gave everyone in attendance the memory of a lifetime. He danced, smiled, played bass and keys and sang. It was joyous to witness. The set list was amazingly different of course. My highlights were The Waterboys and Bill Withers covers but my favourite had to be 'Beautiful Strange'. It gave me goose bumps and tears!

I can only imagine what a double rollover lottery winner must feel like but that night as I was ushered out to make way for the second show I felt like one. I was walking on Cloud Nine for days. His music will continue to enthral for generations but his finesse as a live act will never be equalled. At every gig I have attended since he left us, I wish I was at his. Thank you Prince for the absolute best night of my life!

ACADEMY 1

21 FEBRUARY 2014, MANCHESTER, UK

I WAS THERE: SHANE WETTON

It had been a while since last seeing Prince. He hadn't toured the UK for a while but had played a couple of one-off shows and performances in 2011. Social media had become huge and Twitter was definitely the place to be. An announcement came that Prince was coming to the UK to play a series of intimate shows in intimate locations and announcements would be done through fans. It was also made clear announcements would be instant and late. Shows were for the fans and priced low.

One by one shows were announced, all in London and all with only a few hours notice. The only one I had any chance of attending was Shepherd's Bush, as it was a weekend and the announcement gave me a few hours to get there. Unfortunately I was in bed feeling like shit. There was no way I could travel, stand in a queue outside in all weathers and then possibly not get in. I read every comment about all of those shows and was made up for my fellow fans that had been lucky enough to get in, but gutted for myself. The reviews of the Shepherd's Bush show were outstanding.

Those of us outside London were hoping for some shows further north and whilst Prince was handing out a Brit to Ellie Goulding live on TV, tickets for Manchester went on sale. Typically these were the only tickets to go on pre-sale, the only ones available through the usual avenues such as Ticketmaster, and would be fully priced.

Tickets flew out. I tried, I really did. Tickets would be available on the door but how many and how early? Thanks to the social media relationships I had struck up I managed to secure tickets for all four of us... the youngest would finally see Prince live. The rest of us would finally see him again!

February 21st arrived and we met up with Mark, who had kindly offered me his spare tickets, and made our way to the show. In 2007, I'd bought a polka dot shirt and had Minneapolis printed down one sleeve for the 21st show in London and decided to wear it for this show again. When we got in, the girls made their way to the front of the arena while I stayed back with my wife, Anita. We took a couple of pictures as we knew once the show started that pictures were banned and we certainly didn't want to be thrown out.

After taking a couple of pics, a couple of men walked over. One was very tall, well built and wearing a security badge, the other a little smaller but still athletically built. 'You guys ok?' the security guy asked, I panicked a little but calmly said we were fine, just taking a couple of pictures while we could emphasising we wouldn't be taking any more. Looking at the shirt, the smaller guy asked if I was a big fan. 'Yes, massive fan. Been a fan for years,' I replied. 'You like to dance?' he asked. 'Yes,' I said. 'I mean really dance, get funky,' he continued. I remember my answer to this day, word for word, 'Is there any other way...?' 'Wanna dance with Prince on stage tonight?'

Well, what would you say? What would anyone say? I was ushered to the side of the stage and eventually joined by four others. We were told the show would start soon and after a few minutes Prince would say something like, 'Where are my dancers?' That would be the cue. We were told to go on stage and dance, not to touch Prince unless he approached us but apart from that - have fun.

Once the 'no phones' speech by Hannah was over, Prince opened with 'Funknroll' and as promised, a few minutes in, we were summoned to the stage.

Now, there's a very well used picture of Prince playing at Manchester that night. It's one of the few official photos and it shows clearly how small that stage was and just a few feet away from Prince is Ida's set list. That's the spot where I stood. I remember being conscious not to damage her set list. I was stood right next to Ida and very close to my idol. I'm not in the picture unfortunately so I still have no clear proof, just a very grainy mobile phone image. But I was there, right there. I had my moment.

As it was the opener, Prince played up to the crowd and the song was quite extended so I ended up being there for a good few minutes. We danced, we had eye contact and towards the end he blew us all a kiss but we didn't touch, hug or shake hands. We were thanked and that was it.

I had seen the next song on the set list was 'Endorphin Machine', a song I'd told Anita a few days earlier I was hoping he would play, so when I left the stage I didn't hang about. I got back to my original position and watched the show. It was only later would everything dawn on me. The smaller of the two security guys was actually Josh Welton, the husband of drummer Hannah and a large part of Prince's sound at the time, playing keyboards and his producer in the studio.

A few moments stood out that night. One thing was the very heavy rock sound while another was the length of the songs. We'd got so used to hearing medleys and snippets of songs but this night most songs were played at length. The first part of the concert relied heavily on the rock sound – 'Screwdriver', 'She's Always in my Hair' and 'I Could Never Take The Place of Your Man' were followed by 'Guitar', 'Plectrumelectrum', 'Stratus' and 'Fixurlifeup'. The arena was bouncing, as were the crowd.

Then there was a medley segment and 'Forever in my Life', during which Prince and Ida had a 'bass off'. Just hearing this song was enough, but to have it played this way definitely gave it something extra. The usual tracks followed - 'Love Bizarre', a surprisingly lengthy 'When Doves Cry', 'Sign o' the Times' and 'Hot Thing' kept the atmosphere flying and the fans were loving it. 'Nasty Girl' and 'I Would Die For You' took us into 'Purple Rain' which was its usual sublime brilliance. I think this was supposed to be the end.

It was subsequently reported that a further show was planned that night but didn't materialise. Prince kept playing. The first encore started with 'Let's go Crazy'. I wonder whether this was supposed to be the opener for Show Two? Us lucky enough to be there basically saw two shows in one. 'Let's Go Crazy' paved the way for 'U Got The Look' and 'Play That Funky Music', one of the few funk-based tracks of the night, along with 'Funknroll' and 'Musicology', which would come later. A bit of a slower section followed with 'The Love We Make' and a cover, 'Liathach'. I wasn't familiar with the title but knew the song. These two songs brought things down a bit, but not in a bad way. In fact, it was just what was needed for a moment before Prince turned it up a notch again.

A hit trilogy of 'Take Me With You', 'Raspberry Beret' and 'Musicology' soon had people dancing and singing again ahead of a rocky finish. An instrumental version of 'Cause and Effect' started the guitar-based finish, followed by another two covers. The Clash's 'Train in Vain' was a bit of a surprise and then we had the more familiar 'Crimson and Clover' to finish off. Or so we thought. Prince came back one more time, one more song, 'Bambi'. It had been years since I'd heard this live. What a song, what a performance, what a night! Two and a half hours later it was done. I didn't have tickets for tomorrow night. If this was to be the last time I saw Prince for a while - even ever - I was happy.

I WAS THERE: MARK WARE

The second to last time I saw Prince live was 22nd February 2014 at the Manchester Academy (Students Union). I was absolutely gobsmacked to get a ticket for this gig (I made sure I went armed with my passport and proof of address as security around ticketing was tightened up). The atmosphere was electric with a more than half the set being keyboard-based *Sign o' the Times* era material. There was some fantastic guitar work too and it lasted over three hours after a surprisingly early 7pm start.

I WAS THERE: MICHELLE JUSTICE

My favourite ever Prince concert in terms of performance was, poignantly, my last. He brought me to tears. He looked amazing with the Afro. The guitar solos and the atmosphere were electric, and he brought the house down with his rendition of The Isley Brothers 'Live it Up'. I still can't believe he has gone!

I WAS THERE: SAM BLEAZARD

On the last tour I persuaded my good friend Martin - who missed out on Shepherd's Bush - to come and see Prince play in Manchester. He was effectively playing in a student union building at Manchester University. It was another one of these first come, first served-type things. He had appeared on the Brit Awards one evening. James Corden was presenting it and was bantering with him. Prince didn't play at the Brit Awards but he rocked up in this black hat with the band who were also in black. It was a bit odd. Prince and Corden took a selfie.

The reason I remember is that on the night, without any warning, they uploaded tickets to Ticketmaster and it sold out in seconds, because it was going to be in a tiny venue in Manchester. I paid through the nose to get resale tickets for that, and persuaded Martin, my friend from Stockport, to drive up there with me. It was literally within 24 or 48 hours. 'Come on, this is it. This is your chance. You missed Shepherd's Bush. You're getting lucky because you're going to get to see him.'

Standing in daylight and queuing in Manchester's university campus to get into a Prince show was just another one of those surreal moments. It was a long line. Prince was really into security at the time. He was very focused on people not filming his concerts or taking pictures, so there was a lot of security around mobile phones and a lot of rules, which meant it took quite a long time to file in. When we eventually got in, it was a small square black room with a stage and nothing else in it. I remember walking in and getting as close to the stage as we could.

On stage there was a mic stand with a gold Prince symbol glued to the front of it. That was it, nothing else, and I can remember my mate saying, 'Does this seem like a wind up to you?' It seemed so ridiculous, as if somebody was playing a joke about Prince playing at Manchester University.

Prince played a brilliant set once more. It was the only Prince gig my friend ever saw and I remember chatting to him on the way home and saying, 'The thing about Prince is every gig is as good as the last, they're all different and he always ups his level.' It was just Prince in pure rock mode most of the time. He had a bit of an Afro. It was like he didn't care so much about all the millionaire trappings he had at that point, or all the elaborate and expensive guitars he owned, the purple pianos and the limos. He just used to rock up in black with an Afro like when he was a kid, with a Gibson guitar, and he'd just wander around tearing it up. It was a back to basics thing. It was like he wanted to feel what it was like when he started out, like a garage band.

Not everyone liked it. People who'd seen him do the big elaborate O2 shows were not as keen. To some it seemed a bit raw and not really polished. But I think he was trying to give himself a shot in the arm, an adrenaline hit, so that he could feel vital again about his music. And I think that's also why he was doing a solo piano tour at the end. I think he just wanted to strip it all back and really get to the essence of the music.

Prince was performing a *Piano & A Microphone* show that I never saw because he never made it to the UK. He died during that tour. But he had dates in the UK that we tried to book from Ticketmaster. I remember on the morning buying tickets, but he cancelled at the very last minute. There were terrorist attacks in Paris at the time, and there was a theory that Prince got quite spooked by that.

I WAS THERE: DEBBIE COPPINGER

We left our home in East Lothian in Scotland at 11pm on 21st February and arrived at the venue at 4am. We were the first people to arrive. We took a walk around the venue. My excitement was reaching fever pitch. We decided to try to have a few hours sleep in the car before joining the queue at around 8.30am. We were numbers 41, 42 and 43 so almost guaranteed a place near the front. I started talking to the guy behind us in the queue only to realise it was the same person I had been conversing with via Twitter on February 13th, the false Tweet day during the *Hit and Run* tour as we were both wandering around London trying to locate where the gig was to take place. Sadly it never happened. Alan and I are still very good friends.

My eldest son was also at this gig, his first ever Prince concert. How lucky was he? When we were allowed in we just happened to pick the queue where the person in front's ticket wouldn't scan which meant what seemed like hundreds of people went past us. The closest we could get was about the fourth row, which is still very close, but I was very sad to have missed out being front row.

Prince absolutely blew us away with three hours and 15 minutes of pure genius. We walked away with the biggest smiles and lost for words worthy enough to describe what we had just witnessed. I feel so honoured to have been there.

I WAS THERE: KATE AMY SHINGLER

I've been a fan since I was 5 years old. My mum always says I saw a music video on MTV and it just captured me. I can't remember what the song was to this day.

The first gig I went to was Hammersmith Apollo. The last gig I went to was just awesome. I bought tickets to Birmingham with 3RDEYEGIRL on the *Hit and Run* tour and then the day after Heart FM phoned me and said, 'Do you want tickets?' All of my friends and family had entered a competition for me and I was the one that won. So it was like, 'What are you doing tonight Kate?' and I was like, 'Oh, I dunno' because it didn't register, and they were like, 'Do you wanna go see Prince?' I literally ran round the office like telling everybody that I'd won tickets.

This was in Birmingham, the old NEC. But before that I'd gone to Manchester once, so really small, six seats from the stage. That was the closest I'd ever been. Manchester was my favourite. I was on my own as well, because nobody could come with me, so I just went on my own and booked a hotel. You bought a ticket in advance but it was standing so I got there four hours early and had a number on my hand, I was number 109 or something. You know on that song where the guy goes 'no running, no running, there's enough room for everyone'? That's literally what somebody said to be because I was running to get my space. So Prince must have known what we were like, it was just madness, carnage everywhere.

Mum says I was always a little bit different than everybody else in school and she never wanted to stop that little thing that I had. 29 years later here I am, still jamming.

I WAS THERE: TERRY NEILD

Like most of his fans, I first heard a few songs in the very early Eighties that didn't get anywhere in the charts. I was only 13ish at the time. He was different sounding and very sexual if you like skinny black guys - I don't! Then came the break through tracks – 'Dirty Mind and 'Controversy' and then '1999' exploded and I remember everyone at the time going mad over it. Then I bought everything he released up until his death. What a shit year that was for my favourite artists.

I saw him five times over the years but the best was at Manchester Academy. It was one of his small *Hit and Run* shows, announced only a day or so before. We heard he was playing and queued up for nine hours in the rain and cold just for a chance to get a ticket. Luckily they were handing out handmade wrist bands with numbers on them so you knew you would get in. We made some new friends in that line that night. Finally we got in and what followed was a three hour OMG show. We were about ten feet away from him. He looked relaxed and just never stopped blasting out the hits, new and old. My feet were killing me after being stood up for so long but we carried on dancing until the end. We waited another two hours in the venue because the rumour was he was going to do one of his legendary after show gigs but after two hours we all gave up. What an amazing artist. One of the best we will ever, ever have. He is sorely missed.

I WAS THERE: RACHAEL MILLIGAN

I saw the *Hit and Run* tour in Manchester. I live in Scotland and Ali rang me up and said, 'If I get tickets will you come this weekend?' and I went, 'Yeah, okay - I'll come'. So I drove down to Manchester. I remember it was cold. So I met Ali and we'd booked a place to stay and we'd gone for something to eat and then we heard on the radio that he was gigging already and he was gonna do a second gig, so we jumped in the car and raced round to the venue and sat outside to try and get into the second gig. But there wasn't one. Everybody had gone home and there wasn't a second gig.

Rachael Milligan was at the Manchester Academy gig

So the next morning Ali made us queue up at 10 o'clock. It was freezing - we were chuffing freezing! I was drinking gin and tonic from a tin. I had a bag full of tins. The group in the queue were amazing, they were sharing seats, blankets, food – it had a whole community feel to it. I ate everyone's food, everyone's picnics, I shared the tinnies and that was it. I nicked a hat off some bloke behind me who was lovely called Rich, a friend for life, and we got our photos taken. And then we realised Prince was only letting you in if you had ID and we got our tickets off a bloke so we were freaking all day, thinking we wouldn't get let in. Anyways, the doors opened and Ali legged it and I lost her completely. So I'm stuck in the middle of this mosh pit - god knows where Ali is - and I'm right next to Prince and he comes on and I can smell this most gorgeous smell in the whole world – was it called Paradise?

He played everything - old stuff, new stuff, the works - and he was playing with 3RDEYEGIRL. They were very, very good, and they videoed it and the next day it was on YouTube and I saw my hand!

I WAS THERE: SHANE WETTON

As it turned out it wasn't to be the last time. I saw Prince the next night, same venue, but he wasn't playing or at least not when I saw him. I didn't have a ticket and following the emotion of the previous night I was happy to sit this one out. I didn't think I could top the previous night and hadn't intended going. Anita kept telling me to go. I wasn't so sure. I had family stuff I had to do. I'd promised to visit my elderly Nan that day and so that's what I did.

When I got home I checked Twitter to see what was happening and queues were beginning to form in Manchester. I lived about an hour and a half away. Eventually I gave in. I jumped in the car and drove, not really sure I'd get there. I did. I joined the queue and waited.

The queue started moving. I wasn't optimistic as the process of writing numbers on the hands had stopped before I arrived so I resigned myself that I wouldn't get in. After a while the queue stopped. I was right. I was about 50 back and nowhere near the door. I decided to wait a while though. The queue started moving again about 20 minutes later. I was getting closer - close, really close. With just two people in front of me the barrier was shut. That was it - I wasn't getting in. I mean, I really wasn't getting in.

I could hear the concert start – 'Let's Go Crazy' – and the show continued. Do I wait? Maybe as people left others would be let in? Frustratingly, people would leave or be removed but no-one was being let in. The crowd outside started to disperse. I was getting tweets about the show and others saying 'hang on in there'. I still didn't feel optimistic and I was right not to be. I had two choices. Drive home or sit on a cold wet Manchester pavement and listen to the show. I chose the second option. Why not? Who wouldn't?

The show went on... and on... and on. Prince was on fire, you could tell... and hear, clearly. I decided to go to the stage door at the back of the venue. There wasn't any way I was getting in but there wasn't any way I was leaving either so I tried my luck. After one of the encores, the stage crew must have thought it was finally over. Prince played over three hours that night. I'm not surprised if the crew thought it was over. The stage door was opened so Prince's car could be driven in... Prince had other ideas. The door stayed up longer than it probably should have and I had a perfect view of Prince walking around backstage while the crowd begged for more. He was casually strolling around in his hat like he didn't have a care. The door eventually closed again and within minutes I could hear him playing again. The car stayed inside the venue and left a while later.

The security used indoors to stop photos being taken was replicated outside. I couldn't take a photo. I could have tried but as I was stood alone, not in a crowd as I would have been if I was indoors, I might have got away with it but there was no chance. To be honest, I'd always honoured the 'no phones/cameras' rule so why would this be any different?

And so that was it, the story of my two nights in February listening to and of course watching Prince, from within a few feet and from the other side of the wall. Both special memories, and whilst I was to see the two shows in May at the Manchester Arena, both of which were as unbelievable as ever, it was the two nights in February that will forever have a place in my heart.

ARSENIO HALL SHOW

5 MARCH 2014, HOLLYWOOD, CALIFORNIA

I WAS THERE: ALEXIS PARIS

My first experience of seeing Prince very close up, when there may have been only four feet between us, was when me and my friend were at the infamous club Glam Slam located at 333 Boyalston Street in downtown Los Angeles. I can't remember if he performed that night or not - we attended the club a lot – but we went upstairs for something and when we looked to the right Prince was standing there in the flesh, in all red, talking to a female. I don't know if it was work-related but it seems they were having a deep discussion and it wasn't his Queen Mayte. My friend said, 'Go over there and say something to him. Say hello.' I told him, 'Noooo, I'm not getting my feelings hurt', as we knew sometimes Prince could be rude at times. But Prince was looking at us as if he would've obliged. My friend insisted and I still said no. Who knows what Prince would've said?

The other time was on the new *Arsenio Hall Show*. The show was over and as I was leaving the show and headed toward my car who should appear but Prince. He had been on the show talking about himself which also had performances by him and his band 3RDEYEGIRL and the lovely Liv Warfield, a dynamite singer. Prince appeared in the backlot with a few guys and they were going inside one of the trailers. My friend, who was ahead of me, tried to run back but they whisked Prince so fast into the trailer.

LG ARENA

15 & 19 MAY 2014, BIRMINGHAM, UK

I WAS THERE: ANDY CLOSE

I saw Prince live three times, once at Maine Road in Manchester and twice in Birmingham, the last time being the *Hit and Run* tour in May 2014. Even in his mid 50s finish his set but continue jamming for a while and even do a surprise encore. Before a couple of shows he would appear to pop his head through the curtain and the crowd would go wild. Prince had a presence about him. Just being in the same arena or stadium you could feel his aura. Every lady in the crowd wanted him, and every man wanted what he had! Each time afterwards, for a few days, the guitar riffs would be running through my head constantly. A true legend. Maybe one of a kind.

I WAS THERE: AID COOPER

I went to *Lovesexy, Batman* twice (Birmingham and London) and Wembley Stadium, on my birthday. In the early Nineties, I had tickets for the one that got cancelled at Blenheim Palace and Birmingham at the NIA where he walked off stage because the sound was bad. The last tour was *Hit and Run Part 2* in Birmingham. I went on the Thursday (I paid for that) and the Monday, when I got free tickets right at the front. My mate phoned me up on the Monday morning asking me all about it. He said, 'I'm gutted.' He worked in a music shop and I said, 'What do you mean?' and he goes, 'I left work at quarter to 5, Prince's guitar tech came in and did bits and pieces and left them loads of tickets.' So we got free tickets and our name was on the door and all he kept saying was, 'I made those guitar leads'.

I WAS THERE: GILLIAN DONOGHUE

I first heard Prince whilst living in the USA – it was the album *Purple Rain* and it was 1985. I saw him live three times, on the *Lovesexy* tour in the late Eighties, at Maine Road on the *Nude* tour in 1990 and then in 2014 in Birmingham. All three concerts were brilliant. At one of the earlier concerts, Prince performed partly on a huge bed on the stage and on a motorcycle! The 2014 concert was excellent also, and I took my 21 year old daughter with me. At the end, after the encores, some people started leaving, but lots stayed and kept cheering, us included. Prince came back on stage and said, 'They told me that I have to stop at 11, what do ya'll think about that?!' Everyone who was left in the venue screamed and shouted and moved forwards! The band then continued with 'Housequake' and more songs for another half an hour - it was wonderful!

I WAS THERE: LOUIS HOWELLS

The first time I saw Prince I was 6. My Mum is a huge fan so my sister and I were brought up listening to his music. We walked into the 02 and the security were surprised how young I was and asked if they could take me on a tour of the arena before everyone was let in. I was then was allowed in the VIP suite before the concert. I spent the concert singing every song at the top of my voice and dancing.

The last time I saw Prince was in May 2014 at Birmingham. We arrived really early at the arena and I was number 13 in the queue. My Mum had to ring school and make an excuse as to why I wasn't there. While on the phone there were really loud building works going on onsite. We got away with it though!

A small amount of people were let into the arena early to check out the merchandise first and queue before everyone else. We stood queuing and we heard music. It was the sound check! I snuck round the corner and could see the band and Prince through a gap in the door. The concert was amazing and when Hannah threw her drumstick into the crowd and a guy caught it, one of the security said to him, 'It's his birthday, would you give him the drumstick?' and the poor guy handed it over to me.

Along with my dad, Prince inspired me to become a musician. He was and will always be a genius.

I WAS THERE: LEE BETTLES

I saw him over 30 times altogether. There's just so many highlights. There was never a bad show. I travelled to France, to Spain, to America. I went to America for the *Musicology* tour. The last show I saw was in the May of 2014. It was the Hit and Run Phase 2 shows.

It was at the NEC and I went to the second night. He's still the only person that can elevate me to another place. I just remember thinking, 'There he is again. He's back, he's here.' He did over two hours and he didn't even seem to break a sweat. He just loved performing. He adored it. That's all he lived for, to please the fans.

He was funny. He was energetic. There was a great piano set. I like the raw funk stuff. His latest band, 3RDEYEGIRL, were a bit more rocky. I never thought, 'This is going to be the last time I see him.' To this day I still think, 'This is a terrible dream and I'm going to wake up and find it's not real.'

From every gig I came away thinking, 'I've just witnessed the greatest entertainer that there's ever been.' And no one will ever touch him. It was a privilege to be in his presence for two hours.

I WAS THERE: BEN MARSHALL

I discovered his music back in 2005 or 2006 when I used to browse the music section at my local library. I came across *The Hits/The B-Sides* album and the cover intrigued me. Who was this cool dude with the oddly-shaven beard? I'd never heard anything so different in my life and down the rabbit hole I went, exploring his career via Prince forums and bootleg download sites. I became obsessed very quickly and followed his career, finding his *3121* Vegas shows and searching for the shows that made up clips for his British Rock and Roll Hall of Fame induction. I watched the Superbowl 2007 performance and was mesmerised and I knew I had to go and see him live.

I was too young when he came to

Ben Marshall discovered Prince's music at his local library

London in 2007 and I wasn't allowed to go alone, and I kept missing out every time he came back to the UK only to play *Hit and Run* shows in London or Hop Farm in Kent. I knew I had to be patient and wait for a show closer to me.

Finally in 2014 I got my chance. It was the first time he'd played Birmingham in over 20 years and even though it was a Thursday night and I was working in a school and had to be up the following morning, I jumped at the chance and parted with my 120 quid. I remember driving there straight from work and being so excited walking to the arena bathed in purple light. I made my way inside after the doors opened and walked past the standing queue. It looked rammed. I sat near the arena doors waiting to go in and heard them sound checking 'Funknroll' and it hit me I was actually going to see him. But it didn't feel real until I could see him on stage.

Three false starts and 40 minutes later than stated, he finally walked out and the best gig of my life commenced. My first thought was, 'OMG, he really is small!' I was there on my own so had enough room with an empty seat next to me to dance my backside off. He played all the hits and guitar solos galore and I lost it when he performed 'Electric Intercourse' for the first time since 1983. Within a beautiful piano and microphone medley laden with his slow hits, his vocals sounded incredible. Onto the funk with 'Controversy' and '1999' and I remember dancing until my feet hurt and even more so when the sample section came on. The second he hit 'Hot Thing' I cheered so loud. It was one of my favourites and I couldn't believe he was singing it. I knew he'd not played the guitar solo on 'Purple Rain' for ages and opted instead for piano solos and vocal flutters, and so when the intro kicked in and he walked out holding a guitar, I lost my mind as I knew he would play it. Indeed he did and it was a moment I'll treasure forever. The lights went up and I started to make my way down, ready to run for my car. I asked a steward on the way down if it was the end and she told me, 'He's not sticking to his set list tonight so I'm not sure.'

Just as she said that, he came back out and said, 'There's a strict curfew but we're gonna try to jam until they shut us down' and launched into a blistering cover of 'Play That Funky Music'. The steward told me I could dance in the partly empty seated section next to us. And dance I did, with the Purple One blowing my mind with a brilliant guitar solo to end my night of purple highs. I ran back to my car and it all seemed so surreal - did that really just happen? I managed to get retweets on Twitter off all of his 3RDEYEGIRL band members, and it really was the best gig I've ever been to in my life. I will treasure it forever.

I went on to attend an impersonator gig of a friend in Birmingham whose partner I met at the concert through social media. I kept an eye on future gigs and was ready to attend his *Piano & A Microphone* show in Birmingham but it was cancelled. Obviously I was devastated when he passed, but I did attend the tribute gig at the Hammersmith Apollo a couple of months later with performances from Larry Graham, CeeLo Green, Morris Day and The Time and Mark Ronson, who did a DJ set. I also attended the *My Name is Prince* exhibit at the O2 in London. My favourite tribute band is the New Purple Celebration who I've seen three times.

ARENA

16 MAY 2014, MANCHESTER, UK

I WAS THERE: KATIE TREMBATH

The last time I saw him was at Manchester Arena with 3RDEYEGIRL. Once again he didn't disappoint. It was awesome. I so wanted to be one of the girls in the band. I truly love him. It would have been amazing to see the *Piano & A Microphone* tour but unfortunately he cancelled coming to London after the Paris attacks. I went to see The Revolution on Valentine's Day in 2019. They were so good. It was very emotional. Now I need to see NPG. Hopefully we will have more from The Vault.

He will live on forever in my eyes. No one will ever compare to him. He's a true legend. I can honestly say I love everything he has done. I find genius in everything. Until the end of time – well, my time - I will listen to him everyday.

Katie Trembath's Prince tattoo

CAFÉ DE PARIS

20 MAY 2014, LONDON, UK

I WAS THERE: ROB STAPLES

I first heard the remote rumour of a secret gig about a week before on Wednesday 14th May 2014. A link to a website had been circulated briefly and then disappeared. The public website was www.autismrocks.com and had a simple info flash:

Ticket for the Cafe de Paris show
Ad for the Café de Paris show. Photos thanks to Rob Staples

'In aid of our brand new charity, Autism Rocks, Sanjay Shah, founder of Solo Capital, will be hosting a spectacular, not to be missed event! Featuring a performance by a multi-award winning Rock and Roll Hall of Fame Artist.'

You have to understand how it was going down in London in spring 2014. Prince had been announcing his guerrilla *Hit and Run* gigs at short notice via social media and the whole Prince community was literally on red alert for the next announcement. We all had Twitter notifying us of anything, everything that could vaguely resemble a clue to the next venue Prince would be playing. And Prince had strange gaps in his *Hit and Run II* tour the following week so we were all on hyper alert for news of after shows and one-off gigs. Any Prince fan will see the words 'Rock & Roll Hall of Fame' and immediately make a connection with Prince, with him receiving this legendary title back in 2004. So I went into full on purple detective mode...

The website was basic, but that was consistent with Autism Rocks being a new charity. I noticed that there was a Home link, and low & behold there was a CONTACT link which took you through to a message board. I sat there at the end of a busy day at school (I'm a headteacher!) and just thought well, you don't get anything in this life if you don't ask. So I quickly fired off an email, telling them how much I supported the charity and sharing some the work we do with the wide range of autistic children at my school. Amazingly, we had just run a whole school autism awareness week, so I shared information about that. I then went on to share how, as well as my day job, I am a huge Prince fan and it would be great to get an invitation to support the event. I was thinking, 'I doubt anything will come of that, but at least I tried...'

Imagine my surprise when, almost immediately, I got an email from Sanjay directly thanking me for my support and advising that he would send over an invite including a way to donate and obtain tickets to the event! Well you can imagine my reaction. It's probably best if I leave it to your imagination, actually... It involved lots of 'OMGs', 'I can't believe its' and everything else from little yelps to screams of excitement I think the cleaners at school thought the head had finally lost it! Had I really been invited to a secret Prince gig?

With a weird nausea rising in my stomach, I clicked through the links for the first confirmation that we were definitely talking about Prince. And there was Prince's official publicity shot for the *Hit and Run II* tour, providing an inviting backdrop to an information flyer. With those amazing eyes twinkling knowingly at me, I tried to take in all the information as quickly as I could.

Tuesday 20th May – one of the strange 'gaps' in Prince's UK schedule; he will have just done the second Birmingham gig and needs to be up in Glasgow for 22nd May. Prince is never one to hang about when he's working.

Café De Paris – great venue, Prince loves it and has played there twice before, once in 1998 and once in 2007. Perfect for this type of intimate occasion.

I clicked through to DONATE and was presented with an option to .... Donate and get a ticket!

There were two pricing levels: one which matched the earlier information on the public website for the VIP section. I know the Café De Paris and I knew that that meant sitting in a boothed area, luxurious, but away from the stage. There was no way I was going to pay that much... I had already spent about that this year on Hit & Run I & II combined. It just wasn't possible.

And then my heart started really racing as I realised that there was the second option for general admission and access to main floor standing at a quarter of the price! Really? To see Prince in that intimate venue, at a private gig? And with the option to queue and be front row? If I was saying my OMGs earlier, now I had descended into expletives of joy! This was going to rock!

But there were a few problems. All over the information, everywhere, it said in big, bold letters: 'ALL INFORMATION RELATING TO THIS EVENT SHOULD BE KEPT CONFIDENTIAL. NO RECORDING.' So I had multiple dilemmas, and I had to sort them out fast. How many tickets do I try to buy? How many tickets at £250 a pop do I have the money to buy? Who is on the list of people I would love to give this chance to? Who can I trust enough to share this with? Are they free on Tuesday and are they willing to pay £250? (It's a no-brainer to me, but not everyone thinks like me!) How can I sort this before the tickets disappear? What the hell am I going to wear to Café de Paris?

This was going to cause tensions within the Prince community. We all had 10, 20 or more people that we could think of that we wanted to get to the party. But it was being made very clear to us that any breach of confidence would result in potentially losing our own chance. So some really difficult decisions had to be made and they had to be made fast. We didn't know the venue capacity and all I had in my head was, 'If this is anything like Ronnie Scott's, these tickets are going to disappear in moments.' This was not easy and some people got it right, others might not have done in the heat of the moment. That's life. It wasn't that anybody didn't want the whole Prince Army assembled….

So within 10 minutes I had called round, secured the commitment of two mates, including my best pal and all time Prince buddy, Matt Osgood, and bought three tickets with the last bit of money left on my credit card. An email popped back to confirm, with three e-tickets attached. We were in!

What then followed was a week of exquisite torture. To know that you are going to such an iconic venue, to attend an exclusive, secret gig, with great pals, to see Prince – AND NOT TO BE ALLOWED TO TALK ABOUT IT! Well that was pretty hard, I can tell you. And then there were the moments where I began to suspect it was a huge scam and the paranoia set in… did the website really look genuine? Why did all the links disappear the next day? Why was the currency in dollars? And why hadn't they spelt Café de Paris correctly on the flipping tickets?

Of course, I had four Prince arena gigs to keep me occupied in the meantime, but that made it even harder. Seeing all your Prince Army pals and knowing that you couldn't say anything; knowing that you were in and they weren't… it was genuinely hard. A few hinted conversations here and there quickly established those that were in the know… 'So what are you doing for the rest of the week, after Birmingham on Monday?' was a good one. In huddled corners and private chat rooms, we were able to release some of our excitement and start planning logistics and stressing over dress codes. But it was all overshadowed by the fear that it could be ripped from us at any point. So we had to follow the rules and protect the significant financial risk that we had all put on what could have easily been a complete scam.

The day itself finally arrived. Maybe 20 or so people I knew through Prince-related social media turned up and we queued in anticipation. Finally, we were let in and glued ourselves in front of the stage for another hour or so, until the lights went down and Prince strolled on stages with the 3RDEYEGIRL band.

Prince was on fire. It was just incredible to see the emotion of his performance up so close. It's only really when you can see into the whites of Prince's eyes that you start to get a proper sense of the craft of his performance; clocking each crowd response, anticipating where to take the vibe next and allowing 400 people to enter his soul. It's his capacity to deep create empathy through music which never ceases to astound me, and being there to see it from 5ft away is an indescribable privilege. My dear friend Farzana was invited up on stage to dance with Prince and gave him a hug after.

Being a fan of Prince was filled with these magic moments. Moments that came out of the blue, filled you with awe and excitement, and stayed with you forever. Some might say I was a lucky git to get in to that Café de Paris gig, but it wasn't just a dose of good luck and help from my friends that got me stood in that spot – it was also through quite a bit of hard work, financial commitment and focusing of my priorities and time to pursue my love for the Man.

Now I know you have to just make those moments happen before it's too late.

I WAS THERE: FARZANA JALALI

It was 2014 and it was during the *Hit and Run* concerts and I'd heard rumours of a charity concert Prince was doing for Autism Rocks. I managed to get a ticket and turned up at the Café de Paris in London to wait a full 12 hours until the doors opened. I was first in the queue and we'd all been asked to dress up as it was a VIP event. When we got in, the venue was small and I was at the front of the stage, about a foot away from the stage which was only a few inches high off the ground. When Prince came on stage, I could count his eyelashes, I was that close. I'll always remember his flawless skin.

During 'Kiss', he pointed to a girl to my right to invite her up on stage but she froze. I remember thinking, 'Point to me! I promise I won't freeze!' He pointed to me! I jumped the rope barrier and was up on that stage in a flash. I'm not the type of person who likes being on a stage but at that moment, all I could see were the front two rows of faces of people I knew and I didn't care because I was on stage with Prince! I danced - probably badly - and was overwhelmed with what was happening. I suddenly realised, that I couldn't see Prince so I looked behind me and he was stood with his arms folded watching me! beckoned him back to the front of the stage and he showed me some dance moves and I copied him.

I cannot begin to explain how I was feeling - disbelief, exhilaration, shock. I don't think I was breathing! The song ended and I knew that I didn't want this moment to end but I didn't have the capacity to speak any words so I opened my arms and Prince walked over to give me a hug! I remember feeling his shoulders and his scent - sandalwood. I then came off the stage and returned to my friends who were so thrilled but that's when I started to hyperventilate and actually thought I'd have a heart attack! That moment was one of the best moments of my life.

I WAS THERE: MATT OSGOOD

This was another invitation only gig and this time expensive at £300 plus with a contribution to the *Autism Rocks* charity and only a few fans but lots of people and celebs who supported the charity in attendance. Straight after work, and luckily just around the corner, I met up with my best mate to right the wrong of him not coming with me in 1998. We were off to see Prince together at Café de Paris!

Queuing outside, we met with a few more fans that we had got to know while queuing outside Koko all day earlier that February. Once inside, the 20 or so of us headed directly to the stage front forgoing the drinks and nibbles. This time the wait was not so long and the guests were entertained by a DJ set from Trevor Nelson. Whilst we'd been front row at a Prince gig and after shows before, none of them were at quite a small stage as this one! I don't recall much of a long wait. Maybe I was buzzing about being in such a small venue and up front and – wow, just wow! - clearly knowing the gig was for a more casual audience, Prince and 3rd Eye Girl rocked with pretty much just the hits! Starting with 'Let's Go Crazy' and then not really letting up for the next hour or so and ending with '1999' and then an encore of the synthesiser set of just him on stage having the time of his life joking around. This gig bounced from start to finish and all for a great cause Blissful stuff!

I was also there for what sadly turned out to be his last ever UK gig on 2nd February 2015 at Koko for the *Autism Rocks* charity and for the 21st/22nd September O2 gig and after show at the Indigo where Amy Winehouse guested with Prince on a version of 'Love is a Losing Game'. I was at Bagley's Warehouse too in the Nineties, but while that was an interesting event, it was not a gig I personally enjoyed that much.

SSE HYDRO

22 MAY 2014, GLASGOW, UK

I WAS THERE: MARK HUTCHISON

I met my current girlfriend, Wendy, in August 2014. (As a side note, her hairdresser is called Lisa. Yeah, you know I sang 'Computer Blue'….). After a few weeks, I noticed her singing along to a lot of my Prince music - some well known, some not so. I figured she was into Prince to a degree. After listening to her talk about artists she'd seen live, and the list was extensive but very ordinary, I told her I had to take her to see Prince.

I had just been to see him in May 2014 at the SSE Hydro in Glasgow. What I loved about this gig was that me and my friend Colin McAndrew had a first timer with us in

Gally, a mutual friend. Before the gig, Gally harped on about seeing Paul Weller live and how 'this won't be as good'. He also stated his favourite three Prince songs were 'Let's Go Crazy', 'Take Me with U' and 'Raspberry Beret'. So we get into gig, having paid £186 per £65 ticket. Worth it? Damn straight. We were pretty much stood in the front row and Prince opened with three songs... 'Let's Go Crazy', 'Take Me with U' and 'Raspberry Beret'. Gally was blown away. That concert for me was deep in so many ways - his first time back in Scotland since 1995. For the first time, I had tears in my eyes at a Prince gig. During a stunning version of 'The Beautiful Ones', it really did touch my soul. It was Prince on his finest form. He had the audience in the palm of his hand. Up in the rafters, down in the basement. Everything in between. It was a stunning night. Unknown then, but like a fitting farewell to Scotland. We came out of that gig and Gally had this to say as soon as we stepped into the cold Glasgow night: 'That was the best concert I've ever seen.' And that said it all.

21st April 2016. I'm upstairs, playing FIFA on Xbox, *Gold* playing on my Echo Dot over the muted Xbox. I'm winning 2-0, with 30 minutes to go. Wendy is working. She's a masseuse and works in a hut in the garden. The hut is all heated, wired up, etc. And I hear her shout from bottom of stairs. 'Mark, have you had the news on?' My first thought is, 'She never stops work, must be bad.' I walk to the top of stairs. She looks up at me and says, 'Prince has died.' I knew from her tone, her look, that this was no bad joke. The 10 feet walk back to the room seemed to take forever. I picked up my phone, looked at Facebook and saw Colin's post first. I cried. A deep, hurting cry. I messaged Colin. All I said was, 'What the fucking hell!? I'm in shock. I don't know what to say.' Colin replied, 'I'm coming down.' Yes, he drove over 100 miles from Inverness to Fife and we sat in the car, started with 'Sometimes It Snows In April' and cried. For an hour, maybe three, barely speaking at first then talking about the concerts like only Prince fans will understand.

I never got the chance to take Wendy to see Prince.

FIRST DIRECT ARENA

23 MAY 2014, LEEDS, UK

I WAS THERE: DANIEL PAYNE

I got these tickets at the very last moment - and I'm so pleased I did – just a week before the gig. After queuing for the morning I managed to get in the first row right at the front! He performed 'Dreamer' and closed the set with 'Sometimes it Snows in April'. Little did I know this would be the very last time I would ever see him. I was 42. He was 56 years old.

Daniel Payne's tickets for the First Direct Arena show in Leeds

I WAS THERE: FIONA BROOMFIELD

Prince and 3RDEYEGIRL came to my home city of Leeds in May 2014. This was my third Prince gig - *21 Nights* in London was the time before and the first time I experienced Prince live was in Sheffield, when I was 16 years old. That was just after the *Symbol* album came out, which was the soundtrack to my sexual awakening. Years later I am on another level of excitement when he's on stage in my home city and rips through his epic back catalogue - to the pure delight of this adoring Yorkshire posse. It was perfection. From the second he appeared on stage in Leeds to long after he left the room I felt like I was literally on another planet. It doesn't feel like you're at a gig when Prince is on stage. You are, but something else happens. It feels like your body, brain and soul are electrified. The music, the lyrics and energy literally pulsate through you, awakening every sense and emotion. I felt so unbelievably alive in that room. It's the biggest thrill I can describe, and so deeply spiritual too. It's as arresting as it is affecting. The energy created there and the feeling was something special and it will stay with me forever. It was the last time I saw Prince. Thinking of it brings tears to my eyes, and a lump to my throat. I know I won't ever experience that again, and am lucky and honoured to have experienced it at all. It was a gift. Three times a gift. And its still with me. He's always in my hair.

I WAS THERE: STUART WILLOUGHBY

At Prince's UK show at Leeds Arena in May 2014, I was standing at the front right before show kick off when I started talking to two guys of about 50. We began discussing Prince shows we had seen over the years, and inevitably we discovered that we'd been at lots of the same ones. Next to me was a young woman of about 20 and she started talking to me about Prince after overhearing us. 'I've waited my whole life for tonight,' she said. 'It's my first ever Prince show.' 'Welcome to the dawn. It'll be the greatest night of your life', I said. 'Do you really think it will be?' she asked, laughing. 'I have heard that he's an incredible performer,' she said. 'You won't see anyone better,' I said. 'You'll be crying like a baby by the end of the night.' She laughed, saying she didn't think she would be, and five minutes later Prince walked onto the stage and the band launched into 'Let's Go Crazy'. At the end of the show the area cleared a little and I spotted the young woman. She waved to me and came across to say hello. As she got nearer I could see that her face was literally soaked in tears. 'Do you have a tissue?' she asked and we both laughed. 'Was it the best night of your life?' I asked. Her reply? 'You KNOW it was!'

ROUNDHOUSE

4 JUNE 2014, LONDON, UK

I WAS THERE: GINA JOYCE

The Roundhouse was the last Prince show I went to. I was only six months post having a hip replacement. I could walk without sticks, but only just. I also had a bad chest infection and wasn't feeling great, so for the first time ever I only bought a ticket for the earlier Roundhouse show instead of for both. I really regret that now. I went with the same friend I went to all the Prince gigs with. She was working so I got there extra early to get in the queue for us both, and we had an amazing spot at the stage, just a few rows back from the front and dead centre to the mic!

When Prince first came on stage I thought how he'd aged. We were very close to the stage so looking straight at him. Of course he had his Afro hair now too, which I was never a fan of. I think that definitely made him look older, and like many fans I much preferred his North Sea Jazz/Montreux look/haircut.

He played an amazing set list and as usual received totally amazing reviews in the media afterwards. 3RDEYEGIRL were also excellent, and they played an amazing slow version of 'Let's Go Crazy'. A thumping 'The Max' with awesome deep, loud bass towards the very end got us fans jumping around and dancing. It seemed very strange saying goodbye to my friend inside the venue after the first show had ended. She was going to the second show as well!

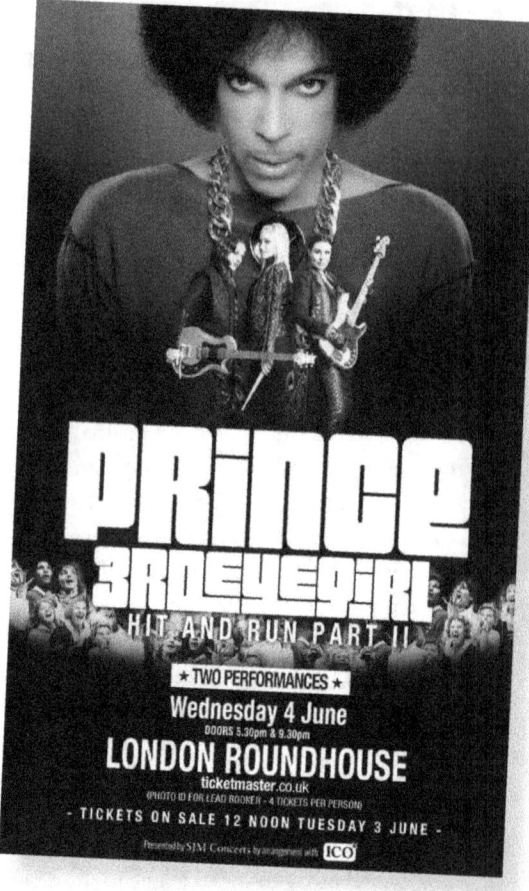

I WAS THERE: NICOLA WAKLEY-WAKE

The last time I saw him live was when he did the *Hit and Run* tour in London 2014. I saw him at the Roundhouse with 3RDEYEGIRL. It was a stunning performance, so intimate and exciting as you only knew where it was on the day or day before. He was magnificent. There was a strict no camera policy (the person next to me had their phone confiscated) but I managed one photo and one video.

I WAS THERE: PED MILLICHAMP

I saw him several times – at Wembley Stadium, the O2, Ronnie Scott's and the Roundhouse. In 1988, aged 12, I listened to a Paul Gambaccini radio show about him. I was hooked from then on. I discovered the back catalogue of his albums and then what followed. I visited Chanhassen aged 17 with my dad and tried to get into Paisley Park without success.

My first gig was around 1994. The Roundhouse was mesmerising. It was the first time I'd seen him up close. I was frozen in awe throughout the whole gig. It was absolute velvety bliss! The news of his death was a shock. I was on my way to an Arsenal game with my son and an Arsenal player! I'd give anything to see him one more time. Prince has always been there for me. Any stage of my life or whatever mood I'm in, I can put on a particular album or song.

I WAS THERE: VANESSA WRIGHT

The last time we saw Prince.

My partner and I had been part of the mayhem that was the *Hit and Run* tour that year having been lucky to see Prince all over the UK at many venues big and small thanks to social media and the Prince Army. We managed to get tickets to both gigs that night at the Roundhouse. Having watched a phenomenal first set, the heavens opened outside and I did not fancy going out into the rain to the back of the queue to get a soaking. I asked a kindly-looking security guard, showing him our tickets for the second gig, whether we could stay inside and shelter until they were ready to open for part two.

The security guard took pity on us and hid us, along with four other couples, round the back of the venue out of sight. Just before they opened the doors for the second set, he came and got us and told us that he would let us in first! Having a bit of a phobia of crowds and a fear of being squashed, I had never been to the front of a gig before. I was slightly anxious but also excited that I would be the closest I had ever been to a living legend.

The second set was just as good as the first and we were fortunate that a big man protected us from getting squashed in the throng of the crowd. We were front left of the stage. The last song before the encore was 'Something In The Water Does Not Compute'. Prince came over to our side of the stage. We were singing the song at the top of our voices. This song preceded the *Hit and Run* tour that was circulating on YouTube - a refreshed version we loved from the moment we heard it. Prince was singing it right back at us. Our eyes locked with the great man. He was smiling. We were smiling. It was spine-tingling and a moment we will never forgot. We were so close to this genius it was electrifying. He was gone way too soon, but I feel incredibly lucky that the last time we saw him was this great encounter. Gone, but never forgotten.

I WAS THERE: SAM BLEAZARD

The last time I saw him was at the Roundhouse in Camden, which was a variation of the *Hit and Run* tour. These were the last two shows I saw Prince play, although I never dreamed that it would be. I just thought he was immortal on some level and that he'd go on forever. He always seemed like quite a youthful guy anyway. A lot of what I'd read about him was that he was very clean living. He'd been into veganism for a long time before it became a hip thing to do. Obviously, he kept really bad hours, but nobody would have predicted that would die when he did.

The Roundhouse was a venue I'd never been to before. It's a bit like the Indigo at the O2. What I loved about those types of venues is that they're wide – they're panoramic and landscape, so everyone gets a good view of the stage. We were on the floor at the Roundhouse. It was really jam-packed because people were clamouring to get close to the stage. The first show was almost an afternoon/early evening thing, and I can remember Prince playing really interesting stuff like 'A Case of You' by Joni Mitchell, and an unusual version of 'Purple Rain' that was all built around a long piano intro. It wasn't guitar-based at all, and was a really moving performance. It was one of those songs where you think, 'Well, how can he wring anything else out of this?' because he must be so sick of playing it. For me it was an incredible and emotional show.

I stayed behind because I had a ticket for the later show, and a friend of my wife's came with me. And this is the myth and the legend of Prince, because the second show was very different. He had a different outfit on. He played very different material. I felt like I saw two different people. The second one was more like a party, with the band playing party songs. It was, 'Hey, it's Saturday night, let's party' so there were a lot of upbeat hits. The afternoon gig was more thoughtful.

I WAS THERE: DIANE ELIZABETH RHULE

My dad had his albums and I got hooked on *Purple Rain* at the age of 8. I saw him on the American Music Awards in 1985 and couldn't believe how beautiful and mysterious he was. The love affair started from there. I first saw him at Wembley Stadium in 1993. I went with a boyfriend and his friend. We got a spot half way from the stage. I was absolutely gutted as I desperately wanted to be closer. Because of that I didn't enjoy the show.

Including after shows I must have seen him around 40 times. Manchester G-Mex in 1995 was great, purely because he saw me on the front row and then got his security to take my phone number. Second, the Café de Paris because the night was absolutely amazing. The atmosphere was so electric you could almost feel the music was another level. There were lots of celebrities in awe of him there and he was in such a great mood too. And then there was the Rio restaurant in Vegas. He played to around 15 of us. It was a bit too jazzy and rocky at times but we felt very lucky to have witnessed it.

The Roundhouse in 2014 was strangely perfect. It felt like he gave it his all that night. I even said to a few people that if I never saw him again that that was ok because I would never see better. He played all the hits and more. His voice was on point. He was in a good mood and was full of energy. The venue was perfect and the crowd were totally up for it. My Facebook post from the night of the Roundhouse gig says, 'Did that just happen? Best gig ever!'

I WAS THERE: PETE HOLDEN

I saw Prince play one of his Roundhouse shows in London. It was actually my last night in London after living there for 33 years and it was certainly a fitting finale. He was, I have to say, amazing that night. I went with an old friend, Campbell Stevenson. The Roundhouse show was stunning and lasted about two and a half or three hours - and it was his second show that day. I thought we'd be into a long Prince funk work out but he actually played pretty much all of the hits and Prince classics. He was bright, funny, communicative, relaxed and very physical and showed no sign of his age. He certainly didn't look like someone who was plagued with physical pains and restraints, which made his death two years later all the more surprising.

It wasn't the first time I'd seen Prince. In the Eighties, a friend of mine's then wife was his wardrobe mistress when he played Wembley and I also saw him at Earls Court. Our guest tickets that time were rubbish side of stage seats but it did mean we got to see him get in the lift thing at the back of the stage for his grand entrance. It all went very Spinal Tap the night we went and the doors failed to open for him!

There was also a tale Lisa the wardrobe mistress told us about the Wembley show, which started with the band onstage first and Prince appearing at the side of stage and then running across the front with his guitar, dropping to his knees and sliding between Wendy's mini-skirted legs whilst grabbing her skirt with his teeth and coming up the other side to hit his first note on his guitar. To execute this manoeuvre, the stage had to be very clean and shiny and Prince needed a pair of toughened and especially 'slidey' trousers. One night, an hour or two before stage time whilst sorting out his stage gear, Lisa realised to her horror that his special trousers weren't in the wardrobe and must have been left in the Sketchley's (dry cleaners) at Holland Park. She was given a flashing light police escort through the rush hour streets. Although it was past closing time when she got there the shop was being refitted so, after banging on the windows and shouting, 'I've come for Prince's trousers', she was able to get in and get back to Wembley with them just before Prince called out for his special trousers to be brought to him!

PAISLEY PARK

20 OCTOBER 2014, CHANHASSEN, MINNESOTA

I WAS THERE: DAVID J BAYLISS

Another fan won a competition and was invited to Paisley Park where Prince would perform. Only those in the know were invited and around 50 people turned up. Prince rocked the place and with only 50 fans attending everyone had the perfect view of the Minneapolis Genius.

We were in Chanhassen - Merry, her hubby and I. There is still no announcement of a show. Thank God for Merry, who had multiple devices. She was texting on one and tweeting on the other. She was on it! We eat, shower and get dressed and... wait... and wait....

Merry is trying to get a hold of Dorothy to get clues. All the while I'm thinking, 'Oh Lawd, Prince done kidnapped Dorothy and flushed her phone down the terlit.' But finally we got word. We go to Paisley Park and immediately get accosted by security. Anyhoo, they let us dweebs stay and then the Cool Kids arrive - Jesse, Kathy Drews and the others. Oh man, we are in there! I hid in Jesse's pocket to get in.

I'm in Paisley Frickin' PARK! We dance, we hug. It was a Purple Love Fest and then... The doors to the big room open and there they are! Prince and 3RDEYEGIRL! They were in full swing with 'Let's Go Crazy' reloaded. I don't know how I got so close, but I was under the mic and it sounded great! 3RDEYEGIRL were amazing. Ida was holding it down and Donna was doing crazy hand tricks on the guitar. Hannah had a drum solo that I felt in my chest and made it look so easy! She smiled the whole time. And Prince? Oh snap, my heart just skipped a beat thinking about it. His voice was clear and strong. His guitar was afire and he looked even younger up close! Chile, that man was cute.

Prince came off the stage as 3RDEYEGIRL continued playing. He stood watching them, assessing their positions on the stage. He then made his way back on stage and walked right passed me as I tapped his shoulder. He continued to performing, playing classic songs. At the end of the show Prince again left the stage, dressed in white with stubble on his face and wearing a beanie hat! He looked absolutely stunning as he walked away and I felt the urge to approach him. As he walked away with that Prince swagger, his arms swinging, I got close and grabbed his hand as he walked about eight steps before I came to my senses and let go. He didn't seem to mind and I watched him walk behind a curtain and he was gone. Afterwards I regretted invading his personal space and acting on impulse and felt a little daft behaving in that manner. But after he passed the memories of holding his hand and being so close to the greatest musician to have ever walked the earth will stay with me to my dying day.

I visited Paisley Park many times especially PJ parties. There was a night when Judith Hill played a set in the Love 4 One Another room. As Judith sang and fans enjoyed the performance from the table I was sat at I noticed some flashing feet walking into the room. Again dressed immaculately in white, he was wearing pumps that flashed red lights when his feet hit the floor, something that only Prince could pull off. There were about four rows of fans watching the show but being so short Prince could not see Judith. He then started jumping up, trying to catch a glimpse of Judith on stage, but was struggling. He then started to put his hands on fans shoulders and jump up to get a glimpse. The amazing thing about this story was that none of the people he put his hands on to lift himself up looked behind them and so they had absolutely no idea it was Prince jumping up trying to see!

I've been with him since 1979 when I bought my first Prince album. I love him even more today. His music liberated me to be ME and he brought some of the best people on Planet Earth into my life.

Prince gave me this goofy grin and I've been giving it to everybody I see. Prince had a great sense of humour. He once tweeted that I looked like Phil Collins!

KOKO

2 FEBRUARY 2015, LONDON, UK

I WAS THERE: CHRIS HARRISON

This all started with an email to advise us of a special gig for the charity Autism Rocks.

The £100 for two tickets was quickly despatched closely followed by train tickets and accommodation and we were advised it had to remain a secret or the gig would be pulled. To the day and we hit the queue fairly early and there was already a buzz around the media that the purple one was in town! The time quickly passed and we were allowed into Koko and ushered upstairs.

Once up there it became apparent we were going to watch Prince from a set of stairs! I wasn't having this and went to see if we could upgrade somehow. This was met with short shrift and I was told that unless I had a black VIP wristband then tough! At this point I realised there was a box of the said black wristbands sat on a wall next to the girl on the door. I used my sales and customer service skills to get in her good books and with a little deflection technique whilst she was busy I helped myself to a couple of VIP wrist bands. I made my exit, tracked down my wife and we very quietly slipped on the VIP wrist bands, headed to the floor and made our entrance, grabbing a glass of Verve Cliquet on the way in!

Needless to say the gig was incredible. 'Dreamer' was off the scale for me and we had an incredible night and finished the night with a big bottle of complimentary champagne. Prince rocked as always. This was the last time we got to see the great man and all I can say is thanks for the music and the memories.

I WAS THERE: CHRISTOPHER GRIFFITHS

I had somehow managed to get on the mailing list of the charity Autism Rocks and lo and behold I was invited to a private performance from Prince and 3RDEYEGIRL at the Koko Club in Camden. Little did I realise this would be the last time I would see him. Having met with my friends and spent the day in the local pubs which had been commandeered by the purple crowds, I had probably enjoyed one too many and sadly, although not a complete wash out, thanks to being inundated with free champagne at the venue itself, the show was a bit of a blur. Somehow I managed to acknowledge every song I had ever heard him perform from 'Let's Work' to a cover of Paloma Faith's 'Only Love Can Hurt Like This' but I promised myself that the next time I saw him I would not get to that state again.

Christopher Griffiths was very excited to see Prince

I WAS THERE: LEONIE CONROY

I went to Wembley for the *Lovesexy* tour for my 14th birthday. I'd been into Prince since I was 10. We were sat far back so I couldn't see much other than a big screen but it was amazing because I felt like I'd found my kind of people. People were dressed up in the costumes. Another memorable one I went to was in Brixton in 1998. I took a friend that was not a Prince fan. She stood at the bar all night and got drunk and I stood at the front on my own.

Manchester Academy was also memorable. I went to both nights. I queued with Paul and Kat for ten hours. I got front row. It was just amazing. It was so personal, so close. 'Sometimes it Snows in April' was a fabulous moment - it reminds me of when my mum died and I'd never heard him play it live before. It was a really emotional thing. But it wasn't sadness. It was a mixture of sad and happy. I was so close. I was literally stood underneath the microphone. I was just in awe of how tiny he was. You forget how small he was because he was such a big character. And he had such big thighs. I was thinking, 'We could share clothes!'

The 'My Name is Prince' exhibition was a little bittersweet. I didn't go. I wasn't sure I was ready for it at the time. A lot of people went and I saw the footage online and didn't really feel the need to be there. I didn't feel I was missing anything. A lot of people follow Prince-related artists like NPG. I don't. It's only ever been him. I miss him.

I was between jobs when the *Microphone* tour was announced and I thought about going to Minneapolis. 'Shall I just whack it on the credit card?' But I thought he was coming to Europe so I didn't.

I went to the last performance he did in the UK at Koko's, for Autism Rocks. I got VIP for that. I didn't know I had VIP. I was there with my friend Nathan and I said I wanted to be at the front of the queue. We were sat in the bar. He said, 'Don't worry, it'll be fine. I've got something up my sleeve' and he didn't quite tell me what it was until 20 minutes before and we just walked straight through. Jimmy Carr was there, Alan Carr, Noel Gallagher. In any other situation I'd be a little bit starstruck but the fact that I was there so see Prince - who was a star to the stars - meant I wasn't bothered who was stood next to me. And we walked out of the show afterwards and it snowed in central London. It was such a surreal feeling. I'll never forget that.

I WAS THERE: NIGEL GOWINGS

The last time I saw Prince was at the Koko Club in Camden, 14 months before we lost him. This would turn out to be Prince's last ever UK gig. I had been lucky enough to see Prince at Koko the year before this, when he and 3RDEYEGIRL performed several late announced gigs that fans would have to queue hours for and pay for tickets on the door. This gig was a charity gig organised by Autism Rocks. My son Luke - of course a big Prince fan - was working at an advertisement company in London at the time and had been offered tickets for the show. The concert was hush hush and if lucky enough to be offered a ticket a donation of £50 was paid and the ticket asked to keep the venue and the show a

Nigel Gowings saw Prince's last ever UK show

secret to avoid a rush of fans to the venue on the night.

So I felt so excited and blessed to have a ticket for this as it was always so good to see Prince in a smaller intimate venue. My son and I arrived that cold February night and we were given wristbands to the lower standing area of the venue. Again, there were many celebs at the show but this time we were rubbing shoulders with them.

The comedian Romesh Ranganathan was stood near us. I just couldn't wait to see Prince up close and we managed to get ourselves quite near the stage. On came Prince with his big cool Afro, a hair style that he had gone back to in recent years. Unusually he opened with 'Purple Rain' and of course the crowd went wild. He followed that up with a cool slowed down version of 'Let's Go Crazy' that he had performed over the last year or so with 3RDEYEGIRL. We were so close we could see his eyes clearly.

The special moment that will stay with me forever was when he sang 'Let's Work', this song being one of my favourites. My son and I went wild and we started singing and began to jump up and down and sing every word. There was a moment during that song when he looked at us both and smiled, which even made the woman in front of us turn to see what he smiled at. Only a small moment, but one that will live with me forever.

He played his usual two hours plus, thanked everyone and left the stage. Little did I know that would be the last time I would see him alive and my last ever concert.

Thanks for the memories Prince.

CENTRE BELL

23 MAY 2015, MONTREAL, CANADA

I WAS THERE: RIZWAN

Prince had announced a surprise concert in Montreal, only three days prior to the show. I hadn't heard about it. On the day of the show, Saturday, a friend and ex-band mate of mine called me up and asked, 'Do you want to go a Prince concert?' With no hesitation, I said, 'Yes!'

At the beginning of every super star concert, there's always the anticipation of the star making his or her first appearance. Prince's people teased the audience. At first, they shut off the house lights maybe 20 minutes or so after 8pm. The audience would erupt in applause and screams. Maybe ten seconds later, the house lights would come back on, indicating the show hasn't started yet. They did this four times.

When the lights went down for real, we heard the voice of a young woman, super casual-sounding - I think it might have been the voice of the super model-looking blonde female virtuoso drummer. She was greeting Montreal while nicely asking us to put away our cell phones because our devices couldn't possibly capture the magic of the show, and if Prince decided to go crowd surfing, how would we be able to hold him up if we were holding onto our phones? 'We like him, please don't let him fall.'

With that we heard samples from classic Prince songs, including the words spoken by a computer voice in the introduction of '*1999*', 'Don't worry, I won't hurt U. I only want U2 have some fun.'

Hannah Ford Welton's drums kicked in, for the bluesy song 'Wow!' Prince and his band, 3RDEYEGIRL, were looking larger than life as we could only see their shadows on the giant curtain. They were pacing themselves, repeating the verse music without Prince singing the verse, only playing lead guitar. The curtains came down with the first verse of the song. It starts off with the words, 'Hello, how are you?' Prince repeated the 'hello' part.

After 'Wow' the band seamlessly went into the intro to 'FunknRoll' and the mood went from blues rock to upbeat funk. The first few songs of a Prince concert usually leave me feeling the same way. At first, I feel that everyone is excited to see Prince. He often starts off the show with songs from the current album, which a lot of the audience may not know. The first few songs go by fast, almost in a blur, people enjoy it, sort of, but I for one feel that a portion of the crowd isn't getting what they had wanted and expected.

We heard the rocking 2007 song 'Guitar' playing next. Donna Grantis, the young female guitarist from Toronto, played the guitar solo for this song and Prince made sure to let us know, 'From Canada - Donna Grantis!' She rocked it of course. I feel her guitar playing has truly solidified since she began playing with Prince in 2013.

The two girls in front me who were standing along with everyone else decided to sit down after the first few songs, while everyone else around was still standing. I assumed that they were not necessarily here to experience a power trio rock experience, heavy on the guitars. There were some girls behind me, one of whom represented another type of Prince fan. She kept yelling out things like, 'I want you to have my children!' Prince couldn't hear her from where we were sitting, but good for her for speaking her mind at a Prince concert.

Around me, there was also the type of audience member that was familiar with Prince but felt the need to exclaim during the show, 'I didn't know Prince could play keyboards that well!' Duh! Prince can play every instrument better than most people!

The type of fan I am... well, I am the musician that became a musician after having been inspired by his musical career. I wanted to play every instrument like Prince did. I wanted to arrange, write and perform my own songs too. I wanted to select different musicians to back me up for different shows that I had done. I also know virtually every Prince song there is to know, when it was released or not released, who played in it if anyone other than Prince, along with any other info I could find.

A lot of people that like Prince's music, like certain styles of his, like perhaps only his pop and R&B stuff. This is an important issue to raise, when it comes to Prince, because Prince was considered a cross-over artist back when he started. He was reaching out to the audiences that loved R&B as well as reaching out to rock fans. Prince himself was a fan of both Led Zeppelin and James Brown so naturally sometimes he sounds like Led Zeppelin, sometimes like James Brown. Sometimes he sounds like both.

Prince music also happens to have more sides than just funk and rock. He's released instrumental jazz albums, an acoustic guitar album, a mostly solo piano and vocal album and there's a 28 minute live rock funk song called 'The War' out there somewhere. He's done nothing but experiment throughout his career and me and many other connoisseurs have been seeking out all of these treasures, whether officially released or not.

Prince and 3RDEYEGIRL then rocked the house with the 2014 rock instrumental piece 'Plectrum Electrum', with all sorts of rockstar guitar poses and choreographed cool stuff from the musicians.

The band also played the chilled groovy but still rock version of 'Let's Go Crazy' with Hannah Ford Welton's awesome drumming and the fuzzy bass solo from Ida Nielsen. It was the same rearrangement that they debuted when Prince won the Icon award in 2013 at the *Billboard* Music Awards.

I am such a fan that I had taken the music off that televised performance back in 2013 and listened to it on my iPhone. In fact it was as though several of the music playlists that I made to listen to was being played on this night by none other than Prince himself, with the three gorgeous and talented women of his band 3RDEYEGIRL, as well as Joshua Welton, Hannah Ford Welton's husband, on keyboards, three back up singers and three horn players, appearing now and then on stage for various songs.

I had sensed there was some angst with the audience. Even myself, a die hard Prince fan, wondered if the show was going well at this point. The band was flawless, and the songs amazing, but the energy in the room was maybe lacking.

They touched on a few of Prince's pop classics, 'Controversy', then 'Raspberry Beret' and 'U Got The Look', all songs I still listen to among the new stuff. Maybe Prince felt something. He asked the audience during a thumping song if we were happy to be here, and he immediately said that he was happy to be here. Yes I was happy. I felt like this was Prince reminding us: hey! It's me Prince! I've come here to play for you… I'm happy to be here, aren't you?

Then they played 'Don't Stop Till You Get Enough', the classic Michael Jackson song. He played this in 2013 when I saw him, and then again this Saturday night. I loved hearing him do it again. That seguewayed into 'C.O.O.L.', written for the band The Time in the '80s. Ida Nielsen's bass guitar was super funky, she was the back bone of the band but her bass could have been even louder. There was the repeated call and response part in the end of the song: 'Montreal!' 'What?' 'Are U hot?' 'No!' 'Do you know why?' 'Why?' 'Cause you're cool!' 'Cool!'

The crowd was warming up. Prince often tested his audiences in the beginning of his shows. In one of Prince's concerts in Montreal a few years before, the first 45 minutes of the show consisted of Prince and the NPG improvising instrumental music that no one has ever heard. Prince didn't even sing! After that they had disappeared to the back stage, came back and started playing the hits, with Prince asking, 'Who was that before?'

This night, after the song 'The Breakdown', a slow song from *Art Official Age*, the lights on stage went off and Prince and the band disappeared for a few minutes. My friend asked me, as if things were not going well, 'What if the band slipped out?' I replied, resenting the implication, 'Don't worry, they're coming back. The show isn't over till the house lights come back on.'

Prince eventually came back on stage, by himself, and told the crowd, 'Sometimes the band and I get into arguments about which songs to play…' Immediately we heard the guitar intro to 'When Doves Cry' and the audience went wild. Everyone stood up, including the two girls in front of me. We all heard Prince play this classic in the old school way, with the old school beat, but with some new twists. I had seen Prince do something similar in 2012. Back then, he did a show in Montreal where during one part he was all alone on stage, played samples of his hits on a keyboard, like some beats and other parts, while singing bits of the song, and it was incredible. It was like a DJ/musician solo performance. What he did this night was a more refined version. This performance included the whole band. What's really cool about this was hearing the old beats as they sounded in the original recordings. They also played 'Sign o' the Times' and '1999'. It was a party indeed. Prince also played a full 'Hot Thing', so funky. He kept saying, 'It's Saturday night!' He invited members of the audience on stage to dance. He told the audience in the balconies, 'I want to see guys and girls dancing!'

Then there was a quiet section, with Prince on keyboards, alone. He started with 'Diamonds and Pearls'. Then he played 'How Come U Don't Call Me Anymore'. This solo piano and vocal performance was so beautiful, it really hit me. We saw stars on the big screen behind him. Then he sang 'The Beautiful Ones'. After that I heard the very familiar drum machine beat from 'Forever In My Life', with only Prince's vocals over the beat. Then came 'Little Red Corvette' in a rock ballad style, completely different from the original, but a song everyone in the house knew and loved. Prince's guitar playing on this was just incredible.

At this point, two pretty ladies that were very late to the show, made their way to the two empty seats on my left. One of the girls asked me as I let her pass to the seat beside mine. 'Did he play 'Purple Rain' yet?' I smiled and said, 'No'.

Then there was 'Nothing Compares 2 U'. In this version, we heard a church organ playing in the beginning, while Prince sang the first verse. The whole band with the horns and back up singers joined in and the audience sang along during the famous chorus. Prince rearranged that song many times for the stage and this night was as great as it has ever sounded.

And then there was 'Kiss'. On the big screen behind the band, we saw the giant image of Prince wearing shades from the original 1986 music video, doubled as though they were facing each other. Prince gave a performance worthy of his status as a show biz legend, a final Broadway style pose and he said. 'Goodnight!'

After some waiting, cheering, the band came back on. They began with a cover song 'The Sweeter It Is' by The Soul Children. The three back up singers had a verse and they each sounded amazing. And then came 'Purple Rain'. I've heard the song countless times and seen him play it live at least six times. But I was enjoying Prince and the band do the song justice. Confetti was being blasted up into the air, as the guitar solo began. The little pieces of paper flew across the venue, reaching to audience members all across and people tried to catch them.

The pretty girl to my left kept trying to catch one of the little rectangular pieces of paper, but failed. I managed to catch one. As it came to a point where there was no more confetti floating our way, Prince was playing his most famous guitar solo, I turned to the girl beside me, smiled and offered the piece of paper I caught. She was the girl that had come in late and asked me, 'Did he play 'Purple Rain' yet?' She smiled, took the paper and gave me a genuine thank you. I turned and there was Prince starting to sing the part of the song where everyone in audience sings along.

Prince and the band said goodnight again, and left. The audience wouldn't have it and kept cheering. At one point, the audience started chanting 'Olé… olé, olé, olé'. Eventually Prince came back.

They began with the song 'Mountains' from the 1986 album, *Under the Cherry Moon*, the same album as the song 'Kiss'. 'Mountains' had been one of my favourites since I was a teenager, a guilty pleasure. I never put this song on for my friends, or recommend it to anyone. Not only did I listen to this song regularly this year, but I would listen to the rare extended version of the song, with several minutes of Prince and the Revolution jamming. It's a pop song, kinda funky, but not particularly cool as 'Gett Off' or 'Sexy MF'.

This night, Prince and 3RDEYEGIRL were reviving this song. They played it in a very, very funky way but still true to the original arrangement. This performance took the song to a higher echelon of funk. I was speechless. My guilty pleasure of a song, that I never listened to with anyone, was now being played on stage.

This had turned into a very Eighties night, with Prince sometimes saying things like, 'Remember the Eighties?' and 'Any Eighties babies out there?' But we also visited the Seventies with a complete version of the classic funk song by the band Wild Cherry, 'Play That Funky Music' with the famous lyrics, 'Play that funky music white boy!' It turned into an extended jam. At one point I wanted to turn to my friend, with whom I played funky music years ago, and say to him, 'Now THIS is FUNK!' Instead, I just relished in the awesomeness.

'The Dance Electric' followed. This was one of Prince's lesser known songs from the mid-Eighties. Even I don't even have a decent recording of it. Prince asked the audience to take out our phones! He was doing that thing where the audience holds up their phones, shining a light each. Prince said to us, 'See what we can do with just 3 days notice!'

With the show coming to an end, we heard the intro to 'Housequake'. 'Does anybody know about the 'quake?' 'We do!' If you only have five minutes, watch the performance of 'Housequake' from the concert movie *Sign O' The Times*. This was one of the funkiest performances of all time. If you watch that, then perhaps you will know about the 'quake. This night, Prince was doing an updated version of 'Housequake', asking the audience to jump up and down, and that original beat sounded funky! There were solos from the girls - man can Hannah Ford Welton play those drums, with Donna on guitar and Ida on bass.

The final song was one of Prince's many past 'radio staples': '*I Would Die 4 U*', from the Oscar-winning *Purple Rain*. Excellent, and with the original beat. After saying goodnight and leaving the stage, the house lights came back on. Finally we knew it was time to leave.

Days later I asked my buddy who told me about the show and who went with me what he thought. He said it was one of the best shows that he had ever attended. What a night. Prince had won… again and hopefully always.

HIT'N'RUN PHASE 1

25 SEPTEMBER 2015

PRINCE RETWEETED MY REVIEW: SAM BLEAZARD

I'd been writing about Prince on and off for a while. He was working on a couple of albums at the time, and one was called *Hit and Run Phase 1*. He'd started experimenting a little bit with electronic music, and with elements that were a bit more contemporary. He also had a young guy in his entourage called Joshua Welton, who was the husband of his drummer at the time. Prince decided to team up with Josh and make an album with him, which was a bit Marmite to say the least. A lot of his fans didn't like it. They thought it was too electronic and a bit throwaway. He was even taking elements of songs he'd recorded before and freshening them up, giving them a new feel. My friend Keysha Davis runs a website called the *CocoaDiaries.com*, featuring arts and culture, which I've written articles for over the past 10 years.

Sam Bleazard's album review got a retweet from Prince on Twitter

I also shared that review on a Prince fan page, more for enthusiasts to read – never thinking for a moment that Prince would ever see it. In the review I said that Prince had taken a bit of a risk, that it was a creative approach and he wasn't resting on his laurels, I'd played it to my kids and it made their ears perk up. It wasn't about being a snob about music - it was about just keeping your eyes and ears open.

One Sunday a few days later I was at a party with friends, and Keysha called me up and said, 'Something weird's going on with the stats and the analytics on the site. Thousands of people have just clicked in the last 24 hours. I think it's your Prince review.' She's also a big fan so it was a great moment.

Prince was a very late entrant to social media. He had a real love/hate relationship with the Internet, although latterly he went on Instagram, and he also had a Twitter account. When Prince retweeted my review he'd put the words 'creative approach' in the link. People from all over the world who followed him suddenly zeroed in on it. Prince read my review and shared it with his fan base. To this day I'm very proud of that.

PRIVATE PARTY

1 JANUARY 2016, GOUVERNEUR BAY ESTATE, ST BARTS

I WAS THERE: NICOLA WAKLEY-WAKE

The last time I was in close proximity to Prince was New Year's Eve 2015 in St Barts, in the Caribbean. He performed on Russian billionaire Roman Abramovich's super yacht (I was on a yacht right next to his yacht) did everything I could to try and get an invite; alas my powers of persuasion didn't get me there, but I felt enormous comfort knowing he was so close. Then the world changed forever. But he is like the gift that keeps on giving, I still devour everything that is released. It still feels like he's close. Haven't come to terms with his passing; don't think I ever will. Just feel so thankful for the moments had, little things show us he's still there in spirit. He was caused a lot of tension in my marriage over the years, as I would put seeing him before ANYTHING! My husband doesn't get it, and he never will. Prince was my first love and he will never be replaced.

Premiered at Paisley Park Studios on 21 January 2016, the *Piano & A Microphone* tour had been scheduled to start in Europe in December 2015 but the European leg was postponed. 20 shows were performed in total, with the Atlanta shows scheduled for 7 April postponed until 14 April because Prince was diagnosed with severe influenza.

I WASN'T THERE: CHRISTOPHER GRIFFITHS

In November 2015, it was reported that Prince was once again returning to the UK but this time without a band. It would be just him, a piano and a microphone. Venues were confirmed and dates were set. This was my chance to reconcile for my previous state at his last visit. I planned on attending the Birmingham show at the Symphony Hall but then all were cancelled at the last minute due to Prince's reaction to ticket touting websites and simultaneously (though not confirmed) the Paris attack at the Eagles Of Death Metal concert at the Bataclan. The tour was then rearranged to begin at Paisley Park and makes its way to Australia, New Zealand and across the US. I thought it would only be a matter of time before it would be rescheduled for the UK, but sadly that day would never come.

The Australian leg of the *Piano & A Microphone* tour was announced at short notice. Prince played four shows over two nights in each of Sydney and Melbourne with one show in Perth.

HAMER CONCERT HALL

16 FEBRUARY 2016, MELBOURNE, AUSTRALIA

I WAS THERE: RAJ NATALY

I went to the 9th August 2007 Indigo after show party. It got to about 1am and I was about to go. As l was exiting the

Raj Natalty's son got tickets for the Melbourne show

door Prince was next to me – OMG! I went back in and managed to take some amazing photos without my phone being taken off me. I saw the *Hit and Run* show at Birmingham NEC in May 2014. He was on fire that night and played a lot of tracks off Hit and Run which I loved. I lost my voice that night. I was in Australia to see my children when Prince suddenly announces he's in Australia. I then flew to Bali for five days whilst my son Ryan tried to get tickets. On returning to Melbourne I found out he'd got two tickets and the look on my face….

This concert was so stripped back it was as if it was you and him in your front room. Strangely I cried at that concert, it just got me. And that was the last time I saw him as he sadly passed away in April of that year. Prince, I will be eternally grateful for all the pleasure, joy and excitement you have given me. I remember the first time I saw you, in London for the *Parade* tour, and how you blew me away with your album, *Dirty Mind*. Rest in peace.

I WAS THERE: THEO KYRIAKIDIS

I was at one of his two shows in Melbourne the day Vanity died. A sadder than usual Prince, he apologised for being a little down and quiet.

ARTS CENTRE, MELBOURNE STATE THEATRE

17 FEBRUARY 2016, MELBOURNE, AUSTRALIA

I WAS THERE: DIANNE GILLIS

On 5th February 2016 Prince shocked fans with an out-of-the-blue announcement that he would be commencing his national tour within the month. The tour press release says, 'For those blessed enough to attend, everything about these exclusive performances has been carefully considered to deliver a special one-in-a-lifetime experience. Tickets will go on sale for all Australian shows at 12pm on Tuesday February 9.'

Talk about short notice! Four days until tickets became available and he'd be here a few weeks later. I had to get myself a seat, and considering how small the venue was it was not going to be easy. And they weren't cheap. Tickets started at $500, going up to thousands for premium.

Tuesday morning I got myself ready with laptop, iPad and mobile phone all at the ready. As the clock hit 9am I jumped straight on and got straight through to ticket selection and then, just like that, the site crashed! Those lucky enough to get straight through snapped up all available seats. It was a logistical nightmare. I just cried in disbelief, I felt sick to my core, I had never missed a Prince performance before.

Friday morning I had a niggling feeling. A little voice inside my head said 'go look for tickets'. Little did I know that the tour promoter had made an announcement that morning that 'extra' seats had become available and would go on sale at 9am. I jumped on my computer, opened up the ticketing site, clicked on the show, selected my date and selected 'best available' for the seating category. At this stage I didn't care as I just wanted to go. And what happened next still blows my mind. The best available seats were selected for me and they were front row centre! I screamed my head off!

The night of the show came quickly. We made our way to The Arts Centre, picked up our tickets and wristbands and made our way to our seats. I was right in front of his piano stool, so close that I could almost touch the piano if I leant over the front stage.

The concert was surreal. Prince was amazing, dreamy even. His voice was simple perfection. I sang along with him, sometimes a little too loud that at one point I'm sure he side glanced over in my direction. I didn't care, I was in my element and when he began to play the opening chords of 'Purple Rain' is when my tears began to fall. They fell because I was in the moment, they fell because I could feel his energy, they fell because I could see his emotion, they fell because at that exact point I turned to my partner and said, 'I'm never going to see him again.'

I'm not sure if he heard me or just saw that I was crying uncontrollably. But as soon as he finished playing and whilst everyone was applauding on their feet he – Prince - walked straight over to me, leant toward me and in the same seamless moment our hands reach for each other's. Prince was holding my hands in his! I couldn't believe it. All I managed to say to him was 'thank you and I love you'. He gave me that coy little smile of his and whispered 'thank you' and then went back to his piano to play for us again.

I was on my feet. I was dancing. I had strangers around me all hugging me because Prince touched me, and touch me he did. The show took on a different level of excitement. Prince took it up a notch, everyone was up on their feet. We managed to get him out for an encore and he played and played and played. And as he said his goodbye, he again walked over to me and took my hands in his, this time I said, 'Goodbye', and with an almost saddened look on his face he nodded and walked away.

April 22nd, 2014. I woke to a simple message from a friend, 'Sorry for your loss.' What followed that message was a feeling of disbelief. I woke to the news that my beloved Prince was found dead in his home, Paisley Park. He was found alone, in an elevator. It seems he got to punch that higher floor that he sang about after all. I was still on a high from seeing him only nine weeks earlier, still on a high from being seated only a few feet away from him, still on a high from having him walk over to me and take my hands in his. I can still see his smile and feel his eyes pouring into my soul, I can still feel his soft gentle hands, I can sometimes even still smell him....

The weeks passed by and slowly I began to make connections all over the world, connecting with like-minded fam, from generous souls taking my handwritten notes to stick up at Paisley Park to gorgeous girls that I've laughed, sang and danced with, girls that I now call my sisters. We don't mourn artists we've never met because we knew them. We mourn them because they helped us know ourselves.

HAMER CONCERT HALL

18 FEBRUARY 2016, MELBOURNE, AUSTRALIA

I WAS THERE: PAUL KOSTROMIN

I took my best buddy - a keyboard player - who was a mild Prince fan. I said, 'Come on, you need to see Prince.' He never had and I'm thankful that we did as he passed only a few months after these shows. This was a beautiful concert hall, with just Prince on the piano and nothing else sound-wise that I could tell, no triggered sounds. It was very pure and so clever how he stripped back the songs and the set to suit just him and the piano! We all knew 95 per cent of the songs, so your mind would fill in gaps in the music and Prince, being so clever, didn't overplay but had space in the music. It worked brilliantly!

My buddy, who went in with reservations, couldn't believe it. His comments were mainly about his voice being superb with such range and dynamics, which of course you heard much more in this setting. Again, moving from one song to another effortlessly, he must have played 30 to 40 pieces in part or whole. It was stunning.

OPERA HOUSE

20 FEBRUARY 2016, SYDNEY, AUSTRALIA

I WAS THERE: LOUISE STAFFORD, AGE 14

The third and last time I got to see Prince was when he came to Australia. I had been living in Perth for 12 or so years at this stage and I missed out on seeing him when he last came to Oz as it was just after my having a baby. As soon as I heard he was coming over again I had to book a ticket! The problem was he was only playing in Brisbane, Sydney and Melbourne so I thought, 'Okay, I'll book to see him play at the Sydney Opera House.' I have an aunt that lives in Sydney so I thought, 'I'll swing a visit in to see her and see my man Prince and get a little kid-free time by myself.' So I got all my ducks in a row, flights booked and everything, when a week later his tour company announces he's coming to Perth for the first time ever! He added Perth into his tour dates and I could've died. I knew I couldn't just sell my Sydney ticket because of his tight anti-scalping security ticket pick up procedure so there was nothing more I could do but go ahead and buy another ticket for his Perth show. I mean, what is a girl to do? Three weeks after his Sydney gigs he would be in Perth, I would be home and there was no way on Earth I would be sitting on my sofa while Prince was turning the town purple.... and I'm so glad I had the privilege to see this unforgettable performer play his final shows before he left us. His gig in Sydney at the iconic Opera House was just breath taking. He had each and every one of us in the palm of his hand. He never missed a beat. His songs just flowed into each other seamlessly and all this only using his piano and a microphone. It was seriously like watching a great artist like Michelangelo painting the Sistine Chapel... I had tears in my eyes throughout both shows that I witnessed. However, I sensed something wasn't right with Prince. I thought that he looked ill and it felt like he was saying goodbye to his fans by gifting us with such a special, intimate and raw treatment of his songs. He still interacted with his audience with lots of humour and anecdotes about how he came up with certain songs, so it never felt sad or nostalgic, but I had just pure fascination and disbelief at his talent.

I felt so lucky to have been able to see him live. I was in awe every single time....

ASB THEATRE

24 FEBRUARY 2016, AUCKLAND, NEW ZEALAND

I WAS THERE: ANZAC

As soon as I found out Mum was taking me to the Prince concert, thanks to the generosity of a fellow fan we met at the Brisbane concerts in '12, I kept telling her that I was going to meet Prince. At the '12 concerts I met Shelby J, The Twins, Maya and Nandy McClean and John Blackwell, and said 'Hi' to Ida Nielsen, so of course I think I'm going to meet the man himself!

We didn't begin the night at the front row of the theatre - our ticketed seats were upstairs, second back row of the theatre - but I was dancing away to the funky music at this once-in-a-lifetime event when Prince started singing 'Kiss' and he missed a line because he was watching me dance! He got up from the piano, stopped playing, walked over to me, reached down and lifted me on to stage with his own bare hands. The crowd went wild! Then I started dancing when he started the song again and they went crazy loud wild! I danced like I've never danced before, and the look on Prince's face was priceless – he was obviously enjoying my company on stage. At one point I went behind him to dance and he turned around to keep an eye on me near the candelabra set up with candles on stage.

He had a beautiful chuckle in his voice when he changed the lyrics from 'I think I wanna dance' to 'I think HE wants to dance!' When the song was finished he motioned with his eyes and a tilt of his head that it was time for me to leave the stage. He got up from the piano, gave me a high five and I hopped off. The crowd went wild again! Everyone around me was congratulating and hugging and high-fiving me. I felt amazing! He then played a really long version of 'Purple Rain', one of my favourite songs, and left the stage with his cane at the end of the concert.

Leaving the theatre, and standing out the front, everyone was coming up to me telling me how awesome I was and getting pictures with me. One lady said she just wanted to touch me. I felt like a real celebrity. Later I was interviewed by Michelle who runs the Prince Worldwide Fan Club on Facebook. Thanks to everyone who came up to me on the night – you all made me feel like a million bucks! But most of all thanks to Prince! I will never forget my moment with you.

PARAMOUNT THEATRE

28 FEBRUARY 2016, OAKLAND, CALIFORNIA

I WAS THERE: JACE WITMAN

After first seeing Prince in 1992, I saw him a dozen moretimes, including his *Piano & A Microphone* show at the Paramount Theater in Oakland of 2016. By 2016, I was in my mid-forties and when I heard he was touring alone, basically doing a concert version of his piano medley, I had to be there. Of course this time I bought tickets on my phone while at work. The tickets were maybe ten times more expensive than the first show, with the two tickets totalling more than $500.

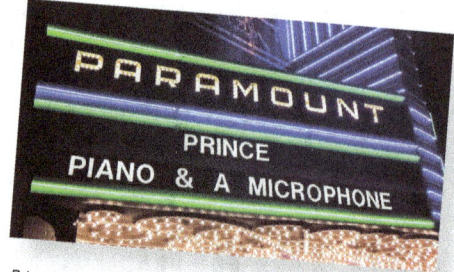

Prince played Oakland's Paramount Theatre in February 2016

That day, I drove to Oakland with my girlfriend who had never seen Prince live. This time, standing in line, I saw old friends and that sense of excitement was still there. Once inside, I bought a concert t-shirt and programme. The venue and the vibe were more intimate and it was there that I noticed that the crowd was older than I expected. My girlfriend laughed at me and said something along the lines of, 'Have you looked in the mirror lately?'

As we stood in the lobby, waiting to be let into the auditorium, my girlfriend said, 'I know these tickets weren't cheap. Do you want me to give you some money to help pay for them?' I answered, 'You're right, they weren't cheap. They were worth it though. This is going to be special.' I refused her generous offer.

Inside, the stage was lit only by candles and the vibe was sombre and respectful. Once again, as the lights went out, and the screams of the audience filled the room, I had that feeling. I was in the right place at the right time. For over an hour and a half Prince sang, told stories and even got up and did a little dance and mesmerised us, with nothing between us. There were no distractions and pyrotechnics, just a genius on stage. On the drive home, my girlfriend said, 'Wow, you were right. That was special.'

Prince was gone less than two months later. Those tickets were priceless. I've been to shows by The Time, Sheila E. and The Revolution since Prince's passing. Not only is the tremendous void felt at all of those shows, but I've noticed that the excitement doesn't seem the same for the audience and that feeling that I loved of right place at the right time is also absent. This is no indictment of the talents and abilities of all these other great musicians that played with him, but it just makes clear where the magic came from.

ORACLE ARENA

4 MARCH 2016, OAKLAND, CALIFORNIA

I WAS THERE: JENNIFER ZAJAC WINTERS

There was a last minute announcement for Prince's ticket sale for *Piano & A Microphone*. Luckily I was able to get the tickets thanks to Mike in the kitchen who knows I'm a Prince fan. Who knew it'd be the last time I'd see him? I got diagnosed with Stage 3 breast cancer on March 25, Good Friday. Chemo started April 14th and Prince died on the 21st. To hear his performance on the piano was the most incredible performance I'd ever seen. It was the light before the darkness.

I almost didn't go on March 4th, since my last concert almost two years earlier on March 15, 2014 was truly a dream come true. My purple streaks in my strawberry blonde hair and the same lace I wore at San Francisco's Cow Palace for the *Purple Rain* tour in 1985 were the cool part of my outfit. We arrived real early and that allowed us to be second row, stage left. I knew something magical was going to happen. First, Prince wiped his forehead with a black small towel and threw it in the crowd and I caught it. Yes, I have his DNA safely placed in my hope chest - I was thrilled! Little did I know it was going to get better. Prince starting pulling girls up on stage and amazingly I was pulled up by his band mate. Others stayed stage left, but I grooved all the way across and got right next to where Prince was spinning his classics. I kept trying to make eye contact with him. We were so close, but he'd keep looking down. Later, my friend said when I danced around in a slow twirl, he'd look at the crowd and give a 'check her out' look and I had no idea. It was so hard to believe I danced three songs up there by him. He eventually exited fast since too many people were let on stage. No cell phones allowed, so no photos, but I will never ever forget jammin' with the Purple One. I still haven't gotten over it, but I did beat the cancer... got over that. Prince and I have a spiritual bond somehow... I'm sure lots do.

THEATRE MAISONNEUVE

21 MARCH 2016, MONTREAL, CANADA

I WAS THERE: RIZWAN

In the early 2000s, I had scored access to the soundcheck of one of Prince's concerts. At first, my brother and I were at some press room at the Bell Center in Montreal, with maybe 30 or more fans. We heard faint traces of live music. We were eventually taken to the first few rows of the Bell Center, and as we walked in, Prince's band, the NPG, was jamming. Me and my bro took seats in the center, second row. After not too long, my brother told me to look behind. I did. I didn't see much. He said to look again. A few feet away appeared a silhouette of a man wearing a hat, sitting down. It was Prince. I must have thought what everyone thinks when they see Prince for the first time up close: 'Holy crap, it's Prince.' He started talking into his microphone, still at his seat, saying, 'I want the distortion on the bass to sound like a motorcycle.' He soon got up and made his way to the stage. Prince and his band began playing. One of the songs was a song from *Graffiti Bridge* called 'Elephants and Flowers'. I don't think this was ever in his set lists for shows. They played older songs that us fans always listened to, but they sounded so much more evolved. I don't even think he would play these songs for real big shows. It was incredible. I was freaking out inside. We kept quiet in between songs.... we didn't applaud. We were that small a group, and it was a soundcheck, where people usually don't applaud. At one point Prince and the NPG played a cover song, it felt like Joni Mitchell, but I didn't know for sure (it wasn't 'A Case of You'). After the song, Prince asked us, 'Does anyone know who wrote that?' Everyone kept quiet. I wanted to say Joni Mitchell, but wasn't sure. I'm not going to say something I'm not sure about in the presence of Prince. Prince said, 'Joni Mitchell' Oh man! I could've sounded so cool but kept my mouth shut!

He tests his audiences, at least it has been the case every one of his shows I have been to. This show was announced on a Friday, and it took place the next Monday, March 21st. A piano and a microphone, a one man show and the man was Prince. The girl beside me was told by her male companion, 'I heard it's a two hour show.' The girl replied, 'I would be happy with one hour.' I felt the same. I mean, I'm a die-hard fan but I wouldn't expect more than a one hour show if it was just Prince on stage with a piano.

The audience was all ready by 10pm. At 10.20pm Prince hadn't taken the stage yet. We heard some orchestral music while people took selfies and ushers kept having to ask people to put away their phones. Finally the lights went down.

There were almost two dozen candles on stage and a piano with an empty chair. We heard more pre-recorded orchestral music for a few minutes, watching kaleidoscope visuals projected on the back wall and on the piano on the stage. No Prince yet. Testing!

After the music stopped, we saw Prince's sillhouette, standing with a cane, on the back wall, looking like a total high class pimp. The square door rolled up and Prince walked on stage. He circled the piano twice, like a lion circling his prey, and then sat down to play.

He began with 'Joy in Repetition', one of my all time favorite songs. He played 'Elephants and Flowers' and songs that were never released as singles or B-sides in addition to the major hits. His rendition of 'Elephants and Flowers' brought a tear to my eye. Right after, he ordered someone to turn the house lights on and I cringed. I didn't want the people around me to see that tear going down my cheek.

He spoke, amazing the audience. He made us stand up, sing, clap, laugh, cry and dance. He played his early stuff – 'Do Me Baby', 'I Wanna Be Your Lover' - and played material from throughout his career. I heard 'Black Sweat' and 'Kiss'. He sang 'Take Me With U' but in between verses he pretended he was writing it and also made fun of his own lyrics. He asked, 'How do you touch a place in a person that call's out names?' and then pretended to wonder where to go next with the lyric writing.

He talked about his father's piano, which no one else was allowed to play in his father's presence. Prince could only practice on it when dad was gone. He said he had learned how to play by watching his father play and because he wanted to impress his mother. There was a bluesy 'U Got the Look'. He played 'Cream' and actually screwed up on the lyrics but recovered. He said, 'I wrote this in front of the mirror. Maybe that's why I always get stuck on that verse.'

He had a tablet in front of him, laying on the body of the piano, and he would swipe the screen on the tablet in between playing notes, seeing pages with the lyrics. He did a little medley of songs with some beats and samples. He sang 'Hot Thing' and you better believe that everyone was on their feet! He sang 'I Would Die 4 U', Bob Marley's 'Wait in Vain' mixed with his own lyrics and music and 'Nothing Compares 2 U' and 'Purple Rain'.

The show lasted just about two hours and went by like a breeze. It was incredible from beginning to end. It was Prince's music, raw, some songs in arrangements I never imagined I would hear. One man on stage, a piano and a microphone, and the man was Prince.

If that wasn't enough, all the audience got a CD copy of the new Prince album, *HitnRun Phase 2*, on the way out.

On 14 April 2016, Prince performed what was to be his last ever show. The performance had to be rescheduled as Prince was ill the week before.

FOX THEATER

14 APRIL 2016, ATLANTA, GEORGIA

I WAS THERE: MARK HEAD

The last time I caught him was on the last night he ever played, once again at the Fox Theater in Atlanta on April 14, 2016. I was at the early show that night – just me and my wife. He put on an unbelievable performance – just him and a piano. We of course had no idea what would happen one week later but after the shock of it all I remember thinking how poetic it was that, as big of a fan as I was and am of this man, it is pretty cool that my first and last live experiences with him took place in the exact same place, 23 years apart.

Mark Head's ticket for the Piano & A Microphone show

QUAD CITY INTERNATIONAL AIRPORT

15 APRIL 2016, MOLINE, ILLINOIS

A private plane carrying Prince makes an unscheduled landing around 1.35am local time. Price is taken from the plane and rushed by ambulance to a local hospital for treatment.

PAISLEY PARK

21 APRIL 2016, CHANHASSEN, MINNESOTA

Prince was found dead at his home in Minnesota at the age of 57, after police were summoned to his Paisley Park estate and found his body in a lift. He was last seen alive at around 8pm the previous evening and his body discovered around 9.40am the following morning. He was pronounced dead at 10.07am.

I HEARD THE NEWS: RICCI TERRANOVA

I was at work. Everybody around me knows I'm a huge Prince fan. I have the miniature guitars on my desk. Everybody knows he's my favourite artist and has been for many, many years. And the people around me are all into music. Somebody turned to me and said, 'Something's happened at Paisley Park.' He said, 'It's breaking news, something's happened at Paisley Park.' Then the reports started coming out that paramedics had been called and so forth and then it broke that it was Prince. I was alone because my wife had flown to Scotland for a funeral. She wasn't here with me. I sent her a WhatsApp message saying that Prince had passed.

It still hurts, because the affection I have for Prince is, I'm sure, is the same affection many people have. I never got to meet Prince. I've met so many celebrities in my life and I always said I would throw away all those experiences to just have two minutes with Prince, just to shake his hand and say 'thank you' because I felt he was there for me at a time when I was not confident as a young man. Listening to him and listening to his lyrics and seeing him were very inspirational. So I really felt like I'd lost a friend that I've never really introduced myself to. But I felt that he was friend to me.

A good friend of mine had told me that he was playing these piano and microphone shows and he had texted me and I remember writing back to him saying, 'Oh my god, I am so excited to see him do this, just him and a piano.' Because it had been five years since I had seen him live so I thought this is going to be absolutely amazing to see him without a band, with just a piano and a microphone.

I'm still devastated by it, I really am. I really thought we were going to see him grow older. I was excited about where he was going to take his music. Now I look forward to hearing all the unreleased music that they will release from The Vault but it's difficult for me to believe that he's gone.

We don't consider ourselves fans because he didn't believe in the word 'fans' and that it sounded like you were fanatical. We consider ourselves to be members of the purple family. That's how all of us that are in these Facebook groups consider ourselves to be - members of his family.

He was such a good person. People who don't know him that well may not know what a good person he was, how much he gave to charities and to humanitarian causes without drawing attention to himself. All of this is now coming out about how generous he was and what a genuinely good person he was. If you think about his career and how long he was in the spotlight, he never got arrested and nobody ever came out and said he was doing this or was doing that. He just made his music and shared his talents with all of us. I have a six year old daughter and feel very good about teaching her about him. He definitely was a role model for people who wanted to use him as a role model.

I HEARD THE NEWS: SAM BLEAZARD

It was really surreal. I was at a work function in London. I heard the news on a Friday in a packed bar. There was a girl who worked for me at the time who decided to leave the company. I was sad to see her go as she was a hard working member of the team. We were having drinks at a bar near King's Cross. At some point my personal phone, which was in my back started going off, and there were a few moments where it just felt as if it was just going off constantly, because I had it on vibrate. It was just buzzing and buzzing and wouldn't stop. People were texting me saying, 'Have you heard the news?' 'Have you heard about Prince?' 'Prince is dead. What do you think about this? Is this true? Is it a wind up?' I remember it was dark and I stepped outside the party.

The first thought I had was, 'I'm never going to see him play live again', and I hated that because I really loved those live shows, and all of the amazing memories they'd given me over the years. I knew there would be more of his music to listen to because of everything that was recorded but not yet released. Even knowing that I was going to be able to hear more of the amazing music that was locked away in Prince's vault didn't make me feel good. I would have traded all that 'new' or unreleased music just to see one more concert.

There were some great quotes from people in the music industry afterwards. Katy Perry said, 'And just like that… the world lost a lot of magic.' And that's how I felt about it. Prince always suggested possibilities, and that there were no limits to your imagination. It felt like he could always come up with some sort of inspirational concept, album or song, and new ways of looking at life or love. He was always restless. He got bored. He was always trying to make live concerts interesting, and he also had a great sense of what a party should be. On one level I think he just saw his concerts as parties. That's why a lot of the time they went on so long. Although he was an incredibly well rehearsed person, he also loved a bit of space and spontaneity, to do something organic, and I think that's why towards the end of his career he did things like the O2/Indigo and the *Hit and Run* thing. He was desperate to keep it interesting for himself. It wasn't like a Lionel Richie concert where you hear 'Easy' and 'Three Times a Lady' and then the house lights go up. He was always testing himself. He made a joke in one of his songs about, 'the only competition is, well, me in the past'.

I HEARD THE NEWS: CHRIS CARRY

Prince was one of the pioneers of using the Internet to distribute music to fans without the use of a record company. For a fee, you could join the NPG online community and have access to buy rare or unreleased recordings directly from Prince. I did. I bought downloads of unreleased albums, special fan only videos, new web only tracks, etc. Anything that was up on-line I probably bought over the space of a couple of months. One day the web site disappeared. It never came back. Not only that, but all the music and video downloads those of us who had spent our hard earned wedge on were no longer even playable. The technical widgets in the software we use to download licensed music were simply revoked by Prince.

This was and still is in my opinion robbery. There were utter nonsensical and cryptic comments made about how basically we were lucky to have this treasure trove for the time we had it but 'Prince has now moved on'. Then he started suing anyone who put his picture up on the Internet, including loyal fan sites or even random users who might have innocently been playing a Prince song in the background while they recorded a home video with their kids. I loved the man but jaysus he could be an utter tool sometimes.

Amanda and I travelled to London in 2007 to attend evening 19 of the *21 Nights* tour, on September 16th. Oh man, what a show. You had to be there. If you have seen the video of Prince playing the Superbowl half-time show, that was the same year, same band, same stage etc. Awesome. The London shows just left you wanting more.

It was announced that on June 16th 2008 Prince was going to play Croke Park. I decided I was going to go all guns on tickets. I bought seats at the side of the stage. They were a horrendous price. Seriously expensive, particularly when money was tight, but this was Prince. They sold 55,000 tickets. Two weeks before the show Prince pulled the plug. No significantly clear explanation given as to why, it just appeared to be a random decision made on a whim. It was rumoured that Prince had expected to sell more than 55,000 tickets two weeks before the show. He didn't understand the walk up on the night or buy the tickets the day before mentality that a lot of Irish music fans have. It was disappointing and symptomatic of a guy who appeared to have lost touch with reality or stopped caring about his fan base.

So, coupled with the robbery from the web site and then the cancellation, I said 'enough, I'm voting with my feet on this.' When the Malahide Castle gig was announced I stubbornly entrenched those same feet in the deepest of emotional concrete and did not buy a ticket. I had to fend off the 'you got your ticket, right?' and 'sure I'll see you in Malahide next week' comments from all and sundry, with a flat 'nope, I'm not going.'

I still listen to Prince all the time. I play his songs on the guitar. Like Bowie, we've been lucky to have shared some of his timeline in history. Unlike the guys in Mozart or Beethoven's time, the legacy of Prince's music as he played and presented it himself will be with the earth forever, for future generations to admire. I suspect those generations will be more than a bit envious of the fact that we were here when we were.

I shall miss Prince everyday.

I HEARD THE NEWS: CHRISTOPHER GRIFFITHS

There are few days that feel like somebody preemptively hit the record button and it is readily available to vividly playback every second. April 21st 2016 was one of those days, much like September 11th, 2001. There's no comparing the two situations but both had major impacts on me.

I used to jokingly say I always felt that Prince was someone who I would probably still see play live to my dying day as an old man. Having read close to everything I could find on Prince, I always felt his lifestyle and self-care made him somewhat invincible. I genuinely thought of him as someone who, despite being exactly 30 years my senior, would outlive me. But that all came crashing down when I happened to be working from home and watched the events unfold from the get go on Twitter when seeing early reports of 'An incident at Paisley Park'.

Fans paid tribute after Prince died. Photo Christopher Griffiths

I thought nothing of it at first, but then there was the updated report, now described as 'a fatality'. Again, I thought nothing of it and had an instant assumption and somewhat naive confidence that maybe a technician might have had an accident. As the reports begun to multiply and worries were aired on social media, I began to feel a sense of dread and as a heavy user of social media, shared the link with the caption 'seriously hoping it's not….' Suddenly I started seeing my idol's face all over Facebook and Twitter. What felt like just a few seconds later, a friend commented on my status with 'confirmed'.

Then came the news bulletins and incredible outpour on the TV and radio stations. When BBC radio 1 played 'Purple Rain' and 'When Doves Cry', reiterating the news of his passing, is when I broke down, realising I'd never get to see him again. When I received messages of condolence of his passing it almost felt like a dark reflection of when I was inundated with text messages from friends and family telling me he was finally coming to the UK. It was like a close family member had died. He was so present in my life and it took a long time to process.

I've been greatly fortunate to have not had anybody close to me have an untimely death and feel like I have the ability of accepting loss when somebody grows old, but this was the first time I really struggled with someone's passing. By April 21st 2016, I had been a devoted fan for over a decade and had seen him perform live 16 times, followed every single piece of news and even named my wife and I's dog after him. I don't think there's a single day I haven't played his music. It is cliché to say, but his music had become the soundtrack to my life and his work ethic was most definitely an inspiration to me. I am forever grateful that I was able to live in the same time period and see such an icon so many times.

I HEARD THE NEWS: JOHN ADDISON

I have a gazillion Prince stories. Concerts, Paisley Park, after shows, etc. The greatest show I ever saw was at City Winery, and that was pretty deep into his career. I had just finished flying a trip that ended up in San Francisco. I ran from one side of the airport to the other to catch a flight to New York. I was standing, waiting for the tram, huffing and puffing, when my phone rang. It was my good friend Sean Smith. Sean and I attended the same flight school, and had recently trained together as sim partners in Captain upgrade class. 'Hey John. I heard about your boy,' Sean said. 'Who?' I asked. 'Prince.' 'What about him?' I asked again. By now I'm getting a little annoyed. Sean is cool, but all my friends consider me the expert on all things Prince. 'He died,' Sean told me. I hung up. That was the last thing I expected to hear, and I wasn't ready to process the info. The tram pulled in, and I sat down, pulled my phone back out.

In today's messed up era of journalistic integrity, there was actually one reliable source for celebrity news. I googled TMZ and felt the earth sway beneath me as I read of Prince's death. I turned off my phone. This was too much. Plus, I was dressed in uniform in public. I had to hold it together. I boarded the plane to NY. The flight attendant noticed something. 'You OK?' she asked. 'No, I'm not actually. Prince just died.' She didn't believe me.

I sat in my seat and hoped against hope that this was some fucked up Internet hoax.

After 30 minutes or so, I pulled my phone back out and connected to the Internet. Right away, I saw multiple voicemails and texts. I couldn't hold it in any longer. I cried, and read the messages and news reports. Then I started playing my favourite Prince songs, which made me feel even worse. The flight attendant who had greeted me came by a few times, but I just waved her away. No more Prince? No more new music, concerts or after shows? A piece of my heart was gone, and musically I have never been the same.

I HEARD THE NEWS: EMMA BAILEY

Sadly I never saw him live. I first got into him in the early Nineties and was probably a 50 per cent fan – I bought his albums, etc. but I never got right into it. But back then I was heavily into the rave scene and we used to put on events so that took up most of my time. Then we had a nightclub so that also swallowed up my energies. Then children came along and when Prince was in the UK, the timing was never right – I was on honeymoon or my kids were new born. So I always looked for an opportunity to see him live but never quite got there. When he died, I began to delve deeper into Prince's back catalogue and watch a

Emma Bailey realised too late what she'd missed. Photo by Debra Parry Photography

lot of concert footage and it's since then really that I became a superfan. So I am really gutted now that I never got to see him live - it's my biggest regret in life! So now if I like someone I make a real effort to get to their concerts as it's taught me that sometimes you don't know what you've got 'til it's gone!

I HEARD THE NEWS: GINA JOYCE

I'm truly thankful I went to the shows I did. I've so many wonderful memories. My world literally fell apart when he died as he was truly unique, one of a kind, and there will never be another like him, of that I'm sure.

I cried for months and months and felt embarrassed for doing so. I kept apologising, and people couldn't understand how I could get that upset over a celebrity/musician. But of course the fans understood completely. We'd grown up listening to Prince. His music was all I ever listened to. I wasn't interested in seeing anyone else live. I just felt this connection to Prince. I'm also a Gemini and he'd always been such a massive part of my life. That will never change.

My son says that our large kitchen looks like a shrine. I've always had a Prince wall filled with framed pictures, but since his passing I've added to that considerably. I also have an illuminated letter P, a Paisley Park official tambourine (from the exhibition at the

02), purple lanterns, etc. My most recent addition, to my family's shock and dismay, is a lifesize Prince cardboard cut-out I had made. The photo is taken from the Hop Farm concert, because he looked amazing at that show. This stands in the far corner of our lounge, and brings a huge smile to my face every time I see it!

I HEARD THE NEWS: LEE BETTLES

I used to sell motorcycle insurance. I was driving home in my electric wheelchair from work to my house. I'd known that he'd been poorly because the week before he'd had this supposed flu issue and had to have an emergency landing. I got home and my partner's phone beeped. She looked at it and she said, 'I think you'd better sit down.' I said, 'Why? What's the matter?' and she said, 'I just need to talk to you.' I was getting really worried that it was something to do with family and asking, 'Is it this? Is it that?' She said, 'No, no.' and I said, 'For God's sake, next thing you'll be telling me Prince is dead.' And she just looked at me and said, 'He is.' I turned the television on and then my phone blew up and I just didn't answer it. I was just distraught. I don't think you ever get over it. I think you learn to live with it.

Four years on, I'm still not over it. I can still get upset looking at his image. Just listen to the last *Piano & A Microphone* shows.

The Gala show at Paisley Park in January 2016 was recorded. It was filmed professionally by Prince's people. And there is a bootleg of the soundboard of that and it is phenomenal. He's talking to the audience about his family, about his father. He's preparing for the memoir. He's getting used to talking to people. I think he was tired but I don't think he was ready to go. I still think he had stuff to do. He was preparing to do the book. He wasn't somebody who had run out of things to say or new adventures. Every album was a new adventure. The year before he died he put two albums out on the same day. It's a tragedy, a life cut short.

I adored him. I've gone vegan partly because of him. He once said, 'I am of the world but I am not part of it.' I loved how he encouraged people to celebrate their differences. In the struggles that I have every day he inspires me. He really does.

29 APRIL 2016

15 of Prince's albums made it into the UK chart as fans rushed to buy his music following his sudden death. Six were in the top 40, with *The Very Best Of*, *Ultimate* and *Purple Rain* at two, three and four.

31 MAY 2016

A report from the Midwest Medical Examiner's Office in Minnesota said Prince died from an accidental self-administered overdose of the painkiller fentanyl.

22 AUGUST 2016

Officials investigating Prince's death said that pills seized from Paisley Park were mislabelled as hydrocone, a weaker opioid than the dangerously powerful fentanyl.

12 OCTOBER 2016

Prince was a new entrant in *Forbes* magazine's list of top-earning dead celebrities. His pre-tax income in the year to 1 October 2016 was estimated at $25m (£20.5m), putting him fifth in the list. Michael Jackson topped the list with an estimated income of $825m (£672.8m).

10 FEBRUARY 2017

Universal Records announced it had struck a deal giving it exclusive licensing rights to much of Prince's private archive, including his 'highly anticipated trove of unreleased works' and 25 albums released through NPG Records, the label Prince founded.

18 APRIL 2017

Court documents revealed that some of the pills discovered at Paisley Park were from prescriptions in the name of his friend and bodyguard.

MY NAME IS PRINCE, THE O2

27 OCTOBER 2017 – 7 JANUARY 2018, LONDON, UK

I WAS THERE: KATIE TREMBATH

I went to the *My Name is Prince* exhibition at the O2. My husband surprised me with the tickets for Christmas. I just sobbed because I'd taken his death really hard. I was on Fentanyl at the same time and I'd been rushed to hospital the day before and was really ill from taking them. So I feel pretty lucky I'm still here. So to get to go to this amazing experience of all his things was awesome. I sobbed even louder when I saw they were VIP tickets. I got to hold his one million pound guitar. As you can imagine, I cried. I still can't believe it now.

Katie Trembath at the My Name is Prince exhibition

HIS LEGACY: SAM BLEAZARD

Throughout his career he united audiences, attracting black and white, straight and gay, male, female and latterly young and old across generations. And while his outlook became more conservative in some ways, his ability to move audiences with intense raw emotion, party funk and hard rock, but also tender ballads, was unparalleled. I met and was introduced to people from all over the world at his concerts. I saw him open a show with 'Purple Rain' with my Dad in tow and took a close friend with a life threatening illness to Paisley Park to hang out in his 'house'.

It's interesting now that, with the passing of time, a number of the things that Prince railed against - the unfairness of music industry contracts, the lack of royalties for artists in the Internet age and mobile phones killing off the live experience at concerts - all turned out to be fairly accurate predictions of where we'd end up.

'Dearly beloved' I've been through a lot 'in this thing called life'. I've lived and loved and been lucky enough to share a number of incredible experiences with like-minded souls, some of these occurring at Prince's best live shows. I've joked on and off that I never had religion, I had Prince. It was his musical universe that was frequently inspirational to me over the years, not least because it encouraged me to learn to play more than one instrument and have a musical life of my own. His fearless, imaginative and unique approach to music and entertainment in all its many forms caused me to believe that I could be so much more than I thought I could be. It made me question who we are as people and why we love the way we do, but always helped me to enjoy life in the moment and party 'like there ain't gonna be another one'.

Futuristic and visionary, eccentric and whimsical, creative and idiosyncratic, raw and visceral, single-minded and unique. In the words of his own hero Sly Stone, I want to thank him 'for letting me be myself again'.

His name was Prince and he was funky.

HIS LEGACY: RIZWAN

A boy, who was a Michael Jackson fan, asked an older girl which concert she would love to see. She replied 'Prince'. Expecting to hear 'Michael Jackson', the shocked boy asked, 'Who in the world is Prince?' That boy was me of course, and once I was exposed to Prince's music, a few years later through *Batman* and then *Graffiti Bridge*, something in my mind was unlocked. I became open to multiple genres of music and became a Prince fan.

Besides beginning a never ending collection of Prince songs, my taste in music in general evolved and I began to explore the world of music as both a fan and a composer. He taught me that a musician can play various instruments and write a large quantity of songs in his own studios, producing himself and using different genres of music as colors, to craft his sonic paintings. Prince was one of the most successful examples of a self produced musician in the history of music. While always writing new songs, he also reshaped his hundreds of classic songs many ways throughout his career, allowing them to evolve on stage, with as many different and amazing musicians as he wanted. Countless musicians of today state Prince as one of their influences.

MORE GREAT PRINCE MEMORIES...

I WAS THERE: EARL RUTLEDGE

I was in St Paul performing and one of my co-workers knew someone in his organization and we got the chance to go the studio. I remember it well because not only did we meet him but got a brief tour of his studio. I was amazed that he rehearsed as if he was performing in real life. He had on clothes like he was performing and I remember the hair do. Also the beautiful pictures he had on the wall like Apollonia, and others involved in his life. We didn't stay long because we heard Janet Jackson was also in town and we tried to rush to meet her but she had already left. But we were VIPs in Prince's club when he had a club and I remember meeting the drummer from Sounds of Blackness there. I must say the ladies there were beautiful and dressed very well and I heard Prince might choose a lady from the club to be in his video.

RADIO CITY MUSIC HALL

26 MARCH 1993, NEW YORK, NEW YORK

I WAS THERE: WENDY BRIODY

That year my two friends and I queued up and got tickets for the three nights. One night some of his security said they saw me with a camera and wanted me to go with them but I refused, I was wearing my painted Prince Jacket.

Anyway each night on a particular song they invited people on stage. On the 26th I was in the second row on my own, towards the end, after folks had been on stage I went to the stage, I'm not sure how I got there and as I stood there

Prince came over. I did a praying motion with my hands, and he leant over and asked my name.

I said "Kiowa", he said "do you want to dance?" I said "OK" even though I can't dance, so I got on stage and Prince whispered "I'm going to sing this song for you". He smelled amazing and his eyes were incredible.

I WAS THERE: ROALD BAKKER

I got his autograph after the Antwerpen 1988 show. I followed his car to the hotel and waited at the entrance for him to leave. When he did I just asked for it but he said no. But while in his car he opened his window and said, 'Okay, gimme a pen and paper.' I also got his handkerchief in a club in Amsterdam after the August 19, 1988 show. He was standing behind us and going to the dance floor and returning to us. Whilst he was taking off his leather gloves I asked if I could have them. He laughed. After a minute or so, he tapped me on my shoulder to give me his black and white polka dot kerchief. The best shows I saw were at the Celebration 2002 shows. He was extremely relaxed and those shows were amazing. I have two set lists from these shows.

I WAS THERE: SONNY BENUDIZ

I saw him around 10 years ago at the Staples Centre, Los Angeles. The rumour was he was going to play at the House of Blues on Sunset Strip, he finally hit stage at 2am and finished at 4am. It was insane.

ROSEMONT HORIZON

18 SEPTEMBER 1988, ROSEMONT, ILLINOIS

I WAS THERE: TONY KIENE

For me, September 18, 1988, was a night that was 10 years in the making and one that I will never forget. I discovered Prince in the summer of 1978 when on a whim, I traded my 45 of The Jackson 5's "Dancing Machine" to a friend for his eight-track copy of Prince's debut album *For You*.

I knew absolutely nothing about Prince, whose album had only been out a few months. But I was simply mesmerized by the album cover. 'Who was this dude?'

I asked myself, 'and how can he look so mysterious, yet so cool?' Moreover, my parents had just bought a new eight-track stereo and I figured this was my chance to break it in.

I played the album from beginning to end. After hearing its exquisite a cappella harmonies on the brief, yet awe-inspiring title track to the dynamic drums and blistering guitar work of the finale 'I'm Yours' (and everything in between), I was entranced. I hadn't heard a lot of music during my young life, but I'd certainly never heard anything like this. From that moment on, Prince was my guy.

By the time I was 12 — and in my mind old enough to attend my first concert — the 1999 Tour was making its way across the Midwest. In my hometown of South Bend, Indiana, some of the bigger touring acts would occasionally play the Notre Dame ACC, but you generally had to drive to Chicago or Indianapolis to catch a concert of any note.

However, the 1999 Tour would swing even closer with scheduled stops at both the Genesis Center in nearby Gary as well as Kalamazoo's Wings Stadium.

Unfortunately, my parents did not agree that I was old enough to see a concert, much less a Prince concert, as they'd heard from others about the salacious material on *1999*. Of course, unbeknownst to them, I often borrowed Prince's vinyl discs *Dirty Mind* and *Controversy* from a teenager down the block and simply hid them in the sleeves of other albums I owned at the time such as Earth, Wind and Fire's Raise and Kool and The Gang's Something Special.

The music and imagery from *Dirty Mind* alone would have undoubtedly shocked them and placed my entire Prince collection at risk. So, not wanting to cause any additional waves, I abandoned my protest at not getting to witness Prince live in 1982 or 1983.

When *Purple Rain* arrived in theatres in July of 1984, it showcased Prince's fabled talent as a live performer that so many of us youngsters had yet to truly experience. Still, as Greg Tate of The Village Voice would later note in rather colourful prose, those going 'gaga' over *Purple Rain* who hadn't witnessed Prince live hadn't seen 'shit.'

The *Purple Rain* Tour eventually came and went, and again, I had to settle for watching Prince videos on MTV and ultimately, the home video release Prince and The Revolution: Live, which featured one of the final *Purple Rain* concerts. And although it was brilliant, it was still not like being there in person.

Then, there I was in September of 1988 — 17 years old and three weeks into my senior year of high school — waiting to board a fan bus sponsored by a local record store for the ride to Chicago's Rosemont Horizon and Prince's second stop on the North American leg of the Lovesexy Tour.

Aside from the *Hit n Run* shows of 1986 and a handful of local gigs in '86 and '87, Prince had not properly toured the US since the *Purple Rain* Tour; he spent three consecutive summers in Europe instead. Now, after two hometown gigs at Bloomington's Met Center, *Lovesexy* was in Chicago for a three-night stand; the second of which was the show I saw.

Nearly thirty years later, it remains one of the most thrilling experiences of my entire life. Prince took us to church that night, as he did with everyone on that 44-city tour across three continents.

Over the next two decades, I saw Prince perform live on dozens of occasions in at least a dozen different cities. I saw many shows from several eras, the only constant being is that I never left disappointed. Prince delivered every single night, whether he was in an arena, theatre, small club, somewhere outside, or at one of his impromptu gigs at Paisley Park.

Scores of his fellow artists have called Prince the greatest live performer of his generation if not of all time, including Bruce Springsteen to whom some have gifted the same label. That said, I believe that Paul Westerberg (a local legend himself) said it better than anyone else possibly could have when describing the first time he saw Prince live in the early 1980s: "[Another musician] turned to me and said 'I'm fucking embarrassed to be alive.' And that's how I felt. He was so good. It was like, 'What are we doing? This guy is on a different planet than we are.'

It was showmanship, it was rock & roll, it was fun, it was great… He'd play Jimi Hendrix-style, between his legs and behind his back. And then he'd do the splits. He could put the guitar down, and Jimi would become James Brown. He could hold the crowd like Mick Jagger, but could Mick Jagger play the piano like that?

Mind you, again, this was in the early days. Prince's live shows only got better in time.

THE GARAGE

15 MARCH 1995, GLASGOW, UK

I WAS THERE: ROBERT FIELDS

I got the phone call in my office in Gordon Street in Glasgow early, around 10ish on the Thursday morning. It came from Wet Wet Wet's manager, Elliot Davis. He told me that he had just had a call from Prince's people to say that Prince was available for an after show gig that night after he had played his gig at the Scottish Conference and Exhibition Centre. The wife, being a massive fan, had her tickets months in advance.

Basically, Prince was skint and did the same in all the British dates. The hall had to hold 500 to 700 and it was a £15 a head. A fee was agreed - £15,000 - and was to be given in a brown envelope at the end of the night. Would I like to attend? I got in early before the doors (10ish) and got right down the front at the barrier. I watched as the production - PA and lights - were put in place. The stage was set up and ready for the wee man to appear straight after his other gig which meant no kit or backline arrived till it was loaded out of the Exhibition Centre. He eventually took to the stage around 2am. He did an amazing gig and then took the money and ran. The gig I saw was a different one to the one that he played earlier for the wife and her mates song-wise. He was renowned, after all, for haemorrhaging songs at an alarming rate (triple and double albums, etc., etc., and his record label had lost patience with him and his demands. His own label, Paisley Park, folded in 1994, hence the impromptu gigs to make cash) so the set I got after talking to my wee wife was different material in general from hers and in my own wee humble opinion we got the better, more interesting set, and certainly historically-wise the better one.

I WAS THERE: PAT COLLINS

The first time I met Prince, I was 16 years old. My friends and I saw him at a concert in Chicago in 1982. We went to an after party and he was standing on the steps of his tour bus, eating Jay's potato chips. He said hi and waved me towards him. I went and my friend followed. We spoke for a moment and I noticed that his bodyguard, Chick, had moved my friend away. I got scared and I ran away. The next time I met him was at the Long Beach Arena during his Purple Rain tour. We spoke about his previous albums and such. He introduced me to Vanity, Stevie Wonder and Eddie Murphy. Everyone was very nice and it was a great after party. He had a Golden Masquerade ball at Glam Slam and gave me a heart-shaped basket of his perfume and toiletries. My friend Pam and I enjoyed drinks in the VIP section. It was very wonderful. I've encountered Prince on a couple of other times but the last most memorable time was his show at the Hollywood Bowl. I was a VIP guest of Laurence Fishburne. The show was amazing and the after party was at the Roxy. I received a great gift box from Prince. The box included a picture and lyric book from his Emancipation set. I also received an NPG hockey jersey, Emancipation boy shorts and a hat with his symbol on it. I've seen every show in every town I've lived in from 1981 to 2015. I love him so much! I am still grieving. I planned to see his last tour but I didn't make it.

O2 ARENA

AUGUST & SEPTEMBER 2007, LONDON, UK

I WAS THERE: JESS HOWELLS

It's hard to define a relationship with an artist. Some have a deeper meaning, a 'debt' which is owed. Others are just here for the music. I can't define my mum's relationship with Prince, but I know it's special. I've always known it's special, but I've not always truly understood the 'hype'. It's 2007 and Prince is on his infamous 21 Nights tour in London. My mum has been to almost every single one. She comes home as I wake up to go to school, she gets changed and heads straight back out for work. This is borderline insanity, surely? I want to see for myself what my mad mother is going on about. So, I go with her. Just me and my mum. She's the happiest I've ever seen her, and I'm starting to realise just how deep this relationship is. I'm still confused though. We arrive at the O2. This venue is the size of a planet and my excitement is definitely swelling as my mum introduces me to all of her friends. Her 'Prince' friends as we call them. Friends she would never have met had it not been for Mr Nelson. This is definitely the first real exciting thing that has happened to me, but of course I still think Prince is overrated (I might be 12 but there's still no excuse). I don't know how many of you remember Prince's 21 Nights at the O2, but it was a bloody good first gig. As it was my birthday, the security guard let me go in to have a sneak peek at the stage before the gates were opened. All I remember is thinking, 'Well, this is definitely the most rock and roll thing I've ever seen.' This man has a stage the shape of his symbol at this huge arena? And that was the turning point.From that moment onwards, I started to truly understand just how much Prince meant to so many people, not just my mum. 11 years later and I will never experience anything that comes close to those nights I saw Prince.

AFTER WORD: SUE HOUGHTON

Like a lot of people, I first noticed Prince with the advent of the *Purple Rain* album. In fact when questioned it's fair to say I'd probably answer the question, 'What's your favourite Prince song?' with 'When Doves Cry'. I've always been a fan of his guitar skills. My liking for the Purple One grew due to assistance from my friend Ali, whom to this day is still my guru when it comes to all things purple, paisley or funky.

1986 heralded the *Parade* tour which the album was the unofficial soundtrack to his second movie, *Under the Cherry Moon*. Pre Internet you still had to buy tickets the old fashioned way so at the tender age of 17 my mum and dad dropped us off at Wembley Arena and we joined the massive queue just to buy tickets! Tickets secured, I recall a desperate search to find something purple to wear for the gig itself. In the end though we failed in our attempt.

Authors Sue Houghton (left) and Alison Howells DiMascio (third left) with Julie Garner and (right) Jeanette Norton

The day of the gig, we spent the day shopping and I remember there was a gigantic poster advertising the *Parade* album on Oxford Street. Finally we were at the gig. There was no support band but the arena was filled with the beautiful harp music of Andreas Vollenweider and black and white balloons (I admit I snaffled one).

Finally it was time for Prince and The Revolution to take the stage. As soon as they came on, everyone stood up (which is fairly normal) and then, as people couldn't see they started to stand on their seats and then the arms of the chairs, Thankfully security made everyone get down because I don't think any of us could have kept our balance for two hours!

As I was still fairly new to the world of Prince, I'm afraid to say that at the time I didn't know all the lyrics fully to 'Raspberry Beret' but the crowd seemed to know it word for word and Prince didn't need to sing any of the first verse.

The *Parade* tour was probably more pop than funk, like earlier Prince shows, and obviously he made a return to that style over the years. It was a great night and I was smitten forevermore.

Over the years we've watched him play with The Revolution, The New Power Generation and 3RDEYEGIRL. Sometimes he's played alone. For some shows there has been no support act whilst sometimes we've been blessed to have some legendary artists as support acts. Depending on the show, you may even have been fortunate to catch a guest on stage. You could watch him play the same tour more than once and it would be a different set list every night. From our first gig in 1986 to our last in February 2015 we have seen him a lot of times – Ali more than me - but at some point I lost count. Each one was awesome in different ways.

But what makes you a fan? Whether you got to see him 100 times, only once or maybe never got the chance, merely the fact that you love his music should be enough to have enjoyed reading this book. We hope you have enjoyed reading it as much as we have enjoyed collecting all the stories.

So what now? Like all great artists there's now a gaping purple hole in the gig calendar! As fans we would sometimes have a long wait between tours but now I guess we can either try to fill the void with tribute acts or maybe catch The Revolution or NPG when they tour; still worth a watch. You can take a pilgrimage to Minneapolis and visit Paisley Park - something Ali and I have done. It's a great way to meet with more fans. Hopefully the estate will release some of the many shows that we know were meticulously recorded. We live in hope....

ACKNOWLEDGEMENTS

Alison Howells DiMascio

I never thought I'd be involved in something like this so I would firstly like to thank Richard for bringing me on board. I'd also like to thank: my Mum, for being my partner in crime on the Prince front since the Eighties, never censoring lyrics I listened to and for driving me around for hours, whether it be camping out for tickets or trying to find a cinema playing a Prince film - you're the best; my husband Gareth for his patience and understanding; the next generation of Prince fans, my gorgeous children, Jessica and Louis; Sue and Rach, my sisters by heart; Julie and Jeanette, my purple sisters. Most importantly, everyone who took the time to share their memories with us and help to keep his legacy alive. Thank you and L41A.

The message Alison left at Riley Creek

Sue Houghton

I'd really like to thank everyone who has made the effort to contribute a memory to this book, you guys make it a book worth reading. Also: shout out to all the Facebook groups that have allowed us to ask for memories through them; to Jeanette Norton and Julie Garner, the best Minneapolis travel buddies a girl could have; to my sister (from another mister) Rach Milligan, who has become a Prince fan following years of indoctrination!; my brother Richard Houghton, who encouraged us to do the book in the first place and has done the heaving lifting with the editing work; to Ali, without whose encouragement and guidance through the years I would not be such a huge Prince fan. And last, but by no means least to Prince, a truly inspirational, amazing artist without whom none of us would be reading this right now.

Alison Howells DiMascio and Sue Houghton would like to thank: Kefle J Callender and Kitty Pilch-Hopkins, creators of The Great Purple Ride.

Richard Houghton

I would like to thank: Alison Howells DiMascio and Susan Houghton for their endeavours; Neil Cossar, Liz Sanchez and Emily Powter-Robinson at This Day In Music Books; goldiesparade.co.uk and princevault.com, both of which are comprehensive online resources detailing Prince's tours and gigging history; Andrea Foy whose book *Prince and Me: His #1 Fan* is available from all good booksellers; Tony Kiene and the *Minnesota Spokesman-Recorder;* Nigel Molden, for permission to quote from his book *The Centre of a Revolution – Live Events at The Polytechnic 1965-73;* Chris Carry at chriscarry.com; Bill Houghton and Sid Houghton for the comic relief; and Kate Sullivan, who keeps the engine running.

PHOTO CREDITS

Page 264 (clockwise from top left): Gina Joyce; Louise Stafford; Lee Hawker; Gina Joyce. Page 265: Nadeem Masood. Page 266: Nadeem Masood (main); Sam Bleazard (inset). Page 267 (clockwise from top left): Christopher Griffiths; Sean Cockwell; Gina Joyce; Louise Stafford. Page 268: (clockwise from top left) Sam Bleazard; Gina Joyce; Kelly Fournier; Christopher Griffiths. Page 269: Nadeem Masood.

WERE YOU THERE?

We hope you've enjoyed reading this book. Perhaps you have concert memories of your own. If you saw Prince or any other major artist in performance we'd love to hear them at iwasatthatgig@gmail.com

www.ingramcontent.com/pod-product-compliance
Lightning Source LLC
Chambersburg PA
CBHW081708100526
44590CB00022B/3693